Dismembering Lāhui

Election of Kalākaua in 1874. Mechanical reproduction of a painting by Peter Hurd for American Factors, Ltd., ca. 1949, courtesy of the Bishop Museum, Honolulu. CP 126,133.

Dismembering Lāhui

A History of the Hawaiian Nation to 1887

Jonathan Kay Kamakawiwoʻole Osorio

University of Hawaiʻi Press
Honolulu

04 05 06 07   6 5 4 3

Library of Congress Cataloging-in-Publication Data
Osorio, Jon Kamakawiwoʻole
Dismembering lāhui : a history of the Hawaiian nation to 1887 /
Jonathan Kay Kamakawiwoʻole Osorio.
p. cm.
Includes bibliographical references and index.
ISBN 0-8248-2432-6 (acid-free paper) —
ISBN 0-8248-2549-7 (pbk. : acid-free paper)
1. Hawaii—Ethnic relations—History—19th century.
2. Hawaii—Race relations—History—19th century.
3. Racism—Hawaii—History—19th century.
4. Hawaii—Politics and government—To 1893.
5. Hawaii—History—To 1893. I. Title.

DU624.6 .O86 2002
996.9'02—dc21   2001058302

University of Hawaiʻi Press books are printed on
acid-free paper and meet the guidelines for permanence
and durability of the Council on Library Resources.

Designed by University of Hawaiʻi Press Production Department
Printed by The Maple-Vail Book Manufacturing Group

Contents

Illustrations and Tables

TABLES

Preface

I have written this mo'olelo over a considerable span of time. The research and initial chapters I began writing while I was an East-West Center grantee and a Ph.D. candidate more than ten years ago. So this mo'olelo has a history that is inextricably tied to my own personal stories—the development of my career, the children I have helped rear, the marriage that has nurtured me, and the passing of beloved friends and family. Events in the present also affect my mo'olelo, my history, my story even as I tell it. In every conceivable way, this mo'olelo of mine has been shaped almost completely by the circumstances of the years in which I have been on this earth: my race; my rearing; the languages I speak; my religion; the 'āina, the land itself. In these ways, the mo'olelo is mine, the individual shape and context that I give it.

Of course, there is the larger part of this mo'olelo that no more belongs to me than the 'āina belongs to anyone. This is the mo'olelo of the Kānaka Maoli, the 'Ōiwi, the Native people, the Hawaiians, however we name and understand ourselves. This is our history. It is like the 'āina, to be shared with one another, to be fought over, to be transformed by our own works and ideas, to be utterly destroyed by the flow of change, as Pele does on Hawai'i, to be reborn alive with the new vegetation of Hi'iaka. Yet the mo'olelo does not belong to us as a people either, so much as we belong to it. Our history owns us, shapes and contextualizes us.

Then there is the mo'olelo that the haole, the foreigner, the Europeans and Americans, understand as history. This tale is bound like a possession, literally and figuratively, as a book, and as a framework of ideas, methods, and ideologies. It is bound by copyright and it will be referred to by the publisher as property. To the extent that this book reflects a trend in historiography, it belongs to that discipline whose practitioners may mark it; cite it; argue over it; ridicule it; use it as binding for other ideas, methods, and ideologies; use it to justify its very existence. To the extent that Western historiography offers anything usable at all to Native peoples whose worlds were "discovered," claimed, converted, colonized, this history may reveal whatever sense of the past can possibly be shared by colonizer and colonized. So what sort of moʻolelo is this? It is the only one I can tell.

I am indebted to so many individuals for the support, advice, and active editing that they have provided for this book. To my colleagues at the University of Hawaiʻi, I give my heartfelt gratitude. In particular, I wish to thank David Hanlon and Lilikalā Kameʻeleihiwa, whose examples and mentoring I have enjoyed for over fifteen years. I am simply blessed by every friendship. No one represents that better than Tori Spaulding, who read my drafts, offered suggestions, called me on the passages that were unclear, and, ultimately, demonstrated that a Vermont malihini could find a history written for and by ʻŌiwi convincing. Finally, I am indebted to those lessons taught me by my family, my parents and siblings, my wife Mary, and my children. I hope that this book clearly imparts our values to the reader and our belief in the wonder of our people: their talent and ingenuity, their aloha and enduring will.

1

Aupuni

In the summer of 1887 a small group of haole (white) men, fired by a tempestuous meeting of their organization, the Hawaiian League, that had taken place a few blocks away, climbed the staircase leading to the offices of His Majesty David La'amea Kalākaua. They carried with them a hastily composed document that came to be known as the Bayonet Constitution, which they forced the king to sign and by so doing effectively surrendered his executive functions within the government to them. This mo'olelo (story) is about that event and its place in a complex, though not surprising, unfolding of other events.

Why tell this story? Why not tell the mo'olelo of the overthrow less than six years after that event, or of the annexation by the United States and the resistance offered by the 'Ōiwi (Native) patriots in the period in between? Those stories are worthy indeed, with high drama, romance, heroic Native figures, villainous haole, and a soulless, imperium-bent America "consummating" the relationship with its reluctant, even hostile bride.[1] Or perhaps it would be worthwhile to retell the story of Cook's execution, from the viewpoint of someone who can, at least, claim an ancestral connection to his killers. That is another good story, worth telling and retelling.

By comparison, the Bayonet tale is a squalid one where few of the major players can claim our automatic sympathies, from the king, who has been characterized as weak, cowardly, hedonistic, and inept, to someone like the constitution's composer, Lorrin Thurston, whose ambitions sprang from his racist belief in America's destiny and his own white-skinned superiority. Yet this mo'olelo is not about that event only. For how was it that a constitution could affect the society at all in 1887? A mere fifty years earlier, Thurston's constitution would

1

have been gibberish, even to the few 'Ōiwi able to read and write in English, much less to the growing numbers of our ancestors who could read and write in their own language. One article alone from that constitution would have confounded every single Kanaka Maoli (Native Hawaiian) alive in 1837:

> Every male reside of the Hawaiian Islands, of Hawaiian, American, or European birth or descent, who shall have attained the age of twenty years, and shall have paid his taxes, and shall have caused his name to be entered on the list of voters for Nobles of his District, shall be an elector of Nobles, and shall be entitled to vote at any election of Nobles provided: That he shall own and be possessed in his own right, of taxable property of the value of not less than three thousand dollars over and above all encumbrances, or shall have received an income of not less than six hundred dollars during the year next preceding his registration for such election.[2]

Fifty years previously in 1837, it would have been inconceivable that Ali'i (the traditional ruling families and original members of the House of Nobles in the kingdom's first constitution) could be elected by human beings. As descendants of chiefly families whose rank equated them with akua (gods), and as akua themselves, they surely were not chosen by the people to represent them. Even Kauikeaouli, son of the Conqueror Kamehameha and Mō'ī (paramount chief) of the archipelago in 1837, was merely the first among several ranked families who could trace their chiefly genealogies back for a hundred generations. Although he could select those chiefs to serve in his councils, he could not define someone's chiefly lineage. So it was inconceivable that a collection of well-to-do foreigners and Kānaka Maoli would have been able to koho (choose or elect) someone to be Ali'i, even if they had had any idea what an election was. More than that, Kānaka Maoli would have bristled at the suggestion that haole should be involved in that sort of process at all.

In fact, the entire article with its references to property and income qualifications is a startling demonstration of how much the millennia-old culture and society had changed in less than three generations. In 1887, the Kānaka Maoli understood the language and implications of Article 59, but once Kalākaua signed the constitution, his people, accustomed to the rule of law, saw no alternative but to obey it. So the mo'olelo of the Bayonet Constitution is not about the political climate of 1887, but about how it was that the traditional concerns of chiefly politics came to be contests over elections, constitutions, citizenship, and legislation in the first place.　　　　-

This story is more than a tale of racism, intolerance, and greed, though these are certainly part of the moʻolelo. It is more than just another example of the twisted nature of nineteenth-century colonialism in the Pacific, though, again, this is part of the history. It is more than a revisionist account by another Native historian challenging the typical haole histories that have little understanding of our culture and often a limited understanding of their own. Finally, it is more than a study of men and women who have been largely ignored in previous histories, but whose stories are worth telling.

This is a new moʻolelo, one that has never been told in quite this way before. It is a story of how colonialism worked in Hawaiʻi not through the naked seizure of lands and governments but through a slow, insinuating invasion of people, ideas, and institutions. It is also a story of how our people fought this colonial insinuation with perplexity and courage. But ultimately, this is a story of violence, in which that colonialism literally and figuratively dismembered the lāhui (the people) from their traditions, their lands, and ultimately their government. The mutilations were not physical only, but also psychological and spiritual. Death came not only through infection and disease, but through racial and legal discourse that crippled the will, confidence, and trust of the Kānaka Maoli as surely as leprosy and smallpox claimed their limbs and lives.

Mai Kīnohi Mai

Samuel Manaiākalani Kamakau introduced his recounting of the first legislatures in the Hawaiian kingdom between 1845 and 1852 with these lines: "In the old days it was tabu for the high and low chiefs (aliʻi and kaukaualiʻi) to confer together. In matters of life and death or in difficult questions of policy it was for the high chiefs alone to decide; they held their counsels in secret, and the ruling chief acted upon their counsel. It was by his action that their counsel became known. But that time was past and a new era had come."[3] Originally published as a series of newspaper articles in the 1860s, Kamakau's histories are one of the few written accounts of prehaole chiefly society.

Much of the content of *Ruling Chiefs of Hawai'i* deals with Hawai'i Ali'i Nui (chiefs of high rank) just before the coming of Europeans. The author portrayed these stunning, powerful chiefs in rich and often glowing detail. When describing the affairs of his own period, especially the legislature, Kamakau was more somber and often skeptical of the benefits of Western culture and haole customs for the Native people. He noted, for instance, that "it was difficult to find men to represent the country districts" and went on to dismiss the early legislatures by saying, "although a good many laws were passed and the commoners were not successful in getting their side represented, the laws were light" (pp. 396–397).

It was an interesting summary for a man who could, in 1869, look back on a legislative career that spanned nearly twenty years and three different constitutions. His experience with government led him to make sobering evaluations of the directions that the kingdom had taken in politics, in commerce, and especially in social values. In 1869 he wrote:

> The younger people are beginning to follow the foreign teaching. They are not a race of beggars who go begging from door to door however much they may trouble their blood relations in this way, but it is an old custom when a man is on the road to ask and receive entertainment. They were taught not to take but to ask. The poor, blind, lame, and crippled, were seldom seen; they were cared for by relatives, orphans were unknown. If one found a waif and attempted to take him in and make him a kind of servant, his blood relations would come and snatch him away unless he were being brought up like an own child. But today the government is doing the asking; it is sending papers from one end of the group to the other and asking what each will give.[4]

Kamakau did not predicate his evaluation of his time on a flattering view of the traditional chiefly society. He wrote about the capacity of Ali'i Nui to oppress the Maka'āinana (the people of the land), Kaukauali'i (lesser chiefs), and even kāhuna (priests, teachers, and scientists). Furthermore, he realized that foreign ways and foreigners themselves could not be summarily expelled, but in some respects the new foreign teachings were creating a society in many important ways inferior to tradition.

How should we understand his ambivalence? His chapter entitled "Hawaii Before Foreign Innovations" is a series of mixed signals on

Figure 1. Samuel Manaiā-kalani Kamakau. Lahainaluna graduate, writer, historian, superintendent of schools, and member of the House of Representatives from 1851 to 1876. From the Ray Jerome Baker collection, courtesy of the Bishop Museum, Honolulu. CP 21,360.

the subject of public morals. He denounced "the old days" with tales of infanticide, polygamy (p. 234), and homosexuality, and still contended that because the chastity and purity of the young were guarded carefully in the old days, "Today, licentiousness is more common than formerly" (p. 235). Along with recounting examples of murderous and vengeful Aliʻi, he described the aloha that existed between Aliʻi and Makaʻāinana, acknowledging that "the chiefs did not rule alike on all the islands."[5]

That may have been an aspect of Kamehameha's aupuni (the government) that Kamakau preferred over the previous chiefly rule. With the end of conquest had come the end of warfare, and the aupuni could proceed to incorporate law and tradition to keep the land at peace. However, Kamakau was also clear that the lāhui,[6] the people themselves who made up the nation, were imperiled by the changes in government and society. He was most decisive when it came to evaluating who were the primary benefactors of the economic and political changes, writing: ". . . but the foreigners who had waited a long time to take the land for themselves were all ready, and when the doors were thrown open for natives and strangers alike they could well laugh; land was what they wanted. . . . His [Kamehameha's] children do not get the milk; his adopted children have grasped the nipples and sucked the breasts dry" (p. 407).

His clarity when speaking of haole who made themselves wealthy at the expense of Natives is arresting because he also praised those foreigners such as the Reverends William Richards and Richard Armstrong, who, he believed, had done much to promote the welfare of Hawaiian people. Speaking of Richards in particular, Kamakau said, ". . . but for the chiefs high and low, for prominent people, and for the humble as well who were in trouble, he was a father and leader who could explain what was right and what was wrong" (p. 406).

If there is one common and consistent thread that weaves throughout *Ruling Chiefs of Hawai'i*, it is that Kamakau was faithful to the idea that good rule came from good and strong leaders. Thus, in the Hawaiian text he always referred to Kauikeaouli, the Mō'ī who had granted the first two constitutions, as Makua (Father) and lionized him as a righteous and proper chief, while at the same time acknowledging the weaknesses of the system that Mō'ī had helped inaugurate.

In 1845 Kamakau added his voice to the thousands of petitioners to the Mō'ī, all of them concerned that foreigners were being placed in high government positions in the ministry or cabinet to the exclusion of Native Ali'i. His letter represented the views of "some old people" who had lived in the time of Kahekili and Kamehameha I [late eighteenth century]. In the letter Kamakau revealed the anxieties and uncertainties of the kānaka, and expressed his own as well. He called on the Mō'ī to reassure his people that the changes in government would not leave them behind.

> The old men said "in the time of Kamehameha the orators *(po'e kākā-'ōlelo)* were the only ones who spoke before the ruling chief. . . . When the chief asked, 'what chief has done evil to the land and what chief good?' then the orators alone were able to relate the deeds of the chiefs of old . . . and the king would try to act as the chiefs acted who did good deeds in the past." Then I said, "Dependence upon those things which were done in the past is at an end; the good which is greatest at this time is that which is good for the foreigner. At the

time when the government was taken we were in trouble, and from foreign lands life has been restored to the government." . . . The old men said, "We love devotedly the King, Kamehameha III; but perhaps the kingdom would not have been taken away if we had not lost the good old ways of our ancestors and depended on the new good ways" (pp. 399–400).

Throughout Kamakau responded to the old men's apprehensions with his own opinions, demonstrating to the Mōʻī that not everyone feared the government's policies. In fact, Kamakau wrote that he disapproved of the people's rejection of foreign laws, saying that the rulers of Britain and France "believe that the Hawaiian group has a government prepared to administer laws like other governments and hence it is that they allow Hawaii to remain independent" (p. 400). He concluded by saying, "We ought therefore not to object to foreign officials if we cannot find chiefs of Hawaii learned enough for the office" (ibid.).

Discussions like these, not only between ruler and people in Hawaiʻi but among the people themselves, reveal some of the political complexities of a community struggling to cope with change. What is also interesting is the discourse on history in which Kamakau and "the old men" engaged.

Ka wā mamua and ka wā mahope are the Hawaiian terms for the past and future, respectively. But note that ka wā mamua (past) means the time before, in front, or forward. Ka wā mahope (future) means the time after or behind. These terms do not merely describe time, but the Hawaiians' orientation to it. We face the past, confidently interpreting the present, cautiously backing into the future, guided by what our ancestors knew and did. But there was one of the new products of Western education, less than eight years out of school, proclaiming that the lessons of the past did not apply any longer.

Nevertheless, he represented the positions of the old men anyway, perhaps because he could read and write and they could not, or because his own Aliʻi status[7] demanded that he convey the Maka-ʻāinana voice to the Mōʻī, or perhaps because he recognized the limitations of his own opinion despite his knowledge and Western education.

In 1845, Kamakau was also young, a mere thirty years old. It would have been hewa (wrong) to simply dismiss the words of his kūpuna (grandparents or elders). But he quite clearly symbolized a new circle of Natives who were coming of age in a very different world than their elders had known. Armed with a literate education and a better knowledge of the outside world, and yet disarmed by the sheer weight of change that was descending on the Islands, Kamakau and other youthful leaders sought to clarify and mediate those changes for the rest of the kānaka. Perhaps they also believed that, in time, they would be the Native officials chosen to replace the foreigners in the cabinet ministry and privy council.

Kamakau was never one of those so chosen, and there were precious few Natives in the privy council and cabinet in any case. Though he became a district judge and a representative in the legislature, by 1869 he knew that Kauikeaouli's promise to give the high positions to Native chiefs who had been sufficiently trained would not be realized in his lifetime. In May of that year he published the letter he had written to the king in *Ke Au Okoa* and the king's response, preceding it with these words: "A learned man had arrived with knowledge of the law, and the foreigners who were holding office in the government hastened to put him forward by saying how clever and learned he was and what good laws he would make for the Hawaiian people. The truth was, they were laws to change the old laws of the natives of the land and cause them to lick ti leaves like the dogs and gnaw bones thrown at the foot of strangers, while the strangers became their lords, and the hands and voices of strangers were raised over those of the native race. The commoners knew this and one and all expressed their disapproval . . ." (p. 399).

Kamakau was not the only Native leader to express in their later years a bitter resignation about the unfulfilled promise of their Western education and knowledge. Others who had also served in the kingdom's legislature shared similar views, though few had the kind of literary forum that Kamakau had. One who did was Davida (David) Malo, graduate of the same school that educated Kamakau, member of the first legislature of the kingdom, teacher, Christian preacher, and eventual critic of haole. Born at the end of the eighteenth century, before there were constitutions, before there were legislatures, indeed before there was a Christian mission, Malo, like Kamakau, straddled an age of incredible change. This was a time when the young aupuni[8] was pressured by foreign threats and by severe internal distresses of disease and social disorder. These pressures strained chiefly leadership, causing the Aliʻi Nui themselves to execute changes in the administration of government and even in the traditional religion.

Transformations: 1795–1829

The Aliʻi Nui were dramatically affected by catastrophic challenges to their traditional leadership coinciding with Kamehameha's conquest at the end of the eighteenth century. The Conqueror had initiated some of these challenges himself, creating new administrative structures and establishing more concentrated centers of power around himself and his close supporters.[9] More important, Kamehameha's military supremacy suppressed the power of other Aliʻi Nui, whose rivalry with one another had contributed so much to the competitiveness and vibrancy of Hawaiian society.

Davida Malo was born in 1793,[10] fathered by a warrior named Aoao who had apparently followed the Conqueror. His genealogy was hardly spectacular, but Malo was hānai (literally, to feed; it meant to adopt) to ʻAuwai,[11] one of Kamehameha's kākāʻōlelo (orator, advisor). Undoubtedly, Malo's intellect was aroused and initially shaped by a very traditional sort of education, one that in older times might have elevated him to a position of some influence. Such influence would certainly have been constrained by his low rank. It is doubtful that such an individual would have been able to distinguish himself in traditional society except as a competent and loyal chiefly server.

Coinciding with the reorganization under Kamehameha and his heirs was the arrival of American Congregational missionaries and the spread of their influence after 1820. Malo was an early and important contributor to their efforts, and like many of the Aliʻi Nui who placed their faith in the political as well as the spiritual possibilities of the new religion, his mana (power) came to be based on the success of the mission.

Without a doubt, however, the most important change was the collapse of the Native population. David Stannard's 1989 analysis of the horrific consequences of introduced epidemics beginning with Cook and lasting throughout the nineteenth century[12] has been interpreted by contemporary Native historians Lilikalā Kameʻeleihiwa and Kanalu Young as having severely disrupted Aliʻi Nui leadership as well. Young has written, "Compared to the makaʻāinana (producer class) the Aliʻi Nui constituted a smaller population. Consequently, losses from their ranks would seem more severe, because of the potential problems lack of leadership could bring and also because there were fewer of them to begin with."[13]

Stannard's estimate of a prehaole population of 800,000 is a projection, of course, and has been challenged as extravagant. But even that challenger postulated that a reasonable estimate would have been closer to 500,000, meaning that the depopulation at the end of the nineteenth century would have been 92 percent rather than 95 percent.[14] Clearly any kanaka in the kingdom, including Malo, lived with the understanding that, as a race, they were in great danger.

It is that context that enlivens Lilikalā Kameʻeleihiwa's analysis of the Christian mission's success in the Islands. The reasons that Hawaiians were converted to the new religion, she has argued, are not to be found by analyzing Christian doctrine or missionary policy but by understanding the traditional culture, especially the kanaka understanding of the akua, their Aliʻi, and the relationship that tied spiritual and material realities together, known as pono (balance or harmony).

Pono was a state of balance between numerous dualities: light and dark, sacred and profane. There were akua (gods) for warfare and akua for planting, and caring for these deities was a significant part of any ruling chiefs' obligations. But above all pono was a balance between what was male and female, a balance that was maintained for centuries by the ritual separation of men and women known as the ʻAikapu (sacred eating) and by the rigorous observance of the ʻAikapu by everyone, especially the Mōʻī. Ultimately, the successful rule of any Mōʻī depended on a healthy, *growing* population. Kameʻeleihiwa wrote: "Certainly epidemic disease and massive death were signs of loss of pono, but Kamehameha—who ruled at the time—was the epitome of a pono Aliʻi. He was devoutly religious . . . and carefully respected the advice of his Kahuna Nui and Aliʻi Nui councils. . . . The people loved Kamehameha because he put an end to war and gave them peace, but for all his efforts he could not give them life."[15]

For Makaʻāinana the concept of pono[16] linked them as well as the Aliʻi into a relationship with the powerful gods whose mana made the miracle of life possible. This meant that they were to be productive as planters of taro and as fishermen; but also as crafters of the beautiful kapa cloth and moena (woven mats) that achieved such high quality in Hawaiʻi. It was the produce and art work of the Makaʻāinana that nourished and adorned the body of the Aliʻi and graced their residences. At the same time it was the Aliʻi whose presence and disciplined behavior also guaranteed that the akua would continue to bless the endeavors of the people as a whole.

The great dying disrupted the faith that had held Hawaiian society together for centuries. In November 1819, less than six months after the devout Conqueror's bones were hidden away, his sons and heirs, Liholiho and Kauikeaouli, sat with their mother, Keōpūolani, and the Kuhina Nui, Ka'ahumanu, who was more than an aunt, and ate together, breaking the 'Aikapu.

Kame'eleihiwa leaves no doubt that the 'Ainoa (free or profane eating) was instigated by Ka'ahumanu, one of Kamehameha's favorite wahine, his Kuhina Nui (high councillor) and daughter of one of the Conqueror's most able Ali'i Nui supporters. Indeed, by that act, she demonstrated her own mana and force of will by convincing the Mō'ī Liholiho to break the longstanding religion. However, by this same act, she reduced herself and her chiefly relatives to the status of human beings, no longer a divinity.

'Ainoa was accompanied by increasing alcoholism among the chiefs and people and by mounting epidemics that caused the decline by one-half of the population between 1803 and 1831.[17] Perhaps these things were not perceived as mere coincidence by the Hawaiian people. There is evidence that Natives saw the growing presence of foreigners in the Islands as contributing to the miserable fortunes of the Hawaiian people. Many of them, even as Christians, wished the haole would simply go home. At the same time, the haole and their new religion promised to rescue the people and their chiefs from the social breakdown that accompanied the 'Ainoa by introducing a new commitment and discipline—namely Christian prohibitions, which were understood to replace the old kapu, the rules that had once demarcated the sacred distinctions between chiefs and people, and men and women.

It was Ka'ahumanu herself who arbitrated the presence and influence in Hawai'i of the American Board of Commissioners for Foreign Missions (ABCFM) until her death in 1832. She was the kingdom's most powerful individual. Beginning in 1825 she and her chiefs initiated a system of laws based on Christian morality and behavior known as prohibitionary or sumptuary laws. These laws not only altered traditional morality and custom, but also resulted in the Natives' abnegation of their own culture and values as well as in their reliance on foreigners to tell them what was pono.

Kame'eleihiwa has argued that the mission's promise of new life (ola hou) figured prominently in the Natives' acceptance of the new religion. Steeped in a religious tradition that regarded all life as a spiritual power, the Hawaiians' turn to Christianity is understandable, especially because it appeared that the old akua had, for some reason,

Figure 2. Kaʻahumanu. Kuhina Nui for Kamehameha and his heirs and regent from 1824 until 1832. This Aliʻi Nui was important to the success of the Christian mission in Hawaiʻi. Lithograph by Langlume, courtesy of the Bishop Museum, Honolulu. CP 29,142.

turned their faces away from the kānaka. In 1823 the high chiefess Keōpūolani took missionary William Richards under her wing, helping him establish a church in Lāhainā. Here she was behaving as a traditional Aliʻi Nui, appealing to the power of the akua to bring life to the land, but it also seems that she feared for the destiny of her own soul, begging the mission to baptize her as she lay dying. The ABCFM missionaries' refusal to baptize someone so briefly under Christian instruction[18] is a testament to their extraordinary self-indulgence, but it is also illustrative of the power of this Christian ritual, even in its infancy in our Islands. The church became an institution promising life when death was everywhere, and the eventual conversion of Hawaiians by the thousands must be understood in the context of a time when their own religion, akua, and Aliʻi could not prevent them from dying.

Of course, as Kameʻeleihiwa has reminded us, the missionaries could not save them either. The key to the mission's success was not that Christianity began to halt the downward slide of the Native people. Christianity succeeded as the Aliʻi Nui accepted the new religion and incorporated it into their own rule and into Native society at large through the institution of new kapu.

For Kaʻahumanu and her Council of Chiefs, the institution of sumptuary laws signaled their commitment to the new deity. These laws, proclaimed between 1825 and 1829, created drastic revisions in kanaka ways of life. In particular, laws prohibiting fornication (virtually any sex outside of marriage), although enforcing monogamy and church-ritualized marriage, may have had much to do with encouraging a society-wide infiltration of the church's influence. Church attendance was not mandatory, but observance of the Christian Sabbath was. Eventually, these laws would not only prohibit socially unredeeming activities like murder and theft, they would also prohibit behavior that was intrinsically native, such as ʻawa drinking and hula.

Kameʻeleihiwa asserted throughout her work that heeding the advice of haole missionaries such as William Richards, Richard Armstrong, and Gerrit Judd was the fundamental reason for the passage of laws and for the institution of a Western economic system that ultimately dispossessed the Natives of land, identity, and nationhood. This is a correct assessment. However, it is precisely where Kameʻeleihiwa ended her analysis that mine begins. The sumptuary laws proceeded to change the relationship between the various elements of Hawaiian society by creating kingdomwide regulations, granting to the state, for instance, the right to intrude into the kanaka family in ways that had not been allowed or ever before imagined. The laws criminalized not just ordinary behavior (sex and ʻawa) but hula, the culture's highest artistic expression.

In other words, the power of haole advice came largely as the result of the destruction of Native self-confidence in their own institutions. Law drove a wedge between Aliʻi and Makaʻāinana by creating a new layer of authority between them, a layer that neither could control. The kānaka accepted haole morality and law as rituals that could or would restore balance and health to their society. However, this acceptance requires a closer analysis. Foreign ways were not accepted uncritically. Native conversion to Christianity and Western laws enabled haole to become powerful authorities in Hawaiian society while managing the systematic destruction of the relationship between chiefs and people. It was the dismembering of that relationship that crippled the Natives' attempts to maintain their independence and their identity.

Conversions

The first class of Hawaiian students at Lāhaināluna in 1831 was like no other class of students in the Islands. For these were not simply Maka'āinana or Ali'i learning to read and write, these were the promising young men (women were not included) who would further the cause of literacy and knowledge of the foreigners' world.

Among these young men was Davida Malo. His age when he entered school was thirty-eight, old in a society gripped by one plague or another. His selection as a student was based, as were the others in his class, on his conversion to Christianity and his personal tie to the Reverend William Richards.[19] However what surely distinguished him more was an aggressive and incisive intellect, noticeable to his teachers from the first.

In many ways, this man helps define his generation and symbolizes the ambiguities of his age. For without an outstanding genealogy, he was, nevertheless, a significant historical figure in a society that had once acknowledged only those individuals with exalted blood-

Figure 3. Davida Malo. Graduate of the first class from Lāhaināluna, educator, writer, advisor to Ka'ahumanu, and representative in the first legislature. Malo's Christian convictions did not overwhelm his concern about the growing foreigner population. Courtesy of the Bishop Museum, Honolulu. CP 29,202.

lines. As a constant critic of an encroaching Western culture, he was, notwithstanding, a most significant asset to the spread of that culture. As a Kaukauali'i, he spoke and behaved more like an equal to the Ali'i Nui.[20] Malo is a symbol of the confusing and often contradictory choices that faced Hawaiians as they modernized their government and society in the early 1840s.

Malo was no ruling chief. Kame'eleihiwa listed him in her Table of Lesser Konohiki as a chief of low genealogy.[21] Of the forty-four graduates of the first class at Lāhaināluna only two names beside Malo coincide with the 218 lesser konohiki listed by Kame'eleihiwa. One name, Kahele, is listed as a chief of high genealogy,[22] but it is unclear if this is the same individual who attended Lāhaināluna between 1831 and 1835. The name, after all, is a fairly common one. The same holds true for Rikadi Kua'ana, whose genealogy was a question mark for Kame'eleihiwa. The Lāhaināluna student roster[23] only lists the name Kua'ana, another fairly common name.

Possibly there were one or two men in the first class at Lāhaināluna who were descendants of Ali'i Nui or who may have been konohiki themselves. There was a student named Kuluwailehua that Kame'eleihiwa listed as an intermediate konohiki, but even she could only guess at his genealogy.[24] It can be said that within the Kamehameha aupuni the classmates at Lāhaināluna in 1831 were, at best, chiefly servers, nothing more.[25]

At least in Malo's case, a better record of his words and attitudes exists than of his genealogy. In 1898, Nathaniel Emerson, missionary scion and, incidentally, a member of the Hawaiian League that had forced Kalākaua to sign the Bayonet Constitution, wrote the introduction to Malo's *Moolelo Hawaii*, also known as *Hawaiian Antiquities*. In addition to making extensive editorial remarks wherever he believed Malo to be in error, Emerson bemoaned the fact that Malo's intolerance for his people's traditions caused him to "cover with a veil of contemptuous silence matters, which if preserved, would now be of inestimable value and interest to the ethnologist. . . ."[26] Emerson went on to say: "But it is not to be wondered at that David Malo should have been unable to appreciate at its true value the lore of which he was one of the few repositories. It could be expected only of a foreign and broadly cultivated mind to occupy the stand-point necessary to such an appraisal."[27]

Describing the Native, even one whom Emerson regarded as among the best of them, as incapable of judging objectively what was good and evil, harmless, or depraved in their own culture is most ironic. In the first place, there is some truth here. Natives indeed became confused the more intensely they accepted Christian doctrine (Emerson actually used the word "warped" to describe Davida Malo). Furthermore, Emerson claimed that only the more sophisticated foreigner could make the real and appropriate judgments about culture and history that the recent and sincere Native convert was incapable of making. Yet, it was Malo himself and young men like him whom the mission began to prepare to lead the aupuni into the modern world. It was not a role that the Aliʻi Nui, at least, expected either the mission or its school at Lāhaināluna to play. Even the mission's stated aim was merely to spread literacy and Christianity throughout the kingdom. That this was to be their students' lifelong work was not in doubt even as late as 1835, when Levi Chamberlain, the schoolmaster at Lāhaināluna, decided that ten of the most promising graduates, including Malo, would be retained "as monitors of particular classes . . . as teachers in our children's school, as assistants in translating into their own language . . . and we strongly hope that a few of them may eventually enter upon the study of theology and be able to preach the gospel to their countrymen—a point greatly to be desired."[28]

So Malo and other lesser-ranked individuals were to be the conveyers of haole education and theology to the Makaʻāinana. That was a sensible decision from the mission's point of view. By 1835 there were less than fifty ABCFM workers in the field, not enough by themselves to spread literacy and religion to nearly 100,000 kānaka. In 1841 the *Polynesian*, a government-run newspaper edited by an American named Jarves, claimed that it was schools like Lāhaināluna that were providing critical new leaders whose literacy and familiarity with Western political concepts set them apart from the older Aliʻi Nui. When the Rights and Laws (kānāwai) of 1839 was drafted, that newspaper claimed that chief credit was to be given to Lāhaināluna graduates and undergraduates "everyone of whom went forth as an unfledged patriot . . . in book learning far above those of their rulers."[29]

For the haole-run newspaper to print such a provocative statement is interesting enough. What the Aliʻi Nui might have made of Jarves' editorial apparently did not matter in 1841. Yet the editorial was misleading. Whether Jarves knew it or not, the kumukānāwai (constitution; literally, foundational law) was composed and drafted by William Richards, with Lāhaināluna graduate Boas Mahune merely assisting.[30] Still, the editorial was not meant to praise Mahune. It was trying to make several important points: first, about the importance of Western education, and second, that there was nothing inherently superior about "the rulers" that could not be outstripped by lesser ranks armed with that Western education.

Malo himself provided such an example for any haole looking for evidence of the "rise of the common man." Malo moved to Lāhainā around 1823, perhaps at the invitation of Keōpūolani herself. He was specifically mentioned by Kamakau as instrumental in saving Reverend William Richards from being put to death for libel against an Englishman, Captain William Buckle, in 1827.[31] According to Kamakau, it was Malo's reasoning with Ka'ahumanu that convinced her to overturn the ruling of her own chiefs, making, as Kamakau claimed, "enemies for herself of the [British] consul, the foreign merchants and of Boki and Manuia of her own people."[32]

For the Kuhina Nui to take the advice of a Kaukauali'i and overturn the decision of Boki, her own cousin, is not so astonishing if we

Figure 4. Lāhaināluna. Established in 1832 to train Native teachers. A number of representatives received their education here. From the Hedemann collection, courtesy of the Bishop Museum, Honolulu. CPBM 77,961.

understand that Boki was one recalcitrant Aliʻi Nui when it came to cooperating with the regent's sumptuary laws. In fact, the high chief owned a saloon in Honolulu, dispensing liquor in open defiance of the ban on alcohol. So Kaʻahumanu's decision, although perhaps calculated to put Boki in his place, was also a defense of her own Christian kapu and added to the prestige of men like Malo who were close to the church.

The establishment of the school at Lāhaināluna for the training of future teachers for the kānaka also guaranteed a future of service for those who were sent. What service was expected of them? Initially, it was intended that they would teach and preach, but within a decade the graduates were being touted by the haole as the best pool of new political leadership available.

Perhaps we should not be surprised that the aim of schools like Lāhaināluna was changing. The conditions facing the missionaries in the 1840s were more hopeful for them than they had been in the 1830s. Certainly, Christianity's place in Hawaiʻi was no longer so much in doubt as it may have been even in 1835. By 1846, 22 percent of the Native population was registered as members of a Protestant church, as opposed to 0.7 percent in 1835. By 1853, virtually the entire population had an affiliation with some Christian denomination.[33] To the extent that the missionaries had succeeded in planting and nurturing the seed of the new religion, it is not surprising that the missionaries would begin to consider the implications of these changes for their own destinies.

A good example of this change in the social landscape is to compare the mission's handling of the Holmans with its handling of Gerrit Judd. In 1821 Thomas and Lucy Holman, members of the first mission company, were sent back to Connecticut because Thomas was charging Natives for his services as a physician. The attitude of his brethren, Hiram Bingham in particular, was that capitalism was at odds with the values and ideologies that the mission was determined to instill in the Islands, and for that reason Thomas was excommunicated and dismissed for, among other things, covetousness.[34]

Exhibiting a less than committed attitude toward the church's work and displaying too much worldliness, Holman and his wife were sent home. What else could be done in 1824? What little haole population existed at that point (whalers, traders, and beachcombers) hardly made up a society of people appropriate for even an excommunicated missionary.[35]

But by the late 1830s, it was possible for a mission physician, Gerrit Judd, to resign his post in the mission in favor of more lucrative political and economic opportunities serving the Mōʻī.[36] On the eve of Judd's resignation, his wife Laura wrote:

> My husband's practice in the foreign community increases every day, and if our rules allowed him to receive pay for it, a day's earnings would support his family for a week. It does not seem right to draw our support from the treasury of the A.B.C.F.M., when ample opportunity is afforded to take care of ourselves without abridging our usefulness to the nation or mission. I have written to my friends to send no more boxes of donations, but to turn their charities in to more needy channels. . . . Lands and herds belonging to the mission will soon be productive, and will make it independent of the board for support. That is as it should be. "Let us provide things honest in the sight of all men."[37]

By the mid-1830s then, even with Native membership in the Christian church still below 1 percent of the population, the social landscape had altered favorably for the missionaries. The foreign community was now large enough to permit missionaries and their families to conceive a bright future in the Hawaiian Islands. By the 1840s, resignation from the mission to engage in business and politics was a fairly standard practice. Another example was the incorporation of missionaries Amos Starr Cooke and Samuel Castle in 1850 into what would someday be one of the largest and wealthiest of the sugar companies.

Of course, conversion of the kānaka was the primary mission, but conversion to what? The specific goal of Christian conversion was complemented by the broader and no less significant vision of "civilizing" the Natives. Hiram Bingham, leader of the first ABCFM contingent, understood that the process of conversion was concerned with more than spirituality. In his memoirs, he stated that in addition to turning the Native from their "idolatries and oppression" the mission was, ". . . to introduce and extend among them the more useful art and usages of civilized and Christianized society, and to fill the habitable parts of those important islands with schools and churches, fruitful fields and pleasant dwellings."[38]

In 1839, another member of that first company, Artemis Bishop, claimed that it was not only religious conversion, but the conversion of the entire Native way of life that was needed to save the kānaka from extinction. That included, Bishop believed, a drastic transformation in the political authority of the chiefs, especially their control of the land:

> but this is the fault of the system—a system without any checks and balances to preserve it from despotism. But it has become antiquated and ready to die. Christianity having removed the bloody features which were necessary for its stability, it is now tottering to its fall. But while it exists, its influence will operate to keep the mass of the people so degraded as effectually to prevent them from the full formation of character upon the principles of moral rectitude. Their pleasures consist in idleness and the low indulgence of sensual gratification. No enlightened mind needs to be informed that such a people cannot continue long to increase in numbers when they come in contact with the vices of those who visit them from civilized countries.[39]

Bishop's dark vision of what might occur, the virtual extinction of the Native people within sixty years without serious political, social, and economic reform, was the vision that was conveyed to the chiefs

Figure 5. The Chiefs' Children's School, also known as the Royal School, established 1839. Every Native ruler after Kauikeaouli and many of the nobles were educated here. Photographer unknown, ca. 1889, courtesy of the Bishop Museum, Honolulu. CP 103,126.

and to the students at mission schools. We know, for instance, that Native haumāna (students) and their haole instructors at Lāhaināluna wrote about the "era of darkness" that existed before the arrival of missionaries: "Listen, you who are reading this, you (now) see what life was like in these islands in olden times. The land was shrouded in darkness; with evil and grief; and pain and death. It was a pit, a dark pit, a pit full of filthy things, a death pit, an ever burning fire pit; that's where all of Hawaii's people lived in olden times! Now the light has dawned but some people prefer darkness because of the sins they have committed. Where are we turning our face, ahead to the light? Back to the darkness?"[40]

The ABCFM was a mission that owed its formation and driving theologies to the Great Awakening of eighteenth-century colonial America. Like the originators of that revival, these missionaries were always concerned about how personal salvation was complicated by issues of free will, obedience to "the authority of governors," and the importance of conversion itself. They also knew that the eternal "felicity" of heaven could never be attained by those who were corrupted by the temptations of the flesh. The mediator for Calvinists was the Bible. The ability to read, understand, and interpret scripture and gospel was the key: "Herein God deigns to confer a singular privilege on his elect, whom he distinguishes from the rest of mankind. For what is the beginning of true learning but a prompt alacrity to hear the voice of God?"[41]

For the missionaries, several of whom were graduates of Andover College and strongly influenced by the revivalist teachings of Jonathan Edwards, conversion to Christianity separated human beings in ways barely distinguishable from any class system except, perhaps, for its continuation into eternity. In the 1750s, Edwards had preached on several occasions that those who earned Heaven did not necessarily earn a place at the right hand of God, but that there were "many mansions" in heaven to accommodate more than one kind of individual soul. More important, ignorance of the gospel would not spare the Native Hawaiian any more than the recalcitrant Yankee from the wrath of God and the awfulness of hell.[42]

Thus Reverend Bishop could argue that "every foreign visitant and resident in the islands, whether he is aware of it or not, has the power to exert, a great moral influence, whether of virtue or vice, on the untutored natives about him."[43] It was a glorious work that the missionaries imagined for themselves. If they were in competition with other foreigners who would use the Natives' "tendencies" toward licentiousness and drunkenness for their own despicable rewards, so be it.

Their work was also something that missionaries considered a noble sacrifice for which they were paid very little. In time that conception of themselves helped them and their children justify the enormous wealth that they accumulated in Native lands, with Native labor, and by way of the Native government that missionaries helped design. Calvinism, which did not adhere to such frivolous rituals as chastity or poverty, freed the ABCFM missionaries from feeling any shame for their astonishing self-enrichment.

But their financial success did raise questions about missionary intentions, questions that were asked even before individual clerics began to accumulate land and profits. Kamakau believed, for instance, that the Ali'i Nui Boki, cousin of Ka'ahumanu, was corrupted by foreigners who hated missionaries: "Boki, whose conduct of the government for a few months was so admirable, fell under the influence of certain foreigners like Consul John Jones [American], Mr. Stephen Reynolds and the British consul, who feared the conversion of the chiefs and commoners to the word of God and used to remark, 'If the missionaries stay we shall have to go, if they go we will remain.'"[44]

The competition between the ABCFM missionaries and the more secular foreign business community never really ended. In 1851 the disputes between them erupted into a constitutional dispute that involved Natives as well as whites. In the end, of course, the missionaries did not go, but neither did they remain missionaries. Although the ABCFM mission had the firm support of Ka'ahumanu and most of her chiefs until her death in 1832, the growth of the missionary influence thereafter was by no means stable or uncontested. But Ka'ahumanu did leave a body of laws supporting the church's influence. The new Kuhina Nui, Kīna'u, a granddaughter of the Conqueror, steadily maintained the government's support for missionaries despite real resistance from the Mō'ī, Kauikeaouli.[45]

The fact is that Hawaiians were kānalua (of two minds) about the new religion even in the 1830s. For Natives like Malo, educated in the mission schools and groomed to take up teaching and preaching, the changes in the physical and social landscape were double-edged with promise and anxiety. Their success in helping create a literate society from a nonliterate one in less than a generation suggested a promising future for Hawaiians. On the other hand, the stability and progressiveness of Hawaiian society also promised to lure more and more haole to the Islands.[46]

The expanding presence of foreigners fostered uneasiness among the Maka'āinana, but also prompted the remaining Ali'i Nui and Mō'ī to consider ever more radical changes in the political system to achieve the respect of foreign residents and their governments for Hawaiian laws. Among these changes was the creation of a state based on democratic principles of representation. The Maka'āinana, who made up the vast majority of the population, were to be given a voice in that government. It was individuals like Malo, with no outstanding genealogy but acclaimed by the haole missionaries for their knowledge and leadership, who were called on by the people to represent them before the Mō'ī. These same individuals, a very different elite from the chiefs of old, may have been ambivalent or even contemptuous of the Native past, but they also bore an equally strong apprehension of haole in their future.

2
Law and Lāhui

To a people living happily in a pleasant land with purple
mountains, sea-girt beaches, cool breezes, life long and natural, even to extreme old age, with the coming of strangers,
there came contagious diseases which destroyed the native
sons of the lands. No longer is the sound of the old man's
cane heard on the long road, no longer do the aged crouch
about the fireplace, no longer do those helpless with age
stretch themselves on their beds, no longer do they remain
withering in the house like the cane blossom stalks plucked
and dried for the dart-throwing game. We are praying to God
that we might reach the length of life of our forebears. We
build churches, labor day and night, give offerings to charity
and the Sabbath dues, but the land is become empty; the old
villages lie silent in a tangle of bushes and vines, haunted by
ghosts and horned owls, frequented by goats and bats.

Samuel M. Kamakau, *Ruling Chiefs of Hawai'i*

In 1839, the Reverend William Richards, the king's personal teacher,
conducted a series of lectures on political economy "among the chiefs
and favorites of the King." Among those favorites were Boas Mahune
and Davida Malo, two of the first graduates of Lāhaināluna.[1] Mahune
and Jonah Kapena, a clerk in the first legislature of 1842, assisted
Richards in the composing of the Rights and Laws of 1839, the document that paved the way for constitutional government and private
ownership of land.

These young men met regularly with the Mō'ī and his privy council, which included the highest-ranking chiefs and haole missionary

advisors such as Richards, Gerrit Judd, and Richard Armstrong. According to Kamakau, "the minds of the chiefs became enlightened" about the purposes of constitutional government and the development of capitalist economy.[2] But the new knowledge brought confusion. Kamakau wrote, "Some think that the changes in government came about so soon because the king, chiefs and their favorites were trained in political science only and knew nothing about the land and the daily life of the people and the way the chiefs of old lived. Others think that Mr. Richards was the cause of the government getting into the hands of foreigners."[3]

In any case, the Rights and Laws of 1839, published in Hawaiian as He Kumu Kanawai a me ke Kanawai Hooponopono Waiwai, made startling changes in the authority of the chiefs and the Mō'ī by pronouncing "God had bestowed certain rights alike on all men and all chiefs, and all people of all lands."[4] This declaration positioned everyone, chiefs and people, kānaka and haole, into one definition of people, all entitled to the rights granted by God. Under the paragraph entitled "Protection for the People Declared" the declaration stated that ". . . chiefs and people may enjoy the same protection, under one and the same law . . . and nothing whatever shall be taken from any individual except by express provision of the laws."[5]

With these paragraphs the ultimate responsibility for the maintenance of the land and the people in Hawai'i passed from the ancient line of Ali'i and the gods they represented to the newer and much less understood authority of law. When Kauikeaouli signed an amended form of the twenty-four-page-long declaration on 8 October 1840, he established the kingdom with few specific directions on how laws were to be constructed. Yet the Maka'āinana were to have a voice, if not a hand in their making. Over time this innovation would hasten the severance of the ties between Ali'i and Maka'āinana. In that first legislature, Maka'āinana would have comported themselves very carefully in the presence of Ali'i Nui—very carefully indeed.

The Constitution of 1840

The first constitution of the aupuni was drafted by William Richards and approved by Kauikeaouli's signature at Lua'ehu, Maui, on 8 October 1840. Among historians it had mixed reviews. Kamakau lauded it for clearing up confusion and inequities of taxation, noting that, "Before the constitution was granted the people were not treated equally; some were favored and some burdened and distressed; and heavy taxes fell oppressively on the common people."[6] But American legal scholar Henry Chambers called it "crude and loosely drawn" and appeared more impressed that a "savage" king had deigned to grant constitutional rights to his people without being asked for them.[7] However, both the Hawaiian and the American analysts agreed that the principal changes inaugurated in 1840 were to theoretically limit the authority of the Mōʻī and to include the Makaʻāinana as lawmakers. For the next five years the constitution provided a basis for representational government while the Aliʻi and the Mōʻī continued to exert a very traditional kind of authority.

Even more critical changes to the structure of government came with the drafting of Organic Acts between 1845 and 1847 by newly appointed Attorney General John Ricord, a New York lawyer who arrived in Honolulu in 1844. These laws provided separate departments, or ministries under the king, to be staffed by senior officials and known as the Ministries of Interior, Foreign Affairs, Public Education, and the Treasury. The ministries replaced various functions of the Executive (the king), theoretically leaving the king to oversee them all. As such they were tremendously important to the day-to-day running of the nation and to the process of legislation. Three of the four first ministers were haole; two of them, Richards and Gerrit Judd, had come to Hawaiʻi as missionaries.

It seems that no one in government save perhaps William Richards, who had designed the kumukānāwai, gave much thought to how the representatives of "commoners" would participate in the legislature. For several reasons, it is doubtful that Richards or any other haole had any high expectations of the first "Makaʻāinana" legislature. Gerrit Judd, writing to the ABCFM in 1838, voiced this opinion: "There is much agitation on the public mind. The influence of the missionaries, especially those lately arrived, is very decided against the ancient system of government. The 'rights of men,' 'oppression,' 'blood and sinews' are much talked of, and a sort of impatience is perceivable that changes are made so slow. The probable consequence is that the people and the chiefs will not come up to our expectations as to reform and we, at least some of us, will be looked on with suspicion."[8]

Some in the foreign community were indeed suspicious of missionaries. The Makaʻāinana had deep misgivings about any haole participation in the government, especially their overwhelming presence as cabinet heads. The Makaʻāinana expressed their dissatisfaction with these appointments in an extraordinary outpouring of petitions warning the Mōʻī and the legislature against giving the foreigners positions in the government and ownership of land. The legislative journals of the first few sessions do not clarify whether the Makaʻāinana petitioners received much support from their elected legislators.

Only Kamakau's report of who sat as representatives in 1842 remains. He listed seven individuals, including himself and Malo representing Maui.[9] He also detailed the laws passed by that legislature sitting together with the former ʻAha Aliʻi (Council of Chiefs), known after 1840 as the House of Nobles. His account delivers a sharp objection to the limitations of democracy in that first legislature and even a recognition of how those limitations were defined by race.

In 1842, both Houses cooperated to pass laws on schools, taxes, and judicial process, but when it came to the appointment of new governors for Maui and Kauaʻi, only nobles were allowed to vote. This was probably due to the fact that the governors were themselves higher-ranking Aliʻi and it would have been quite strange for the lower ranks to have the power to select them. Kamakau tells us that the nobles were unanimous for making Kekauʻonohi, a granddaughter of Kamehameha, the governor of Maui, when Lāhainā was still the capital and residence of the king. John Young Jr. (Keoniana) did have a high chiefess mother and his father had been the respected American military adviser to Kamehameha, but Kekauʻonohi clearly outranked him, and she was related to the Mōʻī. So they voted to send Keoniana to Kauaʻi. But Richards objected, saying that Keoniana understood English better and would "make a better escort for the King and represent him better before the officers of the battleships and with the delegates from foreign lands." Kamakau was astonished when the nobles gave up and John Young became governor of Maui: ". . . for I had believed that the ballot was really to determine the election according to the will of the greater number, but here the chiefs had given up their will to that of a single person."[10]

If even the Aliʻi prerogatives could be overridden by a haole advisor, what exactly was the role of a lower-ranked representative in that period? How clearly would the first representatives, even those who had been educated in the forms of law and exposed to the teachings of William Richards, have understood their mission? Kamakau seems to indicate that, at least, there was some confusion.

The Constitution of 1840 stated that the nobles and the representatives would sit separately but could also meet in joint session. Were it not for those joint sessions, there would be no record of those representatives before 1851, the first year that a legislative journal was kept in the lower house. As it stands, only sparse references to the rep-

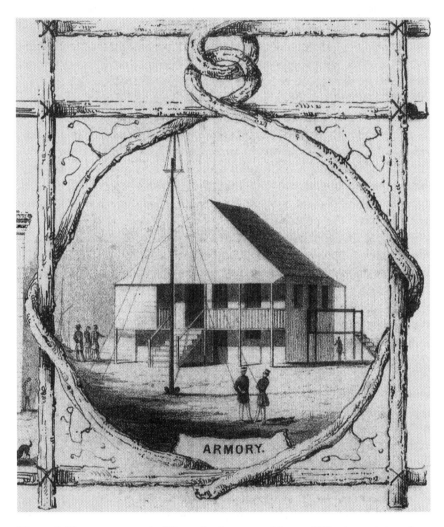

Figure 6. The government building, also known as Mauna Kilika (mountains of silk) for the women who attended sessions of the legislature in their finest wear. The building was secured by Kekūanaōʻa for the nobles and representatives and remained the seat of the legislature from 1845 to 1852. Drawing by Paul Emmert, courtesy of the Bishop Museum, Honolulu. CP 99,491.

resentatives in the proceedings of the Council of Chiefs exist, which has prompted most historians to conclude that the representatives rarely initiated legislation.

What then were they there for? They must have asked themselves the same question. For although the institution of representative government was new, there were many ways, traditionally, for lesser chiefs to advise the Mōʻī. This is how Malo described it: "If the lesser alii desired to consult with the king on some important affair of government, perhaps war, the king would send a message to the kalaimoku [chief councillor] to come and hold a privy council with him; and having given attention to what they had to say, the king dismissed them." [11]

The Kālaimoku that Malo spoke of here was an especially trusted individual who advised the Mōʻī in secret and whose advice superceded the opinions of the lesser chiefs. [12] Again, from Malo: "If, however, the king saw that what the chiefs advised was in disagreement with the councils of his kalaimoku, given him in secret, he openly expressed his disapproval. This was the manner in which the assembly, parliament of the chiefs [aha olelo o na lii], conducted their deliberations." [13]

Who was the Kālaimoku in 1842? Kameʻeleihiwa believes that it was William Richards. That would explain why the nobles deferred to his opinion about the governorships despite their unanimous and opposing opinion. Of course, the fact that the most trusted advisor of the Mōʻī was a haole missionary meant that the changes in the political structure of the kingdom were most heavily influenced by foreigners.

On the eve of the annexation of Hawaiʻi an American law professor, Henry Chambers, wrote that the Hawaiian king granted constitutional rights to a people who had not demanded them (actually implying that Kauikeaouli must not have known what he was doing). Chambers did not appear to understand how the Mōʻī and the Aliʻi Nui had come to depend on the advice and council of missionaries. More important, Chambers glossed over the fact that the first constitution did not merely provide a basis for Makaʻāinana to participate in lawmaking, but it also regulated the participation of haole in the government. Constitutional law also made an immediate and lasting impact on the relationships between the Aliʻi and the Makaʻāinana. It was, in fact, the Makaʻāinana who first observed that foreigners were replacing the chiefs as the principal authorities in the government.

By 1840 much of what had constituted Hawaiian society had been disfigured by sixty years of association with Europeans and Americans, but the values that tied the people to the Ali'i had not changed significantly. Although those ties were no longer based on the sacredness of the chiefs, the social ties of mutual responsibility and a powerful aloha continued to shape the kānaka responses to the Mō'ī, the Ali'i Nui, and the government itself. The evidence for this is the thousands of kānaka who appealed to the government between 1842 and 1852. Their petitions, though representing different Native communities from Waimea, Kaua'i, to Miloli'i, all made the same entreaties. They all expressed concern over haole ownership of land and presence in the highest councils of government, but they also, without exception, sought reassurance that the Ali'i Nui were still their chiefs.

The Native Petitions

The legislative records of the years between 1840 and 1845 include dozens of petitions to the government. In some cases, the authorship of these is known; in others, we can only guess. In some cases, petitioners signed their name or represented their concurrence with an "X." In other cases, the same individual who drafted the petition might sign the name of hundreds of people beneath it. In some documents the language is exquisitely poetic; in others, it is brief and direct. But all of the petitions expressed the common fear that the government was deserting the Maka'āinana.

In August 1845, Z. P. Kauma'ea, a Lāhaināluna graduate and representative in 1846, drafted a letter backed by "more than 1600 of your true servants in Lāhaina" reminding the king and the Kuhina Nui, the chiefess Kekāuluohi, of their previous petitions. Kauma'ea wrote:

> Our wishes at this time, are the same as those expressed by us to you, it shall never change, because we are positive of the troubles that are sure to come to your government, to ourselves even to the first and third generations after us. If we have erred it is but proper that you two show us wherein we your humble servants have done so. . . . We still look with pride to the glory of our Rulers and of our services under you. But with all this you have seen fit to surrender your throne to the care of the foreigners. . . . Alas, for now you dislike us and you together with your chiefs have turned and followed the advice of the foreigners.[14]

Fear of foreigners was only one of the reasons the Maka'āinana petitioned the government. They also used the occasion to remind the king that they belonged to him. In another petition from Lāna'i, said to have been signed by three hundred people, the Maka'āinana told the Mō'ī that neither the size nor the wealth of the nation mattered as long as the nation was theirs:

Below is what we desire

1. For the independence of the Hawaiian government
2. Refuse the foreigners appointed as ministers for the Hawaiian Government
3. We do not want foreigners sworn in as citizens for Hawaii . . .
7. Do not be afraid of our petition for you are our father.
8. Do not have any fear—because your Government is not very rich, of your own people.
9. We do not want you to open doors for the coming in of foreigners. [15]

The people of Lāna'i emphasized the Maka'āinana belief, an ancient belief, that any threat to the Mō'ī and to the government was a threat to their safe existence as well. But the petition also acknowledged the shared weaknesses of both the government and the people. In this and other appeals, the people were not critical of the Ali'i because they could not protect the kingdom from foreigners. Rather, they criticized the Mō'ī for not recognizing the threat that the haole posed to all of them. What concerned them most was not seizure of the kingdom by a foreign government, but that foreigners would replace them as the people of the land.

For this reason governorship of the land was the overriding issue of consequence for the Native people. In 1845, Malo, who was not a representative that year, and Kauma'ea were among those who drafted the Maka'āinana petitions that were sent to the Mō'ī, the nobles, and the representatives. One that was sent from Kona and bore more than three hundred signatures clearly made the chiefs responsible for what they perceived to be a terrible trend:

The things we think proper, if the nobles agree with us are these: You chiefs must not sell the lands to the white men nor to the foreigners. . . . We object to this practice of the government in this respect, the granting of rights of citizenship to foreigners, as being improper in our opinion. . . . The dangers we wish to set before you are these: If the chiefs are to open this door of the government as an entranceway for the foreigners to come into Hawaii, then you will see the Hawaiian people going from place to place in this world like flies.[16]

Of course, control of the land was important to haole as well. Certainly, they recognized the opportunities for wealth. In fact, haole businessmen and missionaries had already formed a model sugar plantation by 1835 and, as small an operation as it was, had turned a modest profit. But even missionaries like Richards, who may not have had any intention of becoming businessmen, believed that no truly civilized country could exist without private property.

As far as the missionaries were concerned, the strange and, for them, uncertain land tenure was the cardinal reason for the unabated depopulation and despair within the Hawaiian community. In 1846 the minister of the interior, Robert Wyllie, sent a memo to the fifty mission stations asking their recommendations for halting the precipitous decline of the Hawaiian people. Nearly all of them responded that Hawaiians could only be saved by ending the "oppressive nature of their *Ali'i* and *Konohiki* land tenure system."[17] Most revealing was the answer from missionary J. S. Emerson, Nathaniel's grandfather: "I think two things are requisite to make the people industrious and provident. First, the feeling that the land they cultivate is their own, for themselves and their posterity. Second, the feeling that the land is of real value, and capable of being improved in value, and that all improvements are private gain."[18]

Private ownership of property was the key element of a society's recognition of individual interests. For the missionaries who claimed to be the protectors of the Maka'āinana, only the dissolution of their "servitude" to the Ali'i could end the cycle of ignorance and indolence by replacing it with a community of individuals who worked for their own interests on the land and defended them in the legislature.

So even as the missionaries sought to break the ties that bound the Maka'āinana to their "oppressive" chiefs, the people were pleading with the Ali'i to maintain and strengthen those relationships to protect the race against the foreigners. The petitions to halt the growing presence of the foreigners in the Islands made up most of the communication between the Maka'āinana and the legislature between 1845 and 1846. Despite what was surely an overwhelming expression of the public will, the legislature refused to accommodate any of those three requests (not to make foreigners subjects, not to make them officials, and not to give them land), instead backing the decision of the Mō'ī and his council "with no dissenting voice." [19]

A New and Strange Elite

In this altered political society where aliens could achieve the status of chief councillors and where even Maka'āinana could address the Ali'i Nui, the function of the Mō'ī was critical. In 1845 Maui Representative Kauma'ea described the Mō'ī as a father to the people and insisted that the Interior Ministry's function was principally to seek the "harmonious living together of each King or Chief with their people. That the supreme ruler is the Moi: that his own laws which he makes for the kingdom do not affect him . . . that he is responsible for all of the troubles that may be against his kingdom . . . that the laws of the kingdom affect everyone who breaks them." [20]

Figure 7. Kauikeaouli (Kamehameha III) and his family, ca. 1852. Proceeding clockwise from the center is Hakaleleponi Kalama, his wife; his heir, Alexander Liholiho; Lota Kapuāiwa; and Victoria Kamāmalu. The last three were all children of Kauikeaouli's aunt, Kīna'u, and the high chief Kekūanaō'a. Courtesy of the Bishop Museum, Honolulu. CPBM 41,657.

Kaumaʻea described a very traditional sort of Mōʻī. Such a ruler would have been the source of all kauoha (decrees) and, thus, above the law. But the 1840 Constitution constructed the "king" differently. Although allowing that his duties included the execution of the laws of the land as well as treaties and decrees with other countries, his duties were "all, however, in accordance with the laws."[21] The same constitution thrust the responsibility for lawmaking on the legislature, a body that included Aliʻi Nui, Kaukaualiʻi, and Makaʻāinana.

In 1840, however, a Hawaiian understanding of representative as lawmaker was several years away. Kaumaʻea offered a simple enough definition for the representatives: their role was simply to counsel the Mōʻī, who actually had the full responsibility for the laws. Initially, they would have seen their appointment as an elevation of their status to a kind of konohiki, a chiefly server, and thus would have taken their cues from the higher-ranked Aliʻi.

The idea of representative as konohiki is sensible because of the nature of the business conducted by the legislature. Domestically, there were three areas of concern for the new government: dispositions of lands, taxes, and education. In traditional times, the konohiki would have been responsible for overseeing the lands entrusted to them by a ruling chief. That would entail making certain that the land and the Makaʻāinana who lived on it were productive. That also meant that they acted as collectors of tribute (hoʻokuapōlaʻo) as well as land managers.

Most of the representatives had positions in one of these areas. Some of them were employed as tax assessors for their home district, and Z. Kaʻauwai (representative from 1851 to 1855), who came from a Maui chiefly lineage, was appointed to the Board of Commissioners to Quiet Land Titles in 1842. In fact, Kauaʻi Representative S. P. Kalama, who would serve one of the longest continuous terms in office (from 1853 to 1870), was listed as konohiki of Kalihikai, an ahupuaʻa (land division) on his island. As such, he wielded very traditional kinds of authority, with the right to place kapu on fish and timber.[22]

But as educators some of the early representatives were something other than traditional konohiki. Several began their careers as teachers: Malo, Kamakau, and Kaumaʻea were retained as teaching assistants at Lāhaināluna[23] (a special distinction), and at least two representatives rose to the position of district superintendent of the schools on their islands. Malo was superintendent on Maui. Kahoʻokuʻi, who represented Kauaʻi in 1851 and 1852, was superintendent on that island in 1848. However, many of the legislators were also schoolteachers, including Oliwa ʻĀlapa (representative, 1845, 1846), A. Moku (representative, 1854), and Samuel Kamakau, who began his prolonged legislative service in 1851 and continued intermittently until 1876.

These kānaka were the symbols of the new Western and Christian knowledge that had been the cornerstone of their education. Malo was regularly called upon to preach, not just to his people but to gatherings of white clergy as well. It is likely that their respect for William Richards and later Richard Armstrong and Gerrit Judd was cultivated in those mission schools and churches, and not just the result of the nobles' deference to a Kālaimoku (chancellor).

Moreover, as educators they had something distinct to offer the Mōʻī in the way of counsel as spokesmen for the literate, educated, and presumably converted Makaʻāinana. It wasn't long before the representatives' voices not only were heard, but on occasion even overwhelmed the order of the assembly. By 1843 the *Journal of the Legislative Council* frequently noted Malo arguing and petitioning with the nobles, and by 1848 at least one joint session was interrupted by an exasperated argument between nobles Kānehoa (James Young), G. L. Kapeau, and Representative Kaʻauwai.[24] Debate between the representatives and the traditional wielders of authority certainly indicates that some alteration of their relationship was already taking place.

It is hard to say what exactly that alteration was. It is not known, for instance, what it was that Kaʻauwai and the two nobles were arguing about. Kaʻauwai had a Maui lineage; perhaps the argument was an example of one chief challenging another. Kapeau, in fact, was challenged by other representatives, including Kamakau, who asked in 1852, "by what right" had Kapeau been included in the House of Nobles?

One important change, however, was that law was confusing the once very distinct lines between ruler and ruled. Over the long run the legislature equalized Natives of high and low birth, especially after haole entered the House of Representatives in 1851. The role of the legislature itself was ambiguously defined in the first constitution, which named the fifteen chiefs composing the House of Nobles to act as the government council along with the Mōʻī.[25] Unequal by tradition, but cast as equals by the constitution, the legislature was the arena where every social change demanded a political response. At first, both Ali'i and Maka'āinana tried to maintain the old, familiar relationships. Over time that became impossible.

Modern or Traditional Rights?

Regardless of how the legislators came to their position, whether they were Ali'i Nui who were specifically named in the constitution or whether they were nominated by the Maka'āinana, their behavior in the legislature, at least until 1846, suggests a very traditional role. They were simply advisors to the Mō'ī, while haole made the important changes in the structure of government. In 1844, Richards recommended that the king hire John Ricord to be the nation's chief legal officer. By 1846, Ricord had drafted a series of Organic Acts that created the various departments and had also designed a land commission[26] to see to the privatization of lands in the kingdom. He became the Hawaiian kingdom's first attorney general in 1845 and authored the kingdom's first Civil Code.

Ricord was a good example of everything the Maka'āinana had to fear. Whatever his intentions were, the fact that foreigners with no experience whatsoever with kānaka were given such authority to determine the course of government validated Maka'āinana concern. The fact that these same haole were setting up rules for the distribution of land was another reason to be apprehensive.

Their petitions reflected those fears and communicated much more than political or even economic concerns. At stake here was not just the disposition of lands and the passing out of political offices, but the whole question of identity. Petitioning was the Maka'āinana's opportunity to reinforce the traditional relationship that existed between them and the Ali'i as well as to define them both together as a people unified against the incursions of foreigners. As one petitioner stated in 1848, "This is independence; that your gracious Majesty, Kamehameha III, be King, and the Chiefs of your kingdom be your assistants, and also your own people."[27]

It was a relationship that ultimately both the Mō'ī and many of the chiefs rejected. In the Legislative Council's reply, printed in the *Friend*, August 1845, the nobles and representatives, with no dissenting voice rejected nearly all of the Maka'āinana objections, agreeing only that matters concerning taxation still had to be worked out. This response, signed by Keoniana, but probably drafted by Judd, imagined a kingdom in which both foreigner and Native honored and respected the Mōʻī and his law: "Shall foreigners who become officers take the oath? If not, then they have a chief in another land, and Kamehameha III is not their proper sovereign, and they will not act righteously between the King and their own countrymen. But if they take the oath of allegiance to Kamehameha III., will they not be faithful to him. And will they not cease to have regard for the chief they have forsaken?"[28]

That this proposition would gradually be revealed as little more than wishful thinking (or intentional subterfuge) should not obscure the fact that there were powerful incentives for the legislature to accept this notion as fact. Because there was nothing that the kingdom could do to prevent foreigners from coming ashore, the next best thing was to prevent them from making mischief or, better still, incorporate the mana of the foreigners under the control of the government. As Minister of Education, William Richards informed them during the session, "regarding the Naturalization of foreigners . . . [he] said that it would be one of the means whereby the King could govern them as he is doing to the Natives."[29]

What a compelling idea that would have been to the members of the legislature and to the Mōʻī. Legislators like Malo and Kamakau were aware that Europeans had already staked out most of Polynesia and had been busy helping themselves to the Marquesas, Tahiti, and Aotearoa, toppling, or at least humiliating, powerful lineages along the way. Yet in Hawaiʻi, despite unequal treaties and a temporary seizure of power by the British,[30] Hawaiians still ruled, with white men working for and under the Mōʻī, their status made plain and firm under the law. Kauikeaouli had seen fit to congratulate himself and his good fortune while commiserating with the fallen Pomare of Tahiti in 1845. In a letter that he wrote to her he said: "Just before this, I had a problem similar to yours, although yours is the graver situation. In my time of trouble certain people stood by my side to aid me. I had a haole who had sworn an oath before me, to have no other sovereign but myself, and he worked with vigor as is the haole way, quickly deciding what was for our good and what should be done. . . . Here I reign with the support of some righteous haole and I think therein my government shall endure in times when I am again troubled by foreign governments."[31]

Haole working for the government were more than a talisman to keep the foreign powers at bay. They were evidence that some kind of sharing could take place without losing everything. As such, the haole were powerful additions to the body politic as far as some of the chiefs were concerned. In 1845 the Aliʻi still held on to the economic strings, namely the land. With this power still intact, it was not unreasonable for the Mōʻī to envision a nation strengthened by haole so long as they were carefully controlled by the granting of lands and offices. Such haole would continue to run interference with their home countries and prevent a repeat of the 1843 seizure by the British. It is even conceivable that the chiefs saw their role in very traditional ways. If it was haole power that mattered in the world now, then it was up to the Aliʻi to mediate that power to the rest of the community in the same way that the sacred chiefs had once mediated the power of Kū and Lono.

Had Malo, as one of the drafters of those petitions, been in office in 1845, would the chiefs' reply have been uncontested? Although he realized that there was little that could be done to prevent the Islands from being overrun, Malo believed that the only thing that could save the Hawaiian people were rulers who would behave responsibly toward the Makaʻāinana. In an extremely provoking and aggressive article Malo had long before revealed his distaste for much of modern society and the chiefs who gravitated toward it. In 1839 he wrote for the *Hawaiian Spectator:* "But from Liholiho's time to the present, the chiefs seem to have left caring for the people. Their attention has been turned more toward themselves and their own aggrandizement, and they do not seek the welfare of the people as a nation, and therefore they are more oppressed at the present time than ever they were in ancient times."[32]

For Malo, who feared that the nation was already passing into the hands of haole, it was not the power of the foreigners that was needed, but closer ties between the classes of Hawaiians and a more determined effort from the chiefs to work for the peoples' advantage. There is no question that Malo expected little to be gained from foreigners who, he claimed, had "lent their whole influence [hooikaika loa], to make the Hawaiian Islands one great brothel." For the chiefs to behave like chiefs, they needed to be better at resisting the worst of the foreign influences.

But Malo also worked for the Westernization of the Hawaiian political system by his support of constitutional government, which called for, among other things, a relegation of the power of the Mōʻī under the law. This substituted the concept that the "law" was the actual sovereign for the centuries-old one in which the Mōʻī was answerable only to the akua and must certainly have discomfitted the lower-ranking members of the legislature who would be expected to meet with, and possibly confront, higher-ranking chiefs in the crafting of those laws.

No wonder that Malo and his fellow representatives treaded very lightly when they took up their positions in the legislature. For them to conceive themselves as lawmakers would not only have been impertinent, they would have had to be willing to usurp the traditional right and power of the Mōʻī to make the kapu, something none of them, including Malo, was prepared to do in 1845. But having been elevated to the status of one who could sit in council with the chiefs, neither Malo nor his colleagues could resist the opportunity to behave like true konohiki. They could and would advise the Mōʻī about the status of his realm.

For Malo and Kaumaʻea, who were both out of office during that critical year when the petitions were flowing in, this meant proposing a stronger cleaving to the subjects and a withdrawal from foreigners. But for the others, that may have meant simply endorsing the king's decision and working to implement it. After all, the legislature knew that the chiefs' response to the petitions would be unpopular. The *Journal of the Legislative Council* tells us: "Mr. Richards then offered a few suggestions how best to appease the people when the Representatives returned home, as it was thought that the people will get angry because their petitions were turned down."[33]

The petitions and the chiefs' response signal an alienation between Makaʻāinana and Aliʻi, and for the representatives, summoned from the lower classes yet expected to behave like chiefs, their response (and alignment) in this matter was a crucial political decision. For it was easy to see by the government's response that the powerful men surrounding the Mōʻī were not as concerned about the growing presence of the haole in the Islands as they were of the potential for the Makaʻāinana to upset the order of business. Anyone who read the *Friend*, the principal missionary newspaper, recognized the Makaʻāinana position when the petition from Lāhainā was published in the summer of 1845:

Is it proper for foreigners to take the oath of allegiance?—There is perhaps a difference of opinion among foreigners on this subject; but among us, the common people, there is no difference of opinion. If it is proper for foreigners to become Chiefs, and the greater part of the nation is to become theirs; it is proper for foreigners to take the oath of allegiance under them (i.e., under foreigners) and let the nation become a nation of foreigners. But if the nation is ours, what good can result from filling the land with foreigners? Let us consider, lest the land pass entirely into the hands of foreigners.[34]

The nobles and advisors surrounding the king certainly understood this position, but they were apparently not convinced that the haole posed the biggest danger in 1845. For instead of attempting to quiet the fears of the Maka'āinana, the nobles tried to stifle the "dissent," even going so far as to accuse Malo of helping to incite a revolution.[35] Ironically, it was the support of his haole friends in the mission that helped clear Malo, a situation that quite sufficiently indicated where real power already lay. Kauma'ea, the only other representative to take the side of the Maka'āinana, wrote these bitter words to the legislature in 1845, signed by fifty-two Hawaiians:

> We heard on the 8th of June 1845, of this thought of yours. You are angry because of the petitions from Maui. Is it cause for your anger if we petition for the clarification of the right and wrong of an independent government's action at this time? Is anger the right thing for an independent government? And is not petitioning allowed by the [kanawai] that was made by an independent government? Petitioning was agreed to by you and anger is forbidden you by law. If you are not angry you will not take court action against those of us [makou] asking thus, "whose ideas are these [No wai keia manao]?" This thought is for all of us [No kakou pu keia manao] [translation mine].[36]

It is fascinating to watch Kauma'ea flirt with the definitions of independence (the word he used was kaokoa, which means to stand apart, or to separate). It is almost as if he had already acknowledged that the government meant to set itself apart from the people and thus, perhaps, had no right to prosecute them for behaving as independent (individual?) citizens.

No matter what reasons can be argued for the legislature's failure to object to the inclusion of haole as citizens, whether it was that they were intimidated by the Ali'i Nui, deferential to the wishes of the missionaries in the ministry, or simply operating from the conviction that the decision was for the Mō'ī to make, it is quite obvious that they did not faithfully represent the wishes of the Maka'āinana in what was the most crucial and controversial issue of the pre-Mahele legislature. Perhaps that was because the legislature was not designed to represent the wishes of those people.

The most important political question of 1845 or of any other year for the kingdom was "to whom does the nation belong?" The question is complicated because of the various ways that we might define the word *nation*. For the haole that word can mean the country, its government, or the people it rules. But for Hawaiians, two words were necessary to convey the meaning of nationhood: aupuni, the government established by Kamehameha, and lāhui, which means gathering, community, tribe, and people. But what lāhui most often refers to is the Hawaiian race. It is possible that Hawaiians came to accept the presence of haole in the government without ever acknowledging their right to be part of the race.

It is also apparent that the members of the legislature may have construed that question differently than the Maka'āinana. For Maka-'āinana, the nation existed for all Hawaiians, chiefs and commoners alike. For the legislators the whole issue was complicated by several irremediable facts. One was that there was really no way of getting rid of the haole. As the government said in its reply to the petitions: "Shall not foreigners come on shore? They do come on shore. Can they not be permitted to live on shore? According to the treaties they can. Who shall be their proper sovereign? . . . Foreigners who take the oath of allegiance can apply to only one sovereign, viz: Kamehameha III.; he will adjust their difficulties in a proper manner, and they will render important services to Hawaii, *their land*" [emphasis mine].[37]

The chiefs and the legislature sought to bind the haole ever closer to the Mō'ī through ties of sacred obligations (the oath of allegiance), the granting of titles, and ultimately through the gift of land. It was nothing short of dispensing a konohiki status, which would, in 'Ōiwi minds, bind those haole to reciprocal obligations to the Crown and to the Maka'āinana as well. It is not surprising that the Native people would bitterly resent the elevation of foreigners before them. What would be surprising is if the representatives had not felt uneasy as well at the fact that this new nobility should so quickly establish themselves as permanent holders of the higher cabinet offices. Kauma'ea himself drafted one of the most pointed criticisms of foreigners in a petition sent from Kona in 1845: "Furthermore we must consider the nature of the foreign officials. Trouble to our Native government is their nature [ano]. Those of foreign lands do not petition. They are helped by war vessels, with the hand turned against us, without love for us all. . . . If perhaps, we are opposed by those of another country and go to war with them . . . will they die together with us the true people [kanaka maoli]? They will run perhaps and not stay and help us kanaka maoli. They will not wish to die with us all, and give their lives, and their dollars to the war." [38]

Representative government to the Hawaiians in the 1840s was a most ironic institution. Designed to give a voice to the people, it operated as a structure that would mediate and amplify the king's voice to them through their own representatives. Proclaimed to be an integral step in the "civilizing" of the Hawaiians and their society, it served to promote some very traditional ideas about service to the Ali'i. Professed to be the vehicle that would bear the Maka'āinana from an ignorant and lethargic servitude to the status of free men, the new laws also reinforced the Hawaiians' fear that they were being cast off, to sink or swim on their own in a rising wave that was bringing, as Malo put so well, "large and unfamiliar fishes from the deep sea." [39]

The mission assumed that the gift of a liberal constitutional government would persuade the Hawaiians that they had come only to save them. But Hawaiians, fearful of the future and wary of those very foreigners, tried to cling even harder to the chiefs whose exercise of power they, at least, knew and understood.

Over the next four decades, Hawaiians would learn to use and master the haole democratic system. Representatives would, within a decade of the first legislature, come to be lawmakers with real and informed constituencies. Hawaiians would come to accept the presence (and even the arrogance and wealth) of the haole in their midst, while electing them to office, marrying them, and entrusting them with their estates. But two important things remained constant. The "common" Hawaiians would continue to believe that their best hopes for survival as a people were symbolized by the Ali'i Nui and the Mō'ī, and the haole would continue to regard the Native people as hopelessly inferior because of their loyalty to their chiefs. Looking back in 1915, a missionary descendant and former conspirator to overthrow the monarchy in 1893 could admit that the Hawaiians never lost their identification with their chiefly rulers:

> It was in vain to explain the principles of constitutional government
> to the aroused and jealous supporters of Kalakaua; it was only adding

fuel to the fire to warn them that the inevitable result must be loss of independence, because the industries of this country, largely controlled by foreigners, would never consent to be taxed and exploited by the acts of an irresponsible ruling class. These statements were flung back at those who made them, as proof that they were making insidious attempts to do the very thing that they gave warning of and that true patriotism was to oppose them and smash their ideas at all hazards, and unite in upholding the King. [40]

3

ʻĀina and Lāhui

On the whole it is doubtful whether the Native race will be
able to withstand the shock which the overwhelming wave of
Anglo-Saxon energy, enterprise and cupidity has given it. If
the transforming influences of the gospel have come in too
late to save the nation from extinction, it will only be because
the nation was too far gone to be saved.

E. O. Hall, *Answers to Questions*

The single most critical dismemberment of Hawaiian society was the
Mahele or division of lands and the consequent transformation of
ʻāina into private property between 1845 and 1850. When it was concluded, the Mōʻī possessed more than one million acres of the kingdom's 4.2 million acres, 251 konohiki and Aliʻi Nui owned or possessed about a million and a half acres, and the 80,000 Makaʻāinana
had managed to secure about 28,000 acres among them.

As significant an event as the Mahele has proven to be, historians
have seen it as a way of making specific indictments either of Aliʻi or
of colonialism. No one disagrees that the privatization of lands proved
to be disastrous for Makaʻāinana, yet the focus of every study, from
Jon Chinen's 1958 work to Kameʻeleihiwa in 1992, has been to try and
establish the principal responsibility for its "failure." Because missionary advisors who designed the land division intended to destroy the
interdependence between konohiki and Makaʻāinana in the first
place, the Mahele was hardly a failure at all. Furthermore, insofar as
the Mōʻī and the legislature intended to provide a framework for
Makaʻāinana to eventually accommodate a new economic and politi-

cal system, only the eventual removal of Native Hawaiian tenant rights made the Mahele the economic disaster that it was for the kānaka.

The Mahele took five years to accomplish. It began auspiciously enough with an Organic Act creating the Board of Commissioners to Quiet Land Titles on 10 December 1845. The privy council recommended this course to the legislature in response to the growing tension between foreign residents and kānaka over land. Since June of that year Maka'āinana had been sending petitions to the legislature warning the government not to sell lands to foreigners. On the other hand, both the foreign resident community and recent European colonial acquisitions in Polynesia pressured the Mō'ī and the legislature to consider drastic changes to the ancient land tenure system.

The changes began slowly, with the legislature approving a very

Table 1. Legislative Council, 1848. (Mō'ī: Kauikeaouli; ministers: Keoniana (John Young Jr.), Interior; Robert Wyllie, Foreign Affairs; Gerrit Judd, Finance; Richard Armstrong, Education; John Ricord, Attorney General)

NOBLES [a]	REPRESENTATIVES
Julie Kauwā Alapa'i	Hulu (Maui)
John Papa 'Ī'ī	Z. Ka'auwai
J. Kā'eo	W. Kahale (Maui) (Hawai'i)
Hakaleleponi Kalama (Queen)	Daniel Kawaihoa
Kānehoa (James Young)	Kekino (O'ahu)
Paul Kanoa	Kekuapāni'o (O'ahu)
Kaisera Kapa'akea	Wahine'ike (Hawai'i)
George L. Kapeau	Wana (Kaua'i)
Luka Ke'elikōlani	
Mataio Kekūanaō'a	
A. Keli'iahonui	
Keoniana (John Young Jr.)	
Laura Konia	
Beneli Nāmakehā	
Nueku Nāmau'u	
Abnera Paki	
Jonah Pi'ikoi	

Source: Lydecker, 1918, *Roster Legislatures of Hawaii*, 25.
[a] *Females are in italic type.*

limited and experimental sale of lands to Maka'āinana in Makawao, Maui, and Mānoa, O'ahu, in January 1846. Eighteen months later the legislature cautiously moved to allow foreigners to claim possession of properties they were currently holding, but on a less than fee-simple basis. Foreigners were not allowed to sell such properties to anyone but other Hawaiian subjects. Six months after that, in December 1847, the Mō'ī and privy council established a Mahele Committee to allow the Mō'ī and konohiki to separate their one-third interests from each other and provide a means of accounting for the one-third interest belonging to the Maka'āinana.

Change accelerated after that. On 27 January 1848, the Mō'ī and the 251 konohiki agreed on the separation of their lands and informed the Maka'āinana that they were entitled to initiate their own claims before the Land Commission. In March of that year, Mō'ī Kauikeaouli officially ended the chiefs' and king's portion of the Mahele by separating his own interests as a konohiki from the king's interest as the head of the kingdom, willingly giving up nearly one million acres to the government—close to half of the lands he had claimed—and thus claiming fee-simple title to the remainder. The chiefs were informed that by extinguishing the government's one-third interest in the lands they claimed with a commutation fee of one-third the value of their lands, they would be awarded fee-simple title to their awards "subject to the rights of Native tenants."[1]

At the same time Maka'āinana were informed through newspaper publications and through notices posted in the churches that they too had the right to claim lands on which they lived and cultivated taro. By the time that the Kuleana Act of 1850 authorized the government to award those claims that had been surveyed and approved by the Land Commission as fee-simple properties, only 14,195 claims had been received, resulting in the Land Commission making only 8,421 fee-simple awards. All in all, Maka'āinana secured 28,658 acres under this legislation, leaving the king, government, a few chiefs, and a growing number of capitalized haole with most of the land. Historians and economists have concluded that the Mahele, whether a huge political fiasco or a devious theft, disinherited the vast majority of the kānaka.

It is doubtful that Kauikeaouli had any intention of swindling his own people of their lands, or that any of the Native Ali'i and leaders had any idea of how immense a social, economic, and political transformation they were unleashing when they acted to form the Land Commission in the first place. At the same time, it is possible to believe that not even many haole in the kingdom saw past their own immediate opportunities and did not foresee the extent of change that would take place. Although the Mō'ī's missionary advisors certainly envisioned private land ownership as a conversion that was critical to their vision of the Native destiny, it is certain that the Mō'ī himself acted from entirely different understandings and presumptions than those of the New England-born missionaries.

In 1850 one thing he understood was that the lāhui was in crisis. Nothing that the government attempted in its formative years had assuaged the rapid and seemingly unstoppable decline of the Hawaiian population. Indeed, the early 1850s brought some of the worst scourges, including an outbreak of smallpox in 1853 that killed thousands of Hawaiian men and women. To say that the society possessed insufficient health care to deal with diseases like smallpox is to significantly understate the problem. In truth, the government possessed very few of the institutional bulwarks—even effective quarantine laws —that might have mitigated or contained the suffering.

One result of the great dying off of Hawaiians was the weakening of the traditional land tenure system that had sustained the pre-Contact chiefdoms. The labor-intensive subsistence economy and extensive cultivation of the mauka (upland) areas had been the basis for, and also a sign of, a healthy and prosperous civilization. This system was especially vulnerable to rapid depopulation, which inexorably led to the abandonment of thriving lo'i (taro patches) and homesteads as the labor needed to maintain them continued to diminish. Nevertheless, this weakened system might well have survived in some kind of altered form had it not been for the Mahele.

Traditionally all of the land was the responsibility of the Mō'ī, who was required by ancient custom to place the chiefs in jurisdiction over the land and the people on it. Kauikeaouli's difficulties began with the depopulation of areas that had once been thriving agricultural communities, important to the collective food and revenue base of the entire society. The fact that lands lay in want of cultivation undoubtably is what prompted the kingdom to offer tax relief to any Maka'āinana willing to undertake the cultivation of "undeveloped" lands in 1847.

However, the external pressures at the time may have had a stronger influence on the king. In February 1843 British Admiral George Paulet forced the Mō'ī to yield the sovereignty of the nation to his control. The subsequent restoration of the kingdom a few months later by Admiral Richard Thomas did little to reassure the Mō'ī that foreign governments backed by warships would acknowledge the commercial treaties that existed between Hawai'i, Britain, and the United States and abstain from simply helping themselves to Hawaiian lands. Indeed it was the "aggressive policy of the French and . . . rumors of filibusters who were said to be about to descend upon the islands from the California coast . . ."[2] that prompted Richard Wyllie, then minister of the interior, to suggest, "it is only private property that is respected, and therefore it would be wise to put every native family throughout the islands, in possession of a good piece of land, in fee simple, as soon as possible. If danger come, we shall then have done our duty in providing for the poor natives, and if it do not come, we shall only do them justice; for by the principle adopted by the Land Commission, the poor natives are entitled to one-third."[3]

In 1845 the Board of Commissioners to Quiet Land Titles consisted of five members. Headed by William Richards, the commission included Attorney General John Ricord, Nobles John Papa 'Ī'ī and J. W. Kanehoa, and Representative Zorababella Ka'auwai. The particular principle referred to by Wyllie asserted that the "tenant" held a third interest in the land, the "landlord" another third, and the king the remainder. One problem with these designations was that they could not be adequately described within the customary definitions of Hawaiian cultural practice. The Ali'i were not landlords who owned the land and its produce. They were konohiki who had responsibilities to administer the land and whose responsibilities extended above and below them. The Maka'āinana were not tenants, entitled to live on and work the land only as long as they paid for it in produce or labor; their entitlements were fundamentally different. Kame'eleihiwa has written:

> In practical terms, the maka'āinana fed and clothed the Ali'i Nui, who provided the organization required to produce enough food to sustain an ever-increasing population. Should a maka'āinana fail to cultivate or mālama his portion of 'Āina, that was grounds for dismissal. By the same token, should a konohiki fail in proper direction of the maka'āinana, he too would be dismissed—for his own failure to mālama. The Ali'i Nui were no better off in this respect, for if any famine affected the 'Āina, they could be ousted for failing to mālama their religious duties. Hence, to mālama 'Āina was by extension to care for the maka'āinana and the Ali'i, for in the Hawaiian metaphor, these three components are mystically one and the same.[4]

Kame'eleihiwa argued that Hawaiian society just before the arrival of the Europeans and Americans in no way resembled that of feudal Europe because of the Hawaiians' sense that the land itself was alive and conscious. Untroubled by Judeo-Christian theology that placed human beings in a position of dominance over the earth and its other creatures, Hawaiian political systems favored not one political class over another, but the land—'āina—over the others.

The Mahele was a foreign solution to the problem of managing lands increasingly emptied of people. But Kauikeaouli's extraordinary choice of an alien solution is understandable because the pressures placed on him and his administration to reform and liberalize the land system were themselves alien. Those pressures came from trusted haole advisors. Even the most well meaning of them viewed Hawaiian society as no different than the feudal "dark age" from which European society was still emerging. The Land Commission's final report confirmed this belief: "But perhaps the greatest benefit that has resulted from the labors of the Commission, coupled with the liberality of our late Sovereign, is the securing to the common people their Kuleanas in fee simple; thus raising them at once from a condition little better than that of serfs or mere tenants at will of the konohiki, to the position of absolute owners of the soil."[5]

Of course, as owners Maka'āinana could be divested of their property through sale and through other less scrupulous means without the weight of tradition, custom, konohiki, or Mō'ī to intercede on their behalf. Instead, conflicts over land ownership would become the proper sphere of laws after 1852, and, accordingly, the process of legislation became much more tightly defined with the Constitution of 1852. As the political roles of king, cabinet, noble, and representative were more clearly defined, all that was left to do was to declare that the Maka'āinana were individually responsible for their own fate. Minister of Education Richard Armstrong took the passage of the Kuleana Act to deliver not only a prescription to the Hawaiians but a critical judgment of Hawaiians as well: "If you now continue poor, needy, living in disorder in miserable huts, your lands lying waste and passing into other hands, whose fault will it be? Whose but yours? Some say this country is going to ruin through your laziness and ignorance. Is it so? Then be it so no longer! Rouse up and act as those wish you to do who have a real regard for your welfare!"[6]

An ideology of individual liability is what continued to separate haole and Hawaiian worldviews even as the very structures of life were being reconstituted, leaving very little that was recognizably Hawaiian in their place. The principal restructuring may have been the land tenure system, but the foundation for the "successful" results of the Mahele was the redefinition of power and political relationships that took place in the society even as the legislature, in 1850, began discussing the need for a new constitution.

The Disabilities of Aliens

In July 1850, the legislature decided to allow haole who were not naturalized to own and sell lands in fee. The timing of this decision, coming nearly a month before the Maka'āinana rights to land were made explicit in the Kuleana Act, suggests the favoritism with which haole were treated over the Maka'āinana. A closer analysis reveals the complexities that confronted the Hawaiian government in dealing with issues of citizenship and nation building. For one thing, Maka'āinana had been making land claims even before the Mahele of 1848 that divided the lands between the konohiki of Kamehameha and the Mō'ī himself. Kame'eleihiwa has written: "The Land Commission had begun receiving claims from the maka'āinana over a period of two years previous to the 1848 Māhele of the Mō'ī. These claims were to include Native and/or foreign testimony to corroborate that the claimant had indeed been in residence on the 'āina in question since before 1839. . . . At the time, the term maka'āinana included foreigners who had sworn an oath of allegiance to the Mō'ī. (Many of those foreigners, however, retained dual citizenship.)"[7]

So, in other words, the debate was not over whether haole should own land, for some already did. Before 1850, ownership had been linked to citizenship, a linkage that had been fought and lost by the Maka'āinana in 1845 and 1846 when the legislature and the cabinet disregarded their petitions. But when the nobles in the Legislative Council introduced their Act to Abolish the Disabilities of Aliens to Acquire and Convey Lands in Fee Simple Title on 9 July 1850, they met opposition from the representatives. The Journal of the Legislative Council reads: "A long debate was had over this Act. The Nobles were all in favor of passing the Act, but the majority of Representatives were against it, because they were afraid the foreigners who were not Naturalized would own all the lands and someday there would be trouble."[8]

It was one thing for the government to give up the right to exclude all haole from citizenship and rights in Hawai'i (at least the Ali'i and the Mō'ī could offer the argument that these few whites had willingly made themselves into subjects, even though many of these naturalized subjects retained their citizenship in their own native countries). It was quite another that any and every haole resident was to be allowed what had once been reserved exclusively to the chiefs and the people: control and use of land. The day after the bill was introduced O'ahu Representative 'Ūkēkē objected, saying: "We have discussed this Act at length in order to more fully understand it, and you Nobles have given some very good reasons for why this Act should be passed; therefore there is nothing against the passage of the Act, but I believe it is proper for me to tell you why I have opposed this measure, it is because my constituents the common people have requested me. The people of Laie at Koolauloa have informed me that they are in great distress, because Chas Kanaina had leased the lands to the foreigners and they were not living in harmony."[9]

'Ūkēkē's words tell us that the Maka'āinana were very much aware of what was going on in the government, at least where their interests were concerned. They deferred to the nobles whose "very good reasons" for passing the Act are not specified in the minutes, but raised their concerns nevertheless. 'Ūkēkē's language left some ambiguity about whether the representatives were going to continue resisting the measure, but Richard Armstrong, minister of education and member of the privy council, came to the bill's rescue.

> Richard Armstrong one of the consulting members immediately asked the speaker, "Are the foreigners that have leased the lands of Kanaina those that are not naturalized?" The members of the Council answered, some of them are naturalized foreigners and some of them are Natives. Some of the Nobles then remarked, "this Act does not refer to the foreigners who are naturalized and have become subjects under the King, and there is nothing in the measure that is objectionable, because it covers every point." Ukeke was therefore convinced of this and he was in favor of its passage.[10]

This discussion shows how easily a specific piece of legislation might confuse and deflect political opposition. 'Ūkēkē's resistance was tied, after all, to the simple truth that the Maka'āinana did not want more foreigners to control land. More foreigners meant more competition for the 'āina, a competition that the Native people felt they were losing. Armstrong confounded the issue by questioning whether 'Ūkēkē's people were having difficulties with naturalized or unnaturalized haole. On hearing that they were naturalized haole and Natives, the nobles dismissed 'Ūkēkē's objection as irrelevant to the specific nature of the Act and the representatives quickly retreated.

Also worth noting is that this discussion shows the distributions of political power in 1850. The representatives had done their duty by voicing their objections to a bill that they knew would threaten their constituents, but were fully prepared to let the nobles decide the issue no matter what their reasons. As konohiki, that would be the extent of their responsibility. Moreover, even if they had wished to, they could not have outvoted the nobles, who had a twelve to eight majority over them. That would remain true until 1851.

But they also acknowledged that the nobles did have reasons, significant ones in fact, that were obvious in the very language of the Act. This was not just some gratuity offered by the Mō'ī to his favored ones, nor was it the nobles finally acknowledging that fee ownership of land was some universal right. It was politics and politics only. The ulterior motive of giving the haole land was to secure (at last) their obedience to the laws by granting such ownership. The Act read that any aliens who purchased lands, along with their heirs, executors, and administrators:

> shall in all cases of dispute in relation to his rights, title or interest in any land he may acquire in fee simple, or any part or parcel of said land, submit the same to the judicial tribunals of this kingdom, and abide by the final decision of those tribunals without seeking the intervention of any foreign nation or representative; and in case he shall refuse to do so, his estate and all his right, title or interest shall cease and determine, and the same shall be forfeited and escheat to the Hawaiian government: And further provided, that no deed or other conveyance of land in fee simple to any alien shall be of any validity or effect, unless it contains a clause providing for such submission, forfeiture and escheat.[11]

If the naturalization laws of the mid-1840s were supposed to secure the support of a new and dynamic constituency of haole, they had only barely succeeded at the end of the decade. By 1851, of almost 1,600 haole only 676 had been naturalized in Hawai'i, and 428 of those naturalized were Americans.[12] The majority of haole were foreign nationals still and, although technically bound to honor the laws of the kingdom, in reality they were likely to claim the protection of their motherland whenever they were in trouble with local author- ity or impatient with the progress of their commercial interests.

For the Hawaiian government this, of course, had been the critical issue from the instant that the Mō'ī Liholiho had first granted permis- sion for the ABCFM mission to come ashore. To allow foreigners to reside, preach, work, invest, marry, and serve in the government also involved the difficult task of defining those foreigners, not for their sake, but for the sake of establishing the king's government as a legit- imate and respected institution. Native people, whose suspicion of those foreigners was so well expressed in 1845, were willing to make their own, individual accommodations with haole (their willingness to elect them into office was one example), but it was the constitutionally created kingdom, itself a foreign establishment, that was continually at risk. Meanwhile, every law that the legislature adopted that made it easier for foreigners to make their homes and their fortunes in Hawai'i tended to have powerful and lasting effects on the Native people. The best example is the 1850 Kuleana Act, which institutionalized private land ownership for the Maka'āinana.

Dismembering Maka'āinana

The Kuleana Act, passed by the legislature in 1850, allowed Maka'āi- nana the right to claim lands on which they had built homes, tended lo'i, and in other ways cultivated as property in fee simple. This Act also called for the legal dissolution of their traditional status even to the point of changing their identity. Maka'āinana who applied for kuleana lands were renamed hoa'āina (literally, friends of the land), which the law translated as tenants.

It is not possible to determine just how many Hawaiians refused to apply for lands or to present themselves to defend their claims specifically because of their reluctance to alter their status and their traditional rights. After all, there were many reasons to avoid making claims before the Land Commission, including economic ones. Sur- veyors' fees, no incidental cost, had to be borne by the claimant. But more important, the typical award was somewhere in the neighbor- hood of three to ten acres, enough to include a good lo'i perhaps, but not enough to ensure that the 'auwai (irrigation system) would be left intact at the point where it joined with the stream. Finally, the cost of securing one's own land had to reckon also the cost of offending the konohiki who had previously claimed the 'āpana (piece of land) upon which the claim was located.

The price of securing a kuleana award cannot be evaluated simply in monetary terms. Its most enduring cost was the ending of an official recognition of the appurtenant rights of Maka'āinana. On 6 August 1850, a legislative act set out rules defining and "guaranteeing" the hoa'āina appurtenant rights to gather timber and thatch and secure water and rights of way. This was the legislature's recognition that the relationships in Hawaiian society had been severely altered. It was yet one more intrusion of law into the lives of the Native people. Although it was still theoretically possible for each hoa'āina to reach individual agreements with their landlords (whether they were the familiar konohiki or not), ultimately their rights, and only those rights, were to be secured not by tradition but by statute and judicial decision.

The problem, for the hoa'āina, was that the new rights were more capriciously rooted than the customary rights had been. In 1846, the legislature had established that each hoa'āina had rights to taro patches that existed on his property and to lo'i he constructed on unoccupied lands. Furthermore, the law entitled Maka'āinana to a fairly comprehensive array of gathering rights, including fishing, all of which entitled them to offer gathered items for sale.[13] Those rights were substantially reduced by Section 7 of the Kuleana Act. Specifically, the rights to extend one's cultivation into previously unculti-vated lands and to fish in the ahupua'a disappeared, and the gather-ing rights were limited to the hoa'āina's personal use.[14]

In the 1858 Supreme Court decision *Oni v Meek* it was held that "the rights of native tenants, both under ancient custom and prior leg-islation, were abrogated and superseded . . ." by Section 7, not only reinforcing the replacement of custom with law, but also establishing that rights were not considerations that could be sanctioned by tradi-tion and negotiated between konohiki and "tenant." In other words, the relationship that had defined both Ali'i and Maka'āinana for cen-turies was replaced by legal definitions of rights, definitions that could be altered by each new statute and each new decision. In the 1980s, legal scholar Maivan Clech-Lam made this analysis of *Oni v Meek*: "In sum, Oni stands for three propositions. First, notwithstanding the Declaration of Rights [1839], which permitted dispossession only through express provision of law, the court will infer the loss of cus-tomary rights in an informal agreement between tenants and konohiki that the old order had ended. Second, customary rights also ceased upon acquisition of fee simple title to a kuleana. Third, Section 7 of the Kuleana Act listed the only traditional rights statutorily still available to kuleana awardees, and to non-awardees who had repudiated the old order." [15]

Of course, it had been possible under the kapu system for Ali'i to deny access of certain lands to Maka'āinana and even dispossess them, in a sense, by the appropriation of resources that they had previously enjoyed. Such a dispossession might be a sign that the chief was greedy or inept and the people were not required to stand for it. One could always leave the ahupua'a of one's birth and try to find another Ali'i to serve elsewhere. [16] Such a recourse was certainly not unheard of at that time. The Kuleana Act, however, prevented such an escape by giving rights and responsibilities the rigidity of written law that held for the entire archipelago.

More than that, one can see a dreadful logic in the gradual replacement of konohiki rights and obligations as they pertained to the 'āina and to the Maka'āinana. In 1847, the konohiki were forbidden to exact labor from their people. The following year, the Ali'i Nui and the Mō'ī each began making their individual land claims. Finally, when the kuleana awards made the people's right to land explicit in 1850, the konohiki were later forbidden to alienate a single right that was guaranteed the hoa'āina by law. From the Maka'āinana point of view, then, the law was systematically rending all traditional ties to the chiefs. If the konohiki had no right to their labor and could not deny them access that only the law guaranteed, then what was left to obligate the chiefs to the people? The fact that the government, the Mō'ī, and the konohiki spent the better part of two years busily dividing up the land between themselves before addressing the concerns of the Maka'āinana could not have been reassuring to the latter.

There can be no question that the Mahele, which allowed private ownership of land, also established the indigenous occupants, both Ali'i and Maka'āinana, as competitors rather than as caretakers of the 'āina. After 1850, Native people were forced to appeal to the courts to allow them to fish, to gain access to irrigation water, and even to farm and graze lands that were unoccupied. For the most part, these decisions, [17] even when they resulted in favor of the hoa'āina, only conferred rights that they had once universally enjoyed. Thus, law became the arbiter between a family that the law itself estranged.

Hawaiians at all levels of the society bore the cost of this change.

Elimination of the konohiki rights to the labor of the Maka'āinana made them dependent on capital they did not possess to hire labor, but also eroded, in some cases, their sense of obligation to the Maka-'āinana cum hoa'āina. Reverend Artemis Bishop's letter to Armstrong in 1850, although not evidence that the chiefs were collectively trying to punish the kuleana awardees, nevertheless indicates the tensions that private land ownership created. Bishop wrote: "The word has gone forth from the chiefs to all their konohikis to forbid all such makaainanas who get their land titles, the privileges they formerly enjoyed from the kula (lands) of the landlord. . . . They are not to pull grass for their feasts or ilima for fuel, nor go into the mountain for any ki (ti) leaf . . . or timber of any kind. . . . It has nearly raised a rebellion among the people of Waianae . . . they say the chiefs have no aloha for them." [18]

Such claims reinforced the perceived need for laws to protect tenants from what the haole believed were punitive and despotic Ali'i, though in fact there is no evidence to suggest that konohiki and hoa-'āina were incapable of working out mutually beneficial arrangements, as they had done for centuries. But again, the legal system made those arrangements less and less likely. *Oni v Meek* also established that "it was not in the power of the *konohiki* had he been so disposed, to alienate a single right secured by law to the plaintiff." [19] Whatever arrangements the konohiki made to allow the former Maka'āinana to remain on the land, they could not invoke time-honored reciprocal duties.

Traditional political and social relationships between the principal classes of Hawaiians were not merely eroding by the middle of the decade. They were being intentionally dismembered, forcibly and zealously separated from each other, as a result of missionary and American ideologies and their projection into political practice through the law. Dismemberment can also be taken to mean that neither Maka-'ainana nor konohiki were still the principal members of the society and that those designations were to be replaced by new ones—subject, representative, noble, and king. At the same time, and virtually with the same laws, haole were insinuating themselves to fill the spaces created by that dismemberment. They began with oaths of allegiance, they progressed to recognizing themselves as legal titleholders to the land, and they capped it off by taking over the House of Representatives in 1851, after awarding suffrage to haole whether they were citizens or not.

Incorporating the Alien

The kingdom's preoccupation with the rights of foreigners to own land dominates the first written laws that deal with the naturalization of foreigners through the taking of the oath of allegiance. In August 1838, Kauikeaouli signed a document known as "Alien Laws," which, according to Hawai'i Territorial Archivist Maude Jones, was "never promulgated into law,"[20] but formed the basis for the eventual definition of citizenship in the kingdom. The first two articles of the law described who were proper subjects of the realm. Those who were not born in the Islands, born to Natives living abroad, or born aboard a ship belonging to the Sandwich Islands were aliens unless they took the oath of allegiance. The succeeding eight articles determined that although the government could not divest aliens of land for a minimum of ten years from the date of acquisition, all such land and improvements belonged, ultimately, to the government.

The final article dealt with the rights of a foreigner to marry a Native woman. It was this article that aroused the most debate within and outside the government. It provided that an alien wishing to marry a Native woman was to place a bond of $400, "promising to make the Sandwich Islands his home for life." That bond was forfeit if the man ever left the Islands, three-fourths of which would be remitted to his deserted family for their care and support. Only a $100 bond was required from anyone willing to take the oath of loyalty "and by this act, renounce all allegiance to every foreign sovereign whatsoever."[21]

The marriage laws most clearly indicate the difficulties of long-term international contact for foreigners and Hawaiians. Perhaps no one saw it with greater clarity than O'ahu governor and noble Mateo Kekūanaō'a. In June 1848, he addressed the legislature, giving several examples of problems that had arisen from marriages between subjects and foreigners:

> After a foreigner has married one of our women and has lived with her for one year, then he deserts her and goes home; the woman is left in trouble under our laws, and is prevented from marrying another husband until after the death of the first husband. Women who are thus deserted by their first husband are left destitute. . . . After a foreigner who has not taken the oath of Allegiance to the country has married one of our women, children are born, and after two years or so, the husband wants to return to his country, taking with him all the children; the wife then comes and complains . . . he then

complains to the Consul who acts, then the Country gets into trouble and the woman also. [In another case] The woman has some property and owns some lands. The woman dies first leaving everything which the husband claim [sic]. He then complains to the Consul of his own country and say [sic], "This is my own land given me by my wife." The land then is lost to the King and the King will be without lands. . . . Again in former times the foreign husbands used to beat their wives, take away the clothes which were given them and sent them away which gave the women lots of trouble. . . . Again, if the marriage of one of our Chiefess had taken place during the time when there was no oath required a part of this country would have been lost to us.[22]

Kekūanaōʻa displayed concerns that were not only pragmatic, such as the disposition of children and assets, but reflected powerful value judgments as well. It is interesting to note that the transgressions that the noble accused foreigners of having committed, desertion and brutality, were the precise accusations leveled at Hawaiian society by missionaries in the 1820s, who ardently believed that the absence of true marriage in Hawaiian culture was responsible for desertion and the absence of any "real" family. The 1824 sumptuary laws forbade "fornication," any sexual act that took place between individuals not committed to a monogamous relationship that had been sanctified by a Christian marriage. That law had prompted thousands of marriage ceremonies among Hawaiians over the years but had not erased the problem of dealing with property difficulties between Hawaiians and foreigners.

Indeed, the politics of marriage and foreign relations was well illustrated in the famous case of William Buckle, an English whaling captain who "purchased" a Hawaiian woman in Lāhainā in 1824 and carried her off aboard ship to Honolulu in what the chiefs and Reverend William Richards perceived as a clear violation of their law. Richard's condemnation of Buckle in a letter written to British authorities resulted in Buckle returning to Lāhainā and threatening to destroy the town unless the missionary was turned over to him for having committed the crime of "killing his good name."[23] Fortunately for Richards, Kaʻahumanu refused to surrender her pastor, but the whole affair only indicated how helpless the kingdom was to control foreigners' behavior.

From the standpoint of respect for the law, it may have been a slight improvement that haole went through the process of actually marrying Hawaiian women before setting up housekeeping in the Islands. Kekūanaō'a's analysis in 1848 indicates, however, that at least in some cases the formality of marriage was little more than a charade for haole who had no intention of spending their lives in the Islands and were determined to make their temporary sojourn as comfortable as possible. The monetary bond was seen as separating the fortune hunters from men of means among the foreigners, and the smaller bond coupled with the oath of allegiance was, so far as the kingdom was concerned, more than ample to test the individual's seriousness about remaining in Hawai'i.

Unfortunately, the worth of an oath was more or less dependent on the worth of the individual, as so clearly perceived by the Maka'āinana whose petition against foreign citizenship was published in the *Friend* in 1845: "Good Foreigners will become no better by taking the oath of allegiance under our Chiefs. Good people are not opposed to us, they do not evade the laws of the Chiefs; they do not wish this kingdom to be sold to others. What good can result from their taking the oath?"[24]

Attorney General John Ricord demonstrated the real value of the oath, which he took just before his appointment in 1844. Three years later Ricord resigned his post, announced his decision to return to America, and asked that he be released from his oath.[25] His request was granted, though not without some fairly complex diplomatic discussions between the foreign affairs minister, Englishman Robert Wyllie, and the American commissioner. Ricord's disavowal of citizenship also aroused considerable public comment. One individual, identified only as "Scrutateur," sent this letter to the *Friend:*

> The King of the Sandwich Islands may, for aught we know, by some inherent right of sovereignty, release any one or all of his subjects, native born or naturalized, from their fealty to him. But neither the King of Hawaii nor the King of Kings can release John Ricord, or any other man from the obligations to the universe of an oath recorded on high . . . and according to our understanding of the King's Constitution and his powers defined therein, he will remain a subject. . . . The King cannot by the exercise of any sovereign prerogative or by the resolution of the Privy Council, abrogate the laws. The law is explicit.[26]

Along with the religious overtones the writer denied that the king could supersede the law, thus claiming the supremacy of haole law over the sovereign power of the Mōʻī. Wyllie firmly contested this position and wrote to U.S. Commissioner Anthony Ten Eyck in an attempt to prevent the issue of citizenship from becoming a diplomatic matter. His words are worth noting, especially his argument that the king was, indeed, sovereign: "I am aware of nothing in the ancient usages of this Kingdom or in the Constitution which disables the King from exercising a power, in a gracious sense, which the Kings and Queens of England, for many civilized Ages, exercised in a penal sense. But even, if there should be anything unconstitutional in the act, so far as the exercise of power is concerned, it is a matter of constitutional and not of foreign remedy."[27]

Wyllie's claim was important for the kingdom in his insistence that the power to define the citizen and the citizen's rights was purely a domestic issue and could not be appropriated as a matter of diplomacy by foreign governments. On the other hand, foreigners who were naturalized in Hawaiʻi were not, themselves, nationless waifs but individuals who arrived here steeped in their own national identities. That presented a problem for some of the haole who sought brides, land, or government employment, because citizenship in Hawaiʻi required that they renounce their former (usually European or American) citizenship.

This renunciation, known at the time as the "abjuration clause," gave way to a compelling debate on the very nature of national identity, rights of nations, and the prerogatives of sovereigns as they came to be written into the naturalization process by 1840. Ironically, it was Ricord, under the pseudonym "Ligamen," who had argued in a letter to the Friend just a few months after taking the oath himself that choosing citizenship was an individual's right, and that ties to one's birth land, although important for sentimental reasons, were not obligatory over one's lifetime.

In reply, Wyllie wrote this analysis (and complaint) of the fact that so many more Americans than Britons were willing to take the oath of allegiance in 1844:

> It would be tantamount to exclusion of British subjects from all appointments of honor, trust or profit under the crown—for not withstanding the arguments and illustrations of Ligamen, the most of them are of the opinion that they cannot legally abjure their allegiance to their own sovereign. That the allegiance of a subject is perpetual and indissoluble, according to the English law . . . America receiving every year by thousands the emigrants of Europe, maintains

the doctrine, suitable to her condition, of the right of transferring allegiance at will. The laws of Great Britain have maintained from all time the opposite doctrine. The duties of allegiance are held to be indefeasible; and it is believed that this doctrine, under various modifications, prevails in most if not all the civilized states of Europe.[28]

Perhaps for Americans who had fought not one, but two wars with England over the right of choosing nationhood, the privilege of altering one's nationality was a matter of right and as simple as an oath, though we would do well to mind the example of Ricord before arguing that the change of nationality was an exercise in idealism and not practical politics, at least for Americans.

In any case, the oath could be a remarkably flexible instrument. There were at least three different oaths issued to naturalize aliens before 1850, when the abjuration clause was done away with once and for all, to be replaced by laws allowing denizens the right to own land and run for public office. One form of the oath, known as the "C" oath, was administered to a single individual, Robert Wyllie, and essentially allowed him to keep his "inheritance" in England. For some, though, the very idea of changing national loyalty was anathema, to be resisted even if it meant loss of livelihood. Honolulu harbor pilot Robert Reynolds, an American, was removed from his position when he refused the oath. For other Americans, the choice of changing citizenship was a problem to be avoided as long as possible. This was especially true of the ABCFM missionaries.

In some ways, missionaries present the most interesting case of all. Because of their stated reason for coming in the first place, serving the spiritual needs of the Hawaiians, one might assume that such temporal issues as national loyalty would have been of rather little interest to them. The official position of the board in New England was that because the mission's presence in the Islands was an act of benevolence, and not to be confused with other foreigners who were there for private gain, their status was separate and special.

Of course, the fact that missionaries did participate in government and were granted extensive gifts of land by the Mō'ī meant that they were not always perceived as being distinct from any other influential and powerful alien, not even by one of their own. In 1844, former missionary and minister of the treasury Gerrit Judd wrote the secretaries of the board saying that, "the missionaries have in fact chosen a position as near as possible to naturalization without taking the usual oath." This coupled with the fact that their children were subjects and that they were given lands when other aliens had to be satisfied with leases had created, in Judd's estimation, a climate rife with jealousy and resentment, mostly by foreigners, of the American church. Judd's solution was that they ought to become naturalized because, "As subjects, his Majesty could at once avail himself of the example, countenance and aid of all the missionaries . . . and thereby the jealousy which now exists towards the mission and towards the Government when it listens to them, be done away."[29]

Ultimately, the haole problems with naturalization were resolved quite discriminately. It was obvious even to the Maka'āinana back in 1845 when they petitioned the government that the methods and rituals of incorporating the haole reflected only one common reality. That reality was that the government was willing to make exceptions for individuals and that those individuals were already powerful. Ricord could retract his oath, Wyllie could compose his own, and missionaries like Richard Armstrong could be given cabinet positions without becoming a subject of the king. On the other hand, the government could be quite strict with less-influential haole like Reynolds.

Seen in this light, the Maka'āinana reaction to the prospect of aliens becoming subjects merely by their word was surely sensible. It was not only that the Natives were possessive of their identity, but the cheapening of that identity outraged and worried them as well. The fact that the government cooperated with the haole to continually redesign the rules by which aliens could become Hawaiians undermined the gravity of citizenship. Put another way, aliens who were naturalized acquired privilege, but Native subjects were less and less privileged by the very same laws that sought to incorporate the foreigners.

Furthermore, the Native petitioners made a very astute point when they argued that good foreigners would not be better on account of an oath. Rather, bad foreigners would have one more opportunity to secure wealth at the expense of Hawaiians: "Who are those who take the oath suddenly? These are the persons. Those who want a building spot, or a large piece of land for themselves; those who wish to become Chiefs or head men upon the lands, and those who wish to marry wives immediately. . . . Do they desire this people to become enlightened? It is not clear to us that they do."[30]

The Natives' distinctions between good and bad haole indicate that their judgments were not racist. However, neither were they shy about making judgments. In the 1850s at least, these judgments reflected their perceptions of whether particular haole had good intentions toward kānaka or were merely selfish and opportunistic fortune seekers. The legislature, by passing a series of laws that would enable denizen haole to own land and hold political office, created opportunities for "good" and "bad" haole alike. This may be why Natives were willing to vote haole into the House of Representatives in 1851; they hoped that good haole would counteract the bad ones.

The Residency Laws of 1850 were part of several attempts to bind non-Natives to the kingdom that had begun a decade before. The first strategy had been to offer them full citizenship, and when less than half of the foreigners took advantage of that offer, the government offered them land. Finally the government granted them full participation, suffrage, and the right to hold office, without the discomfiting necessity of forsaking citizenship in their native country. Here, the legislature made a defining decision to go beyond trying to bind the loyalty of the haole to the Hawaiian nation through appeals to self-interest. When that effort failed the legislators had few choices remaining and were confronted with a foreign community that had taken a controlling interest in the economics of the kingdom and thus could not be denied access to government.

The legislature authorized haole voting and office holding in an act approved on 30 July 1850, three weeks after it permitted foreigners to purchase lands. Land ownership conferred the suffrage on male citizens and denizens alike.[31] Denizens were defined as aliens who had received from the king "letters patent of denization which conferred . . . without the necessity of renouncing his *natural allegiance* [italics mine] all the rights, privileges and immunities of a Native Hawaiian." According to the law, "Said letters patent shall render the denizen in all respects accountable to the laws of this kingdom and impose on him the like fealty to the King as if he had been naturalized."[32] In short, a new category was invented for haole that gave them suffrage in Hawai'i without requiring that they give up their own citizenship.

This law was proposed by haole advisors to the king and enacted to allow and encourage foreigners' participation in the government. Yet the idea of a haole citizenry was by this time quite established through the taking of the oath of allegiance. Denization conferred rights so casually that the very act of taking up residence seemed to carry with it all the benefits of citizenship. Such a practice had few parallels in the world, though American laws in the nineteenth century made it remarkably easy for European immigrants to gain political rights. Historian Kirk H. Porter described the situation in the United States in the 1870s this way:

For the first time the alien found strong champions; for the first time he was really wanted in certain parts of the country, wanted so badly that inducements were held out to attract him. Up in the Great Lakes region—in Michigan, Indiana, Wisconsin, Illinois, and Minnesota—there were vast, uncultivated tracts of land awaiting exploitation. Most of these states had not been organized very many years, and they were eager to grow, to develop their resources, increase their population and their wealth, gain larger representation in Congress, and become important units in the national government. What then could be more logical than to offer the swarming immigrants a hand in the government if they would only come? And a hand in the government meant the right of suffrage even before they were naturalized.[33]

This liberalization of the suffrage laws often provoked a backlash against people whom Anglo-Americans considered inferior or undesirable. Porter described the reaction to one such group, Irish Catholics, in the mid-1840s:

Illiterate Irish Catholic hoodlums promoting a riot at the polls was a particularly offensive spectacle to conservative New Englanders. It is told how they beat respectable citizens, insulted public dignitaries, fought openly with the police, and raised havoc generally. An election was considered an occasion for a grand uproar. And, what was most alarming, they were building up a vast machine to be controlled by shrewd, unscrupulous politicians. . . . To combat the menace a very considerable number of people were ready to form a political party.[34]

Porter noted without a trace of irony that this new organization was known as the Native American Party (historically referred to as the Know-Nothings). The author asserted that the undisciplined newcomers could only distort the meanings of real participation in government and that the owners of that process (the so-called Native Americans) were entitled to entertain strategies that would limit the desecration.

In Hawai'i, although Native Hawaiians made up the majority of the population, many haole, like the Anglo-Saxon majorities in North America, believed that they should properly be in charge. It was their very foreignness that they believed was valuable to the government and the society. Their cultural and racial being, in their minds, gave them certain rights among traditional peoples everywhere and also guaranteed that there could be no successful nationhood in places like

Hawai'i without their participation. One "Brevitas" expressed it this way in 1849:

> In the Constitution of the Hawaiian Islands it is provided that there shall be a "House of Nobles and Representatives." Now, Sir, I wish to know whether it would not be sound policy, to say nothing of *right of representation* to have a certain proportion of the Representatives elected by the vote and from the body of foreign residents upon these islands? It occurs to me that the influence of Anglo-Saxon energy and perseverance in the councils of the nation would operate more than any other cause, to the benefit and preservation of the Hawaiian race, while it would give foreigners coming here to reside, an interest in the affairs of government, which they could not receive in any other way. [35]

In America denization laws were usually repealed when labor quotas were filled. The reverse was true in Hawai'i. Although immigration was seen as diluting and weakening the pure electorate in the American states, many whites in Hawai'i believed that foreign immigration, so long as it was the right kind of foreigner, strengthened the electorate. Strangely enough the Hawaiian denization law was passed by a legislature that included no haole members. This indicates either a major shift in Maka'āinana opinion regarding whites in government or that the legislature, as it had in 1845, continued to express the will of an entity other than the Native Hawaiian public. On the other hand, the continuing downward spiral of the Native population may have signaled to the legislature, at least, that it was necessary to expand suffrage, if not the definition of citizenship.

There was, in fact, rather little debate on the measure within the House of Representatives, but the English-speaking press reacted favorably. [36] The principal argument in favor of the law seemed to be that haole who were naturalized citizens by way of the oath of allegiance needed to secure representation, which would be more effective if all resident haole could vote. Haole believed that this would be an unadulterated bargain for the Natives, who although still retaining their majority status (for the time being) would certainly benefit from a stronger House of Representatives. *Polynesian* editor E. O. Hall published these interesting racial observations in 1849:

> There is one topic on which we should like to have an expression of opinion, and that is, whether the House of Commons would not have a little more energy, and better represent the industry and capital of

the Kingdom, if it was in part composed of naturalized citizens, and not entirely of Native born. We have long thought that some such should have a hand in the legislation and have had serious thoughts of nominating a candidate for the suffrages of the voters of this Parliamentary district. [37]

Historian Ralph S. Kuykendall made a similar point, arguing that this legislation coupled with the Act increasing the number of representatives to twenty-four strengthened that body, with its size and the presence of foreigners within it making it "in fact the abler and more effective branch of the legislative council." [38]

So the legislature sought to "strengthen" itself in much the same way that the Mō'ī had sought to strengthen his ability to govern in the 1840s by appointing haole to cabinet positions. What sort of signal was being sent to the Natives but that their worst fears were being actualized? As their numbers faded, so too did their government's determination to resurrect them, choosing instead to adopt a foreign constituency. The lack of a systematic opposition to the inclusion of haole in the legislature only five years after the outpouring of resistance to their presence and legitimation invites speculation.

One explanation for the lack of opposition is that Maka'āinana had little faith in the legislature and therefore did not much care, at least initially, about its composition. Between 1842 and 1850, there was never a session where all of the seats of the House of Representatives were filled. According to law, a total of eight representatives was allowed membership in the legislature, two each from Hawai'i and O'ahu, two from Maui, Moloka'i, and Lāna'i, and two from Kaua'i and Ni'ihau, to sit with the nobles in council. Yet there were never more than seven representatives in attendance in any year, and in 1847 and 1849, only five members were elected and approved by the Mō'ī. Some of the problems arose from voting irregularities, [39] but the people on Kaua'i simply refused to send anyone to the legislature in 1847:

The Governor of Kaua'i then reported on the election of the three districts of his Island as follows:

The First District said, "There is no use electing a Representative, as the one we elected to the Legislature last time went there and passed a law making us pay $1.00 tax on our dogs."

The Second District said, "There is no use electing a representative because the lands are being sold."

The Third District said, "There is no use electing a Representative as he will then get a swallow-tail coat."[40]

This passage, part of the minutes of the legislature in 1848, was not accompanied by any official comment, but one can hardly imagine that any legislator would have been pleased to have been so casually dismissed by the Maka'āinana. Perhaps the legislature's decision to increase its numbers by liberalizing the franchise to include foreigners is related to Maka'āinana ambivalence to the institution. In any case, the impatience flowed both ways. The Kaua'i governor's report quite clearly indicates the people's dissatisfaction with the performance of the legislature. More interesting are the kinds of accusations that were levied on that body; not only was the legislature criticized for being a useless waste of money, but also that it was inherently helpless to deal with the most critical issue of the period—the future of the Maka'āinana on the land.

As the legislature and particularly the House of Representatives became more powerful, it increasingly was dominated by foreign-born subjects and, after 1851, denizens who were knowledgeable enough about the uses of legislatures and laws to push their own interests to the forefront. A close look at the conduct of kanaka representatives at the onset of these multiethnic legislatures indicates that they initially evinced some confusion over the role of their agency and their own responsibilities within it. They were not made helpless spectators by the haole and their vigorous pursuit of opportunity, but the commerce-driven legislative agendas increasingly forced the kānaka to mediate the needs and demands of their own constituency with the apparent needs and demands of the Western-styled nation that they were also trying to serve. It was not apparent to them that this could not be done.

1851 Election: Haole in the House of Representatives

According to the best estimates, there were about 27,800 votes cast in the kingdom when the polls closed on 6 January 1851. Of these, 13.9 percent came from Honolulu, the only area that published a record of voter participation that year.[41] According to the law in 1851, all Native-born males twenty years and older and all naturalized citizens and denizens were entitled to cast votes for the House of Representatives. In that year, there was a total of 1,600 foreign men and women living in the Islands, about 2 percent of the overall population. Assuming that the ratio of qualified voters to population was not radically different between Native and haole, one would have to assume that white representatives were elected not only because haole voted for them, but because Hawaiians did. Of the twenty-four representatives in the House that year, seven were white.

The fact that Hawaiians were willing to vote for non-Hawaiians is a curious but explicable development. For one thing, the method of voting underwent a significant change in 1850. The election day was standardized throughout the kingdom (the first Monday in January) and from that year on, voters had to present themselves at a polling location and cast their votes for the candidate of their choice. The old system that allowed petitioners to name their candidate and sign their names may have been inefficient and subject to abuses of the "one man, one vote" ideal, but that practice was framed around a political process that Hawaiians found relatively more familiar and comfortable (that is, the petition).

Petitioning is based on a relationship that quite explicitly places the petitioner in a position of subordinance, the very position that defined the Maka'āinana and their successors, the hoa'āina. The petitions used before 1850 stated that the undersigned requested that their nominees "serve with the Nobles" in the legislature, something that was consistent with their cultural norms. Their representatives would convey their concerns to the Mō'ī and the Ali'i while actually depending on the Ali'i to make the decisions, as the ruling chiefs had always done.

However the new law called on the people to choose from a slate of candidates the individual who would serve their interests best. Here, the haole candidates had an advantage because they could put themselves forward for election without having to wait for a few hundred Hawaiians to consider them trustworthy. Moreover, the 1850 laws expanded the size of the House of Representatives from eight to twenty-four members. Theoretically, the law provided more opportunity for Native candidates as well as haole, but there had never been full participation in the earlier, smaller legislature, and there is some justification for the notion that the additional sixteen seats were created for newly enfranchised haole.

There are, unfortunately, no reports on the election results except for a very spotty one from Honolulu. In a (Kona) district where over 2,000 votes were cast, the two haole candidates, George M. Robertson and T. C. B. Rooke, both Englishmen, won over the Native candidates,

Table 2. Legislative Council, 1851. Legislation making cabinet ministers voting members of the House of Nobles and increasing the number of representatives to no less than twenty-four was passed on 30 June 1850. (Mō‘ī and President: Kauikeaouli; ministers: Wyllie, Foreign Affairs; Judd, Finance; Armstrong, Public Instruction)

NOBLES[a]	REPRESENTATIVES
Richard Armstrong	B. Barenaba (Hilo, Hawai‘i)
John Papa ‘Ī‘ī	Francis Funk (Hanalei, Kaua‘i)
Gerrit Judd	P. J. Gulick (Waialua, O‘ahu)
Joshua Kā‘eo	Ka‘ahalama (Ka‘ū, Hawai‘i)
Hakaleleponi Kalama	L. Ka‘apā (Puna, Hawai‘i)
Charles Kana‘ina	Zorababella Ka‘auwai (Wailuku, Maui)
Kānehoa (James Young)	Kaho‘oku‘i
Paul Kanoa	M. S. Kālaihoa
Kaisera Kapa‘akea	J. Kalili
George L. Kapeau	Samuel M. Kamakau
John Kapena	S. Kapehe
Mataio Kekūanaō‘a	M. Kau‘ōhai
Keoniana (John Young Jr)	John Kekaulahao (‘Ewa, O‘ahu)
Laura Konia	William Little Lee (Kohala, Hawai‘i), Speaker
B. Nāmakehā	G. W. Lilikalani
Abnera Pākī	D. Lokomaika‘i (Moloka‘i)
Jonah Pi‘ikoi	A. W. Parsons (Lāhainā, Maui)
Robert C. Wyllie	Godfrey Rhodes
	John Richardson (Honolulu, O‘ahu)
	George Robertson (Honolulu, O‘ahu)
	Thomas C. B. Rooke (Kona, O‘ahu)
	L. S. Ua (Lāhainā, Maui)
	George Belly ‘Ūkēkē
	Wahinemaika‘i (Hāmākua, Hawai‘i)

Source: Lydecker, 1918, *Roster Legislatures of Hawaii,* 32.

[a] *Females are in italic type.*

whomever they were. According to the newspaper *The Polynesian*, less than forty haole actually voted in that district.[42] Rooke and Robertson were the only candidates to advertise in the newspaper, entering a small statement of their candidacy and ideals in October 1850.[43]

Obviously, Hawaiians must have voted for haole candidates, possibly even forsaking their own. One reason may have been the advertisement, though such a small item placed only once in the newspaper could not have had that large an effect on people's choices. It is much more likely that consistent and numerous messages regarding haole candidates in general would have had a stronger effect. Though we cannot be sure how many kānaka read the haole newspapers, there was never any shortage of letters and editorials praising the new liberal voting laws and especially the fact that white leadership would now come to the House of Representatives and enable the people to get their share of consideration in the government.

Because of the Natives' mistrust of haole in their government, however, their willingness to actually place the foreigners in the legislature is quite interesting and certainly indicates that however Hawaiians made their political choices in this period, they were not bigots and made their own judgments about individual haole. Dr. Rooke, a well-known Honolulu physician, was the husband of an Aliʻi Nui (the chiefess Grace Kamaʻikuʻi) and the son-in-law of Kuhina Nui Keoniana. As for Robertson, he received some publicity as a clerk in the Ministry of the Interior in 1848 when he brought several serious charges against Treasury Minister Gerrit Judd for misusing his position and power.[44]

It is interesting that Robertson's attack on a former ABCFM missionary did not hurt him in the estimation of the voters. If Natives did vote for Robertson, and they most likely did, those Natives must also have believed that being an ex-missionary and a favorite of the king did not automatically make one a good haole. Perhaps there were some Native voters in 1851 who hoped that a House that included rival haole might keep other ones from becoming more potent political forces within the government.

More and more, the purposes of representative government became ambiguous as the composition of the electors and the legislative bodies themselves changed. The influx of so many haole into the 1851 legislature until nearly a third were Europeans and Americans by birth profoundly affected that legislature's ability to create a new constitution that would further redefine nearly every aspect of the government.

The new constitution was a familiar one for Americans and Englishmen, but to Hawaiians it severely diminished the authority of the Mō'ī and abruptly changed the membership, rules, etiquette, and power of the House of Representatives. One significant change suggested how very different a haole-inhabited House would be. The representatives were to be a separate body, no longer meeting with the nobles: autonomous and in some ways more powerful than the nobles. It was a heterogeneous group only insofar as it was populated by Natives, native-born and naturalized subjects, and foreigners. The members had definable and homogeneous interests and coalesced into something approaching a class, with individuals sharing some strong, mutual interests.

Nevertheless, they all arrived at the table with very different histories and altogether different understandings of their place. For the Natives, deference to the Ali'i Nui and the king was no less required in the second and third decades of the kingdom than in the first. If anything, protecting the authority of the Ali'i was even more crucial as their status as Natives became more and more obscure. But for the haole, their power and status was invested, at least at first, in the lower House. It would be several years before their numbers would have much weight in the House of Nobles, whose appointments implied either chiefly genealogy or cabinet-level positions.

It was the haole way to be vocal and demand that government address their individual concerns and issues. They had, in fact, secured their place in the society through a steady and determined assertion of their rights and no little intimidation by their home governments. They had also successfully negotiated a place for themselves through a greater familiarity with law. Many of the first legislators, kānaka and haole, were lawyers. As such they provided the kingdom with its only pool of trained bureaucrats, and beginning with the legislature of 1842 a term as representative very often prefigured appointment to judicial office.

In the first decade of Hawaiian legislatures (1842–1851), fifty-one representatives served at least one term in office. Seventeen of them succeeded their terms with a seat on the judicial bench, fully one-third. Nine of these were graduates of Lāhaināluna.[45]

Of the twenty-four representatives serving in 1851, fourteen were either licensed attorneys or judges by 1855. Some of them were already working in the capacity of attorney even before they were licensed. But licensed or not, the presence of so many individuals in the legislature with a practical knowledge and experience with the law

Table 3. Representatives Elected in 1851, Noting Their Legal and Government Experience.

REPRESENTATIVE	YEARS IN THE LEGISLATURE	LEGAL CAREER
B. Barenaba	1851–1852, 1856	None known
Francis Funk	1851–1853	Practiced law 1851
P. J. Gulick	1851	None known
Ka'ahalama	1851	Third circuit court judge 1854, full lawyer 1855
L. Ka'apā	1851, 1854, 1862–1867	None known
Z. Ka'auwai	1851–1852, 1854–1855	Second circuit court judge 1855
Kaho'oku'i	1851–1852	None known
M. S. Kālaihoa	1851	None known
J. Kalili	1851	First circuit court judge 1848
S. M. Kamakau	1851–1856, 1860	Second circuit court judge 1853
S. Kapehe	1851–1852	None known
M. Kau'ōhai	1851–1852	None known
John Kekaulahao	1851–1852	Lawyer 1848, First circuit court judge 1853
William L. Lee	1851	Drafted 1852 Constitution
G. W. Lilikalani	1851, 1853, 1855	Fourth district court judge 1854
D. Lokomaika'i	1849–1851, 1854	Second district court judge 1855
A. W. Parsons	1851	Lawyer, Second circuit court and other courts
Godfrey Rhodes	1851–1852, 1855, 1862, 1864, 1866, 1868, 1876–1886 (noble)	Lawyer, 1853
John Richardson	1851–1859	Partial license, Second circuit court judge 1848
G. M. Robertson	1851–1859	Third circuit court judge 1851, full lawyer 1852
T. C. B. Rooke	1851, 1855	Lawyer, 1844
L. S. Ua	1851	None known
G. B. 'Ūkēkē	1850–1852, 1856, 1860, 1866, 1867	Partial license 1867
Wahinemaika'i	1851	None known

Sources: Lydecker, 1918, *Roster Legislatures of Hawaii;* Friends of the Hawaiian Judiciary History Center, Searching for the Hundreds, 1984.

cannot be ignored. It would be too much to argue that they constituted a class with distinct and separate interests from the rest of the residents and Natives in Hawai'i, but it seems that when the Hawaiian voters went to the polls in 1851, they voted for candidates, haole or kanaka, that knew the law.

By 1855 legislation and judicial reviews were actually completing the separation of kānaka from the land and from the leadership they had known for centuries, leaving them with the vote and a representative agency in the government. The problem was not that the House of Representatives would be an impotent agency. Rather, it was its efficient use of laws and procedures that accelerated the transformation of 'āina into plantations and Maka'āinana into wage labor that hastened the dismemberment of the kānaka from their Ali'i, their Mō'ī, and from so many of their traditions and values.

As American law was grafted onto the Hawaiian political system, it provided for foreigners, and especially Americans, an 'āina of their own. The law was their refuge, a place where all haole, whether they saw themselves as missionary or opportunist (or both), could gather and claim the moral grounds for their presence in Hawai'i. If they identified with the mission of saving Hawaiians, their law was one of the instruments, through the liberalization of voting and property, for the Hawaiians' salvation. If one believed that the world and the Islands would be markedly improved if there were no Hawaiians, the law provided not just the instrument for the dispossession of Natives, but continual evidence of the superiority of the West, a superiority that made that dispossession, in the minds of haole, inevitable.

The haole in Hawai'i shaped their identity around a familiar institution, the law. Their profession of respect for law was sincere. Their ownership of the law gave them a substantive place to stand and defend their "interests." Yet at the same time, the law was fluid enough to change and accommodate their changing status in the Islands. Perhaps 'āina is not a good word for what the constitutions represented to the haole. Moku (boat) might be a better one. Even as Americans were busy occupying this moku of the kingdom, they were altering its course and steering it toward more familiar waters, east to America.

4

A House Divided

His Majesty Kamehameha III, now no more, was permanently
the friend of the foreigner, and I am happy in knowing that he
enjoyed your confidence and affection. He opened his heart
and hand with a royal liberality, and gave till he had little to
bestow and you, but little to ask. In this respect I cannot hope
to equal him. . . . I therefore say to the foreigner that he is
welcome. . . . Welcome so long as he comes with the laudable
motive of promoting his own interests and at the same time
respecting those of his neighbor. But if he comes with no more
exalted motive than that of building up his own interests at
the expense of the Native—to seek our confidence only to
betray it—with no higher ambition than that of overthrowing
our Government, and introducing anarchy, confusion and
bloodshed—then he is most unwelcome!

Kamehameha IV, Alexander Liholiho

With the entry of haole into the House of Representatives in 1851
came astonishing changes in the politics of the kingdom. These
changes were anticipated by foreign observers who felt, at the very
least, that the lower House would be made more efficient and favorable to commerce. E. O. Hall's editorials in *The Polynesian* stressed
this idea repeatedly after 1850: "The interests of commerce, and of the
foreign population generally, require a fair proportion of foreign intelligence and business habits in the legislature; and this we hope it will
have. Its presiding officer should be of that class; one who understands, not the native language merely, but Parliamentary usages, and
the proper mode of doing business. Honolulu is entitled to two repre-

sentatives; and these in our estimation, should be men capable of representing the metropolis of the kingdom, where the commerce and business of the nation naturally finds its center."[1]

A new constitution signed by Kauikeaouli shortly before his death strained the traditional ties linking the kānaka to Ali'i while greatly increasing the efficiency with which business-minded haole could create a new and dynamic market system in the Islands. As the government enlarged the prerogatives of capitalism, the Native legislators, representatives and nobles alike, struggled to maintain a foothold in the political system that threatened to make the Native irrelevant. In the early 1850s that struggle was compromised by their lack of experience with constitutional government and with the surprising aggressiveness with which foreigners pursued political power. It is also true that initially kanaka representatives cooperated with haole leadership in the House.

Just as haole symbolized a kind of empowerment for the king's government when Kauikeaouli appointed them to his cabinets in the 1840s, their presence acted as a buffer against the traditional authority of the Ali'i as the House began the process of securing and defending not only its independence, but more important, its ambitions. Not that haole and kanaka delegates were united in their intentions: in fact, they disagreed over the form and purposes of the legislature from the first day they served together.

Their disagreements were not based on mere competition. Rather, they disagreed over the most important principle of government, namely, whom did they serve? Native representatives declared a sense of responsibility to the people from their districts. In sessions they recited numerous petitions ranging over a variety of subjects including complaints against particular konohiki and requests that poll and animal taxes be made more reasonable.[2] The representatives worked as they had in previous legislatures: they read the petitions to see what the Ali'i thought should be done. But as far as haole were concerned, the people's concerns could be dealt with perfectly well without Ali'i approval, as long as important business was taken care of first.

Led by William Little Lee, Thomas Rooke, and George Robertson, the foreign-born representatives introduced a bewildering array of rules and procedures in the first week of the 1851 session. Although outnumbered by the Native delegates, they made an immediate impact on the structure of the House, recommending the naming and appointments of a half dozen committees, even before the kānaka had any idea of those committees' functions. Thus, the newcomers immediately assumed leadership of the House. Why did the Native legislators, even the experienced ones, permit this?

Although there were talented and cunning newcomers among the Native delegates, only three of these representatives, 'Ūkēkē, Lokomaika'i, and Kamakau, had served previously. There was L. S. Ua, a graduate of Lāhaināluna and heavily involved with the kingdom's educational system. He and Kamakau had both been lecturers at the school in the 1840s.[3] They were joined by Kekaulahao, an experienced attorney who had clerked in the House of Nobles in 1846, and Z. Ka'auwai, an entrepreneur and former member of the Land Commission who had nearly succeeded in purchasing the island of Kaho'olawe from the Mō'ī and the Land Commission in 1849. In fact, most of the Native delegates had some experience with government work before their election. As talented as they were, however, their understanding of their role and the role of a legislature differed greatly from the haole perception.

One week of business in the 1851 House illustrates how differently haole and kanaka representatives conceived legislation. By 13 May, five of the seven white members had introduced bills designed to create infrastructure for commerce in Honolulu. They included a Market Act for Honolulu, improvements to the harbor, construction of a prison, and straightening and widening of the streets. These bills required nothing more than their introduction and referral to committee, which the House quickly dispatched. But between 13 and 19 May, the Native representatives proceeded to read an astonishing number of petitions from their constituents. Among the petitions were complaints from different districts that taxes were too high, that the sick should not be taxed, that konohiki were overcharging former Maka'āinana for grazing rights on kula (pasture) lands, and that their access to the mountains for gathering and subsistence was restricted.[4] As they were read, haole members, usually Robertson, would immediately call for their referral to committees.

For those few Hawaiians who had served in previous legislatures, referral to committee was an innovation, and perhaps an empowering one, as it implied that they need not wait upon the nobles to do something about the petitions. For those seasoned in parliamentary rules, committee work avoided wasting time on issues that were likely to cause extensive debate. But for Robertson, the frustration of listening to one petition after another, many of which involved similar complaints—although from different sources—was simply too much to bear for more than a week. On 19 May he interrupted Ka'ū Representative Ka'ahalama's recitation of a petition from his district requesting that certain taxes be reduced or eliminated. Robertson called for the matter to be tabled. This was a parliamentary ruse intended to silence further debate or consideration. Robertson then requested that: "a rule should be made in regard to Petitions. He thought that petitions addressed to a Member should not be considered by the House. Those addressed to the House only should be considered."[5]

As far as Robertson was concerned, petitions that dealt with similar complaints were indistinguishable from one another. Petitions to individual representatives personalized the issues in ways that the haole considered inappropriate. Moreover, reading these petitions wasted the representatives' time on irrelevancies. Robertson and the other haole delegates were anxious to make the House into an efficient and powerful instrument. They focused their efforts on enhancing economic opportunities, which is not at all surprising, but in doing so depersonalized the power that the government wielded. Robertson's motion mandated that any communication from the people had to be addressed to an impersonal entity, the House itself. Then the petitions would be dealt with, not by individuals, but by committees that would treat them as legal problems rather than as requests for personal redress. The people had lost their voice.

Samuel Kamakau's response signifies quite clearly the differences between haole and kanaka legislators. Kamakau, though unfamiliar with the new procedures, quickly rose to challenge Robertson's request as unrealistic, saying that ". . . the people were not up to such things and that it ought to be left as it is, but to explain to the people of this mistake."[6] As far as Kamakau could see, there was no discernable reason why one petition should be granted a hearing over another simply on the basis of the addressee. Furthermore, as a representative, Kamakau perceived an obligation to protect the people's right to be heard. The conflict was settled when the Speaker of the House tried a compromise: "W. L. Lee remarked that it was against the law to accept such petitions but if a member should receive an important Petition from his District, he should consult with the proper Committee on the matters asked for, and in that way save much labor for the House. But in case this was not done he would introduce an Act relating to the matter."[7]

From Lee's perspective, the actual procedure relating to the framing and acceptance of petitions, though regulated by law, was immaterial. What mattered was saving labor for the "true business" of the House. Reading (and therefore acknowledging) the concerns of individual Native subjects was an inefficient use of the representatives' time and energy.

The depersonalization of the people's petitions allowed the state to distance itself from ordinary people (and their constant complaints) with the implicit promise that a more orderly fashioning of laws would more efficiently deal with those complaints. That, however, was a promise that in the most crucial instances for the Natives could not be fulfilled. What many novice politicians began discovering as early as 1852 was that although there was never any shortage of rules and procedures governing their performance and behavior within the House, there were serious deficiencies in laws that affected their constituents in areas that truly mattered to them.

For example, in 1852 over a hundred subjects in Koʻolauloa, Oʻahu, petitioned the legislature complaining that the konohiki were charging up to $10 (up from $1.50 the year before) for the people to use the kula for grazing: "And because it is quite clear in that law that we have a true right in the kula area, and that law has not been repealed as of the present nor has our right been made invalid with regards to the kula area, and we are still quite convinced that we have a right *because, he has mistreated us,* and have placed an over burdensome charge of ten dollars, we want you to consider this charge. Is this charge proper? Does this action by this konohiki show aloha?"[8] In keeping with the new procedure, the House referred this petition to a select committee consisting of Kaumaʻea, Kamaʻipelekane, and chair, T. Metcalf. Their decision on it had profound implications for the nature and limitations of the law for Natives:

> That if the petitioners have allodial titles, neither this House nor any other constituted power in this Kingdom, have authority to grant said prayer inasmuch as such an act would be in direct contravention of the constitution of this Kingdom, wherein the rights of property are *sacredly guaranteed* [italics mine] to every individual residing therein. That if the petitioners are hoaainas simply (which they do not state) your committee beg to refer the petitioners themselves to the law they themselves have quoted relating to Hoaaina rights, which is plain and easily understood, as their guide, which law, if it cannot be so administered as to secure to them their just rights, your

committee are of the opinion that any further enactment on the subject by this House will prove equally futile.[9]

This was clear enough. There were limits to what the representatives were willing to do given their constraints of laws pertaining to
private property. Those laws themselves had, somehow, been elevated, even sanctified, and although they did not offer the protection
requested—access to kula lands—they could not be altered. The
refusal to answer the petitioners' question, "Does this action by this
konohiki show aloha?" was also meaningful. The acts of individual
konohiki were beyond the scope of laws that sought to treat all parties
as objects, to be judged in terms of their compliance with existing law.
But the petitioners were not concerned with interpreting the law; they
were not asking for legal redress. They simply wanted an outrageously
improper konohiki disciplined so that he would deal with them fairly.

Apparently the law was helpless to treat such Native concerns,
although at the same time it dealt quite well with commerce. Thus,
innovative rules and procedures benefitted foreign agendas while portraying Native voters and their representatives as merely ignorant of
the "proper" uses of the legislature. After haole entered the House in
1851, their rules reduced every piece of public business to its most
efficient fraction. Legislating in the House of Representatives came to
consist of a sort of legal triage in which explicit rules governing the
initiation and referral of bills, when they could be discussed, the language used, and even the kind of paper on which they could be drafted
became the criteria for legitimate and timely treatment. In other words,
the rules governing the structure of a bill could be subjected to end-
less analysis, but the substance of those bills, including their effects on
real people, was not to be discussed. Haole representatives like Robertson and Lee did not care what happened to the common Native
petitioners, and after a brief confrontation, Native representatives
yielded to their "expertise."

Parliamentary procedure was unquestionably the strangest innovation Native politicians encountered. It was haole who brought these
rules into the House in 1851, and it was up to the Natives to learn to
use them correctly. Achieving control or even attaining equal participation in the House meant mastering those rules of order.

All of this exacted a price. It weakened the kanaka representatives' traditional respect for the Ali'i. Without a doubt, the most critical political development in the early 1850s was the growing alien-

ation between these groups at the same time haole politicians were entrenching themselves in the House. These two developments were related as law and procedural matters came to symbolize the system for Natives. Meanwhile the nobles spent entire days on matters of protocol, and sober consideration of bills initiated by others heightened the perception that the traditional chiefs were not equal to the demands of the new order. Innovation and change, it seemed, were being sponsored, inaugurated, and carried through by the House of Representatives.

The Fall of the House of Nobles

In 1851 the House of Nobles and the House of Representatives met as separate and distinct governmental bodies for the first time. The representatives, now under haole leadership, used their new "independence" from the Ali'i to transform their body into an efficient engine of legislation. The nobles, on the other hand, appeared to have no agenda of their own, considering only the bills that were laid before them by the executive branch or the lower House. Nearly all of the new business introduced for their consideration came either by decree of the king and privy council or was sent "up" from the House of Representatives. The nobles were thus much more constrained by the authority of the king and the privy council than were their counterparts in the House of Representatives.

There are two reasons for this development. First, many of the nobles in that body were inferior in rank and status to the Ali'i Nui who had once made up the powerful and venerated Council of Chiefs. In 1851 the House of Nobles consisted of the following individuals: the Ali'i Nui Laura Konia, a wahine; haole cabinet members Richard Armstrong, Gerrit Judd, and Robert C. Wyllie; and fourteen Kaukau-ali'i: J. Y. Kānehoa, Kaisera (Caesar) Kapa'akea (father of Kalākaua), John Kapena, Abnera (Abner) Pākī, John 'Ī'ī, Joshua Kā'eo, Charles Kana'ina, Paul Kanoa, George L. Kapeau, Mataio Kekūanaō'a, Beneli Nāmakehā, Jonah Pi'ikoi, John Young, and Hakaleleponi Kalama, the king's wife. Altogether this "Council of Chiefs" symbolized the diminishing of the chiefly lineages that had once supplied all of the traditional leadership.

A second reason for the diminishment of the House of Nobles is that haole members Wyllie and Armstrong assumed the direction of it in much the same way that haole representatives took over the organization of that House, but Wyllie did not form standing committees. The nobles did not receive or read petitions from the people; they appeared to content themselves with matters of protocol. For example, during the first five days of the session, 30 April to 5 May 1851, the nobles did the following: chose Armstrong and Wyllie as a committee to "bring forward rules for the regulation of this House," accepted the rules, agreed to meet at the home of John Young, appointed a committee to tell the representatives that the king would meet with the legislature on 6 May, discussed the proper use and placement of kāhili (traditional feather standards, symbols of the Aliʻi Nui), and heard the king's speech.[10]

It is evident that the haole organizers of the upper House were not initially prepared to create from the Native Aliʻi a legislative body similar to the senate in state legislatures. Perhaps Wyllie and Armstrong believed that the nobles as symbols of tradition would prevent the representatives from making rash or radical decisions, in the same way that the U.S. Senate is supposed to function. It is also possible that the haole-dominated ministry did not anticipate that the foreigner-led representatives would so quickly assert themselves and turn lawmaking to their own purposes.

This is not to say that the nobles had no important tasks. They considered and amended the privy council's decree for the creation of a Fire Department and Health Department for Honolulu as well as a Market Ordinance, which they promptly dispatched to the representatives for their advice and consideration. As the legislature became the agency by which so many changes took place in the kingdom, it was the House of Representatives that directed those changes.

The differences between the two Houses presented a difficult paradox for the kingdom. The presence of whites in the legislature was the logical end of the policies the Mōʻī and his Aliʻi had favored during the 1840s. To exclude them from the lower House after giving them the highest appointive positions in the realm and after accepting them as full-fledged citizens was logically indefensible. On the other hand, whites appointed to advise the king and nobles did not have the same kind of power as whites elected to the House of Representatives, a power that was independent of the Crown and the House of Nobles.

It is not surprising that it was haole representatives who led the way in the transformation of political power in the 1850s. Lacking any culturally defined relationship with the Aliʻi, they tended to treat the nobles as political obstacles, maintaining an independence from them that sprang in some cases from a deeply rooted disdain. Charles Reed Bishop, entrepreneur-husband of the princess Bernice Pauahi and a representative in 1853, made this confidential evaluation of the Nobles in 1851:

> James Young [Kānehoa] the Govr of Maui, died last week; and has no successor appointed, yet. Lot is sick, some say with consumption. the King is poorly. He drinks a great deal, and, it is a wonder that he is living. His example, and that of *the young chiefs* is having a very bad effect upon the natives, generally, and it is astonishing, considering their power and influence, that the affairs of govt. go on so orderly and sensibly as they do. Lee and Armstrong are the main pillars in the foreign part of the council, that is, they are the most disinterested, responsible and capable. John Ii, Paki, John Young and the govr [Kekūanaō'a] are about the only ones among the chiefs worth mentioning, and they are in a trying situation. [11]

It was easy, and gratuitous, for Bishop to praise the old chief who was no longer living. His comments about the young chiefs' inadequacies, however, are worth a brief note. Two of those young chiefs, Alexander Liholiho and Lota Kapuāiwa, ruled as Mō'ī who were not only respected, but revered by the Natives. [12] It was not at all evident to them that Alexander Liholiho and his brother Lota Kapuāiwa were inferior chiefs. Moreover, the provisions of the Constitution of 1852 and legislation actually prevented Ali'i Nui from displaying the kind of power and authority enjoyed by their forebears. Indeed, as some foreigners observed, the willingness of Ali'i to voluntarily restrain their authority was a significant reason for the success of their government. Charles de Varigny, a Frenchman who served in the ministry of Lota Kapuāiwa, made this observation in his memoirs: "The native chiefs willingly retired into the background. Their ambition did not extend beyond the desire to assist in a task they regarded as beyond their capacities, but to which they all wanted to lend their loyal cooperation. They had but one goal, that of establishing an orderly system of government, of abandoning anarchy and despotism, of winning through their moderation and wisdom the kind of respect they realized they could never attain by the mere exercise of force." [13]

Lee, Bishop, and many of the missionaries who turned from church to commerce and politics justified their manipulation of the kingdom's politics, having convinced themselves that the chiefs were a decadent remainder of an obsolete society. It was not that they had no use for aristocracy, but they were suspicious of aristocracies founded on inherited rank. Most important, they could not bring themselves to believe that the "lower classes" would obey, honor, even love such an aristocracy without the coercion of military force or the temptation of wages. Kamakau put it this way: "The Hawaiian nation loves its king and chiefs. If a chief expresses a wish, his people see to it that his words are not spoken in vain. The foreigners saw this and made this country their home and never thought of returning to their own land. . . . The Hawaiian people welcome the stranger freely; rich and poor, high and low give what they can. The strangers call this love ignorance and think it good for nothing. The love upon which they depend is a love based upon bargaining, good for nothing but rubbish blown upon the wind."[14]

The debasement of the Ali'i was a discourse. It was a conversation that filtered the creation of new laws and affected the direction of the society and government. So it was a powerful conversation. But from the kanaka viewpoint, anything that is voiced has a power, a mana of its own. Native Hawaiians have a saying: "I ka 'ōlelo ke ola, i ka 'ōlelo ka make." [In language is both life and death.] It was meaningful that Ali'i could be openly criticized, and this criticism presaged their actual divestment. Although privately, a cautious Charles Bishop made the same kinds of evaluations of Ali'i Nui, but in time this would be a public and angry discourse. Even a king and queen would not be exempt from its consequences.

It was, of course, the hideous depopulation that destroyed ancient lineages, which had been centuries in the making. In addition, the critique of Ali'i that enabled Maka'āinana representatives to even conceive of competing with Ali'i Nui for leadership had not come only from Europeans and Americans; Christian Native leaders like Malo had criticized them as well. But aside from the fact that religious conversion played a significant role in undermining Maka'āinana devotion to the Ali'i, Malo had insisted that for the nation to thrive the Ali'i had to deserve the people's respect. William Little Lee advanced a similar, though less sanguine thesis in 1851 while he was drafting the new constitution, saying, "It is evident that the old chiefs are stronger in body, mind and morals, than their children will ever be, and when they are swept away the pillars of the nation will have fallen."[15]

Lee, whose constitution created a more business-oriented government, was not so much scornful of the "old chiefs," who he believed were capable leaders in their time, but their time, he believed, was passing:

> I have had a thorough insight into the character of the Hawaiians, sleeping in their huts—eating from their calabashes,—listening to their grievances—redressing their wrongs, and settling their quarrels. Certainly they are a kind and peaceable people, with a superabundance of generous hospitality; but with all of their good traits, they lack the elements necessary to perpetuate their existence. Living without exertion, & contented with enough to eat & drink, they give themselves no care for the future. . . . Now & then we meet with an enterprising native, climbing up in the world, and I feel like crying bravo! by [sic] good fellow! bravo! but the mass of the people, where are they? *I consider the doom of this nation as sealed* [italics mine]. . . . I am just now engaged in revising the Constitution, and I trust that I shall have the wisdom given me to frame it in such a manner, as to secure to the people of these islands for all time to come, the blessings of liberty and justice.[16]

Lee's comments would appear to be nothing more than hopeless double-talk unless he was talking about two different nations and, perhaps, different peoples: the Native kingdom and its replacement. Both he and Bishop were much more careful in their public discourse regarding the state of the kingdom and these letters probably would have embarrassed them had they been made public. After all, there were still the Makaʻāinana, whose numbers, though rapidly diminishing, were large enough to make certain that Native lawmakers would compose the majority of the legislature for some time to come. Controlling the legislature was something else again.

For Native representatives, perceiving the nobles as political competitors, and genealogically substandard ones at that, may have undermined their respect for the Aliʻi. The nobles appeared unable to counter the rising power of the House of Representatives, and the new constitution, passed by the legislature in 1852, granted more extensive authority to the lower House, including the sole power of appropriation. When Alexander Liholiho became the Mōʻī in 1854, he immediately recognized that the representatives had become too independent and too powerful and tried for all of his nine-year reign to curb their power by constitutional amendment.

Constitution of 1852: New Law, New Elite

The Constitution of 1852, drafted by the American attorney and House of Representatives member William Little Lee, is generally credited with having empowered the lower House by separating it from the executive power of the Mōʻī and granting to it the decisive power of spending. Legal scholar H. E. Chambers wrote that "the Lower House now attained to considerable importance."[17]

When Kauikeaouli granted this constitution, he not only forwarded the ideologies of liberal government, he connected the series of political concessions that had steadily incorporated the haole as citizens, landowners, voters, and, finally, as elected officials. Kuykendall wrote about Kauikeaouli's misgivings about the implications of his new constitution. Kuykendall noted that Kauikeaouli had wanted a constitution more like that of Great Britain and that his advisors agreed with him. Nevertheless, the Mōʻī believed it was best for the legislature to choose to reject or adopt the new law.[18]

The legislature approved the new constitution in the 1852 session and the king, Judd, and Wyllie, despite their own objections to its "American" flavor, signed this constitution into existence. The Crown's principal objections were to universal manhood suffrage and representative power. If these had both been fresh developments in 1852, it is unlikely that they would have been seriously entertained. However, voting rights had already been granted all subjects and denizens in 1850 by the Mōʻī and the legislature, rendering them equal before the law. As for the empowerment of the lower House, it is unlikely in the extreme that these concessions would have been made to an all-Native legislature.

According to Wyllie, the king had been reluctant to sign this constitution because "it gave to the people a power which they were not prepared to use judiciously."[19] Why then did he grant it? If democratizing the legislature and the electorate created difficulties for the government, it was partly done to avoid other dangers.

The king signed the 1852 Constitution in the hope of securing the foreigners' loyalty to the Hawaiian government. The haole would support the government because (and so long as) their discernible interests lay in supporting it, and the kingdom would be spared international strife. As for the Native subjects, their emotional loyalty to the kingdom, or at least to the king, was a given, and in any case had antedated the introduction of constitutional government. Allowing Natives

more power and authority in the legislature was a by-product of granting them to haole, but was probably not seen as all that risky, at least
by the Aliʻi in 1852. It is interesting that Lee, who made so much of
liberalizing the government, had no confidence that Native patriotism
would quickly rise above what was little more than a misplaced love
for a "manipulative" chiefly class: "The new Constitution will not be
passed I think, because the King and Chiefs have been talked into the
belief that it is too Republican; but its defeat will only be a temporary
postponement of a certain triumph. . . . The Chiefs begin to be jealous
of the growing power of the people, for you know it is a maxim with
them, that 'Kanakas were made for the Chiefs.'"[20]

So the chiefs, according to this haole belief, merely capitalized on
their subjects' deference. On the other hand, haole like Judd, Armstrong, and Lee took the Natives' deference to them for granted, as
though they could be trusted more than the Native leadership to effectively represent the Makaʻāinana. This was the crux of the competition
between haole and Aliʻi leadership, and in several ways the whites
demonstrated a more forceful leadership. The House of Representatives was already operating as an autonomous body, led by haole
politicians busily demonstrating to the Native representatives what
the institution was capable of in the hands of those who understood
how to manipulate law.

This explains why Native representatives helped elect William Little Lee as Speaker in 1851 and why they would continue to support
haole in that favored position for the next two decades. Those like
Robertson and Lee who were outspokenly in favor of increasing the
power of the legislature were not revered as Aliʻi themselves, but
rather as strange beings who did not share the kānakas' esteem for
the traditional ruling class. It was the foreigners' strangeness that was
steadily altering the legislature with their peculiar rules and procedures, and the fact that they were able to do this with little regard for
the objections of the nobles was not lost on the representatives. But
although the Makaʻāinana may have wondered at the political potency
of the haole, they also understood that part of their power sprang from
their lack of respect for the chiefs.

The first draft of the Constitution of 1852 was written by House
Speaker Lee and initially reviewed by R. C. Wyllie, representing the
cabinet, and John ʻĪʻī, representing the nobles. This committee was set
up on the last day of the 1851 session and despite its significance, it

appears that neither legislative branch discussed the implications of a new constitution before a resolution introduced it in the upper House.

This draft was not so much a liberal extension of the 1840 Constitution and the Organic Acts that followed as it was a fundamentally different philosophy of government and society. It redefined power and political legitimacy. The first of these new definitions was quintessentially American, the separation of powers. The Constitution of 1840 had simply made provisions for elected representatives to help frame the laws. The authority of the Mō'ī, who was at once the executive, a member of the House of Nobles, and chief judge of the Supreme Court, pervaded every aspect of government. The new constitution in 1852 consigned the king and his successor, Alexander Liholiho, to a more limited role as the kingdom's chief executive officer. Moreover the king was to be further prevented from acting unilaterally by the new restrictions placed on his ability to declare war, make treaties, convene the legislature, and grant pardons without the consent of his cabinet and other advisors (known as the privy council).

Although the king could influence the legislature through his ability to appoint members of the House of Nobles, that influence was diluted by the constitutional stipulation that all appointments of the nobles were for life. Also, the chief legislative powers, appropriations and spending, belonged to the House of Representatives. In political terms, this constitution represented not merely the limitations of the Mō'ī's authority but also a concomitant appropriation of real power— spending and lawmaking—by the representatives of the people. In cultural terms, this turned the traditional notion of authority and rule on its head through a legal chain in which, first, traditional authority was subsumed beneath the law, and second, the power to compose that law was appropriated by an institution declaring itself to represent the interests of the people.

Where exactly did that leave the Ali'i? At least one foreign observer noted how severely the House of Nobles would be handicapped by the draft provisions of the new constitution. Swede Abraham Fornander, husband of a Moloka'i chiefess, underscored a critical problem raised by Article 15 of the draft constitution dealing with the appointment of members of the House of Nobles. This proposition would have allowed the House of Representatives to appoint two nobles from each island, with the king appointing the rest. Fornander remarked: "How much independence of thought and freedom of discussion may exist in a House so curiously constituted, is one of these Legislative problems, which Hawaiian Statesmen alone can propound and alone solve. It is certainly strange . . . that our Commissioners should have hit on the very worst plan to procure an independent Upper House."[21]

This article, too, signified the loss to the kingdom of the higher lineages of Ali'i Nui who were dying out and the attempt to appropriate their authority by haole and kanaka representatives. Fourteen Ali'i Nui and Kaukauali'i families tied by blood and marriage to Kamehameha I had composed the original House of Nobles in 1842. There had been no stipulation on the appointment of these individuals by the 1840 Constitution, but they generally reflected those lineages that had formed the 'Aha Ali'i (Chiefly Council) of the Conqueror. Furthermore, it stated that "Should any other person be received into the Council, it shall be made known by law."[22]

There had been no legislative or judicial criteria for selecting nobles in 1840 because the constitution had simply recognized the existence of powerful chiefs, those ranking Ali'i close to the Kamehameha family. Their authority was not constituted by law because it preceded it. Moreover, they were not selected to fill an office of government. The office was created to contain them. But with the passing of fourteen Ali'i nobles (including five chiefesses) between 1841 and 1852,[23] the king and privy council had steadily replaced their numbers, mostly with members who were closely related to the original fourteen, or with haole who had no discernible rank. In 1843 Gerrit Judd was appointed a noble, and in 1851 three of the four new nobles were haole cabinet members.

In the debate over Article 15, it is quite interesting that some of the votes and most of the arguments against this new empowerment of the representatives came from haole legislators. Thomas Metcalf, Godfrey Rhodes, and Henry Sheldon argued that the constitution "was a free gift of the King" and that ". . . the King was but lately the sole lord of all in these Islands and had by his own free will given us all the indistinct rights we possess." This argument was advanced in opposition to both Francis Funk and George Robertson, who claimed that it was the king's rights and prerogatives that were "indistinct" until they were set forth in the constitution. Rhodes, a naturalized Briton, went on to move that all of the nobles should be appointed by the king. J. F. B. Marshall, an American citizen who had not been naturalized, responded that, "as representatives of the people, we should take all of the privileges we could get, and leave the other House, to make any such amendments as they thought proper in these things."[24]

For Marshall, it was clear that power existed to be seized by some entity; it was up to the people to claim whatever authority they could, just as it was incumbent upon the king and the nobles to protect their power. For Rhodes, there were other principles involved, including honoring the position of the Mō'ī, out of a healthy respect for the power he wielded. But for the kānaka legislators, such discussions made little sense unless they accepted the notion that king, nobles, and representatives were nothing more than competing political institutions vying for control of the mechanisms of law.

The representatives did vote in favor of Article 15, in vain, because the nobles simply amended it out of existence two weeks later. As a test of political strength, it was obvious that the nobles still had the upper hand, but the willingness of the Native representatives to challenge the other House by their votes indicates a level of competitiveness that had not existed before.

It was also a competition from which the haole were exempt. The Native representatives did not protest the inclusion of Wyllie and Armstrong as nobles in 1851 (or Judd in 1843), perhaps because they were already recognized as having a separate status of their own. Particular white men infiltrating the ranks of the Ali'i was not a novel development. In some ways they almost appeared to possess many of the qualifications for the status of chiefs. Some, like Fornander, Rooke, and Bishop, married into chiefly society, they possessed lands that had once "belonged" to the chiefs, and they seemed to assume the right and prerogative of rule so quickly and unabashedly. But although they may have occupied a special category, they were never confused with Ali'i.

Ultimately, however, the key to the haole exemption was that they did not belong to the struggle that occupied the kānaka and the Ali'i. For them, it was simply a competition for political power, and one that had to be conducted carefully and sensibly, especially if one was not necessarily connected to the inner power circle dominated by American Protestants. It was the English Catholic Godfrey Rhodes who declared, "by grasping too much after power, we might loose [sic] all."[25] For the Natives, it was a much larger and, to them, more significant discourse about the identity of kānaka now that liberalization, land ownership, and a collapsing population had altered the older social relationships. The problem for Kamakau and the other Natives who supported Article 15 was not whether the king or the legislature should appoint nobles; the problem was that nobles had to be appointed in the first place.

It was not just on the basis of genealogy that Kamakau, in mid-April 1852, rose tò challenge the seating of G. L. Kapeau in the House of Nobles. Kapeau, a Maui Kaukauali'i, had enjoyed a remarkable career after attending Lāhaināluna (he entered in 1837, the same year as Kauma'ea), serving as a secretary to Gerrit Judd in the Treasury and elevated to the privy council in 1846 and to the House of Nobles in 1848. If Samuel Kamakau had chafed under the indignity of observing someone of inferior rank and inferior ability (inferior to his, at least) and a name that defined obsequiousness (Kapeau means "to crawl on one's knees before high royalty") joining the select group of Ali'i, it was not until he was elected to the House of Representatives that he could finally do something about it. As *The Polynesian* reported: "In regard to Kamakau's requesting that the House of Nobles furnish the Representatives the right of G. L. Kapeau to sit in the Upper House: Mr. Sheldon thought the House had no right, under strict reading of the Constitution, to interfere in the matter. That what was required of us was merely to sanction the publication of the law, appointing members. Mr. Robertson differed." [26]

For Kamakau the issue of Kapeau's "nobility" was not merely a personal attack on an individual with a questionable rank, though such an attack was perfectly comprehensible in Hawaiian society. He was, in effect, attacking the entire process by which nobles were selected and legitimized. He questioned the qualifications of another chief because he himself was Ali'i and had the right to do so by his birth rank. On 16 April, before the nobles could even respond to the question of Kapeau, a special committee that included Kamakau and Kauma'ea determined that the seatings of the princes Alexander Liholiho and Lota Kapuāiwa (Kamehameha IV and V, respectively) were unconstitutional because their appointments had to be "made known by law," meaning, according to the committee, that the House of Representatives as well as the House of Nobles had to enact a law "entitling them to a seat in that place." [27]

The idea of kānaka and haole legitimizing the Ali'i, even those of esteemed rank, did not necessarily imply that the Native representatives had forsaken their allegiance to true Ali'i Nui, but that the House of Nobles was not the official embodiment of those chiefs. Only genealogy, by itself, was sufficient to determine who was rightfully Ali'i. For someone of lesser rank, like Kapeau, or no rank whatsoever, like haole, to sit with the Ali'i was a demonstration that the rules by which nobles were selected and the values by which Ali'i existed were not the same, at least where the nobles and the privy council were concerned. Kamakau and the kanaka delegation may have decided that if the nobles were going to debase themselves, there was no reason why the representatives should not have a hand in the process and perhaps elevate, politically, if not culturally, one or two of their own.

Paradoxically, as constitutions ever more liberal, and therefore more haole, allowed the foreigners greater and greater access of all kinds in the kingdom, and as those laws were driven by a hegemonic conceit that all were equal before the law, the Native legislators continued to treat them as special. Far from assuming an air of equality to the whites, the Hawaiians perceived them as different, incomprehensible, and, therefore, exceptional. This despite the fact that haole demanded that their rights should be acknowledged because they were not different from any Hawaiian subject.

Equality and the Exceptional Missionary

Ultimately, the constitution did more than challenge kanaka respect for the Ali'i Nui. Debate over its provisions also contested the more recent dependence on ABCFM missionaries, and especially the kingdom's reliance on them for political as well as religious advice. In all likelihood, it was Robert Wyllie (the representative of the Mō'ī and the cabinet) who drafted Article 23, under Chapter I, The Declaration of Rights, which read, "No clergyman or priest of any denomination whatsoever, shall be eligible to a seat in the House of Representatives, while he continues in the exercise of his ministerial functions."[28]

It certainly was not drafted by the nobles' representative, John Papa 'Ī'ī, who vigorously protested its inclusion. This old Kaukauali'i, who was tied to the Kamehameha family by years of service, especially to the Conqueror's son, Liholiho, had been an early convert to Calvinist Christianity and was a friend and supporter of missionaries in government such as Gerrit Judd and Richard Armstrong. He told *The Polynesian* that the clause had been inserted while he was away on Maui and "that he was entirely opposed to it."[29]

This draft article set off the only vitriolic public debate over any of the constitution's provisions and wound up pitting the three commissioners, especially Wyllie and ʻĪʻī, against each other. But more than a political conflict, Article 23 became symbolic of the tremendously powerful and deeply ingrained resentments that existed among the foreign and Native community, resentments that were complicated by, at times, nonsensical arguments over equality.

The propriety of mission participation in the Hawaiian government is a debate that went back to the 1840s and involved not just the enviousness of the foreigners who were not missionaries, but also the suspicions of the Makaʻāinana, who responded to the ABCFM-dominated cabinet in 1845 by petitioning for their removal. Because their petitions called for the ending of privileges for *foreigners,* the government's refusal of those petitions settled the question, for Hawaiians at least, of whether missionaries could be called into government service.

But for some members of the foreign community, missionaries were a distinct and privileged group that dominated the cabinet and had an altogether unwholesome influence on the Native population, which was ignorant of their designs. Wyllie suggested that the provision was necessary, if only to avoid the potential conflicts with other nations over the predominance of a religious sect whose clergy originated in one particular (and competing) nation: "If the *bare suspicion* of such a political interference nearly lost the King his sovereignty in 1837, 1839, 1849, and 1851 [troubles with the French Catholics] the most obtuse politician must see what *reality* would do." [30]

Another Englishman, Sir George Simpson, felt that mission interference was real and deeply embedded. Simpson traveled with William Richards and Timothy Haʻalilio in 1842, visiting American and European capitals in the hope of securing equitable treaties and recognition of the Hawaiian kingdom. He published these controversial remarks in his 1850 memoirs:

> At first, perhaps, the missionaries could not avoid adopting the Hawaiian language, but in the exclusive use of it . . . the missionaries have operated on the national mind only through the expensive medium of laborious and expensive translations . . . that it enabled them to exercise a censorship such as neither pope nor emperor ever exercised over the studies of their neophytes . . . its mere existence assimilates the Protestantism [*sic*] of the Sandwich Islands, at least in kind if not degree, to that very Catholicism of California which the missionaries of the group are so ready to decry—the proselytes in either case being subject to a tutelage which does not even profess to teach them to think for themselves. [31]

For Simpson to have articulated the idea that American missionaries had appropriated political power through their "acquisition" of
the Hawaiian language was perceptive enough. His charge that
Natives were not being taught to think for themselves, at least where
politics was concerned, was a distortion that is perpetuated by contemporary poststructuralists. As Elizabeth Buck wrote in her 1986
dissertation:

> By the middle of the 19th century language was becoming increas-
> ingly problematic for Hawaiians; the logic of Hawaiian was not con-
> sistent with new social institutions, new laws of morality, and new
> relationships of power. Hawaiians were forced to engage Westerners
> in a language foreign to them; in a language where the strategies of
> discourse and rhetoric were different from the strategies embedded in
> Hawaiian; in a language where metaphors called on a pool of knowl-
> edge, mythic and otherwise, that Americans were privy to but that
> excluded Hawaiians—or to totally withdraw from the arenas of social
> discourse (which many Hawaiians did).[32]

Buck's very deterministic analysis rests on the premise that the
options available to Hawaiians in the mid-nineteenth century were
limited to clinging to tradition while in political retreat, or its inverse,
discarding traditional values while pursuing political power. It was not
evident, though, to Native legislators that these were their options. On
the contrary, government service was, by 1852, normalized as a bilin-
gual, multiethnic activity into which Hawaiians sought to incorporate
foreigners as well as their ideas. It was also evident to them, through
their experience with some of the white representatives, that there
was nothing mainstream about haole culture.

Simpson was undoubtedly making the case for a more general use
of English in the kingdom, but he also indicted the kānaka, whose
helplessness he linked to their trust and dependence on the missionaries. Such dependence, in his opinion, limited the Natives' ability to
think and act for themselves. Several articles in the *Weekly Argus* went
so far as to accuse the missionaries of having actually determined the
election of two Hawaiian lawyers,[33] Honoka'upu and Kekaulahao, to
the legislature from Honolulu in 1852:

> Some days previous, there was a meeting at one of the native
> churches, when the minister admonished his congregation not to vote
> for a WHITE MAN; again, the day preceding the election, they were
> commanded in like manner from the pulpits of both those in Hono-

lulu and that adjacent, seconded by one of the Privy Council. . . . From all parts of the islands we have received information of like measures being actively carried out by the missionaries, to the effect, we suppose, the election of such men as they can make instruments of.[34]

The Polynesian had a slightly different slant on this election, professing that Native voters had merely expressed their displeasure with the fact that Honolulu had been represented by two haole, Rooke and Robertson,[35] the year before.

> Honolulu, which last year was represented by two naturalized foreigners, has this year two native representatives in the lower house; which simply shows that to have a foreign representative, it will be necessary to coalesce, and concur with the natives in the selection of candidates. When foreigners only were offered for their suffrages, they naturally enough felt that they should have at least one, of the two, to which the district is entitled, and accordingly nominated candidates of their own, whom they have elected by very large majorities.[36]

Neither explanation of the Native voting behavior gave any credence to the idea that Hawaiians were capable of exerting much intelligent choice, whether they were influenced by missionary demagoguery or by their own "natural" inclination to vote for one of their own. But it should be noted that a Native petition accused former Honolulu representative Rooke of having bullied voters in his precinct,[37] and the only other haole candidate from Honolulu, William Jarrett, was then being tried in superior court for embezzlement of government funds during his service as auditor in the Treasury.[38]

It was not just the hegemony of missionary authority that the newspapers asserted, but the simplicity and incompetence of the Native voter and legislator. This argument was conducted even more viciously in the *Weekly Argus,* which claimed to represent those outside the inner circle of government. Indeed, they could not put the story to rest without delivering a final insult to the kānaka who had been elected: "We cannot close these remarks without giving rather an amusing anecdote of one of the members elected. A friend met him and congratulated him. 'Well' said he in the simplicity of his heart, 'What does it mean? Elected for what?' 'Why parliament!' rejoined his friend. 'What must I do there. I don't know anything about such

things, what must I do?' These are the sort of people to make a constitution! Verily brethren, it is easier to control ignorance than reason."[39]

Despite the constitution's assertion of equality, there were very
mixed feelings among the foreign community about what that meant
for the Natives. But even the most optimistic of them tended to
believe, as Wyllie did, that Hawaiians needed protection from their
own trusting natures, which was part of the reason for Article 23 in
the first place.

Still, there were not many ABCFM missionaries who even chose to
run for office in 1851, and none of them stood for the House the following year. This may have helped quiet some of the antagonism by
eliminating one more reason for an attack on the ABCFM's preeminence. In any case, the mission's principal objection to Article 23 was
not that practicing preachers ought to hold elective office, but that by
obliterating the people's right to choose them, the government was
setting a dangerous trend. According to the missionary-turned-mer-
chant E. O. Hall: ". . . it is proscriptive in its application to that class
of subjects, and it is also abridging the right of the voters to elect the
man of their choice, should they be so disposed. With the same propriety might they be deprived of the right to vote, and with the same
justice might the entire catalogue of their civil rights be swept away
from them. . . . We should no less oppose the disenfranchisement of
any other class of innocent men in the kingdom, than the one in question. In fact it is the *principle* of disenfranchisement that we object to
altogether, as opposed to what we regard as fundamental 'inalienable
rights.'"[40]

It is noteworthy that Hall, a former secular agent in the ABCFM's
seventh company (arriving in 1835), was able to argue that Hawaiians' right to choose missionaries to represent them should not be
abridged, while writing editorials questioning the Natives' readiness
for the "proper enjoyment" of liberty. In June 1852, he wrote: "We
regard the premature acquisition of liberty, by a so recently barbarous
people, as an experiment with no small degree of hazard; and what
should not be too suddenly thrust upon them, lest it lead to anarchy.
. . . When the Hawaiians are fully prepared for the proper enjoyment
of all the liberties that can properly be bestowed upon them, why not
let them have them. But until then, do not give them a razor with
which to inflict only injuries upon themselves."[41]

Voting and the right to government office, originally granted to haole as political arrangements by the kingdom, were now being claimed by missionary supporters as "inalienable" and linked to the establishment of those very same rights for Natives. Moreover, this claim consecrated the idea that all male subjects were or should be indistinguishable from one another with respect to their standing before the law. Most important, even the conception of Native incompetence was appropriated into this discourse on equality by the suggestion that it was the kanaka dependence, first on the Ali'i and later on the missionaries, that made them unfit electors. Nevertheless, democracy was too important, too sacred, not to make it available to the poor, inexperienced Hawaiians.

As individuals, perhaps, quite a few missionaries were hardly distinguishable from the rest of the foreign community. Even their ambitions and activities in commerce tended to obscure their differences from other haole, especially after the Mahele. But as a group, they benefited from their historic relationship with the ruling family and from the general trust that many Hawaiians were willing to accord them as kahu (guardians). In fact, Hall's argument, that missionaries were no different than anyone else, must have struck everyone as odd, given the special considerations they enjoyed as a result of their close association with the government.

The first three haole to be elevated to the cabinet, Richards, Judd, and Armstrong, were all employed originally by the ABCFM. Richards and Judd had been two of the original land commissioners who had set up the division of the lands. In 1849, Noble Joshua Kā'eo, a blood relative of the Kamehameha line, charged that ABCFM personnel received favorable treatment from the government in the form of land grants at very nominal costs.[42] In response, Keoniana, Wyllie, and Lee conducted a study of missionary land claims and awards in 1850. When they finally published their findings in 1852, Wyllie advocated a peculiar case for making awards of 560 acres available to every current and past ABCFM missionary, even those who had elected not to apply for lands.

Wyllie pointed out that, indeed, twenty members (approximately half) of the ABCFM contingent were purchasing government lands and paying, on the average, 90 cents an acre less than nonmissionaries, including konohiki like Kā'eo, who were paying an average of $1.47 per acre. From this Wyllie drew the astonishing conclusion that the government owed the other twenty missionaries who had not applied for lands the opportunity to purchase lands at the same low rate:

They further assume that Your Majesty may be pleased to allow to the 20 individuals above named, who have not applied for any lands the same favor of 50 cents per acre on 560 acres person, if they should apply for it which averaged for 22 persons, including the ladies, would be 12,320 acres. Supposing this to be done, the members of the American mission . . . would hold 21,850 acres . . . and they would hold them at a loss to your Majesty's treasury of $10,925, which loss, would be a pecuniary favor to each of 39 individuals or families of $280 5/39 [cents] . . . and that is all that every one of the same mission can claim in the future, on the principle of putting those who have not applied for lands on an equal footing with those who have obtained lands and applied for more. [43]

In other words, because ABCFM missionaries had already exacted special favors from the government, they had to be treated as an exclusive group entirely in the interest of giving all of them equal treatment. This flawed reasoning legitimated greater and greater access by haole to the privileges of land and power in Hawaiian society. The logic began with the premise that missionaries had earned the right to outright gifts of land as a return for their services to the Hawaiian people. Hence their willingness to pay for land, no matter how small the amount, testified to their integrity.

Jean Hobbs, in her 1935 study of the land tenure system, tried to dispel "the popular notion that missionaries waxed rich upon large land areas acquired by gift," arguing further that such acquisition "would have been extremely easy had the missionaries been so minded." [44] That would hardly have eased the resentment of the nearly two-thirds of the Maka'āinana who were landless, but, as she also pointed out, the ABCFM people were not supposed to be so minded: "The minutes of the General Meetings of the mission group record many discussions on this point; invariably, the attitude expressed was that acceptance of gifts of land would violate the rules governing the organization." [45]

Some missionaries had no trouble justifying a claim for thousands of acres of the kingdom's lands nor any problem engaging in land sales once they got over whatever initial reluctance they may have possessed. Although certain individuals like Levi Chamberlain, principal instructor at Lāhaināluna, and Lorenzo Lyons, a truly beloved kahu in Kohala, made it a point to avoid acquisition (Lyons eventually received five and one-half acres near his church at 'Imiola), some missionaries and mission agents did, in fact, become major landowners after 1850.[46] Of the seventeen missionaries who had not applied for lands by the time of Wyllie's report, fourteen proceeded to apply for and receive grants over the next three years.

The story told by Representative 'Ūkēkē about Levi Chamberlain refusing a substantial offer of land from Ka'ahumanu may be apocryphal, but it is instructive: "Ukeke related to Rev. Emerson that when Levi Chamberlain had been offered land in Koolauloa by the *Kuhina Nui* Kaahumanu in the early 1820s, he had refused stating, in effect, that his coming to Hawaii nei was for the purpose of teaching the people . . . and not for any personal aggrandizement. It is said that though repeatedly solicited to reconsider, Mr. Chamberlain held to his purpose."[47]

It is true that some of the missionaries did maintain certain personal scruples by refusing to engage in land acquisition and speculation even after the ABCFM ended their support in 1855, but they were exceptional and few. Hobbs' appendixes make it quite clear that some missionaries pursued the buying and selling of land much more aggressively than others. But of the eighty-seven ABCFM missionaries that came to the Islands in twelve companies, only thirty did not possess lands of any kind, and twenty-eight of those had either left Hawai'i or died before the Mahele.

Perhaps that was part of the problem. Some men of the cloth were capable of living up to the ideals and moralities they proclaimed from the pulpit. Such men and women, as individuals, aroused tremendous aloha from their Hawaiian congregations, not only for their spiritual but also for their material contributions to their flock. One example was Lorenzo Lyons, who spent hundreds of hours on behalf of Natives in Hāmākua by helping them make kuleana claims before the Land Commission.[48] But there was more than a little facetiousness in the premier editorial of the *Weekly Argus,* claiming as one of its ideological principles: "We disapprove the active interference of ministers of the gospel in political matters . . . hoping to convince the missionaries of Christ that we wish to regard them in a more sacred and elevated light."[49]

Between the outrage over the mission's purported influence on elections and the stories about missionaries profiting on land deals, there was still the issue of competition between active businessmen and ministers of the gospel who were becoming businessmen. Ultimately, if the individual ministers were going to act like any other haole, seeking fortune and political power, it seemed only fair that they officially declare their intentions by resigning from the mission first.

Both Europeans and Americans benefited from their liberal traditions by having a seasoned historical critique that opposed clergy in the government. In some cases that critique was even incorporated in their own nation's laws. In defense of his position and his English traditions, Wyllie wrote: "It has been the practice of civilized and christian [sic] governments to protect their clergy by law from being called off from, or interrupted in the discharge of their holy calling. Thus in England, though the privileges which are allowed to the clergy are but a faint shadow of those which they enjoyed before the Reformation, they cannot be compelled to sit on a jury. . . . They are privileged from arrest in civil suits while engaging in divine service. . . . He cannot now sit in the House of Commons." [50]

Wyllie did not, of course, discuss the main reason why clergy were prohibited from the House of Commons, preferring not to discuss the painful history of the Catholics and Protestants in England. Hawaiians could hardly have been blamed if they entertained confused notions of the clergy's status. Were missionaries an exceptional class of people whose service to the Natives deserved special consideration toward their purchases of land? Or were they like any other subject in the kingdom whose political rights had to be defended as rigorously as anyone else's?

The House of Representatives voted to strike Article 23 by a count of twelve to eight, with kānaka on both sides of the issue. [51] Meanwhile, Alexander Liholiho, the designated successor to the Mōʻī, broke a seven to seven deadlock in the House of Nobles by voting to strike the article after that House had deliberated for many hours. [52] No friend of the ABCFM, Alexander Liholiho's vote was somewhat surprising because he had been one of the supporters of Article 23 and had spoken in favor of it that same day. Perhaps the fact that there was no majority among the nobles convinced the prince to avoid a drawn-out confrontation from ʻĪʻī and half the privy council and follow the leadership of the lower House. The *Argus*, in fact, used this occasion to attack the manhood of this noble and future Mōʻī: "The Gentleman who gave that vote was not equal to the emergency; he quailed beneath the responsibility laid upon him, and fell short of the high expectations of his friends." [53]

It was just one more irony that Natives were made responsible for an emotionally saturated political issue that divided haole. Although some foreigners praised it as a sensible vote, that was only after *The Polynesian* had taken the time to scold the members of the white community who wished to disenfranchise the missionaries, asserting that their influence was important and salutary, not just for the Natives but for foreigners as well. In February 1852, Hall wrote an almost resentful reminder to the rest of the foreign community about how much responsibility the mission had to shoulder to maintain the Hawaiians in some form of civilization: "What would be the condition of the islands, had the missionaries never possessed any power or influence? And what would soon be their condition should all who are, or have been missionaries, withdraw immediately from the field? How long before the irreconcilable enmities would spring up between the white and colored races? How long before blood would flow and interminable hostilities arise? Who would then control the excited elements? . . . would the person and the property of the white man be safe, as now, in every part of the islands?"[54]

He made a revealing admission that the mission was more than the salvation and protection of Hawaiians; it also existed to protect foreigners. In the end, Article 23, though a critical discourse on missionary behavior, was also a discourse on what could be expected from the Native. The suspicion that they were never more than an absent church away from resurgent savagery would continue to inform and direct the politics of haole in the kingdom. Despite the resentment that the American Protestants stirred among the other denominations and nationalities, they were a useful thermometer and buffer of the Native temper.

Church and state were quite effectively entangled, not by the absence of Article 23 in the constitution, but by the Hawaiians' reluctance to challenge missionary power and privilege without arousing serious misgivings, especially among Native Hawaiians who considered themselves Christians.[55] As white foreigners further enriched and entrenched themselves, Hawaiians found it impossible to criticize them without also denouncing members of missionary families whose behavior so closely resembled that of other haole opportunists. Each time Hawaiians attacked missionaries because of their participation in business or in politics, it was "evidence" of the Natives' ungratefulness and, ultimately, of their own deficiencies.

In 1869, Kamakau tried to explain this paradox by making it clear that it was missionary malfeasance, not some Native misunderstanding of Christianity, that was the cause of the Hawaiians' loss of faith in the mission fathers: "Some of the missionaries thought it wrong to protect this government of God; the kingdom of God is not a kingdom ruled by a king [they said]. Perhaps this was not the king's thought. . . . He did not mean to give up his rule as chief, but to make God the protector of the kingdom and his rule over it. . . . Strange indeed were the hard thoughts of the missionary! . . . So they girded up their loins, sharpened their knives, and chose which part of the fish they would take. . . . Rich, aye, rich! It could be cut up, salted down, hung out to dry . . . until the smell of it was wafted from one end of the islands to the other end."[56]

Kamakau mentioned no names, though he was always careful to single out missionaries who had, in his opinion, earned Hawaiians' trust. Indeed, he lavished special praise on Richards, Judd, and Armstrong for their efforts at establishing democratic government in Hawai'i.[57] But by praising the missionary members of Kauikeaouli's cabinet, he was very clearly justifying the king's decision to elevate foreigners above some of his chiefs. As he had back in 1845, when he had supported the king's decision to employ foreigners in the ministry,[58] this historian continued to believe as late as 1869 that some haole had been good for the kingdom. On the other hand, Kamakau was also determined to remind the nation of Kauikeaouli's intent someday to replace those white cabinet members with Hawaiians:

> It was clear to us from this letter how deeply concerned the king was for our own good and how completely he was working for the good of his own race and how he was giving his own people, chiefs and commoners, the offices which they could fill; and only those which they could not fill were being given to foreigners, and that when the young chiefs were sufficiently instructed in the English language the offices were to be given back to them; and that the new ways of civilized governments were added to the old ways of the Hawaiian government.[59]

This restoration of the cabinet to chiefs had not occurred by 1869 and would not occur until Kalākaua became king. To that extent, both Alexander Liholiho and Lota Kapuāiwa, whose reigns spanned the nineteen years from 1854 to 1873, left something to be desired in terms of their willingness to entrust the kingdom's administration to kānaka (although Lota did serve as minister of war during his brother's reign). Still, both these Mōʻī did reduce, rather significantly, the American missionaries' influence within the privy council and cabinet.

In the end, the conflict over Article 23 did not free the Natives from missionary dominance so much as it created doubt about the sufficiency of Christianity to completely legitimize the Hawaiians as electors and as government officials. Even where their conversion was not doubted (and it was doubted in many quarters), the Natives' Christianity was trivialized by the argument that religion had no place, or at least a very tenuous place, in the practical running of the state.

The eventual distancing of the royal family from the once dominant influence of the ABCFM, however, displaced neither haole nor, for that matter, missionary families from the seat of real power in the kingdom. By the mid-1860s, the kingdom's business was dominated by the growing and exporting of sugar. Those who planted, financed, and freighted sugar and shaped the policies that enabled large-scale plantations to become the economic reality in the Islands were those who wielded power. Many of them bore the surnames of former American ministers of the gospel. These families, Castles and Cookes, Alexanders and Baldwins, Thurstons and Smiths, may not have distinguished themselves as exceptions to the haole tendency to acquire lands and other privileges, but they did become exceptionally wealthy.

Sermons on Wealth and Self-Reliance

The 1852 Constitution preserved some of the Mōʻī's authority over the House of Nobles and granted the House of Representatives both independence and power. This institutional framework enabled greater penetration of Western influence and capital through a representative agency that neither the nobles nor the king were allowed to contain. But what made the House of Representatives most accessible to haole was not simply the articles of this constitution, but the suggestions and claims that were embedded in the laws and in the discussions over those laws. As kānaka learned to question the potency of the Aliʻi and the integrity of the missionaries, they were loudly encouraged to believe that the key to their future was in their own individual hands. Unfortunately, most of the kānaka were required to struggle from a distinctly inferior position. Their resources were meager and their numbers would plummet once more in 1853 with the outbreak of smallpox.

The continual disintegration of the Native population was a significant reality. It suggested, however, different responses depending on whether you were a haole businessman in government or a kanaka. Lee in his 1850 address to the newly formed Royal Hawaiian Agricultural Society rejoiced in the rise of the plantation for what he termed "an advancing step toward the thorough civilization of the Hawaiian race, and the security of its national prosperity and independence." However, in recognition of the manifest downward spiral of the Maka-'āinana, he also professed:

> There is one agent, however that we require, who holds the key of success—the great brawny armed, huge fisted giant called labor . . . now, when the dark cloud, which has hovered above them for ages, is lifting, there is hardly a nation to save. Alas! And must these people . . . perish from the face of the earth? Perish too, not by famine nor pestilence, nor the sword but by the rust of indolence—the canker of sloth? Shall we let them die without making one struggle to save them from the grave to which they are hastening? No, my friends, justice and humanity forbid. Though but a lone remnant remains, let us strive to gird it with strength to wrestle with its approaching destiny; to arm it with the healthy body and vigorous frame, the only weapon that can stay the hand of the destroyer. [60]

Ever so subtly, the symbols of commerce and industry were replacing the traditional leadership of the Ali'i and the not-so-traditional leadership of the mission. In fact, Lee's speech quite neatly appropriated for the planter all of the virtues and justifications of the ABCFM at the same time that it laid complete responsibility for the failure of the mission on the indolence of the Natives. Hawaiians, having failed to be saved by the Mahele, liberalism, and the church, would surely be rescued by the reliable hand of commerce (or perhaps not). [61] Moreover, because the Natives were *portrayed* as helpless and even reluctant recipients of commerce's saving grace, the stage was set for completing the transformation of Hawaiians from the proprietors of the kingdom to a class of wage labor, subordinate to the capitalist haole who possessed the land. Freed from their ancient dependence and freed, as Karl Marx so humorously put it in *Das Kapital,* from the land itself, informed of the missionaries' shortcomings, and with the proper incentives of plantation wages, the Hawaiians could finally secure their real place in Hawai'i.

So what was the place and position of the Mō'ī? In some ways this was the most important political question left to answer. As long as the kānaka maintained their aloha for the Mōʻī and as long as the king was in a position to act on their behalf, the strands of a traditional polity remained. In fact, the more ineffectual the Aliʻi appeared, and the more venal the mission families, the more faith the kānaka seemed to have in the king. When Representative J. W. E. Maikaʻi petitioned to have the king's salary raised to $20,000 a year, to "increase the prestige and better his reign," he also expressed the very tangible nature of the Hawaiians' aloha for their king, concluding, "We are pleased to see much of our tax monies spent for his benefit."[62] It was, perhaps, the most natural thing in the world for Hawaiians to vest their hopes and aspirations in the one powerful Native figure left.

It is more than ironic that the next Mōʻī, Alexander Liholiho, would spend nearly his entire reign trying to tame the House of Representatives and trying to rid his cabinet and privy council of the ABCFM influence. As symbols of what Hawaiians wished so ardently to project—intelligence, ability, accomplishment, and pride—Alexander Liholiho and his brother Lota Kapuāiwa would reign at the apex of the kingdom's stability and prestige. In their battles to reclaim the primacy of the Crown and its independence from missionary control, these Mōʻī reassured the kānaka that they were not being deserted. However, these Mōʻī also indulged the perception that some of their kānaka, the landless and illiterate ones, at least, were helpless children whose continued dependence on their chiefs was an embarrassment to the race.

The haole discourse on equality was riddled with an unsolvable paradox. Native dependence on a monarch meant, to Americans at least, that the people were not yet civilized. Once liberal law weakened the Aliʻi/Makaʻāinana relationship to the point of replacing it, there remained only two loci to attract the loyalty of the kānaka to the state. One was naked self-interest. After 1852, few would argue that Hawaiians had many material interests left to protect in the kingdom. The one remaining locus was the Hawaiians' obvious regard for their Mōʻī, the symbol of their nation, as the sole guarantor of their allegiance.

5
Conventional Beliefs

O kakou e noho nei ma neia Keena na Apanaekolu a keia
Aupuni. O na Elele o na Makaainana, na Lii, a me Au ponoi,
e noho akoakoa ana maanei, ia kakou na mana nui o ke
Aupuni; a aohe mea mana e ae mawaena o kakou a me
ke Akua.

[We who are here together at this moment in this Office are
the three parts of this Kingdom. The Delegates for the Maka-
ʻāinana, the Aliʻi, and Myself, while we exist separately here,
together we are the power of this Kingdom; and there is no
other power between us and God.]

> Lota Kapuāiwa, Constitutional Convention
> 16 July 1864

The Constitution of 1852 tormented the reign of Kamehameha IV,
Alexander Liholiho. As king he spent a good deal of the legislature's
time as well as his own trying to amend the constitution, in particular
those articles that defined the composition and authority of the House
of Representatives. Amendment, however, required the cooperation of
both houses of the legislature. William Little Lee had written into the
constitution a diabolically complicated method of amendment that
was specified in Article 105:

> Any amendment or amendments to this Constitution may be pro-
> posed in either branch of the Legislature, and if the same shall be
> agreed to by a majority of the members of each House, such proposed
> amendment or amendments shall be . . . referred to the next Legisla-

ture; which proposed amendment or amendments shall be published for three months previous to the election of the next House of Representatives; and if, in the next Legislature, such proposed amendment or amendments, shall be agreed to by two-thirds of all the members of each house, and be approved by the King, such amendment or amendments shall become part of the Constitution of this Kingdom.[1]

The king's efforts not only failed but led to mounting confrontations between him and the legislature, particularly the representatives.[2] It was precisely the authority and independence of the representatives as well as the constraints on his own power that Alexander Liholiho was attempting to amend out of existence. Kuykendall discussed those features of the constitution to which the king most strenuously objected:

> . . . the existence of the office of *kuhina nui*, which distracted from the dignity and strength of the kingly office, the defective character of the provisions regarding the succession to the throne; the power of the privy council, which had a practical veto on many of the acts of the king and the cabinet and could interfere seriously with the policies of the administration; the universal manhood suffrage . . . the absence of any property qualification for members of the house of representatives [sic]; the strong position of the house of representatives arising from the fact that all financial measures must originate in that house and from the independent and vigorous course which the representatives followed—sometimes wrongly, it must be admitted.[3]

Kuykendall's judgment of the representatives' errors no doubt refers to the legislature of 1855. On 16 June 1855, Kamehameha IV dissolved the legislature for failing to pass an appropriations bill that would not exceed the government's revenues. The Mōʻī's decision came at the end of an unusually pugnacious session in the House of Representatives that climaxed in a showdown between Kaumaʻea, that now-wizened Lāhaināluna warrior, and the House of Nobles. They fought over an issue that was strange and convoluted, with implications for the power and independence of the House of Representatives from both the nobles and the Crown, but the dispute also allowed the Native delegates to display their independence from the haole.

The proximate cause of their disagreement was the disbursement of money to Dr. George Lathrop, an American physician, pharmacist, and dentist who had diagnosed one of the first cases of smallpox in Honolulu. He presented the government with a bill of $2,500 for his services, which included advising on quarantine measures and helping to devise an inoculation against the spread of the disease. The fact that the inoculation had been largely ineffective and the disease had probably claimed close to 6,000 Native lives[4] since May of 1853 may have been one reason why the nobles decided that his fee was too high by $1,000 and informed the representatives of their decision in early June of 1855. However, there were other reasons for the nobles' decision that had little to do with the fact that the House was liberally spending money that exceeded the revenues of the kingdom.[5]

For one thing, Lathrop was trouble. He belonged to the infamous "Committee of Thirteen," a handful of foreign residents who had pledged themselves to the ending of monarchical government in the Hawaiian Islands. This group, said to represent hundreds of newly arrived Americans in the Islands, apparently favored the overthrow of the king and replacement with a white-led "republic."[6] In the fall and summer of 1854, the Committee of Thirteen created such a storm in the kingdom that Foreign Minister Wyllie raised a small Native army and at the request of the king made inquiries to the United States about the possibility of annexing Hawai'i.[7]

It was Lathrop himself who had accused Gerrit Judd and Richard Armstrong of negligence in the handling of the vicious smallpox epidemic, making of Judd an enemy for life. Lathrop also believed that Natives were no different from "niggers" and required firm governance by whites like himself.[8] Given Lathrop's notoriety, it is not surprising that the nobles were anxious to teach him a lesson and were, perhaps, amazed that the representatives were so insistent on opposing them.

From Kauma'ea's point of view, unchanged since his authorship of the 1845 petitions, the haole was trouble, period. George Lathrop was not the only foreigner who behaved as though Hawai'i was merely a stage for his posturing. After all, the doctor's accusations of Judd and Armstrong, both members of the original Land Commission, resembled nothing more than a power struggle between Americans, competitions that usually ended in trouble for Natives. As for Lathrop's exorbitant fee, there was a delicious irony in the fact that Kauma'ea, who had repeatedly warned the Ali'i about the disruptive consequences of relying on foreigners, was now in a position to defy the Ali'i and show them how costly that dependence would be.

The nobles sent the representatives a resolution reducing the payment to Lathrop, which the House rejected 13 to 9. Then the nobles requested a joint session of the two Houses to discuss their differences, and Kaumaʻea moved to table that communication as well.[9]

All things considered, the Mōʻī's response was hardly severe. He complimented the House for its good work in passing "many worthwhile bills" and merely commented that their inability to complete the appropriations by their scheduled date of adjournment necessitated an extraordinary session. *The Polynesian*'s editor, E. O. Hall, was not so gentle in his criticism: "In reviewing the circumstances of the case, we can but regard the course of the majority of the house as extremely inconsiderate, and to have been dictated more by passion than judgment. In fact there seems to have been a stubbornness manifested by some of the members, that would have been highly commendable had some great principle been involved. But the fact is, the members were carried away by the excitement of the moment."[10]

The fact that only one haole representative had supported the stonewalling of the nobles reinforced, for Hall, the House's action as a Native, therefore injudicious, initiative. But for the kanaka representatives, the "great principle" was that challenging and obstructing the nobles with parliamentary procedures was a watershed on how far they had gone from respectful compliance with Aliʻi and haole leadership. Using the vote to unify most of the Native House members, Kaumaʻea effectively stymied the nobles with procedural rules that he and the others had learned. Their "rebellion" was not only an important lesson about the authority of law; it also indicated Hawaiians' independence from haole dominance within the House of Representatives.

The reign of Alexander Liholiho should not be minimized by his failure to secure his authority over the legislature. He and his successor would prove to many of the Islands' foreign residents that the Native leaders were potent and honorable statesmen, but there is no question that the recalcitrant legislatures mystified and frustrated him. In a special message to the 1858–1859 legislature the king, in measured tones, expressed some of his growing dissatisfaction: "The 105th Article of the Constitution prescribes the ordinary mode of amendment. Without reference to a different manner of revision, clearly founded on the inherent rights of the different Estates of my Kingdom, I am *at this time* [italics mine], content to appeal to the Legislature for such action as will provide an adequate remedy for all existing difficulties."[11] His brother would not content himself with appeals.

Table 4. Legislature, 1855. This legislature was dissolved on 16 June 1855, necessitating the appointment of a special session to complete business, 30 July 1855. (Mōʻī: Alexander Liholiho; ministers: Wyllie, Interior and Foreign Affairs; Allen, Finance; Armstrong, Public Instruction)

NOBLES[a]	REPRESENTATIVES	SPECIAL SESSION: REPRESENTATIVES
E. H. Allen	J. W. Austin	J. W. Austin
Richard Armstrong	R. G. Davis	S. L. Austin
Haʻalelea	J. Fuller	J. D. Blair
J. Kāʻeo	John Papa ʻĪʻī	Preston Cummings
Lota Kapuāiwa Kamehameha (President)	D. K. Kaʻauwai	R. G. Davis
Paul Kanoa	Zorababella Kaʻauwai	S. G. Dwight
Kaisera Kapaʻakea	William P. Kahale	J. H. Heleluhe
George L. Kapeau	G. B. Kalaʻaukane	R. S. Hollister
Luka Keʻelikōlani	S. P. Kalama	John Papa ʻĪʻī
Kekaulahao	W. Kaluna	D. K. Kaʻauwai
Mataio Kekūanaōʻa	Samuel M. Kamakau	J. D. Kahoʻokano
Keoniana (John Young Jr.)	Z. P. Kaumaʻea	S. P. Kalama
Paul Nāhaolelua	Keaniho	Kamaʻipelekane
Beneli Nāmakehā	J. W. Keawehunahala	D. Keawehano
Abnera Pākī (died in office)	W. S. Keolaloa	J. W. Keawehunahala
Jonah Piʻikoi	S. Kipi	H. Kūihelani
Robert Wyllie	R. Koiku	J. W. Kūpākeʻe
	J. W. Kupakeʻe	G. W. Lilikalani
	J. W. E. Maikaʻi	L. Maui
	Paulo	R. Moffitt
	Godfrey Rhodes	P. Nāone
	John Richardson	John Richardson
	G. M. Robertson	R. Robinson
	R. Robinson	Henry L. Sheldon
	Thomas C. B. Rooke	William Webster
	A. G. Thurston	
	Henry M. Whitney	
	H. A. Widemann	

Source: Lydecker, 1918, *Roster Legislatures of Hawaii*, 61, 64.
[a] *Females are in italic type.*

Empowering the Mōʻī

When Lota Kapuāiwa, older brother of Alexander Liholiho, became Mōʻī after his brother's death in late 1863, he refused to take what H. E. Chambers referred to as the "customary oath to support the existing Constitution."[12] A number of political observers had expressed reservations about his ascent because of his well-known opposition to the constitution's liberal franchise and his contesting of the representatives' power while he was a member of his brother's cabinet.

Kapuāiwa's dominion over the constitution itself needs to be analyzed under the broad themes outlined in the first three chapters of this work: conversions, identity of the citizen, the erosion of traditional authority, and the imposition of law. His reign demonstrates how foreign claims and perceptions of nationhood articulated the margins of political change by describing what was just and correct in a "civilized" society, and even what was possible for governments, electorates, legislatures, and kings. But his reign also demonstrates that in 1864, Native legislators, writers, and, most important, the king himself were more than willing to take on those claims and make dramatic assertions of their own.

The foreigners' responses to Kapuāiwa's constitutional initiatives were bound up with a very definite respect for his authority as a king and conflicts about their own place and identity in the Islands. At the same time, they felt that the law still belonged to them. They did not hesitate to instruct the public, especially the Native public, about how law could and should be used. Their ownership of the public media in the 1850s guaranteed that they would control the discussions and debates, so the conflicts that arose between them and kānaka were never equally waged. But those conflicts did confirm the importance of the monarch as the only significant institution able to represent the kānaka.

Lota Kapuāiwa Kamehameha was born on 11 December 1830, the elder surviving son of the high chiefess Kīnaʻu and Kekūanaōʻa.[13] His ascent to Mōʻī, as well as his brother's, is clear evidence that the ancient structure of lineage and status was still trusted despite the ravages of disease and untimely deaths of Aliʻi Nui. On the other hand, it was not a structure intact, having been altered by depopulation and conversion.[14]

His mother was certainly a Kamehameha, daughter of the Conqueror and his Aliʻi Nui Wahine Kaheiheimālie. Her first mating had been with the Conqueror's son Liholiho, Kamehameha II, with whom she bore no children. Liholiho died in 1824. Three years later she took as a church-sanctioned husband the Kaukauali'i Mataio Kekūanaō'a, a match that is said to have sent the regent Ka'ahumanu into a rage.[15] Ka'ahumanu eventually reconciled with Kīna'u (Kamakau said that the reconciliation was on account of Kīna'u giving birth) and the chiefess even succeeded Ka'ahumanu as Kuhina Nui.

Ka'ahumanu's displeasure with Kīna'u's marriage was mostly frustration that there were so few eligible Ali'i Nui for a suitable match. But the birth of children, five in all, certainly made up for Kīna'u "marrying down," because her offspring would constitute a lifting of Kekūanaō'a's status and constitute a pool of potential Mō'ī as the Ali'i Nui continued to disappear.

Yet despite the fact that the princes Alexander Liholiho and Lota Kapuāiwa both represented what Kanalu Young called "the best of the rest"[16] genealogically, it is also true that they were both elevated by

Figure 8. Portraits of Alexander Liholiho (Kamehameha IV) *(left)* and Lota Kapuāiwa (Kamehameha V) *(right)*. These sons of Kīna'u and Kekūanaō'a reigned consecutively from 1854 to 1873. Neither had children to succeed them, and the Kamehameha ruling dynasty came to an end in 1874. Anonymous portrait, courtesy of the Bishop Museum, Honolulu. CP 126,136.

the hānai of Alexander Liholiho to the Mōʻī Kauikeaouli. It was the hānai relationship, and not just Alexander Liholiho's genealogy, that made Kauikeaouli specify him as his heir under the provisions of the 1852 Constitution.[17] Those provisions did not actually require that the successor possess a chiefly rank: "The Crown is hereby permanently confirmed to His Majesty Kamehameha III during his life, and to his successors. The successor shall be the person whom the King and the House of Nobles shall appoint and publicly proclaim as such, during the King's life; but should there be no such appointment and proclamation, then the successor shall be chosen by the House of Nobles and the House of Representatives in joint ballot."[18]

Article 25 had several significant implications that are worth examining. Perhaps when Kauikeaouli approved the constitution, he did not consider it necessary to explicitly require the Mōʻī to have Aliʻi rank in 1852. Anything else would have been unthinkable. Then again, this article mentions nothing about an heir, a delicate sidestepping, perhaps, of the unhappy reality that Kauikeaouli would probably die childless. In any case, the Mōʻī removed any possible doubt by naming Alexander Liholiho, who fulfilled the expectations of the law, at least, when he took the oath swearing to maintain and uphold the constitution.

This article also granted representatives and nobles the right to choose the monarch by joint ballot. This was not such a large legal change from the 1840 Constitution, which specified that the heir would be whomever the king and his chiefs appointed during the king's lifetime, "but should there be no appointment, then the decision shall rest with the chiefs and House of Representatives."[19] Nevertheless, the representatives in 1842 were very different from those of 1854. Had the king died without naming an heir in 1842, it is unlikely that any of them would have had much to say about picking his successor.

In the past the Mōʻī had the principal responsibility for naming his heir. In better times, the heir would have come from a large pool of potential candidates of Aliʻi Nui rank. The choices were often quite obvious and well known, not only to the Mōʻī but to his konohiki. Among the best-known examples, Kalaniʻōpuʻu issued his kauoha (verbal will) that the nīʻaupiʻo chief Kīwalaʻō, son of his union with Kalola, succeed him. In terms of lineage, Kalaniʻōpuʻu correctly chose his own son, but the reality was that his son did not have the support of very powerful West Hawaiʻi Island chiefs. They rallied around

Kalani'ōpu'u's nephew Kamehameha, whose rise to power proceeded with the slaying of Kīwala'ō.

Although successorship was related to lineage, political power that was, in part, military power determined the survival of the new Mō'ī. In Kauikeaouli's time, the collapse of the population and the resulting depreciation of the Ali'i Nui genealogies required a wholly different set of assumptions concerning the heir. Kauikeaouli could not assume, as Kalani'ōpu'u could, that some close relative would assume leadership should the designated heir falter or prove unworthy. On the other hand, the end of chiefly warfare and the dearth of challengers to the heir meant that traditional methods of legitimating the Mō'ī were at least partly replaced by the legitimation of the constitution.

But even the specific and clear wording of the constitution regarding the succession did not interfere with the political realities of 1863. Alexander Liholiho did not specify an heir. He and his queen had produced a son, Albert, whose early and traumatic death appeared to have precipitated his father's sickness and resulting demise. The king's sudden illness and rapid decline was unexpected, and he had made no provision for the succession. Indeed, some of the cabinet officials speculated that Queen Emma might be hāpai (with child), prompting an "investigation"[20] that delayed the actual naming of Kapuāiwa as the heir and new king.

Nevertheless, the primary legitimating factor in 1864 was still genealogical rank. Led by Wyllie, Alexander Liholiho's cabinet proclaimed Lota Kapuāiwa king without ever suggesting that the successorship should be determined in the legislature. However, a small group of unnamed American missionaries, said to be in control of the Kuhina Nui, Victoria Kamāmalu, did oppose the succession. They asserted that she should be regent, following the example of Ka'ahumanu, while the legislature elected a Mō'ī.[21] Evidently, it was as important to the haole who held political office as it was to the kānaka that the king bear the rank and status of the Kamehameha line. It may also have been important, at least for those in power, that the ruler be male. There were several legitimate heirs to the crown in 1864; three of them were women, and two, including Victoria Kamāmalu, had lineages comparable with that of Kapuāiwa. Yet this prince, in 1864, entertained no doubt that he would be named Mō'ī and that there would be no one to challenge his succession. There were no male Ali'i with rank equal to his own.

The scope of this work unfortunately does not allow much more than a slight, but important, digression to mention sex and power in Hawaiian society and in the kingdom. The case can certainly be made that the most powerful of the chiefs after Kamehameha was Kaʻahumanu, whose political cunning was unmatched by anyone except Kapuāiwa. Kaʻahumanu ruled as a very traditional Aliʻi, but although she was not the Mōʻī, she, rather than her son Liholiho, was responsible for the growth of the new political authority based on Christian laws described in chapter 1.

Kamehameha made her Kuhina Nui when her father, Keʻeaumoku, died in 1807. When the Conqueror himself died, Kaʻahumanu used her official position as well as her lineage to assert her dominance throughout Liholiho's reign and into the reign of Kauikeaouli. After Kaʻahumanu, three chiefesses were named Kuhina Nui: Kīnaʻu, Kekāuluohi, and Victoria Kamāmalu. According to the provisions of the 1840 Constitution, the king could not act without the knowledge and approbation of the Kuhina Nui.[22] In 1852, the Kuhina Nui was specifically empowered to veto the acts of the Mōʻī.[23]

Kapuāiwa named his father Kuhina Nui in 1864, and Kekūanaōʻa became only the second male in that position in over half a century. Two things need to be noted here. First, the king replaced his sister who shared his rank with his father whose rank was inferior. Second, Kapuāiwa made this change as a preliminary step to abolishing that position altogether. Eliminating the premier would ultimately involve challenging the constitution, a rigorous test of the new king's political skills. Perhaps he was not prepared to have that contest complicated by considerations of rank and genealogy.

But it is also true that after Kaʻahumanu and Kīnaʻu, the female Kuhina Nui had only rarely challenged the authority of the Mōʻī and were generally content to merely place their signatures beneath the king's. Why were Kapuāiwa and his brother unhappy with the position of Kuhina Nui? Simply put, the presence of a second executive whose approval was needed on any significant matter demeaned the status of the king. Not only was the monarch saddled with a privy council, but also with a second imperial presence who historically had been female.

Ironically, this position was written into constitutions devised by American attorneys and missionaries. In the United States, women held no political offices, were denied suffrage, and in some states could not even control their inherited property. Yet the Americans William Richards, John Ricord, and William Little Lee all believed that it was quite appropriate to reinforce the power and authority of the Kuhina Nui as an equivalent to the king despite the fact that it had become a "traditionally" female office. Perhaps these haole had a much higher opinion of female leadership in Hawai'i than most of their countrymen. Or perhaps they created the law to subtly humiliate the office of Mō'ī.

As for the Kuhina Nui, their rank was equal, if not superior to, that of the Mō'ī after 1854. Kapuāiwa himself recognized that. Nearing death in 1872 and needing to appoint a successor, he asked Bernice Pauahi to become the Mō'ī Wahine, preferring her lineage and abilities to those of the male chiefs Lunalilo and Kalākaua. American law might not have been willing to legitimate female authority in 1872, but the king had rather little problem with it. The kanaka electorate, entirely male, was furiously supportive of Queen Emma over David Kalākaua in 1874. Chiefly rank was everything. Gender, at least at this point, was not the issue for the Natives, especially as epidemics consumed the ancient lineages in the holocaust that was the nineteenth century. In fact, Kapuāiwa's successful termination of the position of Kuhina Nui did not destroy the opportunity for feminine leadership in the kingdom. On the contrary, by strengthening the office of Mō'ī, the king made it possible for a queen to wield real political power.

Between the perilous shoals that represented the diminishing pool of Ali'i Nui leadership, Lota Kapuāiwa was forced to channel his efforts to change the distribution of power in the kingdom between the markers of Western legal precepts. But it was the *conceptual* nature of constitutions as an institution and not the Constitution of 1852 itself that circumscribed Kapuāiwa in 1864. Having refused "the Oath," the king believed that he was not in any way bound to or by it. He did not believe, any more than the most opinionated lawyer, that the kingdom could operate without one.

Historians of that period have focused their analyses on the legal questions raised by Lota's call for a constitutional convention.[24] Kuykendall, for one, never paused to examine the deeper significance of the fact that this Hawaiian monarch felt obliged to provide a constitution at all. Nationhood and constitutions have become such normalized practices in the twenty-first century that we forget that this king was a mere generation removed from Ka'ahumanu, who ruled capably without one. He was only two generations from the great chiefs of Kamehameha's time, who would have considered such a constraint on their authority and the concomitant granting of political power to Maka'āinana unimaginably absurd.

Unquestionably, Hawaiian chiefly society had undergone deep alterations, one of which, the rearing and education of Ali'i Nui, ensured that all of the Native ruling elite, including the chiefesses, were trained in Western political forms at the Chiefs' Children's School. Just as important, Kapuāiwa's own career in government, as a member of the House of Nobles and cabinet minister during his brother's reign, was certainly enabled, in part, by the organizational apparatus set up by the 1852 Constitution. But this Ali'i Nui never acknowledged that it was the legal system that entitled him as Mō'ī. In his first speech to the nobles and representatives of the 1864 legislature, he proclaimed: "The right to the Throne of this country, originally acquired by conquest and birth, belongs hereditarily to the family of Kamehameha I."[25] Kapuāiwa believed that his authority alone was sufficient to challenge that constitution's provisions in Article 105 that amendments were to be secured by the legislature. In fact, the question of the monarch's authority over the amendment process (and ultimately over the entire constitution) had been raised before by Alexander Liholiho in 1859: "Experience has conclusively shown that the Constitution of 1852 does not, in many important respects, meet the expectations of its framers, or of my Predecessor, by whom it was voluntarily conceded. . . . The 105th Article of the Constitution prescribes the ordinary mode of amendment. Without reference to a different manner of revision, clearly founded on the inherent rights of the different Estates of the Kingdom, I am, at this time, content to appeal to the Legislature for such action as will provide an adequate remedy for all existing difficulties."[26]

Alexander Liholiho's choice of words is critically important. Ascribing Kauikeaouli's promulgation of the constitution as voluntary, coupled with his own statement that he was for that time "content to appeal to the Legislature," underscores his assertion that the monarch's cooperation with the constitution had been and would continue to be optional. Unquestionably, this assertion of the Mō'ī's preeminence over the law was the overarching dispute for Hawaiian political society in 1864.

The conflict over whether the constitution should be changed was not the dividing issue between supporters and antagonists of His

Majesty's government. In fact, there was considerable agreement in the haole and Hawaiian press that the very changes desired by Kapu-āiwa were necessary for the sake of the kingdom's economy and political stability. But the issue of whose authority was supreme, the Mō'ī or the law, entangled haole and Natives in a discourse that was not simply about the politics of power, but a deeply meaningful conflict between embedded values and understandings.

Conventional Identity

On 7 and 14 May 1864 the *Pacific Commercial Advertiser* published several editorials and articles relating to the text of Lota's "Royal Proclamation," calling for a constitutional convention to reconsider the 1852 Constitution. Actually, the proclamation published on 7 May was substantially different from the revised version printed in the later issue. The editor was Henry M. Whitney, the Hawai'i-born son of first-company missionary Samuel Whitney. His editorial struck an ominous tone as he attempted to analyze the king's intentions. The text of the later proclamation read: ". . . it is our will to meet Our Nobles and the Delegates of Our People for the purpose of consulting on the revision of the Constitution of Our Kingdom, and consulting upon the public good as well as to provide ways and means to carry on Our Government." [27]

The editorial comment acknowledged (with emphasis) that such a convention could be called to discuss needed revisions to the constitution so long as they were mere recommendations to the 1864 legislature:

> But thoughtful minds have been thrown into a state of alarm by the following clause in the proclamation, to wit, *"as well as provide ways and means to carry on the government."* This seems to ignore the Representative Branch of the Legislature or House of Commons, and call upon a convention to do what *that branch only can do constitutionally. . . .* It would unsettle the present quiet, it would be revolutionary in its tendency, and more unfriendly to the ruling dynasty than almost any act short of positive rebellion. It would unsettle property as well as political institutions. [28]

The almost menacing rhetoric of the weekly newspaper probably sprang from more than one anxiety. The king's proclamation not only challenged the constituted authority of the House of Representatives,

Table 5. Legislative Assembly, 1864. The king granted a new constitution on 20 August 1864 creating a unicameral legislature in which his appointed nobles and the elected representatives would meet and deliberate together. (King: Lota Kapuāiwa [became Kamehameha V following the death of his brother in December 1863]; ministers: Wyllie, Foreign Affairs; de Varigny, Finance; Hopkins, Interior; Harris, Attorney General)

NOBLES	REPRESENTATIVES
Charles Reed Bishop	Edwin H. Boyd*
John O. Dominis*	S. N. Castle* (Vice-President)
Charles Coffin Harris	J. H. Heleluhe
C. G. Hopkins	T. C. Heuck*
John Papa ʻĪʻī	L. Kaʻapā
Kāʻeo (Peter Young)*	J. Kahai
H. A. Kahanu*	J. P. E. Kahaleaʻahu*
David Kalākaua	A. M. Kahalewai
William P. Kamakau*	M. Kahananui
Charles Kanaʻina	S. Kahoʻohalahala*
Paul Kanoa	J. M. Kalanipoʻo
Kaisera Kapaʻakea	J. H. Kamalo
John Kapena	J. K. Kaunamanō* (Hāmākua, Hawaiʻi)
Mataio Kekūanaōʻa (President)	J. W. H. Kauwahi*
William Charles Lunalilo*	J. W. Keawehunahala
Paul Nāhaolelua	C. W. Kenui*
Charles de Varigny*	H. Kūihelani
Robert C. Wyllie	W. T. Martin*
	J. A. Nāhaku* (Kāʻanapali, Maui)
	D. H. Nāhinu*
	D. Nuʻuhiwa
	J. H. ʻŌpūpahi*
	P. Papaua
	P. Paulo
	W. E. Piʻi
	Godfrey Rhodes
	Ūwēleʻaleʻa

Source: Lydecker, 1918, *Roster Legislatures of Hawaii,* 103.

* First year.

it also resolved, unexpectedly, Kapuāiwa's six-month-long silence on the subject of the oath not taken, with an apparent willingness to obliterate that constitution entirely. That coupled with a growing uneasiness in the foreign business community over an anticipated economic downturn integrated many of their concerns into one anxious distress.

Actually, the state of the economy in 1864 was fairly vibrant on the rural plantations, where labor shortages kept the wages at a relatively high level through the mid-1860s. The American Civil War denied the Northern states access to the sugar-producing Confederacy and thus, despite a huge U.S. tariff, the demand for Hawaiian sugar was extremely high.[29] Nevertheless, several businessmen worried that a continuing labor shortage in the Islands would eventually translate into a higher cost of labor and very tight money for the economy as a whole. The *Advertiser,* covering a meeting of the Royal Hawaiian Agricultural Society, editorialized: "The Hon. Judge Robertson, who was in the chair, very justly observed that although some planters in isolated localities, were of the opinion that we had labor enough, the demand for more laborers for so many estates was becoming so great that it would very soon exceed the supply; and consequently, that it would be impossible to resist such a rise in wages as would be very detrimental to all the planters."[30]

The *Pacific Commercial Advertiser* was one of the few publications that opposed increasing the importation of labor from other parts of the world. This too was widely debated in economic, geopolitical, and ideological terms,[31] but the issue of whether the sugar industry was making the fullest possible use of Native labor had a direct influence on the public discourse concerning the reform of the 1852 Constitution. Whitney's editorial, just cited, went on to claim: "If we could but compel our idlers, loafers or vagrants (for such they may well be called) to work, for their own good, and the good of the kingdom, we would at once have a supply of perhaps 5000 able-bodied men and women. It is said that at this moment there are upwards of 500 of that degraded and worthless class in Honolulu alone."[32]

The *Advertiser*'s assertion that part of the economic troubles of the kingdom could be laid at the feet of Hawaiians unwilling to work integrated several foreigner anxieties, especially those living in Honolulu, into a single explanation and a simple solution. Vagrants should be forced to work, thus solving not only the labor shortages of plantations, but effectively removing those individuals from the towns where they, and they alone, were responsible for every conceivable mischief:

Amongst *us*, they live without any social or civil disqualification, rejoicing in their right to eat the bread of their neighbors, to harbor themselves in other men's houses, seduce their wives and daughters, and to vote for such law makers as will protect them, their dogs, and their horses. Ought such men to be allowed to vote at the polls? Would it not be charity in the state to exercise a patriarchal power over such *moths* of society, and as a father coerces his vicious children, so to coerce idlers to eat bread earned by their own hands? [33]

The article expressed fears that are interesting and suggestive enough to explore momentarily. These characterizations of a particular kind of Native, seen as quite prevalent in the population, reinforced a perception of them not only as children, but as potential predators as well. Also, because those characterizations were leveled at the vagrant and, therefore, landless poor, such vagrants were placed outside of and in opposition to respectable Natives who either possessed land or were willing to engage in wage labor. Whitney's articles intended to discourage sympathy for the landless, unemployed Natives and drove a moral and political wedge between those kānaka who had property or jobs and those who did not.

Moreover, disenfranchising the landless clarified the status of haole in the kingdom. They, along with propertied and educated Hawaiians, would be bound together by position, *equalized* despite their racial difference, as a body of sober and responsible citizens. Such equalization between white and brown would take place, however, only when the propertied or wage-earning Hawaiians learned to use their positions wisely.

That meant that the Hawaiians' disposition toward sharing and charity, noted by such prominent haole as William Little Lee (see chapter 4), had to be actively discouraged. The government, and even the church, Whitney argued, had sound theological reasons for denying support to vagrants: "A more common sense view of this was taken by the Christian Emperors of Rome and the primitive Christian church. Idleness was then considered as the mother of robbery. Idlers were then designated *natis consumere fruges*, born to devour that which belonged to others. And they were punished as thieves and robbers, both by the canons of the church and imperial decrees." [34]

Ultimately, Whitney would carry this argument to the conclusion that landless and wageless individuals were not true subjects of the

kingdom and should not possess the rights of suffrage and representation. When a Native representative, Maʻakuʻia, was elected in Honolulu to replace the deceased haole representative William Webster,
Whitney exploded: "Every reasonable man must be convinced that a
property qualification of some kind, applicable to representative candidates as well as to voters, has become a necessity, and is the only
guard that can be established to prevent our Legislature from being
filled with men totally unfit to represent at least the foreign population
and its capital, or to enact laws for the kingdom. Let us have a change
in this organic law of the land, even if the Constitution itself has to be
remodeled."[35]

Of course, this is what both Kamehameha IV and V had been saying since the late 1850s. Altering the suffrage to include only literate
and propertied males had been the centerpiece of Alexander Liholiho's
efforts to amend the constitution. The leading member of his cabinet,
Robert Wyllie, had repeatedly criticized the too-liberal nature of the
constitution. His remarks on universal manhood suffrage and its presence in the American republic seemed especially appropriate as that
nation prepared for a war that was, in part, linked to their own definitions of citizenship: ". . . establishing Universal Suffrage, virtually
hands over the power of governing this kingdom to its *ignorance* and
poverty—a principle which, I believe, will soon, unless corrected,
destroy the Great Confederation and will eventually destroy every
Country where it becomes the fundamental law."[36]

Over the issues of reform, there appears to have been a good deal
of support, at least from the haole press, that the qualifications of the
representatives and of the voters themselves were entirely too liberal.
Kapuāiwa's own statement in the early months of his reign, that "universal suffrage was altogether beyond the political capacity of this people as it exists today,"[37] certainly found some support among the foreign population, even those like Whitney whose parents were
American missionaries. However, the Mōʻī and the haole press did not
share the same reasons for their positions.

Whitney perceived the Natives as people who required strong discipline to curb their natural or cultural tendencies toward sloth, believing that it was appropriate to deny such individuals a common membership as fully enfranchised citizens with the rest of them. Whites,
in other words, did not need to consider themselves linked to those
Natives who did not behave like them. Having defined by constitution

and legislation the qualities of citizenship, certain individuals in 1864 were prepared to acknowledge that some haole had stronger claims to belonging to the nation than some Natives.

When the veteran cabinet minister Wyllie was appointed to assist the king in the making of a new cabinet, Whitney responded by expressing regret that the ministry would continue to be in the hands of a *foreign* element: "He is almost the only existing representative of a policy that is now fast becoming obsolete—the theory that the Hawaiian Government cannot exist without employing aliens, and by *aliens* we mean those who have not become thoroughly identified with the Hawaiian people—strangers, ignorant of our language and wants." [38]

Assigning to individuals like Wyllie the onus of being aliens was done not so much to belittle them politically as to clarify the status of those haole who had deeper, or at least longer, roots in the Islands. Whitney, who bore and used the kanakalike name Wini on his ballots in the 1855 election for representative, made it clear that he represented a contingent of haole who because of their "identification" with the Natives had more legitimate claims to the higher offices of government. "It was hoped," his editorial added, "that he [Wyllie] would yield his peculiar notions, and by the selection of a *Hawaiianized* Ministry, usher in the new reign with an administration that would command the welcome support of all classes, chiefs and commoners, foreign and native born." [39]

Whitney made an interesting use of "classes" here, combining a socioeconomic status with a station based on birthright. It was a deft assertion that the children of missionaries and other early immigrants to the Islands had a particular status that was not shared by latecomers such as Wyllie or the new French minister of the treasury, Charles de Varigny. Whitney, a missionary son and a strong proponent of a business-oriented government, was trying to position a particular element as having a more legitimate claim to speak, not only for commerce, but for the Natives as well. This element was not haole per se. It was a certain kind of haole.

Even before 1864, references had been made in the press and in other public documents to the "missionary party." Although no formal political party existed as such, certain individuals were linked as sharing political and social ideas and qualifications, among which was a strong presumption among them that they represented what was best for everyone. Many of those who belonged appeared to be missionaries and their children, though by no means all of them.[40] Neither William Little Lee nor Charles Reed Bishop were missionaries, but clergy and mission families recognized them as acute and successful businessmen who lived in service to the government and, presumably, the Natives. It was not wealth nor possession of land that set all these men apart; it was a sense that they were *responsible* with their wealth. That is to say, these individuals understood that their ability to make money was directly linked to their continued willingness to minister to the Hawaiians as a way of serving God.[41]

Recognition as a Hawaiianized haole was not necessarily based on nationality. The American missionaries were, without question, a tight-knit group, but it did not prevent them from welcoming and supporting individuals in government like William Webster, an Englishman, or Vlademar Knudsen, who was Norwegian. However, some were seen as true foreigners, especially those like de Varigny, who maintained his French citizenship even after his appointment to the ministry. The *Advertiser* reported, with emphasis: "But we were astonished at the appointment of Mons. De Varigny to the post of Minister of Finance. We had hoped that this government, now in the commencement of the new reign, was at last to become *Hawaiianized,* that those only were to be invited to participate in the government who had cast their lot here, *and had become identified with the country.*"[42]

It is easier to perceive how they saw themselves by noting whom they characterized as outsiders. Dr. George Lathrop, infamous member of the Committee of Thirteen, was certainly one of those who did not belong. In a letter to former U.S. Consul Joel Turrill, Charles Reed Bishop apologetically revealed his great distaste for Turrill's own brother-in-law: "We have among us a set of men with no honesty, no principle except to make trouble, and serve their own ends without regard to the rights of others. Pray excuse me for saying that I consider George A. Lathrop one of the worst of the class I have mentioned."[43]

Just as certain haole possessed a distinct position in relation to other "foreigners," Whitney inferred in subsequent articles that his Hawaiianized haole had a status separate from kānaka as well. When the early January election returns revealed that James Dowsett[44] had not been reelected in Honolulu, Whitney editorialized:

His place will hardly be supplied by either Mr. Kamakau or Mr. Ragsdale. The former has previously sat as representative from Maui, and is well known as one of the finest Hawaiian orators and scholars that we have among us. He will be one of the best native members of the House. Mr. Ragsdale may be considered as the representative of the half-caste population—a portion of our island community which is fast increasing in numbers and political influence, and whose right to a representation in the national councils no one will attempt to question. [45]

Whitney envisioned a kingdom inhabited by several kinds of citizens: Natives, half-castes, native-born and other "Hawaiianized" individuals, and foreigners. "Hawaiianized" delegates (that is, haole who had become "thoroughly identified with Hawaiians") could presumably represent the nation as natives and not as aliens, but Natives like Kamakau and Ragsdale obviously could not replace people like Dowsett, despite their own qualities as kānaka.

If Natives were a separate category, at least as far as the "missionary party" was concerned, kanaka delegates did not apparently take this to mean that they should necessarily oppose initiatives that sprang from missionaries. Indeed, as we shall see in the debate over the constituting power of the constitutional convention, several kanaka delegates agreed with the petition of missionaries O. H. Gulick and J. Porter Green that the convention had no authority to actually alter the 1852 Constitution. [46]

Some very interesting political battle lines were being drawn in the opening days of the convention. Gulick and Green's petition portrayed the convention as a usurpation of the authority of the House of Representatives, a body that technically existed but had not been convened by the king. [47] Their claim underscored the position taken by the *Pacific Commercial Advertiser* and the Hawaiian-language newspaper *Kuokoa* [48] that the people's rights were being trampled because their constitutionally erected safeguard, the House of Representatives, no longer appeared to exist.

The Mō'ī responded with the statement quoted at the beginning of this chapter, that all of the suitable representatives of the kingdom, delegates of the people, nobles, and himself, were present and as the three parts of the kingdom represented all the power and authority that was needed. Moreover, as the king asserted in one address to the convention: "The question has been distorted. Are the rights of the people threatened? No. The electoral franchise is first a privilege, next a duty, but in no sense whatever is it an absolute right. Under a constitutional government the people must be consulted. But who are the people? Is it the dregs of society, the ignorant and improvident, or is it the intelligent element who are appropriately to be consulted?"[49]

For Kapuāiwa and his cabinet, the principal issue was not the protection of rights that had been a mere twelve years in existence, but the protection of the stability of the only slightly older kingdom under his monarchic leadership. He was not denying the importance of an elected legislature. Rather he was attempting to render it a dignity, and therefore a legitimacy, that in some minds it did not possess.

Kapuāiwa supported several constitutional changes that were more or less inseparable from each other. He wanted property and literacy qualifications for representatives and for the electorate. He wanted to confine the franchise to actual subjects of the kingdom. He wanted a single legislative body that incorporated nobles, representatives, and the executive. Finally, he intended to centralize executive authority in himself, ending the office of Kuhina Nui and the prerogatives of the cabinet and the privy council. All of these alterations were calculated to exalt the government by purging it of individuals who were perceived as incompetent or superfluous. Under Kapuāiwa's plan, even the electorate would be reduced to those whose behavior would not embarrass the kingdom. This idea was heavily supported by Wyllie and Charles C. Harris, who reported to the king that not only did the constitution "cramp and circumscribe the authority of the crown" but that "the possession of the right of suffrage by the larger portion of the people, who are unable to exercise it intelligently, or do not value, tends clearly and directly to the demoralization of Govt., and to derogate from its dignity and means of benefitting the People."[50]

One political objective of ending the separate House of Representatives and replacing it with a single legislature of nobles and representatives was to retrieve more influence for the king. But it is also true that a legislative assembly occupied by both the remnants of the Ali'i and established haole who constituted the House of Nobles and the people's popular choices was intended to produce a body that would be more effectual by removing the chief targets of haole political criticism, the "foolish" kanaka voter and the "ineffectual" kanaka legislator.

These constitutional changes were more than simply political strategies designed to strengthen government authority. They were also extensions of a historical and Native discourse on the relationship between Mō'ī and Maka'āinana. Kānaka who refused to work would have been quite unacceptable to the ruling chiefs of old. In the modern kingdom, they were not only an embarrassment, they were a threat to the idea that the Hawaiian nation, represented by kānaka, could achieve and maintain a strong and proud independence among the nations of the world.

Kapuāiwa's dilemma was that as their Mōʻī, he quite clearly represented the entire kānaka, especially with respect to the non-Hawaiian subjects in the nation. Those kānaka who displayed "evident" weakness in the marketplace, ignorance of or resistance to haole law, and illiteracy all reflected badly on the king as well as on themselves. They did not, however, reflect badly on haole citizens, who, by their own assertions, were different and, though different, were as entitled to the fruits of land and power as any Native.

Kapuāiwa's limiting of the franchise to those who were literate and possessed property demanded a leap of understanding in the Hawaiian conception of things that would have been most unlikely two generations earlier—that the former Makaʻāinana, now vagrants, should have any political say at all in the running of the kingdom. By limiting the franchise in these specific ways, he preserved a Hawaiianness to the discourse on political power by recognizing that both kinds of subjects, the landowner and the literate, were aliens as far as the traditional civilization was concerned. Hence his leap was not a leap at all, but a sidestepping of the real issues of political legitimacy. The aliens would vote. Voting was an alien institution. The kānaka would continue to be wards of the chief, as in traditional times, but sooner or later they would either be landed or be employed citizens.

This interpretation explains the fact that resistance to the king's new constitution by Hawaiians was limited to those who served in the legislature as well as American haole whose own political power (most of them were either propertied or had money) was *enhanced* by the new voting restrictions. Neither the newly disenfranchised subject nor the Hawaiian voting citizen protested because each was now defined by the state in ways that gave them a status with which they were either familiar or approving. For the Americans, however, the king's edict was, on many levels, an appropriation of powers that they felt *belonged* to them, especially the power to define the citizen.

Since their arrival, various haole had insistently described and defined the Hawaiians with a status that resonated Enlightenment and/or Christian conceptions of humanity and civilization. When Kapuāiwa appropriated the "dividing practices," he threatened the power relationship that existed between Hawaiians and haole. The liberal (pre-Kapuāiwa) voting laws coupled with the Hawaiians' "obvious" ineptness in government were part of a significant haole discourse. On one hand, this discourse applied the Lockean thesis that liberally interpreted (or God-given) natural rights could not be abridged and therefore existed separately and above the ability of a people to make proper use of them.[51] On the other hand, should the Hawaiian government falter and annexation ensue, it would reflect a natural (or divinely ordered) process for which no one could be held accountable but the Hawaiians themselves.

Kapuāiwa's convention shifted the assumptions of who or what was the legitimating authority of the kingdom. The king was claiming that authority for himself, but his opponents insisted that he and everyone else derived their rights and powers under the constitution signed by Kauikeaouli. Former missionaries Gulick and Parker, who resigned as delegates during the convention's first week, said: "We protest, because we believe that this is a Constitutional Monarchy, and that the Crown can no more claim the powers which it exercised previous to 1852, than it can resume the lands which Kamehameha III separated from his Royal Domain and made over to the Government. We believe that Your Majesty, in ascending the Throne, by that act resumed all the duties and responsibilities which attach to the Throne under the Constitution."[52]

It is not surprising that many of the haole who offered their opinions in the *Advertiser* were so indignant over Kapuāiwa's disregarding of their "sacred" constitution. Nevertheless, there was virtually no direct criticism of the king himself. In fact, critics of the convention continually portrayed it as a strategy of the king's cabinet, asserting that the real struggle was not between king and people but between haole who had the Natives' best interests in mind and those who did not. In a sense, all of the Natives were removed from the center of the controversy, king and kānaka alike, because both the convention delegates and the newspapers that covered them depicted the convention as a struggle between haole members of the cabinet and haole who opposed them:

If, however, as we have too much reason to believe, the Convention is intended to annul or alter the present Constitution, we warn the King's Ministers that they are doing the very thing to destroy the best safeguard of his Throne. In no more effectual way could they impair all its securities, than by thus trampling on the Constitution, which all would sacredly regard, until the Sovereign himself sets an example of disregarding it. *No other Constitution can ever have like sacredness.* If one can be arbitrarily set aside, another can be.[53]

A later story accused Minister Wyllie of having succeeded in stirring voters against foreigner delegates on Kauaʻi and Maui. In both instances the respective governors of those islands were purported to have used their official influence to prevent the election of foreigners. Nahaolelua of Maui is said to have called the haole candidate, Dr. James Smith, an enemy of the people. But again, neither the king, who was present in both instances, nor the governors were given the brunt of the responsibility.[54] Wyllie was framed in the press as the chief instigator of the constitutional difficulties. Even when Kapuāiwa eventually terminated the convention and submitted a constitution of his own devising, the press quickly abandoned a direct assault on the king and resumed harping on Wyllie's "treachery."

The positioning of the established haole as supporters of, among other things, the Natives' best interests required continual adjustments. Such positioning could not allow, at least under the reign of a Kamehameha, a treatment of their king that was in the least bit disrespectful. The king was still the one reliable symbol for the kānaka, the only one that could hope to maintain Native loyalty to a kingdom that was in other ways more and more alienated from them.

No one either in the convention or covering it for the press uttered a word of argument when the Lāhainā delegate Kauwahi insisted that the king was acting properly by attempting to drastically alter the makeup and authority of the legislature:

> What was the King's desire when he submitted this article to us? Did he want to prevent his people from enjoying a sacred right? I do not myself think so. The King is a member of the same race as we are; he is the highest of our chiefs. . . . He has submitted to us the draft of a constitution so that we may discuss and amend it, inviting us to select this and reject that. Why then these feelings of hostility, as revealed in the speeches of certain delegates? Do these persons think they are the sole guardians of the rights of the people? Certainly the rights of the people are also the rights of the king, and of both reciprocally. They cannot be divorced.[55]

This was the problem for the anticonvention delegates and their sympathizers. Their arguments were limited by their unwillingness to confront the king directly. They might have done so by attacking his refusal to swear to the 1852 Constitution in the first place, or by claiming, with some justification, that His Majesty was initiating a power play to increase his own authority under the law. This the delegates and the press steadfastly refused to do. In one of the few letters to the *Advertiser* critical of the king's refusal to swear, the anonymous writer only obliquely attacked the king: "the public are of opinion that the cabinet,—and particularly its senior member [Wyllie]—is responsible for our imperfect constitutional organization of the Government, since the death of his late Majesty. And they are responsible for the imperfect legal titles that may have been given, and the litigation that may follow from otherwise legal acts, but which are not believed to be legal, because the King has never sworn to the Constitution of the land."[56]

When in 1887 haole businessmen would finally succeed in taming, once and for all, the power of the monarch and the Native electors, they would do so by greatly strengthening the cabinet. The king in 1864, though, was quite powerful and the cabinet, including Wyllie, was deferential to his will. There is no doubt that the Mōʻī himself understood this, just as there is no doubt how clearly he perceived his struggle with the constitution. In his last address to the convention—just before he terminated it—he said:

> I would explain my final views on the matter. Universal suffrage cannot coexist with a monarchic form of government. I have no more belief in the stability of a Monarchy based on republican principles than I have on a republic based on monarchic assumptions. A choice must be made: monarchy or republic. In this matter the choice of the majority of the nation has been achieved long since, and so well has it been made that the most fiery partisans of universal suffrage have not dared, not once, to match their actions with their principles.[57]

Even as the king seized control of the laws that changed the qualifications of electors and representatives, the debates among delegates during the convention were never meaningless. For one thing, these assertions illuminated the growing contest for mastery of the more than twenty-five-year-old discourse on identity and control of the state. Ownership was never merely about the physical landscape, nor even about political power. Tenure over the land and resources was linked to the holding of a particular status, having a particular kuleana in the Islands. That was the kuleana of determining the nation's values and mores.

The Moral Imperative of Wealth

In 1864 the chief fear for foreign residents and citizens was not the changes that the convention might bring about but the obvious manifestation of political power and authority by the Hawaiian king. The evident inability of the Hawaiianized haole to determine the outcome of the convention through their public discourses reflected their actual weakness in confronting a determined and effective monarch so long as that monarch had the support and loyalty of the kanaka citizens. As one *Advertiser* reader put it, with emphasis: "it follows beyond denial that the Convention *may do what they please with all of us.* No Constitution any longer interposes itself between us and their arbitrary will. They may abrogate all our privileges; they may enact a despotism, or a State Religion; they may abolish the Courts; they may alter the tenure of lands. *We have no appeal.*"[58]

Kapuāiwa's convention exposed some of the raw and sensitive tissue of the multifarious body politic. The Hawaiianized haole whose influence was insufficient to seize control of the convention probably did not fear the king's intentions as much as they feared other haole who might be frightened into some drastic response. The kingdom, after all, offered a welcome haven for commerce and had maintained to that point a fairly benign political climate. It was also unsettling to the Hawaiianized haole that some of the worst disturbances of that climate tended to come from non-Hawaiianized Americans.

In the late 1830s, haole in Hawai'i perceived the French to be the principal threat to Hawaiian independence, especially after French naval officers and consuls had pressured the kingdom into accepting unequal treaties that played havoc with the kingdom's autonomy. The arrogance of the French greatly disturbed the American missionaries, in part because the French championed the Catholic Church, and in part from sheer jingoism. On the other hand, it had been the British who had actually seized the kingdom in 1843 when the Hawaiian government, on Gerrit Judd's advice, ceded Hawai'i's sovereignty to Great Britain.

American missionaries who claimed to be working to strengthen the kingdom economically and politically could hardly argue to the king and the legislature that the Islands should be annexed to the United States. Yet, that is exactly what Gerrit Judd did in 1853, carrying a secret offer from an American shipping magnate, Alfred G. Benson, to Kauikeaouli to buy the kingdom for five million dollars. By

1854 the French and the British were the least of the kingdom's worries as hundreds of California fortune seekers began arriving in Hawai'i. Their loud aggressiveness is what prompted Kauikeaouli to enter into negotiations with the United States for Hawai'i to be annexed to the United States, but only on the condition that the Islands be immediately admitted as a state.[59]

Kauikeaouli's death in 1854 ended that discussion for all time, at least as far as the monarchy was concerned, but pressures for annexation continued despite firm opposition by the kānaka and from many American officials, in the Islands and abroad. These pressures worried many of the haole business community, who feared that any attempt to take over the Islands or to foment insurrection among the foreign residents would destroy what was, in many ways, a very manageable relationship. In 1853 Charles Reed Bishop wrote: "One of our greatest fears is that under the idea that the new administration [U.S. President Franklin Pierce] will be in favor of general and unlimited annexation (and Cuba & the Hawaiian Islands in particular) . . . the restless characters of California will be fitting out 'Filibustering' expeditions

Figure 9. Kamehameha V (Lota Kapuāiwa) addressing the legislature ca. 1864. Wood engraving by A. Daudenarde, courtesy of the Bishop Museum, Honolulu. CPBM 59,972.

against us, and thereby not only making us trouble, but, destroy in the minds of the natives all respect for, and confidence in Americans."[60]

One reason why some of the more powerful and influential haole were reluctant to confront Kapuāiwa directly over the constitution was their concern about Native respect and confidence. For that reason, setting up "straw men" like Wyllie, Harris, and de Varigny was, perhaps, their most viable strategy. But it is also true that such men did arouse a very real suspicion and envy among the "missionary gang."[61] Haole who identified with the missionaries and missionary-owned businesses attacked those three cabinet members unmercifully, claiming that their foolish and megalomaniacal policies were detrimental to the Natives and to the long-term independence of the kingdom.[62]

It was for the Natives' own protection, insisted several haole delegates, that the new constitution should guarantee the equality of all people. The king's proposed constitution altered Article 1, which in the former constitution read, "God hath created all men free and equal, and endowed them with certain inalienable rights," by removing the words "and equal." The assertion of equality was an especially important contributor to the reorientation of the Hawaiians from Maka'āinana to subjects and citizens. In 1850, "equal rights" was seen to be the kānaka's safeguard against oppression by the Ali'i.

But in 1864, the haole who tried to amend Article 1 by reattaching the words "and equal" made no claim that it should be done to protect the people from the chiefs or the king. On the contrary, they argued that the amendment's principal benefit would be to protect the Natives from whites. Charles Judd, son of Honolulu delegate and former Minister of Finance Gerrit Judd, claimed that: "nothing was meant by the word 'equal' by which to detract from the prerogatives of King or Chiefs, it was merely the expression of the broad doctrine of the equality of all men, whatever be their color, condition or circumstances in life."[63] Reverend Green, whose opposition to the convention's constituting power had not moved him to resign along with Gulick and Parker, added: "Those States that had left out the word 'equal' from their Constitutions, had done so to countenance slavery. The cornerstone of our Constitution should be the principles of liberty, equality of all men, and these words will be a safeguard against the encroachments of the white against the native race."[64]

Taken together these two opinions conveyed the belief that Natives had much to fear from white foreigners. For Green and the

Judds, that belief was entirely sincere. As members and inheritors of the ABCFM mission, they had constructed a separate status and identity for themselves that posited the existence of voracious foreigners—at that point, the foreigners were white—who would quickly and unconscionably divest the Natives from their remaining possessions and possibly from their freedom. Constitutional equality for the Natives guaranteed, at least in their estimation, that dispossession would not single out the Hawaiians just because of their race. Nothing could be done, of course, if certain kānaka's individual incompetence dispossessed them.

Haole supporters of the amendment were not especially interested in dragging out the old claim about equality between the king, chiefs, and people, but Native delegates were. Kauwahi and Kepoʻikai, who had supported the king's right to call the convention as well as the convention's right to draft a new constitution, voted against the amendment, arguing that not only would the amendment place king, chiefs, and people on the same level, but that such equality did not in reality exist. Delegate Kepoʻikai mocked the notion of equality by saying that he would like to wear the cocked hat and epaulets of the governor of Kauaʻi, but they would be taken from him. Not every Native delegate agreed. Waialua delegate Kuaʻea, a pastor who had entered Lāhaināluna in 1847, argued from the Bible that God *had* made all men equal. In the vote on the amendment at least five Natives sided with Green and the Judds, passing it on to the nobles and the king by a vote of 12 to 7.[65]

The other two "estates" made short work of the amendment. The nobles voted 18 to 2 to strike it,[66] and the king delivered his opinion that "He was not prepared to say that God had created *all* men free and equal." Furthermore: "The history of these islands informs us, that there have always been here races of chiefs and common people. The *laws* and not this amendment will protect the native race against the white. This amendment will conflict with the property qualification coming hereafter in the revision, and as the words convey no political rights, they are useless."[67]

Significantly, the king did not claim that *he* would protect the Natives. But in believing that laws emanating from his new order would be sufficient protection for the kānaka, Kapuāiwa was quite consistently moving toward a much stronger and more executive-run nation. His other proposed articles all clearly pointed in that direction, from the elimination of the Kuhina Nui and the inclusion of the cabinet in the legislative assembly, to the king's assertion that, in defense of the government, the freedom of the press could be limited.[68]

Nevertheless, by confining the franchise and legislative qualifications, the Mōʻī and his ministers were also defining that government as married to the prerogatives of commerce and landowners. It was not just law, but prosperity and power that would protect the kingdom's independence, as far as Kapuāiwa was concerned. For the whites in Hawaiʻi to argue anything else was either foolish or fraudulent, because they themselves had placed such importance on the relationship between self-sufficiency, prosperity, and independence.

In one sense, the new constitution validated haole in the kingdom, especially those who by right of birth or by swearing allegiance to the Crown were fully enfranchised. Denizens, it is true, were disenfranchised along with thousands of Natives, but even those haole who *had* sworn their loyalty felt that they had reason to complain. One *Advertiser* reader who identified himself as "a Haole" remarked bitterly: "The King now denies the covenant of his predecessors. He is in no way held by it. Now I would humbly inquire, *are his foreign subjects bound on their part,* having never sworn allegiance to Kamehameha V? Is not the obligation mutual, and if it fails on one side, does it not fail on the other?"[69]

Whether foreign subjects would continue to uphold the law was critically important to the business community that depended so much on political and social stability. There is no evidence that any of the haole ever feared an insurrection by Natives over the new constitution. But there was considerable apprehension that the foreign community, especially Americans, would not tolerate the constitutional changes that Lota Kapuāiwa was proposing. Gerrit Judd, commenting on whether the freedom of the press should be limited in an emergency, said: "One of the great attractions of these islands, besides its climate, has been the freedom of its institutions. . . . Do you think if the press is muzzled, foreigners will come to live under such a government? Natives might allow it, but white men will not be muzzled. Like a volcano it would smoulder and burn within and by-and-by burst forth and destroy the Government itself."[70]

Ultimately, haole fears for the nation's security were well founded, if less than completely ingenuous. Annexation would remove the internal threat posed by foreigners in the Islands, but the kānaka would explode. Charles Reed Bishop was candid with Turrill when he informed him that he would be quite happy with annexation to the United States, but that the Natives would never stand for it, and therefore it was out of the question.[71] Anything that could conceivably rile the Natives, who even after the constitutional changes in suffrage would continue to outnumber the haole voters, had to be avoided at all costs.

It is no wonder that Bishop had no respect for someone like Lathrop whom he viewed as an unprincipled troublemaker. But in fact, Bishop had had his suspicions of Lathrop's shortcomings long before the doctor became involved in insurrectionist conspiracies. Bishop and other haole who had made their fortunes through careful and long-term investments had little use for individuals who failed in business. In one letter to Turrill, Bishop castigated several haole whose businesses had gone bankrupt, forecasting Lathrop's failure as well. His remarks, though lengthy, are worth close scrutiny:

> Some of our planters and merchants are in trouble these hard times, as people should expect to be who undertake to do a large business without experience or capital. . . . Vida owed ten times as much as he was worth, (I think). His affairs will have to be settled up now. You will see the account of his sudden death, in the Polynesian. It was hastened, if not caused, by intemperance. [Crabbe] and Spaulding have dissolved, and he has a family on his hands, to support, and has neither business, money, health or character (that is, good character, in the view of respectable men). . . . Doct. Lathrop is working on the plantation in Kaneohi [*sic*]. He has planted considerable cane. . . . *I think* he has made a great mistake in giving up his profession, a sure, tho' not speedy fortune, for a business that will make him a great deal of hard work and trouble. I don't know how much capital he can command, but I know that he will need a small fortune to accomplish what he has undertaken. He leased the land from Paki, and there is a misunderstanding between them, which was left to Dr. Judd, Dr. Wood and Janion to settle, but the Dr. refuses to abide by their decision. He has lost the confidence of Paki, and I think of the chiefs generally, and some influential foreigners. I confess that I feel an interest in the matter, and perhaps not as much charity for him as I ought to have.[72]

There is an overwhelming sense here of the Calvinist ethic that wretched morals, as in the case of Vida and Spaulding, reflected on their poor business sense, practically guaranteeing their failure. In

Lathrop's case, however, not only did he fail to abide by good, conservative mediation, he appeared to Bishop to be impatient for wealth, unwilling to take the slow, sure path to success.

The very individuals who supported liberal government structures, giving loud, though ultimately temporary support to the kingdom's independence, tended to be the most fiscally conservative as well. Insinuating themselves as protectors of Native interests, they were also fiercely protective of their own economic privilege. When challenged by a renewal of monarchial authority, they briefly lamented the Natives' loss of political rights and, without losing a step, proceeded to assure themselves that the government would continue to protect and expand the commercial interests of sugar in the future.

This assurance came in two forms. One was closer political and economic ties with the United States, which haole pursued with increasing intensity during the economic recessions of 1866 and 1867.[73] The other was an ever more determined effort to occupy the moral high ground of the society. The task for the Hawaiianized haole was to link the moral stature of the nation to its prosperity. If that link were to be accepted by Native rulers and kānaka, the gradual accrual of power to the government could be justified on the highest moral plane, so long as the government pursued policies that were beneficial to business.

Unfortunately for the monarchy that link, once established, competed with the cultural imperatives that defined Native loyalty to the Mōʻī as the symbolic representative of the people. So long as Kapu-āiwa lived, the notion that government belonged to business never quite overwhelmed the notion that the king belonged to the Natives and they to him. This much can be seen when examining the behavior of the legislative assembly during the 1866 session. This legislature revealed much about the discord and tension that underlay two very different interpretations of the state and the king. The discourse produced by Natives took on ever more desperate implications as time went on.

The Legislative Assembly of 1866

The 1866 legislative assembly was made up of twenty-seven elected representatives and seventeen nobles. More than half of the representatives were experienced legislators, and ten of them had served in the House before the constitutional changes of 1864. Some, like ʻŪkēkē, had legislative experience dating back to the early 1850s. Twenty-two were kānaka, but all of them were either native-born or sworn subjects to the king. Twenty-one of these representatives were either lawyers or had been district and police court judges.[74] As far as the "dignification" of the legislature is concerned, we may infer from the property qualifications[75] that these representatives could be considered not only members of the middle class, but also important members of the lower and middle ranks of a governing elite.

Some of the kanaka representatives on being asked to provide the assembly with proof of their qualifications to serve immediately demanded that the nobles also be required to provide similar proof.[76] Minister of Finance Charles Coffin Harris responded to this challenge by Representative Keawehunahala that nobles did not have to qualify because they were appointed by the king himself, who presumably was already satisfied with their credentials.[77]

This early confrontation set the tone for much of this legislature as Keawehunahala and a minority of kanaka representatives continually challenged the upper leadership of the assembly, especially Harris. In general that confrontation was symptomatic of the fact that some of the Native delegates mistrusted the power and authority of the government. They also expressed grave concerns about the predominance and unfair considerations given to haole in the kingdom.

Following that initial confrontation, Harris nominated R. H. Stanley and Marshall Parke, both Americans, to serve as the assembly's clerk and sergeant-at-arms, respectively. Both were incumbents, having served in 1864. Keawehunahala challenged their appointment and nominated Hawaiians in their places, in part because they understood both English and the Native language. But he also ". . . objected to the principle being established that because a man had held an office, and discharged its duties efficiently, he should always be retained in it, especially if he was a foreigner, and it was of no use to throw away money on the education of Hawaiians if they were not to have some of the offices."[78]

The issue of patronage was a harbinger of things to come. Over the next few weeks Keawehunahala, 'Ūkēkē, Kepoʻikai, Pinehasa Wood, S. W. Mahelona, and Luther Aholo would all raise objections to various initiatives proposed by the minister of the interior unless those initiatives favored Hawaiians over haole. Kanaka legislators charged that haole officials were not only favored in the selection process but that they usually made more money than Natives in the same position.

Table 6. Legislative Assembly, 1866. (King: Lota Kapuāiwa; ministers: de Varigny, Foreign Affairs; Harris, Finance; Hutchison, Interior)

NOBLES	REPRESENTATIVES
Charles Reed Bishop	Luther Aholo
John O. Dominis	Edwin H. Boyd
Charles Coffin Harris*	I. K. Hart*
C. G. Hopkins	J. H. Heleluhe
F. W. Hutchison*	T. C. Heuck
John Papa 'Ī'ī	J. G. Hoapili*
Kā'eo (Peter Young)	Hulu'ili*
H. A. Kahanu	S. W. Ka'ainoa*
David Kalākaua	L. Ka'apā
William P. Kamakau	J. Kaha'ulelio*
Charles Kana'ina	N. Kahulu*
Paul Kanoa	C. K. Kakani
Kaisera Kapa'akea	J. H. Kamalo
John Kapena	Kaulia
Mataio Kekūanaō'a (President)	J. K. Kaunamanō
William Charles Lunalilo	J. W. Keawehunahala
Paul Nāhaolelua	L. Keli'ipio*
C. de Varigny	Keohōkaua*
	N. Kepo'ikai*
	J. Kupau*
	S. W. Mahelona*
	J. Mott-Smith
	J. A. Nāhaku
	Godfrey Rhodes (Vice-President)
	George Belly 'Ūkēkē
	H. J. Wana*
	William Pinehasa Wood*

Source: Lydecker, 1918, *Roster Legislatures of Hawaii,* 107.
* First year.

In the first week of May, Harris called for the hiring of a permanent government surveyor to oversee the surveying of the Crown and government lands. He proposed a salary of $2,500 for the two years between legislative sessions. Kāʻanapali Representative J. A. Nāhaku moved to amend by reducing the appropriation to $800. As ʻŪkēkē would later argue, "$800 was sufficient unless the Government wanted to put a foreign favorite into office. Last year there was a native surveyor, but they did not propose to give *him* $1250 a year."[79]

Harris responded to Nāhaku's amendment, somewhat indignantly, that disputes over land were becoming more numerous and the rise in land prices made the higher expenditure sensible. William Pinehasa Wood, a hapa haole (part Hawaiian, part haole) representative from Honolulu, retorted that Harris' motion seemed to be very one-sided, in favor of the government, especially because the public surveyor's salary would not cover the surveying of lands belonging to Natives.

Harris indignantly responded that Wood's remarks: "seemed to give currency to the idea that the King's government were one side, and the people another. . . . It was a pernicious idea, which it would be well to lay aside, that the Government and people were of diverse interests, that the Government were [*sic*] one thing and the people another."[80] Furthermore, the minister argued, the king's and the government's lands belonged to the people and thus the expenditure of public money for a public use was more than justified. His final remarks were also very revealing of just what status the kānaka held in the kingdom when he said, "The King and Nobles were the best friends the people had, and if they failed them, be assured the people of Hawaiʻi had no friends left."[81] That the nobles and the king were the last bulwark of defense standing between the shrinking and increasingly poor kānaka and a hostile world of haole and foreigners was, ironically, an idea that Makaʻāinana back in the 1840s had very clearly articulated.

Despite the minister's rhetoric, the truth was that of the twenty nobles appointed by Kamehamehas III, IV, and V since the year of the Mahele, nine had been haole, and the king's latest appointment, Fred Hutchison, was a prominent plantation owner. Other nobles, including the aforementioned Bishop, were appointed for life during the reign of Alexander Liholiho. Bishop owned stock in several sugar companies, and his bank was the largest single provider of capital for sugar growers in the Hawaiian Islands.

In 1866, one-third of the House of Nobles was foreign-born, landed, and wealthy. Their status rested in some cases on their connection to the rapidly expanding sugar industry, their positions as members of previous and current cabinets, and, in the cases of Bishop and John Dominis, as husbands of high-ranking Aliʻi women.[82] If these were the only friends that the people had left, they nevertheless had very little in common with them.

It was also true that over the years, the government's official activities were more and more compatible with the interests of the sugar planters, to the point where they were almost inseparable. In 1864, the legislature at the cabinet's request established a Bureau of Immigration, an agency that immediately assumed the responsibilities and risks for all of the contract labor that was beginning to flow into the kingdom, principally from China. The ministry trumpeted the bureau as necessary to prevent misunderstandings between laborers and their employers while they were under contract. The bureau also assumed the responsibilities of enforcing the contracts and, as some historians have pointed out, tended to work more on behalf of the employers than the Chinese workers. The bureau also actively recruited labor in China and, later, in Japan and the Philippines. In one eight-year period, the government spent over one million dollars on the recruitment of labor while all of the plantation companies together spent half of that amount.

There were other claims that the kingdom's government represented the interests of the wealthy haole even at the expense of the poor Natives. Harris' response to Wood over the government surveyor's salary indicated a posturing by the cabinet that the government's and the people's interests were inseparable, despite the minority representatives' attitudes to the contrary. Harris even invoked the king as the symbol of the nation when he said: "The Royal Domain would have to be surveyed. Now this was the property of the Nation— of the King as Representative of the People of Hawaii, and this was the true light to regard their King—as the Representative of the nation."[83]

It is doubtful that kanaka legislators needed instruction in how to view their king. But the growing conflict between them and the ministry clouded the real and significant political issues of the day. Spending was power. The small minority of kanaka representatives was merely establishing the idea that their constituents deserved a share of the wealth and prosperity of the kingdom. They did not consider the king their antagonist. In fact, the kanaka minority would later argue that if the king knew of the difficulties that faced his people, he would not object to the reduction of certain taxes that affected their poorer constituents.

On 28 April, Keawehunahala and C. K. Kakani had tried to amend the "horse tax" law from the assessment of one dollar a year per horse to fifty cents. Several petitions from Puna, South Kona, and Koʻolauloa had requested the reduction. Harris responded, asking, "by what financial scheme did they propose to fill up the gap of $37,000 that would be caused thereby?" [84] Kakani was indignant over the minister's remarks. He scolded Harris for asking such a sarcastic question and wondered whether the representatives "had come here . . . and to be pulled about just as the Government liked. The one dollar per head horse was found to be oppressive . . . he supported its repeal without considering how the gap was to be filled." [85]

Over the next week, several representatives offered their opinions about how the government might fill the financial gap. Several solutions called for government officials to take smaller salaries. It is meaningful that the issue of officials' salaries helped the representatives to agree that $1,200 per year was too much to spend on an official surveyor, and Nāhaku's amendment carried—one of the few victories by the opposition minority. But the reduction of the horse tax elicited insufficient support. The minority lost 23 to 14, even after arguing that "the King would never veto the bill if he knew it represented the will of the whole people." [86]

The fourteen who favored the amendment, all kānaka, felt that they represented the wishes of the many Natives who required horses to work their kuleana and to transport children to school. For that reason, de Varigny's comment that "this tax would only be considered oppressive by the indolent and vicious" [87] was not only outrageous, but it tended to place all kānaka in the same category of people who were not entitled to participate in the decisions of the government.

Two very significant and interrelated conflicts converged in this legislature that would define the political agendas of the legislature until the overthrow. The first conflict was the issue of taxing and spending. For the fourteen Native representatives who claimed to speak for a majority of the Native people, the poor kānaka were paying taxes to a government that did not seem to address their interests when it came to the spending of those taxes. Their solution was to limit government spending on anything that did not directly benefit a Native or Native group.

When ʻŪkēkē suggested lowering officials' salaries so that the horse tax might be lowered, Godfrey Rhodes, vice-president of the assembly, argued that, "if salaries were reduced, they would not find good and efficient men to fill their places, and what would become of the country if an inferior set of men were put into office?"[88] Because one of the complaints that all of the kanaka representatives could agree on was that Natives tended to be paid less than haole in the same or similar positions, the legislators understood exactly what was meant by "an inferior set of men."

That was the larger and more grievous conflict, the rising belief that the government's stake in the nation's business was sharply opposed to the interests of the Native people themselves. This was a discourse very unfavorable to most kānaka because the constitution reinforced their political inferiority to the Aliʻi and haole. Already economically unequal, they no longer had a representative voice in the legislature. Strictly speaking, there was no one but the king to represent them.

The *Pacific Commercial Advertiser* had pointed out in January that because of the suffrage qualifications of the constitution, only five hundred adult males out of nearly five thousand had qualified to vote in the District of Honolulu, making the representatives answerable only to government officials and the rich.[89] If the *Advertiser*'s charges were true, then the minority of representatives who opposed the ministry should have been congratulated for seriously considering the needs of people who were, with respect to the government, helpless. Thus, S. W. Mahelona, representative from ʻEwa and Waiʻanae, bemoaned the loss of the "horse tax" amendment by saying that, "All the people from Hawaii to Niihau were in favor of the reduction of the tax, and it was only the Government who were [sic] opposed to it."[90]

If the government was antithetical to the Natives, then there truly was no place for them to turn. Considering the fact that the press and public discourse had consistently portrayed the landless and jobless kānaka as a drain on the society, what little advocacy they still possessed operated from a tremendous social disadvantage. That disadvantage would affect the kinds of political associations that Hawaiians entered into the 1870s and beyond and is the subject of the next chapter.

In some ways, too, the role of the representative was no less problematic than it had been in the early 1840s. No longer were they konohiki cooperating with Aliʻi Nui and Mōʻī to rule over the people. Nor were they the independent body of the 1850s, allying with haole to challenge the supremacy of the House of Nobles. In 1866 and in the years to follow, either the kanaka representatives would come into the legislative assembly prepared to cooperate with the wishes of the cabinet and, presumably, His Majesty, or they would come to speak on behalf of Native subjects whose gradual and sure impoverishment gave them little influence and voice in the kingdom's affairs.

Class and Race

Although Kapuāiwa's constitution increased the influence and authority of the Crown, it did not accomplish several of his other, stated objectives. It did not, for instance, bring greater dignity and solemnity to the legislature. On at least one occasion, the debates between Keawehunahala and C. C. Harris led to a furious confrontation in which all of the representatives and two nobles stood and shouted at the minister of finance, inviting him to "come out of his seat" and fight when he tried to have Keawehunahala ejected from the assembly.[91]

Harris has been described as an obnoxious individual, incidentally a graduate of Harvard, who had little respect for kānaka and an overweening ambition, but in turn they had rather little regard for him. In fact, although Native representatives willing to defy the ministry were in the minority, the fact that all of them and even some of the nobles unified against Harris to protect one of their own underscores the racially divided, economic tensions that accompanied and directed so much of the legislature.

Nor did the laws do much to protect the kānaka from further dispossession. While Kapuāiwa lived, Native Hawaiians made up 80 percent of the plantations' workforce, ensuring that at least some of the benefits of the sugar industry would flow to them. However, his policies tended to undermine that benefit over the long run, especially as the kingdom increased the recruitment of cheaper foreign labor.[92] As the legislature's primary tasks appeared to deal more and more with the demands of the sugar planters, it was left to a small minority of voices to speak on behalf of the nation's kānaka.

It may have been class that demarcated the possessors of wealth and political station in the Hawaiian kingdom, but it was race that determined political legitimacy. The Natives had every reason to complain that the physical resources of the 'āina were slipping away, but for them the critical struggle was always over the haole seizure of the power to define them as a people and in the process determine the nation's values. The discourse of identity was *never* a distraction from the whites' seizure of political and economic control; it was instrumental to it.

One important reason that haole did not rise up against Kapuāiwa in 1864 was that his constitution made political power an issue of class and not race. The new suffrage laws did not threaten their position in the kingdom, but they clearly undermined any kānaka whose land holdings and earnings did not qualify them as fully enfranchised subjects.[93] Although some haole, like Whitney, continued to assert the importance of restoring voting rights to the kānaka, many more would begin to question the wisdom of supporting the kingdom's independence as Native voters and representatives began to insist that the real struggle for the nation was defined by race.

There was also no shortage of haole who were strongly opposed to so powerful a king. Too careful to challenge Lota Kapuāiwa directly, during the reign of Kalākaua they would attempt to join forces with disaffected kānaka. At that time, a powerful opposition party, still in the minority, but financed and organized by powerful and wealthy haole, would criticize and contest all government spending. Most important, though, that party would finally succeed in weakening the allegiance of the Natives to their Mō'ī.

6

Hawai'i for Hawaiians

In that country, a city (encircled by a huge wall) was embattled by their enemies, but the enemies outside were not at all
victorious, and so they thought at length about a means by
which they could be victorious over that city. So they assembled a huge horse figure, hollow within, and inside of this
wooden horse were placed warriors armed with weapons of
war. During the night this horse figure was taken and set up
at a place near the wall adjoining the main gate where one
would enter or exit. At dawn the people of the city saw this
new thing standing outside of the wall, and because of their
excitement and ignorance they fetched the horse, and it was
carried into the center of the city and set down. When the
city's people were busy observing this new thing, then all of
the soldiers from within the horse figure issued forth and took
the whole city captive.

Representative Joseph Nāwahī
before the assembly, 1878

During the decade ending in 1887, the independent kingdom developed a highly profitable plantation economy; modernized its roads,
harbors, and bridges; completed several expensive and substantial
irrigation projects; and broadened its international stature through its
contacts and treaties with other nations. While the Native population
continued to plunge, the numbers of foreigners were beginning to rise,
chiefly the result of imported Asian labor.[1]

Significantly, the bureaucracy of government also grew between
1840 and 1887. Although, as the statistician Schmitt admitted, reli-

able numbers before 1939 are unavailable, statistics of government revenues and expenditures are known at least since 1846, when the kingdom took in $76,000 and spent $78,000. In the biennium of 1886 to 1888, the government spent $4,712,000 of the $4,813,000 it took in.[2]

The nation had modernized, with a government that was increasingly involved with the promotion of capital expansion, aggressively marketing the production of sugar and spending its tax revenues on the infrastructure necessary for increasing production. The nation also modernized its citizenry. A highly literate Native population[3] was being enjoined by a surfeit of newspapers, some of them in their own language,[4] to be quite critical of the administration, both the king and his various cabinets, especially after 1880. In fact, the newspapers played pivotal roles in determining the growth of distinct political parties that were defined by race.

Previous chapters describe the growth of the Hawaiian nation as a gradual accommodation of the haole, first their presence, their religion, their legal system, and finally their economics, into a national order that was designed to separate the Natives from their traditional reliance on the Ali'i and on the 'āina, transferring them to a reliance on Western law, education, and capitalism. Intrinsic to this transformation was the haole claim that it was necessary for the kingdom and its Native inhabitants to embrace, or at least deal with, Western conceptions of modernity for it and them to survive.

This claim was largely accepted by the Hawaiian rulers and incorporated into law by the legion of Native legislators who served the kingdom after 1842. Kanaka subjects were gradually positioned into a devotion to the constituted government that utilized traditional loyalties and dependence on the Ali'i. Both traditional and Western discourses encouraged the Native citizens to *believe* in the legitimacy of the nation as it was being created.

Yet despite the fact that the construction of this nation was based on the inclusion of haole as citizens and as political leaders, it is my contention that most haole did not share the same faith and belief in the kingdom's legitimacy as did the kānaka. The Hawaiians believed that the Hawaiian nation was real; haole did not. The kānaka had no other ruling entity, let alone national entity, to represent them. The haole, even those born in the Islands, had their own "native" countries whose existence and viability was more real to them than was the kingdom. As Native legislators and Native voters debated the directions and meanings of nationhood, they understood how the state had come to symbolize their very survival as a people.

That these differences should have become obvious and critical during the Kalākaua reign should really surprise no one. In essence, the reign of this Mō'ī was all about legitimacy. This chapter describes how Natives, haole, and king fought to contest this legitimacy as Kalākaua ascended to rule. It was a contest for which haole were much better prepared because, in the end, it was monarchy itself that they were opposing. For the Natives, it was Kalākaua whose authenticity—and ability—was at issue. The king, more of whose palpable weaknesses, political and personal, were exposed the longer he reigned, could never adequately represent either kānaka or haole without alienating one or the other.

Twentieth-century historians such as Ralph Kuykendall believed that the important controversies of Kalākaua's reign were about race, but "Hawai'i for Hawaiians," the battle cry for both Kalākaua's supporters and his opponents, had little to do with the haole. It had everything to do with what it meant to be Hawaiian.

Bearing the Torch

After reigning just over a year, from January 1873 until February 1874, William Charles Lunalilo, son of the Kaukauali'i Charles Kana'ina and the high chiefess Kekāuluohi, a member of the Kamehameha line,[5] died of pulmonary tuberculosis without naming an heir to the throne. In fact, he continued the recent trend of Mō'ī refusing to specify their successors. It will be remembered that Lota Kapuāiwa, after apparently having his first choice, the chiefess Pauahi, refuse his nomination, refused to name either the popular candidate Lunalilo or David Kalākaua.

This might well have resulted in a severe constitutional crisis had the prince Lunalilo not been so immensely popular among the kānaka. As Kuykendall noted, when the unofficial plebiscite was held on 28 December 1872, "a large vote was recorded, and it was nearly unanimous for Lunalilo."[6] The kingdomwide plebiscite was Lunalilo's idea, though the constitution specifically designated that the legislature, in the absence of a named heir, should elect the new king from among one of the Native Ali'i.[7] When the legislature met on 1 January 1873, it validated Lunalilo's popular election with a unanimous balloting in his favor over the rival Kalākaua.

Lunalilo's succession manifested differences between kānaka and haole perceptions of the monarch, even while they both mutually supported Lunalilo over Kalākaua. The press, for instance, noted Lunalilo's lack of government experience compared with Kalākaua. On the other hand, they were attracted by his promise to restore the liberal qualities of the 1852 Constitution, and Lunalilo's authentic liberal leanings were well known, in any case.[8] There is no evidence to suggest that any of this mattered to the kanaka electorate, whose attraction to Lunalilo stemmed simply from the fact that he was a Kamehameha when there were not many of them left.

The issue of Lunalilo's rank needs some clarification. His maternal grandfather, Kaleimamahū, was a half brother of Kamehameha I, both sons of the Ali'i Nui Keōua. His maternal grandmother was Kaheiheimālie, who after giving birth to his mother Kekāuluohi was taken from Kaleimamahū by Kamehameha after his favorite wahine Ka'ahumanu was found to be unable to conceive. Thus Kekāuluohi became Kamehameha's punalua (literally, two springs; the child whose mother has more than one mate is daughter to all of them) offspring. On the other hand, Lunalilo's father was Charles Kana'ina, Kaukauali'i of low rank.

To Hawaiians, the genealogical identity of the king *mattered*, whereas haole tended to be more concerned about the destabilizing effects of an interregnum than about who was actually the more legitimate successor. U.S. Minister Henry Peirce and the British acting commissioner Theo Davies, both major plantation owners and factors, requested warships from their respective nations "to serve as a steadying influence"[9] when the legislature met to elect the king, after the plebiscite in 1872.

A number of observers, Hawaiian and haole, believed that the Natives were quite willing to do battle if the proper person did not become Mō'ī. Up until the day of the legislature's confirming election, Lunalilo was uneasy about whom they would choose, even sitting down with Sanford Dole and P. C. Jones to discuss what might be done if the legislature selected Kalākaua. As it turned out, they needn't have worried. The assembly voted unanimously for Lunalilo, especially after they adopted a change in the House rules that required each member to sign the back of his ballot, all the while surrounded by Lunalilo's supporters, who had filled "all available space in the building and in the surrounding streets."[10]

Kuykendall suggested, as did the newspapers, that the legislators

Table 7. Legislative Assembly, Extra Session of 1873. This special session was called after the death of Lota Kapuāiwa in December 1872. The new king, William Charles Lunalilo, appointed new cabinet ministers who took their place in the House of Nobles. The representatives are essentially the same group elected to serve in the 1872 legislature, except that Kona judge J. W. Kupakeʻe died in the interim and was replaced by D. H. Nāhinu. (Ministers: Bishop, Foreign Affairs; Stirling, Finance; Hall, Interior; A. Judd, Attorney General)

NOBLES	REPRESENTATIVES
Charles Reed Bishop	Luther Aholo
John O. Dominis	John O. Carter**
Edwin O. Hall*	G. W. D. Halemanu
Alfred F. Judd*	William Hanaʻike
Kāʻeo (Peter Young)	I. K. Hart
H. Kahanu	D. H. Hitchcock (Vice-President)
David Kalākaua	Alfred F. Judd
William P. Kamakau	Charles H. Judd
Charles Kanaʻina	Simon K. Kaʻai
Paul Kanoa	M. Kahananui
Paul Nāhaolelua (President)	D. W. Kaʻiue
Robert Stirling*	D. Kaukaha
	A. Kaukau**
	E. Kekoa**
	Solomon Kipi
	J. Komoikehukehu
	H. Kūihelani
	J. W. Lonoaʻea**
	W. T. Martin
	E. Mikalemi**
	D. H. Nāhinu
	J. W. Naihe
	Joseph Nāwahī**
	R. Newton**
	P. Nui**
	J. N. Paikuli**
	Z. Poli**
	William Hyde Rice

Source: Lydecker, 1918, *Roster Legislatures of Hawaii*, 124.
* First year.
** First year, 1872.

were intimidated into electing Lunalilo, perhaps because Kuykendall, like so many of the foreign observers in 1873, believed that Kalākaua was the abler and more experienced politician of the two. But clearly, the kanaka electorate saw only Lunalilo, whose genealogical link to Kamehameha, however imperfect, made him the only choice.

For Hawaiians, the king was not an office of the government; he was the symbol of the Hawaiian people, the bodily link to divine ancestors and the greatness of the Conqueror and his times. Kalākaua's qualifications, loudly trumpeted by the newspapers, mattered not at all. In fact many kānaka viewed his candidacy as maha'oi (rude and inappropriately forward). In the public relations struggle that preceded the plebiscite, Kalākaua tried to elaborate his own illustrious lineage and to point out the flaws in Lunalilo's. Indeed, Kalākaua's supporters argued that his ancestors were every bit as exalted as Kamehameha's. His great-grandfathers were two of the powerful "Kona uncles," Keaweaheulu and Kame'eiamoku, who supported Kamehameha's rise to power in the 1780s. Keaweaheulu was a descendant of the 'Ī chiefs, who had controlled Hilo and other districts on Hawai'i Island for many centuries. But for most kānaka, the kingdom could not be separated from Kamehameha, who had united Hawai'i. The nation lived while his descendants lived and ruled. As long as a Kamehameha lived, they thought it improper for anyone to challenge his, or her, right to rule, at least not without warfare.

Lineage was not always the final arbiter in whether one individual or another actually became Mō'ī in traditional society. Kamehameha, after all, became the legitimate ruler because of his success in war. His success signaled his mana, and his mana legitimized his political power. As Queen Emma pointed out, the throngs of people waiting to "tear to pieces [members] who were suspected of opposing Lunalilo" were the physical representatives of Lunalilo's mana. It was altogether satisfactory to them that Kalākaua's supporters, whoever they were, shrank from committing themselves to battle.

Lunalilo's brief tenure of just over a year brings into focus the cataclysmic effects of depopulation. He drank too much, a situation that must have contributed to his poor health, and on two occasions, at least, he ruled indecisively. The most important example was when he considered ceding Pearl Harbor to the United States in exchange for a treaty of reciprocity. He was poorly advised, by Charles Bishop, as it turns out. It was a bad idea, and Kalākaua made the king pay for it politically.

The other example was his hesitation when his Royal Guards "mutinied" against their drillmaster and barricaded themselves inside their barracks. On one hand, their revolt was specifically against the Hungarian instructor, who was something of a martinet. On the other hand, the press portrayed the mutiny as a typical example of the Natives' lack of discipline and a sign of disrespect for the king. Even the suggestion that Kānaka Maoli subjects might not be fully respectful of the authority of the ruling chief had powerful implications, though they would not surface before the rise of Kalākaua.

In traditional times, when there were hosts of powerful Ali'i Nui to challenge for leadership, Lunalilo probably would not have remained Mō'ī even as long as he did. When he died without naming an heir, he guaranteed that the succession would be severely contested. The implication of violence that underlay the selection of Lunalilo became explicit when Kalākaua was elected by the legislature over the popular Queen Emma on 12 February 1874. Following the announcement

Figure 10. The courthouse. This building was the seat of the legislature from 1853 to 1874. It was here that Emma's supporters attacked the Native members of the assembly who voted for Kalākaua to succeed Lunalilo as Mō'ī in February 1874. Photograph taken ca. 1864, courtesy of the Bishop Museum, Honolulu. CP 115,474.

of the vote, the large crowd assembled outside the courthouse on Halekauwila to await the legislature's decision attacked the legislators as they tried to reach their carriages.

The attack was unquestionably conducted on behalf of Queen Emma, who, despite disparagement of her genealogy[11] and her gender, commanded much greater personal loyalty than Kalākaua ever would. Emma descended from the Conqueror's brother, Keliʻimaikaʻi, and as the granddaughter of John Young, she was part haole. She was also the widow of Alexander Liholiho, and as such was the living reminder of his kingdom. Finally, she was staunchly anti-American in her political views and, more important, antimissionary. In her letters to her cousin Peter Kāʻeo, banished to the leper settlement at Kalawao, the queen continually expressed her belief that the missionaries wanted nothing less than annexation:

> The natives are all awake now to the American intention of taking possession of these Islands for themselves, and they oppose them to their faces. Mr. Henry Parker spoke from the pulpit of his meeting house last Sunday advising his congregation to favor reciprocity. [Noble] Moehonua left directly. . . . Mr and Mrs [Liliʻuokalani] Dominis followed. In the afternoon Porter Green preached there on the same topic to a congregation of less than 10. It has taken the Hawaiian Nation nearly 20 years to learn their Dissenting Missionaries' true character, which Alex knew from the beginning. . . .[12]

From the viewpoint of many kānaka, the queen was the more reliable champion of the kingdom's independence, opposing without reservation all measures, like reciprocity, that promised closer ties to the United States. Kalākaua, on the other hand, was far more circumspect, opposing reciprocity only if it entailed ceding kingdom lands to a foreign power.

As one historian put it, "Kalakaua was not a great favorite of the Americans either, but he seemed cooperative and the lesser evil."[13] In fact, Kalākaua had published a public manifesto days before the election retreating from his previous position on reciprocity, which he had once wholly opposed. No doubt he did this to garner American support before the election. It is quite obvious that Kalākaua did not believe that he could secure election without them, with the divided kānaka support for his candidacy.

The newspapers, both English and Hawaiian, came out fully for Kalākaua, forcing the queen to rely on placards, handbills, and posters to advance her candidacy. The night before the election, the *Hawai-*

ian Gazette editorialized that "A King will be more acceptable and undoubtedly be able to give more satisfaction to His people in the administration of the Government than a Queen could possibly give."[14] On 4 February the *Advertiser* issued this most condescending editorial to the queen's partisans: "The Queen is a woman—in the highest sense of the word—whom all have learned to honor and

Figure 11. Emma Naʻea Kaleleonālani Rooke. A descendant of the Kamehameha family and granddaughter of the Englishman John Young. She was the widow of Alexander Liholiho and known as Queen Emma when she challenged Kalākaua for the succession in 1874. Courtesy of the Bishop Museum, Honolulu. CPBM 38,913.

esteem for noble qualities and noble deeds. And while we heartily concede all this, together with that consideration and chivalric forbearance which is due her sex, we must express our profound regret that her partisans have chosen to add to the existing complication of affairs by placing her name in opposition to that of the High Chief Kalakaua."[15]

Whether Emma's gender ever disabled her in the eyes of some Native voters is impossible to say, because this election was not placed before a plebiscite as Lunalilo's election had been in the previous succession.[16] Some of the sentiment expressed even indicated that the Natives reserved a particular aloha for Emma *because* she was a woman. One response, from "the Flower girls of Maemae," was a handbill directed to the wives of the legislators who would elect the king and read:

> Ye wives of the Representatives, beg, coax, and draw the hearts of your husbands to the one you are thinking on. If your husband does not consent to your desire, it will show that he despises you. Husband and wife should be of one mind and not merely companions.
> . . . The spirits of the old cannibal (man eating) women of Wahiawa prophesied last night that we shall be preserved and blessed through the Queen . . . she will look upon us, and we will eat together, talk together, live together, and walk together with her, and she will always assist the poor and distressed.[17]

There were no women in the legislature, nor could they vote. Perhaps the possibility of a ruling queen had a special significance for them. As for the kanaka males, it is doubtful that Emma's gender worked against her or there would not have been so many willing to fight for her at Halekauwila. One placard that circulated in Honolulu read: "It has been published in writing that it will not be well to elect Emma because she cannot wear trowsers [sic] but only petticoats. The answer to this is, it will not do to elect D. Kalakaua, for he will put on trowsers and boots too, and give us all a kicking."[18]

However the Native vote may have divided over the controversy of gender, it is certainly true that missionary descendants viewed her candidacy with some alarm, and consequently many haole were forced to consider Kalākaua more seriously. Yet it was a most reluctant consideration, born from a near total lack of trust and, among some of them, actual contempt for the prince. As Lunalilo's attorney general, Alfred Judd, revealed, "he would almost prefer the chances of a revolution, to the election of Colonel Kalakaua."[19] The American minister, Henry Peirce, found it difficult to take the prince seriously, calling him "ambitious, flighty & unstable . . . [lacking] prudence & good sense."[20]

The electorate was certainly stirred enough. Rallies held in Honolulu brought thousands of Native supporters to both candidates, causing each of them to proclaim themselves the "people's choice." But unlike the previous succession, the selection of this monarch was not to be subjected to a popular vote. In the same editorial that so patronized Emma as a woman, the *Advertiser* also patronized the Hawaiian male voters:

> For a people whose political education was so recent and so limited as that of the Hawaiians, the ordeal of a popular election for a King— a proposition involving something of a contradiction in terms—was not a socially healthy one. Political excitements, without some vital and necessary end in view, and for the general good, are to be deprecated, especially among a people circumstanced like ours. The *plebiscitum* of last year, while it passed off quietly and amicably owing to an enthusiastic unanimity of sentiment among the populace, has become, it is now acknowledged, a precedent we were much better without.[21]

It was an interesting statement that spoke not at all to the very real differences between the two successions. In other words, the hand of the people could be trusted to notarize what was patently the case when Lunalilo was contesting Kalākaua. But where the succession was doubtful, democracy was a bad precedent.

The truth is that neither chief nor people had so seriously contested a succession since the Conqueror's rise to power. Haole were quite anxious about the level of excitement that the election raised, and they scolded the Hawaiians on the day after the attack on the legislators. Indeed, the newspaper accounts suggested how inexplicable Native behavior was to haole even after a century of contact: "We can hardly find words to express our shame and sorrow in view of the lawless and violent proceedings of Thursday last. For the first time in Hawaiian history have we seen a mob of natives, made up of the lowest classes, unreasoning and cruel, and utterly reckless, as all mobs are, but fortunately without any recognized leader of ability, and so without much concert of action."[22]

The mob was cruel. But was it unreasoning? In fact, the men involved in the attack who lined up outside the courthouse were particular, even precise, about whom they attacked. Kuykendall noted that "the wrath of the rioters was directed against the representatives who had voted for Kalakaua."[23] Only Native representatives who had voted for Kalākaua were harmed. Haole delegates were conspicuously exempt. "They declared that they had nothing against any foreigner, but only wanted to get hold of the Native Representatives to wreak on them their vengeance for having voted against Queen Emma."[24]

Figure 12. Representatives W. T. Martin and Moehonua, survivors of the attack on the legislative assembly by Emma's supporters, 12 February 1874. Kalākaua made Moehonua his first minister of the interior and later governor of Oʻahu. Martin did not return to the legislature. Photograph by M. Dickson, courtesy of the Bishop Museum, Honolulu. CP 97,393.

Lorrin Thurston, in his memoirs, noted that haole were relatively safe while the "Emma-ites" committed mayhem against the supporters of Kalākaua, literally tearing apart the carriage that was to be used to carry word of victory to the new king and using its wreckage to beat his supporters and trash the courthouse where the election had taken place.[25] This was not some senseless violence. It was too partisan, too intentional for that. Even the police officers sent to establish control were reported to have "removed their badges" and joined in the fray themselves. The attack on the legislators was not quite a revolution, but it certainly was an extraordinary statement from a people who had suffered a government increasingly distant from them and had responded with patience and petition for thirty-two years. The idea that their own countrymen would support an inferior Mō'ī was more than they could bear.

The battle ended when Kalākaua and two of Lunalilo's ministers called on the American warships *Tuscarora* and *Portsmouth* for troops to be landed to quell the "riot." When the British commissioner had troops landed from HMS *Tenedos,* the Emma partisans apparently cheered, believing that they had come to take up her cause against the Americans, "as it was well known all Britishers were for Queen Emma & they were much disappointed when they found that the British troops joined with the Americans to put the rioters down."[26]

Kalākaua had won his victory, but it cost him dearly. His mana would forever be based on American power and support, a fact that he continually labored against throughout his reign. Until the last of the Kamehameha finally passed away in 1885, his own legitimacy was constantly under attack from a small but very articulate Native constituency whose loyalty to Emma never wavered. Kalākaua was the only monarch of the Hawaiian kingdom to have inspired kānaka to oppose him. The story of his reign, therefore, must begin with the acknowledgment that he operated from a position of political weakness unknown to any of his predecessors. His weakness, as far as some of the Natives were concerned, was not his character or his leadership, but his genealogy. Even in 1874, the kānaka still insisted that their Mō'ī be more than the government's chief executive.

Not only was his Native support suspect, but the Americans and other haole who preferred him over Emma were not in the least bit loyal to him and eventually were quite willing to oppose, even ridicule, him *personally* in the press and in the legislature. That haole were able to treat a Native king with contempt is important, but should not be overemphasized. Surely it stemmed in part from the fact that Kalā-kaua needed, or believed he needed, their support to be king. What was far more important is that there was considerable doubt about whether the Natives would be loyal to this king, a doubt that had never existed before. Elections had finally destabilized one of the last remaining bastions of traditional linkages between the kānaka and Ali'i, though not without considerable help from the ravages of disease and infertility that had all but terminated the Kamehameha line.

The Natives' attempt to assert the queen's succession directly opposed the constitutional invention of the Kalākaua dynasty and, in ways quite reminiscent of tradition, was asserted by warlike gestures and bloodshed. Their defeat warned of the actual supremacy of the haole at the outset of the new regime, for not only were they overcome by foreign troops, but their own efforts were expropriated and used against them in the newspaper accounts that followed. American-born editor Thomas Thrum wrote this attack after the election: "But it appears that we have been so much in the habit of crediting the Hawaiians—even those of the lowest classes—with an almost super-stitious regard for the sanctity of the law and its representatives, that . . . no one seems to have seriously anticipated that they were capa-ble of resorting to the senseless extreme of attempting to coerce the Legislature to undo the solemn and formal constitutional act of the election of a Sovereign."[27]

This editorial reminded the foreign community that Natives, despite their "superstitious" regard for law, continued to be unworthy as citizens of a democracy. Moreover, their savagery demonstrated how clearly they threatened foreign ways and foreigners themselves. Again, the Hawaiian Gazette claimed: "The inevitable moral to be drawn is . . . that the government of the day is not only lamentably weak, but that weakness is fraught with danger to the order and peace of the community and the safety of life and property. But for the pres-ence in our waters—we may say providentially—of the war vessels of the United States and Great Britain, the city of Honolulu and its inhabitants, foreign men, women and children as well as native, would have been at the mercy of a mob of infuriated, semi-savage natives. . . ."[28]

There are such ironies in this statement. Hawaiians who rejected Kalākaua's candidacy because they believed that he did not possess the mana to lead the nation that Emma did were essentially being told how correct they were; that his government was not even strong enough to protect itself *from them*. Meanwhile, the same editorial communicated to the foreigners that despite the existence of "solemn and formal" constitutional processes, the reality was that American and British arms were the real guarantors of the peace. In either discourse, the legitimacy of the kingdom, in 1874, was seriously eroded and it was the king himself, in the face of a mounting number of critics and doubters, both whites and Natives, who would have to reassert the mana of the Mō'ī and the legitimacy of the Native government.

The Native Opposition

The story of the decline of Kalākaua's—and the monarchy's—prestige cannot be divorced from these inauspicious beginnings, but it was the framing of Kalākaua's administration as corrupt, especially after 1876, that played the more significant role. Of all those who accused the king of corruption, the most damaging were Native legislators who represented a strong minority of opposition to the king, his ministers, and their policies between 1876 and 1886.

This Native opposition was born even before the king was inaugurated. Those who composed it were staunch supporters of Emma, including Representatives Joseph Nāwahī of Puna, George Pilipō of North Kona, and John Kaulukou of Honolulu. They formed the nucleus of this opposition over that decade and were joined later by other, mostly Hawai'i Island legislators such as J. W. Kalua of Hilo and John Ka'uhane of Ka'ū. Their strong constituencies and perhaps their affiliation with the haole Independent Party, which also opposed Kalākaua, enabled them to secure continual election until 1886 when National candidates, favored by the king's administration, defeated both Nāwahī and Pilipō.

Nāwahī was, in the political climate of the 1870s and 1880s, what Kamakau had been during the earlier decades, a completely irreproachable statesman from the perspective of both Native and haole electors. He had a Kaukauali'i genealogy. At his funeral in 1896 his eulogist, Reverend Stephen Desha, indicated that "As for his parents, they were not of humble origin, because within their veins flowed the high ranking blood of this land."[29] His father's name was Nāwahīokalani'ōpu'u, which indicated a lineage of chiefly servers to the great Hawai'i Mō'ī Kalani'ōpu'u, uncle of the Conqueror Kamehameha. But as important a symbol as he would be to Hawaiians—the seer Barenaba predicted that he "was the child through whom the bones would live"[30]—he may have been even more important to the haole, especially to the missionaries. For them he symbolized the success of the mission.

He was born in 1842, the year of the first legislature, and was shortly thereafter given to an elementary schoolteacher, Joseph Pa'akaula, to rear. He attended Hilo Boarding School, Lāhaināluna, and the Royal School, all ABCFM institutions.[31] Like Malo and Kamakau before him, Nāwahī became a schoolteacher, in fact establishing his

Figure 13. Joseph Kaho'oluhi Nāwahīokalani'ōpu'u or Joseph Nāwahī, representative from Hilo and Puna from 1872 to 1884. His opposition to Kalākaua led him to the haole-dominated Reform Party. But he was a patriotic supporter of the kingdom's independence. Courtesy of the Bishop Museum, Honolulu. CP 77,056.

own boarding school in Pi'ihonua in 1863 before taking on the post of vice-principal at Hilo Boarding School under the missionary David Lyman. According to his biographer, he taught himself surveying and law, and without instruction managed to earn both partial and full licenses to practice before he was thirty years old.

He was the living promise of the Calvinist mission and an exemplar of that mission's contradictions. He was a Christian Native who was, nevertheless, a firm and lifelong opponent of annexation. He associated freely with the mission children who betrayed his country, men like Thurston and Dole, yet every Native patriotic organization acclaimed him in life and mourned his death.[32] He was educated in the missionaries' system, which aimed to instill the values of individual acquisition and profit among the Natives, yet he was extolled by them for not having used his education to profit from "the many avenues by which his personal benefits and fortunes could be increased."[33]

Supreme Court Justice Lorrin A. Thurston delivered a most ironic eulogy, noting that "His position was established on a firm foundation of truth and ever strong opposition to the mischievous deeds and the powers of the circle of scoundrels."[34] Although some of those in attendance might have thought the judge was including himself in that circle, in all likelihood Thurston was describing the business and legislative supporters of the late king, whom Thurston despised and whom Nāwahī had indeed opposed during his legislative career.

His opposition to Kalākaua sprang from his loyalty to Queen Emma. Nāwahī was one of the six legislators to vote for Emma in 1874, and had Pilipō been a member of the assembly that year, he would have voted for her as well.[35] Their personal stature helped place their critique beyond partisan loyalty to an Ali'i Nui, but this claim requires context. There had, after all, never before been a rival to the throne to stand as a political symbol for a disaffected Native constituency. The fact that Emma's supporters continued, even after the election, to assert her legitimate claim to the throne was unprecedented since Kamehameha had established the aupuni.

In the summer of 1874, a group of Natives circulated a petition addressed to the French consul-commissioner "declaring that Queen Emma and not Kalakaua was the rightful sovereign of Hawaii, and requesting the assistance of a French warship to place her on the throne."[36] The arrest and condemnation of one Native for treason[37] (as well as the lack of French support) may have ended whatever conspiracy existed to overthrow Kalākaua, but it by no means ended the opposition. Several newspapers reported the existence of a Queen Emma Party as early as 1874. Its motto was "Hawai'i for Hawaiians," and its pro-British and anti-American stance, according to the press, was at the heart of a move to secure the election of their representatives in 1876.

The portrayal of the "Emma-ites" as Anglophiles was only partly accurate. True, both her grandfather and stepfather were Englishmen. It was also true that the queen belonged to the Church of England, but it should be remembered that her late husband had imported that religious sect as a political wedge against the predominance of the ABCFM in the business, politics, and society of the Hawaiian Islands. In very much the same way, Emma's supporters, at least, appeared to favor the British only because it was not Great Britain that appeared to be the chief threat to the Islands' independence.

Independence was very much the overarching issue for the 1876 assembly as it dealt with the administration's successful negotiation of a treaty of reciprocity with the United States. Reciprocity was the dividing line between those who were prepared to make peace with the Kalākaua regime and those who believed that their worst fears about this king were being confirmed.

The 1876 elections marked the true beginning of a significant Native legislative opposition to the policies and agendas of the Crown. On O'ahu, there were government and "queenite" tickets that contained the names of candidates loyal to their respective constituencies. Emma's candidates ran under the motto "Hawai'i for Hawaiians," and in Honolulu, two of her representatives, A. P. Kalaukoa and the venerable Samuel Kamakau, were elected. Also elected in Honolulu was Henry Waterhouse, who, although not a queenite, was opposed to reciprocity and therefore was counted as a gain for Emma's party.

The Native opposition included some members of the legislature who, though supporters of Emma initially, tended to be more accommodating to Kalākaua once they were elected. One example was Luther Aholo, who began his service during the reign of Alexander Liholiho and represented Lāhainā in the legislature for over two decades. Though he voted for Emma in 1874, Aholo reconciled politically with the king, eventually parlaying that into the vice-presidency of the assembly from 1876 to 1886.

All together, twenty-seven representatives were elected, but in many instances it was difficult to determine whether an elected candi-

Table 8. Legislative Assembly, 1876. (Ministers: W. L. Green, Foreign Affairs and Premier; W. L. Moehonua, Interior; J. S. Walker, Finance; W. R. Castle, Attorney General)

NOBLES	REPRESENTATIVES
Charles Reed Bishop	Luther Aholo (Vice-President)
Samuel N. Castle*	S. 'Aiwohi*
William R. Castle*	G. Barenaba
Archibald S. Cleghorn**	T. N. Birch
John O. Dominis	Cecil Brown* (replaced S. Kamakau, dec.)
James I. Dowsett**	J. W. Gay*
William L. Green**	G. W. D. Halemanu
Paul Isenberg**	W. H. Halstead*
Simon K. Ka'ai*	E. Helekunihi*
H. Kahanu	J. Kahuila*
Charles Kana'ina	L. Kaina*
Paul Kanoa	D. W. Ka'iue
John M. Kapena*	A. P. Kalaukoa*
H. Kūihelani**	Samuel M. Kamakau (died in office)
William P. Leleiōhōkū*	K. Kamauoha*
W. T. Martin**	L. W. P. Kāneali'i*
J. Moanauli**	J. Kaua'i
W. L. Moehonua*	Edward K. Lilikalani*
John Mott-Smith**	S. W. Mahelona
J. P. Parker	S. K. Mahoe*
Godfrey Rhodes* (President)	J. A. Nahaku
J. S. Walker*	J. L. Na'ili
Samuel G. Wilder**	J. Nakaleka*
	S. M. Naukana
	Joseph Nāwahī
	George Washington Pilipō
	E. Preston*
	H. J. Wana
	H. E. Waterhouse*

Source: Lydecker, 1918, *Roster Legislatures of Hawaii,* 136.
* First year.
** Kalākaua appointees.

date supported the queen's positions or the king's until the assembly actually met. Emma, for one, was uncertain about where some of the representatives stood.[38] But some believed that the election signaled a victory for Kalākaua's opponents and "emphasized the importance of the government having control of the house of nobles."[39]

The 1876 assembly was thus politically divided, not just on the issue of Kalākaua's kingship, but on reciprocity with America. It was Nāwahī and Pilipō who led the attack on the treaty. When despite their "vigorous opposition" the treaty went into effect after the 1876 session, these representatives and a few nobles continued to confront the ministry on issues such as the status of the Crown lands, immigration, and the kingdom's debts and fiscal policies. Although the Native opposition was not able to overcome the king's positions on the first two issues, they did contribute to the public censure of Kalākaua and his cabinet over government spending.

Led by Nāwahī, the Native opposition made their challenge on the first day of the 1876 session when Nāwahī introduced a resolution "asking the right of the Crown Ministers to vote on any question laid before the assembly."[40] He was questioning the status of the ministers who were designated ex officio members of the House of Nobles by the 1864 Constitution. Those ministers should have given the king four votes in the assembly, no small thing because the resolution was tabled by the narrowest of votes. Undaunted, Pilipō proposed a few days later that the legislators vote by "estates"[41] (in other words, the representatives having one vote and the nobles/ministers having one vote). That would have placed the opposition on a more even basis with the king's supporters and left any deciding vote to the president of the assembly, who was Godfrey Rhodes, a Briton, vociferously opposed to reciprocity. It was an astute ploy that was narrowly defeated when the motion to table it ended in a 22 to 22 vote tie and was broken by Rhodes himself, who evidently had no desire at that point to ally himself with the opposition.

He would, perhaps, come to regret that decision. One of the more starkly memorable portraits of that session was the afternoon of 6 June. The Native opposition walked out of the assembly, leaving the noble Rhodes impotently railing against reciprocity, while the assembly voted to congratulate the government for securing the treaty.[42]

The Reciprocity Treaty was not the only significant business of that legislature, but it will be seen that its successful acquisition by the kingdom's planters had the most critical effect on the Hawaiian government and society since the Mahele. Like the Mahele, it was backed by the king and contested by Native representatives. Like the Mahele, it chiefly benefited a small class of haole entrepreneurs and promoted the plantation economy over the still-viable subsistence of the kānaka. But as important as anything else, reciprocity encouraged the alienation of more konohiki, government, and even Crown lands, and it also seriously eroded the economic viability of various kuleana, espe-

Figure 14. David La'amea Kalākaua, ca. 1884. Courtesy of the Bishop Museum, Honolulu. CP 38,025B.

cially on Maui, all the while encouraging larger and larger influxes of immigrant labor, from China, Japan, and Portugal. Ultimately, the wealth that reciprocity brought to the sugar planters stoked their greed and strengthened their resolve to bring the government further under their control.

However, unlike the Mahele, reciprocity was opposed by kānaka who also opposed the Mōʻī. Criticism of the policy that further enriched and empowered the haole also redounded against the king. The criticism that he was unable or unwilling to defend Native interests weakened the links between the kānaka and a ruling Aliʻi and contributed enormously to the rise of a powerful haole-led—and financed—opposition known as the Independent or Reform Party by 1884.

It was important that kanaka legislators took the lead in opposing the king early in his reign. Despite the fact that American haole were strongly supportive of reciprocity and encouraged the alienation of Crown lands, those individuals such as Nāwahī and Pilipō legitimized the eventual censure of the reigning monarch. It was not only that they were Natives, but that they were a very special kind of Native; fiercely independent and honest, extremely articulate, and wielding a morality of thrift, they were extolled by the missionary children for being emblematic of the mission's best intentions. Simultaneously, they were attractive candidates to the kānaka who felt most distant from the center of political power. They were, for the haole, the ideal instrument of the king's destruction.

The Reciprocity Treaty

Once elected, Kalākaua advocated for a reciprocity treaty and referred a petition to the legislative assembly, which they passed as "An Act to facilitate the negotiation of a Treaty or Treaties of Reciprocity."[43] Kalākaua then traveled to Washington, D.C., in November 1874 to personally negotiate on its behalf. In doing so, he made a permanent break between his kingship and the supporters of Emma Rooke.

Emma had never been circumspect about her opposition, not just to the cession of Pearl Harbor, which, she said, made her "blood boil," but to reciprocity itself. In August of 1873, she wrote her cousin about a lecture she had attended in which John Kapena, who would be Kalākaua's minister of foreign affairs, had spoken on a number of issues, including reciprocity: "In the address he took one of the opposition arguments strengthening their reasons for Reciprocity—that everything will come in cheep [sic] and we will all grow rich—Our would-be usurpers lie to us very cleverly." [44]

Perhaps it was simpler for Emma, and therefore her supporters, to remain unequivocal about issues like reciprocity and the place of foreigners in Hawai'i. Their assertion was clear that the nation belonged to Hawaiians, an assertion from which the queen, at least, never retreated. Kalākaua's difficulty was that his claims were more ambiguous. According to the constitution, he could assert his kingship. But his leadership of the people, both kānaka and haole, was entirely another matter. The securing of a legislature sympathetic to the king's policies was important symbolically, because the assembly represented the only official voice of the people, and continual and effective legislative opposition would only serve to remind the voters that the king did not possess the mana to rule the nation.

But a Kalākaua-dominated legislature was also a practical necessity. For one thing, the Reciprocity Treaty would mean wealth for the haole sugar planters in the kingdom. If that alone was not enough to guarantee their support for his reign, ratification of that treaty in the Hawaiian legislature would also demonstrate that Natives in the government—including the king—were willing to continue to endorse haole aims. It was hoped that that would secure their cooperation, if not their loyalty.

Kalākaua's support for reciprocity sprang from his own peculiar relationship with the haole planters and commercial agents who had come to his corner just before the election. In 1873, David Kalākaua, then a member of the House of Nobles, had publicly denounced a scheme, initially approved by Lunalilo, to negotiate a treaty with America that included the cession of Pearl Harbor to the United States. That proposal was so unpopular with the kānaka and a number of British residents that Lunalilo quickly withdrew it. Kalākaua's hostility to the cession of territory became the foremost symbol of his willingness to defend Hawaiian independence from the United States. But to quell haole fears that he was dangerous to their interests in the Islands, Kalākaua had to maneuver carefully with the press.

In December 1873, as he began positioning himself to challenge for the crown, he issued a public statement in which he said nothing about reciprocity, except that he was not in favor of ceding any territory to secure it. But his most important shift may have been to distance himself from Emma's ardent and consistent anti-American stance. Saying that he felt Hawaiians should not fear the United

States as a threat to independence, the prince declared: "A great deal has been said by a few persons in our community to the effect that our natives are antagonistic to the foreigners. This I deny, and I take this opportunity to say that no such feeling has or now exists; for the proof of which I state that during the discussion about ceding Pearl River to the United States, no violence or threats came from any one of the natives, save a fair criticism in regard to the actions of the Ministers." [45]

From the point of view of the Native opposition, the fight over the Reciprocity Treaty with the United States was equivalent to a fight for the nation's independence. In May of 1876, Nāwahī and several others took the floor and delivered several passionate orations against the treaty. Calling reciprocity "the first step of annexation later on," Nāwahī warned that: "this was a nation-snatching treaty, one that will take away the rights of the people causing the throne to be deprived of powers that it has always held as fundamental. If the nobles will see the severe burden that will be placed on the throne of Hawaii, and if they have a royalist sentiment, then there is but one good action to carry it out, that being our unifying and strongly opposing this treaty. . . ." [46]

It was an interesting argument given Nāwahī's own loyalties to Emma, but it was entirely logical as well. If one doubted Kalākaua's reliability as king, one would certainly be apprehensive about his willingness to surrender the nation's sovereignty to a foreign country. This is precisely what the treaty in its latest form threatened to do. Despite the fact that Kalākaua had resolutely refused to entertain the cession of Pearl Harbor to the United States in exchange for reciprocity, he, or at least his cabinet, led by William Green, was willing to accept the treaty as it was amended in the U.S. Senate before its ratification: "It is agreed on the part of His Hawaiian Majesty, that, so long as this Treaty shall remain in force, he will not lease or otherwise dispose of or create any lien upon any port, harbor, or any other territory in his dominions, or grant any special privilege or rights of use therein, to any other power, state, or government, nor make any other treaty by which any other nation shall obtain the same privileges, relative to the admission of any articles free of duty, hereby secured to the United States." [47]

That amendment to Article 4 in some ways was more destructive to Hawaiian independence than the actual cession of Hawaiian territory because it prohibited the king from even leasing lands of the kingdom to another nation. In other words, a foreign power assumed the authority to restrict the use and development of the kingdom's territory, thus compromising the king's sovereignty over it.

Prime Minister William Green asserted that the clause merely stated that the government would not cede any of its territory to anyone, including the United States. Because the government, in fact, did not want to cede any territory to the United States, or to any other foreign country, Green argued that the amendment, "when properly understood, just suits everybody." [48]

It did not suit the Native opposition. They issued a resolution finding "want of confidence" in the ministry and demanded their resignation, insisting that the ministry had acted unconstitutionally. Despite Green's assurances, he had decided, with the advice of the Supreme Court, that the treaty did not need to be submitted for ratification by the assembly in 1876, because the king had been empowered by the 1874 assembly to do whatever was needed to secure a treaty. Pilipō went so far as to demand that the Court confirm that it had, in fact, been consulted, arguing as well that the judiciary was overstepping its constitutional powers.

Green and the ministry held fast, but it is doubtful that they could have resisted a unified opposition from the representatives. Unfortunately for Nāwahī mā (and his group), even the kanaka representatives were divided over the treaty. Although the opposition assured the assembly that reciprocity would "do no good for the natives but only to the rich planters," other representatives believed the ministry's claim that the increased prosperity would benefit everyone, or at least everyone willing to work. Assembly vice-president Luther Aholo scornfully told the gallery: "it is not you, who are loafing your time away here in idle inquisitiveness, that will be benefitted, but those who are away from here attending to their work." [49]

Aholo's claim that individuals, presumably Natives, who were willing to work would benefit from the Reciprocity Treaty was later clarified by Minister Green. Green argued that based on the export of 25 million pounds of sugar per year, the country would realize an additional profit of $500,000 annually with the ending of the two cent per pound tariff. But the minister also addressed an important criticism that had been leveled at the treaty because it would eliminate certain duties from the United States that were significant contributors to the kingdom's revenues: "But it has been said, we *lose* $60,000 in revenue on the duties on American goods . . . it is true we shall have to look to some other source for the $60,000 revenue . . . by a different arrangement of duties and other taxes, the $60,000 can be raised from those who can better afford to pay it."[50]

But although acknowledging that the nation could be weakened by the onset of reciprocity, his argument that the monetary loss could be made up by taxing those who could afford it would ultimately place the kingdom squarely in the path of the planters' and merchants' indignation about having to support the government through their taxes. In fact, shortly after the assembly passed enacting legislation for the treaty, it resolved that the ministers should submit a proposal to raise taxes on personal and real property. On 16 June 1876, Minister of Finance J. S. Walker submitted a plan that would tax money and property at three-fourths of a cent for every dollar of assessed value.

The merchants in Honolulu responded by publishing their objections in the *Pacific Commercial Advertiser* several weeks later. A memorial issued by the Chamber of Commerce questioned whether the loss of duties would amount to as much as $60,000 and proposed that "the elasticity of the revenue consequent on the impetus given to trade, and the increased value of taxable property arising therefrom, may safely and properly be looked to as a natural means of making up the loss." Arguing that it would be "wise and politic to leave untouched the present machinery and degree of taxation," the letter went on to propose a universal income tax "in order to equalize the burdens on the various classes that have to support these budgets."[51]

The assembly did not agree and voted to approve the ministerial plan to tax profits and property instead. Perhaps they did not think it would be all that "wise and politic" to place an additional tax,[52] no matter how small, on people's wages when the legislature was still receiving petitions from the kānaka to reduce or eliminate the horse and poll taxes.[53]

In any case, the size of the tax was merely part of the problem. In the opinion of the haole merchants, the tax itself symbolized the inequities that they were forced to endure. The Chamber of Commerce complained that: "The inequities of the present property tax have been hitherto passed in silence, rather from the smallness of the amount levied, than from any conviction of the equity of the tax itself; and it is our opinion that the increase of the tax recommended by the Minister would be found to be most inequitable and burdensome in operation."[54]

Thus, on the eve of what would prove to be the most profitable era in the history of the kingdom, with production of sugar rising tenfold over the next fifteen years,[55] the merchant community may have been anticipating a time when the sheer volume of profits and acreage under production would make a heretofore trivial tax much more meaningful. As some haole would later argue, the fact that the kingdom was financially supported virtually by the sugar planters and merchants without their possessing an equal say in the running of the kingdom was a situation that could not continue.

Kānaka had a very different perception. For those who opposed reciprocity, the government had acted to enrich the fortunes of haole merchants and planters at the government's own expense. In fact, the government directly financed and assisted the expansion of sugar, and not only by its sacrifice of customs revenues. In 1879, the minister of finance loaned $250,000 to the Bishop Bank of Honolulu, at that point the only lending institution in Hawai'i, to continue capitalizing planters and merchants in the Islands. The 1880 legislative

Figure 15. Ali'iōlani Hale. The government building was completed in 1874 and housed the legislature and the judiciary until the end of Lili'uokalani's rule. This photograph was taken from an upper floor of 'Iolani Palace by J. A. Gonsalves, ca. 1890, and is part of the Ray Jerome Baker collection, courtesy of the Bishop Museum, Honolulu. CP 31,509.

assembly scrutinized this transaction "somewhat critically," [56] especially because it was Bishop's bank that had committed several large
overdrafts with the Bank of California in 1879. [57] Ultimately, the
assembly approved the loan because "there was an imminence of
danger to the business interests of the country, which required the aid
of public treasure." [58]

The notion that the country had business interests was, of course,
dependent on how the country was defined. For the entire nation to
benefit by the expansion of a single industry over all others depended
on a general rise in the welfare of the citizenry, Natives, Caucasians,
and Asians as a whole. This was part of Minister Green's claim that
among the treaty's benefits, the tariff-free exportation of rice would
allow small, independent Native farmers to sell their surplus on the
American market, and a drop in the price of goods imported from
America and the rise of wages would directly benefit the kānaka. [59]

That these things did not happen was, perhaps, not the fault of
Kalākaua's ministers, most of whom were replaced two years later. It
is doubtful that any of them anticipated the extent to which the
wealth of sugar would be concentrated within four or five corporate
giants that would virtually eliminate any significant rivals in sugar by
the turn of the century and, through a spectacular acquisition of land
and water rights, severely limit any rival industry as well. In 1898 the
Hawaiian Commission reporting to the U.S. Congress under the terms
of the annexation agreement could proclaim:

> The large profits resulting from the cultivation and manufacture of
> sugar, where inexpensive Asiatic labor was to be obtained, produced
> the legitimate result of aggregating capital in large amounts for the
> purchase or leasing of sugar lands. . . . The cost of irrigation in sugar
> producing districts is also an obstacle not easily to be overcome by
> the small land holder . . . So that many thousands of the most fertile
> lands in the world have . . . become unattainable by ordinary citizens.
> The large holdings have become larger and the small ones have been
> driven out or absorbed. [60]

The ministers and Kalākaua might be excused for not understanding the implications of reciprocity for a nation in which much of the
capital and lands developed for plantation agriculture were already
concentrated in so few hands. It is interesting, however, that although
so few of the ministers' rosy predictions materialized, Nāwahī and
Pilipō, who were so outspoken against the treaty, came to be seen as

prophets. Nāwahī likened the Reciprocity Treaty to the Trojan horse in a famous speech quoted at the beginning of this chapter. Reciprocity looked so attractive and promised so much, but its real intent was unknown. Once it was delivered, there was no getting rid of it.

The Nation's People

The triumph of reciprocity signaled more than a setback for the Native opposition. Reciprocity also heralded a new fiscal reality for the government, indeed for Kalākaua himself, over the next decade. As the dream of an almost unlimited market spurred the concentration of capital on the development of once-marginal lands (marginal for the production of sugar) and an unprecedented diversion of water to irrigate those lands, the representatives and the king locked into important debates over how the nation's wealth was to be used and especially by whom.

Haole were much less divided over the proper use of the Islands' resources than kānaka. Regardless of whether they were supportive of Kalākaua, sympathetic to continued Hawaiian independence, insistent on the survival of the Hawaiians as a people, or antithetical to all three, the influential and prosperous whites believed that the sugar industry had to thrive and the government should be an instrument of its growth.

Despite their undivided passion for independence, Natives, especially in the legislature, were deeply conflicted over how it would be preserved. Some, like Aholo, believed that the fortunes of sugar were capable of bringing prosperity to all, including the government, but others were highly skeptical, pointing out that the decrease in the kingdom's customs revenues demanded careful spending.

Even before the 1876 session, the two principal haole newspapers generally agreed that retrenchment was a very good idea, especially if it would thwart the ministry's intentions to tax capital and property. The *Pacific Commercial Advertiser* remarked: "While we look forward with solicitude for the consummation of the Reciprocity Treaty, yet knowing the deficiency of revenue which must follow, we should be looking about for every available means by which to meet that deficiency without adding to the burdens of taxation. But aside from the probable contingencies of the Treaty, there still exists abundant reasons why every superfluous and expensive mere adornment of our system should be immediately abolished."[61]

The superfluous and expensive adornments referred to included such measures as "lavish support for a useless military" and "provision for a style of government suited to a nation of sixty million rather than a small tribe of less than sixty thousand."[62] Some of the *Hawaiian Gazette*'s objections centered on military spending, an issue that receives more complete treatment in the next chapter. But its claim that Hawai'i was no more than a small tribe is worth a closer scrutiny for what it suggests about how foreigners and haole viewed the kingdom and the importance of race to their perceptions.

On 4 March 1876 the *Advertiser* printed a strongly worded memorial signed by thirty-eight haole planters, merchants, journalists, legislators, and even Kalākaua's attorney general, addressed to the king. It called for "radical change" in government policy that should include immediate retrenchment "until a large surplus of revenue is secured for internal improvement and the acquisition of new people."

With ratification of reciprocity just around the corner, it is easy to see what the authors of the memorial had in mind: more efficient government spending for projects conducive to the expansion of sugar and a larger workforce. But economic prosperity was not their sole concern. In fact, they made it clear that the government should cease or at least limit the further importation of "unchaste" Chinese males whose cohabitation with Hawaiian women was doing nothing but contributing to their continued infertility. Calling for the introduction of kindred races and an education program of sanitation and personal hygiene for the Natives, the memorial went on to issue this warning to the king: "For let us say, that this is an era of great States, and consider, also, that a State like Hawaii, with a mere brigade of people, with a machinery of government so largely in excess of its needs, with an official expenditure that precludes all hope of internal improvement, and that is not at times sufficient for the preservation of its own peace, can hardly much longer be recognized among the family of nations."[63]

An incredulous ministry responded by pointing out that China had been, thus far, the only lucrative and reliable source of immigrant labor, and that far from being a threat to the Native population, "some of the largest families which have been borne to Hawaiian women have been by Chinese fathers, and that even lower orders of Chinese, and we say this with regret, are, we believe, reckoned by the Hawaiian women to make more faithful and attentive husbands than the similar class of Hawaiians."[64]

It would be difficult if not impossible to prove the truth of that statement, though it was certainly true that Hawaiians and Chinese did marry and that large families in some cases resulted. It was also true that many Chinese chose citizenship, swearing allegiance to the Crown and committing their lives and fortunes to the young nation.

But that was also a problem for at least some of the white community. They believed that Chinese who stayed in Hawai'i after their contract expired were rivals and competitors in business and the mechanical trades. Editor and publisher H. L. Sheldon of the *Advertiser* in an editorial on 27 May 1876 entitled "Shall We Admit More Chinese?" pointed out that there were almost half as many Chinese in Honolulu as all other foreigners, and "The foreign *mechanics* other than Chinese, feel their baleful influence in their theft of trades and their cheaper working of the same. They cannot compete with men who require for food only a pound of rice, and perhaps, a rat, *per diem*, which costs but a few cents, when they themselves require many times that amount to maintain them."

These kinds of claims demonstrate that for some of the haole, thrift was not the primary social concern. The important issue was who belonged in Hawaiian society. Clearly, foreign mechanics other than Chinese had a stake in the Islands that should not be offered to Asians, even if it were true that Chinese willingness to work for less and consume less might actually be beneficial to the planters and, perhaps, to poor and underclass Natives.

But Sheldon had even more repulsive perceptions of Chinese. Married to a Native woman, Sheldon was disturbed by the sexual and familial relationships that he saw as "polluting" the kānaka. In the very same editorial he said: "The Hawaiian feels their baleful influence in the contamination of their natural unchastity, and the habits of social and physical ruin they are everywhere introducing among the women of Hawaii, with whom alone, for the mere gratification of imperative animalism, they seek to mate."

Many haole voiced an understanding of Hawaiians that was, at the very least, paternalistic and condescending. But Sheldon's words remind us that there were fine and ambiguous distinctions between supremacy and ownership. In 1876, it would not have been all that difficult to find an American who conceived of certain people as property. But the American mission, with its New England roots, had historically been very much opposed to slavery in the Islands, and slavery was specifically prohibited in the constitution. Sheldon's editorials may not have demonstrated a slave owner's mentality, but it revealed a more subtle kind of ownership.

By 1876, it was apparent that the presence of "Asiatics" threatened the haole monopoly on many things: commerce, land ownership, influence, and even sexual access to the Natives. One wonders if Sheldon, as the husband of a kanaka, believed that not just the "unchaste" Natives were being sexually polluted by Chinese. If so, there were deeply emotional meanings attached to ridding the kingdom of Chinese contract labor. At the same time, economic realities virtually prohibited the plantations from contemplating an end to the system. Those missionary families who did oppose contract labor were most concerned about the penal clauses of the contract "by which the courts appeared to be arrayed on the side of the master,"[65] making the system, they feared, too similar to slavery to be countenanced forever.

Not everyone in the missionary family was so discomfitted, however. Samuel N. Castle, one of the largest of the sugar producers in Hawai'i, argued that abuses of "coolie rights" were far less likely to occur in Hawai'i than in other places and that "Our 'forced labor' system consists in laws requiring people to fulfill their contracts, specifically. They are just to both parties, and both are protected by them, and he who tries to throw odium on our system abroad as a semi-slave system, or to unsettle it at home, unless he brings something practically better, strikes a serious blow at *every interest* in the country, not the planting interests alone, but the coasting, the mercantile and every other one."[66]

Castle's letters were not so much admonishments to the government, but reminders to former missionaries and missionary children such as Henry Whitney, Samuel Damon, and Sanford Dole, all of whom opposed the current system of contract labor, that the business of sugar was everybody's business. Missionaries did not, perhaps, always agree. Sanford Dole issued a mild criticism of his missionary brethren in the sugar business in 1869 that they were sacrificing principle for profits. Yet as president of the republic from 1894 to 1900, he allowed the system to remain in place.

The problem for haole who shared such principles was that terminating contract labor could only be practically accomplished if there were a local or Native population sufficient to the needs of the industry. The kānaka were still being victimized by diseases, the latest of which, leprosy, was believed to have been introduced from China.[67] In 1864 the legislature, on the recommendation of Dr. William Hillebrand,[68] passed an Act to Prevent the Spread of Leprosy, which committed the government to a policy of segregating victims of the disease from the rest of the population. Eventually, the majority of those afflicted, most of them kānaka, were sent to Kalawao on Moloka'i.

Much has been written concerning leprosy in Hawai'i. Most of the literature, however, is about Damien de Veuster, who committed himself to ministering to the sufferers of leprosy in Kalawao. One reason that Father Damien's example was and is so celebrated in Hawai'i is because of the special abhorrence that Christian haole had, not just for the disease, but for its victims.[69] The segregation policy derived not only from what was then considered to be a medical necessity, but also from a deeply ingrained disgust for its victims as "unclean."

Kānaka resistance to banishment is also well documented, as is their willingness to accompany their afflicted relatives and friends into "isolation," rather than allow them to make their way alone.[70] Even some of the Native legislators fought the isolation policies. On 31 May 1876 in response to a petition from Wailuku that all lepers be returned to their homes, Representative Wana of Hanalei resolved that no more Hawaiians be sent to Moloka'i for the duration of the legislative session.[71] It was tabled indefinitely by a close vote, which nevertheless signaled a strong kānaka revulsion for the policy of isolation.

Natives' response to the disease was inexplicable to haole, who fell back on a familiar interpretation for kānaka behavior. When leprosy showed no sign of abating in 1883, the *Saturday Press* published a series of letters and articles denouncing the administration's laxity in its handling of the disease. One letter revealed how much more important the "leprosy question" was, even than reciprocity, to the survival of the Anglo-Saxon race in Hawai'i: "Instances, not a few, can be recalled by many here where innocent children, young men and maidens, besides numbers in adult life, all pure Anglo-Saxon blood, have been sacrificed to the demon of leprosy—a demon from whose embraces the Hawaiian race, with characteristic fatalism and childishness, has not the will nor the power to flee."[72]

The writer also held that the Anglo-Saxon community, rather than wait for the "overspreading poison to corrupt your blood or forever rob your family circle of its purity and happiness," had to act to protect their families, even from the king, who was willing to "sacrifice the race" to gain a "fleeting popularity" with his own people.

The writer stopped short of advocating revolution, though for those who submitted these letters, the paramount issue of national importance was to maintain the purity and happiness of their own race. But for the government, the continued collapse of the Native population was one of many paradoxes that defied resolution. The influx of the most readily available foreign source of labor was seen, at least by some, to be responsible for the latest scourge that continued the downward spiral of the kānaka.

Between those haole who believed the Chinese to be the worst problem and those in Kalākaua's own ministry who saw them to be the best available hope for the Native population, what could be done for kānaka, who appeared to have little choice between dying or isolation? Some believed that being sent to Kalawao meant nothing more than being buried alive. The historian Daws referred to one Hawaiian name for Kalawao, ka lua kupapau (literally, a hole for corpses). But even more revealing is that in the 1876 legislature, W. T. Martin introduced a bill that lepers be declared dead, and considered alike with those in tombs. The bill passed on its second reading.

The fact that terminating immigration was not seen to be an option demonstrates the power of the economic "prosperity" over the other political and social considerations. Labor would have to come from somewhere if the Hawaiians did not learn to avoid contamination or to be more "sanitary." Of course, if they continued to die off, despite the best advice and counsel of the haole, then it was only a matter of time before the kingdom and its king became superfluous. As the *Advertiser* predicted: "It may be said that as production of material for commerce has not declined but rather increased in the kingdom, and may not be diminished in succeeding years, that consequently revenue will be forthcoming and our political order and autonomy may still go on. But should your people continue to decline, the consideration of Your Majesty as the chief of an independent tribe of people must in such event be so far diminished, that the present courtesy of foreign recognition will be withdrawn."[73]

There is a grotesqueness about this image of an expanded sugar industry churning out produce and profits while the people dwindled away to nothing, but it was also deeply revealing about how important kānaka were to the real existence of the nation. Despite the fact that many haole and growing numbers of Chinese were subjects, having been either born or naturalized in Hawai'i, even haole believed on some level that only kānaka could legitimately be represented by the kingdom of Hawai'i.

But this statement was also a warning that there might not be significant haole identification with the government that would enable the kingdom to survive, nor impel the haole subjects to maintain an independent status, once the "Hawaiian tribe" was reduced to insignificance. Coming on the heels of the king's strenuous support of the merchants' fortunes, it betrayed not an iota of gratefulness, nor that his leadership over them was acknowledged. It was a most important signal to the king and his administration that there was really nothing the kingdom could do to secure their loyalty or even their identification, once the Native people were too weak or too few to defend it. Ultimately, it was a most distressing omen for the kingdom's independence that the most wealthy and powerful segment of the society, including individuals close to the king, considered the kingdom dispensable while the least powerful were the only ones who could legitimize the nation in the eyes of the world.

The assertions of those who argued for more immigration and, along with it, greater availability of land to contain the new immigrants were not exactly consistent with assertions that the validity of the nation depreciated with the decline of the Native population. But these claims were consistent with the tremendous financial opportunity that reciprocity presented if and only if substantial labor and sufficient resources existed.

Haole who warned the king that failure to revive the kānaka would result in the termination of the kingdom apparently did not believe that this termination had any particular relationship to the progress of the sugar industry and the prosperity enjoyed by the sugar planters. But as far as the Natives were concerned, what did the nation's prosperity mean if they themselves did not survive? Minister Green, noting that only one of the signers of the 4 March memorial had "the least drop of Hawaiian blood," put this issue somewhat delicately in his response to the memorialists: "The main object contemplated is the expenditure of public money in importing large numbers of men and women of a foreign race and language, and in which question the Hawaiian race must be so especially interested . . . it would have been eminently proper that they should have largely been represented. . . ."[74]

The banishment of Hawaiians to Kalawao, even as the nation was entering a period of tremendous prosperity, intensified the growing distance between kānaka and the various symbols of their identity: 'āina; the leadership of the Ali'i; and lately, even the Mō'ī. The national prosperity was not something to be shared with kānaka. Rather, this prosperity, sought by the legislature and the king's administration, had little to do with the fundamental pursuit of the Natives, who were simply trying to survive.

When Kalākaua's reign is placed in this context, his policies have a certain clarity. He worked to increase business wealth and investment in Hawai'i, while creating institutions that would help the Natives survive. Concerned with increasing both the wealth and prestige of the government to place it on equal footing with the powerful and wealthy elements in Hawai'i, the king incurred loans from wealthy investors such as Claus Spreckels and spent money on the building of a new palace and a military force. At the same time, the king's motto, Ho'oulu Lāhui (Increase the Nation), directed the king's attempts to look for new (non-Chinese) sources of immigration[75] and older, Hawaiian sources of medicine and medical knowledge.

Even the legislature's ostensibly confusing record during the Kalākaua years needs to be placed in context by this growing distance between haole and kānaka aims in this period. The prosperity-bearing treaty created immense wealth for haole planters and merchants, but also drove a wedge between kānaka who were unsure about the best ways to safeguard the future of the kingdom and the survival of the race. There was a drastic difference between Kalākaua's agenda for independence and that of the Native opposition.

Ultimately, the opposition led by Nāwahī and Pilipō was never able to secure a working majority among the elected representatives, much less command of the assembly, which contained so many of Kalākaua's nobles. Where the opposition symbolized careful spending and husbanding of the nation's revenue, the "King's Party" pursued a much more ambitious and vigorous projection of the kingdom's prestige in the Islands and abroad. Such differences drove the Native opposition into alliance with haole critics of Kalākaua by 1884.

As for the haole, though they were as well represented during Kalākaua's reign as they had been in every previous one, their lack of commitment to the nation became more explicit. So too did the kānaka opposition to them in the elections, and from the beginning of Kalākaua's dynasty could be heard the cry, "Hawai'i for Hawaiians."

But the Native motto "Hawai'i for Hawaiians" was also an acknowledgment that from any perspective, the nation lived only because Hawaiians lived. Far from being a racist ideology, it was a realization, founded on decades of experience with the haole, that the kānaka were truly alone in their identification with the nation founded by Kamehameha. Although that motto may have inspired kānaka to vote along ethnic lines, the white residents did not help themselves by becoming citizens and voting.[76]

It was ironic that the newspapers criticized elections of 1874 and after, claiming on one hand that the success of Native candidates was due primarily to the "wide-spread and unreasoning prejudice that has recently grown up against foreigners,"[77] while gently chastising haole for not putting up more of a fight. Several newspapers ran editorials in 1877 on that very subject, with the *Pacific Commercial Advertiser* attributing the preponderance of Natives in the assembly to "apathy and want of national spirit on the part of the foreigners in this country."[78] In fact, the *Hawaiian Gazette* had argued in 1874 that a large percentage of qualified haole electors had not even bothered to vote, much less stand for election and acknowledged that the typical foreigner was reluctant to become naturalized to "such a small country."[79]

But for the most part, the Native voters were censured for refusing to vote for haole candidates and reminded that it was in their best interest to see to it that eight or ten representatives should be foreigners even if that should entail a constitutional change in electoral law.[80] In a letter to the *Pacific Commercial Advertiser,* one observer, claiming that "The natives are in no way able or fit to carry on any civilized government," made this remarkable observation: *"We cannot keep up our national independence except under the guidance of the foreigner.* It is a great law that where the white and colored races come together, the white takes the lead. And it must always be so here. The natives can no more alter this inevitable law of progress than they can choke up Kilauea by dumping in stones."[81]

There was, indeed, an unreasoning prejudice attending the kingdom's elections during the Kalākaua years, and it sprang from the haole indignation that the kānaka did not trust them and would not rely on them for leadership. By 1884, even the *Pacific Commercial Advertiser*'s editors were ready to acknowledge that the Natives' voting preferences were justified by the foreigners' attitudes toward them:

Men who have come here and made money, instead of recognizing how largely their good fortune is due to the favor that has been shown to foreigners by the native race and native rulers are full of contempt for the Hawaiian and treat him and openly speak of him as an inferior being whose country they have made prosperous and who ought to submit to be ruled by them. The old and time-worn, but ever new and active combat between the men of means . . . and the working classes is here complicated by race prejudice. . . . Suffice it to say that if a number of white men are not returned to the legislature . . . this is the one sole reason of it; they have made the Hawaiians who hold the power of the ballot boxes in their hands, afraid to trust them.[82]

Henceforth, every haole candidate would have to earn the Natives' confidence, a situation the haole found intolerable. Either that or they would have to solicit partnerships with Native candidates who had the support of kānaka. At the same time, the Native voters were offered a peculiar choice: to preserve the nation's independence, Natives were told that they must support the representation of foreigners and haole who were, themselves, not particularly interested in the nation's fate. In every election up to 1887, the Native response to this choice became abundantly clear. Hawaiians would vote for Hawaiians.

The Nation's Prosperity

If contract labor reminded some planters, such as H. M. Whitney, of slavery, even government officials were inclined to agree. William Hillebrand, the kingdom's first commissioner of labor, asserted that "the difference between a coolie [contract laborer] and a slave is only one of degree, not of essence."[83] The issue was important enough to certain white businessmen and planters that when reciprocity became a more realistic eventuality, they began to develop schemes by which an ample labor supply might be obtained without offending their sense of morality.

One of these individuals was Sanford Dole, scion of a missionary family and one of the members of the Hawaiian League that would convey the Bayonet Constitution to Kalākaua in 1887. In the fall of 1872, Dole and others published a series of articles dealing with the population and labor supply. Dole favored a policy of immigration that attracted free labor from all parts of the world, including China, by offering land, wages, and citizenship.

The problem, according to Dole, was that the only available land was held by the Crown and the government. Crown lands were inalienable by a legislative act passed in 1864 and there was a "long existing prejudice" against the alienation of government lands. Dole proposed that these lands should be made alienable and available for homesteading for new and "free" immigrant labor, along with a government program to promote it.

By 1876, the pressure was mounting to end the legislative ban on the sale of Crown lands and to facilitate the sale of government lands. It is not surprising that some of that pressure came from kānaka who were landless. In May, the representatives from Kohala and South Kona read petitions asking that the "remaining Government lands be sold or leased to Hawaiians who have no lands and that konohiki fisheries be made free."[84] Pilipō would later introduce a bill to allow fewer restrictions on access to fishing waters, but no representative was willing to call on the government to make more land available to kānaka.

One reason may have been the inordinate pressure coming from haole to sell off those lands in the interests of the economy. The *Pacific Commercial Advertiser* and the *Hawaiian Gazette* contained a number of articles calling on the government to liquidate some of its property, but not before criticizing the monarchy for its outdated policies: "The old and ridiculous notions of primitive times in regard to the effects of alienating territory should have long since been abandoned, and certainly should not be entertained by governments professing to enlightenment, especially at this time, when it is felt as an imperative necessity that everything will be done that will in any way tend to produce an influx of population. Here alone [in the crown lands] are lands sufficient in area to support a population many times exceeding the number of our entire people, and now hired out to proprietors who might be numbered on a few men's fingers."[85]

The increase of the population was thus bound to the freeing up of the king's lands, an attractive proposition to haole who would not have to make home sites available from their own properties, but of considerably less value for either the king or the kānaka. Nevertheless, the legislature began in 1876 to consider how the Crown lands were currently being utilized. Responding to the legislative request, the Crown Land Commission reported that all of the lands were under lease "except a few small patches," and that revenues had amounted to about $37,000 the year before.[86]

That information was of particular interest to those who felt that the government should pension off the king for his interest in the Crown lands and then proceed to sell those lands to all interested parties: "how much better it would be now—if the government, with an intention to make use of the lands in a proper way, would buy out the right and title of the Crown in them . . . if the government would in exchange for them, guarantee the annual payment of a sum equal to the average yearly rents, we fail to see that it would be otherwise than a fair, legitimate and politic action." [87]

Fair, perhaps, to everyone but the government, which would have to foot the bill for the "annual payment," and the kānaka, who, doubt-less, would never see any of that land. And because so much of the Crown lands was among the best agricultural lands in the kingdom, it is easy to see why haole businessmen favored offering them up for sale. The king, however, had no intention of parting with his lands, and the assembly never came close to delivering the necessary legis-lation. Quite simply, the idea of a landless king was an oxymoron to Hawaiians, because the Mōʻī could not, by definition, be landless.

Nothing is more indicative of this belief than the fact that staunch Native opposition members Pilipō and Nāwahī resisted the sale of Crown lands, specifically the ahupuaʻa of Wailuku, to Claus Spreckels in 1882. Speaking before the assembly, Pilipō said that "taking crown lands away from the crown and giving them to another person is a step toward destroying the independence of the country." [88]

This sale of Crown lands in Wailuku, Maui, was a remarkable inci-dent at the midpoint of Kalākaua's reign. It was given extensive treat-ment in two chapters of Jacob Adler's 1966 work, *Claus Spreckels: The Sugar King of Hawaii*. Adler made it clear that it was reciprocity that drew Spreckels to the Islands in 1876, just as the treaty was being rat-ified by the U.S. Senate. In fact, the news and the millionaire sugar refiner arrived on the same steamer.

Spreckels would play a large role in Kalākaua's political difficul-ties, but he had an immediate impact on the kingdom's economy. Adler believed that it was Spreckels' about-face on reciprocity—he originally opposed it—that encouraged the Senate ratification in the first place. Adler was also pretty clear that Spreckels joined Kalākaua and Walter Murray Gibson in a "regime of political corruption unlike anything known in the previous 40 years of constitutional govern-ment." [89]

Charges of dishonesty in government have been leveled at the king from his contemporaries onward. Most of the charges were never proven. It is not my main purpose in this book to rehabilitate the memory of David Kalākaua, so I hesitate to take too much space refut-ing the charges that the Kalākaua administration was corrupt or that this corruption tainted members of the legislature. I contend, however, that corruption in government has never been limited to the Hawaiian kingdom and, in fact, can be demonstrated as a liability for any government that is intimately involved with commerce, especially during periods of sudden prosperity.[90]

The king's "depravity" was one of several reasons for the opposition raised against him. Portraying the king as a corrupt leader became the best strategy for those who hated him once the other royal challengers died off. Furthermore, those charges found a ready audience of Natives and haole who were *already* willing to challenge the king's legitimacy and his virtue.

In any case, Spreckels arrived in Honolulu with little experience in sugar cultivation, no lands, and no water rights. He possessed capital, however, which allowed him to purchase some 16,000 acres on Maui and lease another 24,000 acres of Crown lands in the Wailuku Commons, a dry and dusty plain that was considered unsuitable for sugar cultivation. Two years later, Spreckels managed to contract with the Crown to build an irrigation project diverting water from the northeastern slopes of Haleakalā, bringing water and tremendous productivity to his own plantations. Although it was his capital, about $500,000, that built the irrigation system, the price for the water rights was a mere $500 per year to the government and, in all likelihood, a payoff to the king himself.[91]

Adler's work treated the construction of this pipeline as an admirable project, even if the unsavory politics that accompanied it sullied the reputations of both Spreckels and the king. It makes no suggestion that the diversion of 60 million gallons of water per day from areas that were the kuleana lands of former Maka'āinana may have harmed their livelihoods. The absence of kānaka from so much of the historical record is a reflection of their disappearance from the political considerations of the kingdom in the nineteenth century. The fact is that we do not know if the diversion of water in the Hāna and Makawao Districts led to widespread migration of Hawaiians from their homes, or if the removal of water may not have significantly depopulated areas above and beyond what the succession of lethal diseases had already done. What was popularly "known" was that the lands and resources of the kingdom were going to waste and that only sugar would bring about prosperity.

Plantation owners, of course, tended to support irrigation of marginal lands for sugar. In fact, two of the established mission-children entrepreneurs, Henry Baldwin and Samuel T. Alexander, were already completing their own irrigation project on Maui that brought water from the same general area as Spreckels' to their plantation at Ha'ikū, but several wealthy haole also believed that the financing of irrigation was the responsibility of the government. In the *Pacific Commercial Advertiser* there were repeated calls for irrigation as a capital improvements project that only the government could afford to undertake, and that would avoid the danger of a "tyrannizing" monopoly.

The monopoly feared in the *Advertiser* was Spreckels, whom many felt represented a new and dangerous player in the race to develop fresh lands and take advantage of reciprocity's rewards. It was an uncomfortable realization that a stranger, a malihini (newcomer) armed with nothing but cash, could so quickly accomplish what most of the planters, after generations in the Islands, could not. Natives did not appear to resist the "Spreckels Ditch." One searches in vain for petitions from the Maui ahupua'a protesting the taking of water, and an editorial in the Hawaiian newspaper *Kuokoa* even linked the millionaire's project to the king's design to revive the Hawaiian race. The article was entitled "Hooulu Lahui": "One of his [Spreckels] ideas concerns the increase and preservation of the Hawaiian race. He will divide those lands into small districts and settle whole families on them. They will plant sugar on shares and get paid for their labors. The country will become prosperous and the people will multiply. Thus the idea of Hooulu Lahui will become a reality."[92]

If some of the kānaka were clinging to the idea that this malihini would save them from extinction, it may have been only because it was so clear that the established haole community was too busy pursuing their own interests to be worrying about them. In any case, the connection of Spreckels with Kalākaua said very different things to different elements in the kingdom and dramatized the ever-widening distance between kānaka and haole within the looming prosperity.

It was a prosperity in which few haole believed the kānaka would participate. It was pointed out in the *Hawaiian Gazette*, in fact, how corrupting money could be and how unfortunate it would be for kānaka to be influenced by it: "Possibly it appeared to the native mind that a speculation—which has in it somewhat of a savor of a monopoly—was a disinterested investment of money in these Islands for the benefit of the nation. . . . Hitherto the Hawaiians have been free from its influence, and happy will it be for them if they never have to contend with its subversive power."[93]

After all those years there was still enough of the missionary in editor Henry Whitney's genes to wish that the kānaka be spared the loss of innocence that wealth, especially the suspicious wealth of the outsider, would undoubtedly bring. The first to be suspected of this taint was the king himself, who abruptly dismissed his cabinet, "rousing them from their beds" at two in the morning, apparently because they were in no hurry to grant the water licenses to Spreckels.[94] But it was the suspicion that the sugar magnate had bribed the king for special consideration of his application that established a pattern of opposition to the king and his administration that would intensify over the years.

The king's apparent culpability embarrassed men like Nāwahī who, because of their aloha for Emma, had to be careful about how much they pressured him. There had never been any shortage of haole support for ending the monarchy entirely, and attacking the king personally increased the danger to the monarchy itself. This is one reason for the seeming ambivalence that characterizes much of the Native critique of the king, as we shall see in the next chapter, while the most vicious and indelicate denunciations came from haole subjects and foreigners.

But Nāwahī mā would be uncommonly direct when the king's transgressions included the dissipation of 'āina. They saw the Crown lands as particularly important to the maintenance of the Crown's political and economic independence from the wealthy and the influential. But there is also no question that those lands were symbolically important and represented a meaningful legacy from the Kamehameha family. Thus, even though Kalākaua's complicity in the Spreckels land purchase was less explicit than when Spreckels obtained his water licenses, the Native opposition brought much greater heat on the king.

In 1882, Spreckels set about to secure clear title to some 24,000 acres of the Wailuku ahupua'a that he had been leasing from the king. The completion of the irrigation project made these once arid lands extremely valuable, but the 1864 legislative restriction prohibited the king from selling the lands to anyone. Undeterred by the law, Spreckels arranged to purchase for $10,000 an undivided interest in the Crown lands "belonging" to Princess Luka (Ruth) Ke'elikōlani, a great-granddaughter of the Conqueror and a half sister to Kamehameha IV and V. As heir (one of the few remaining) of Kamehameha I, Luka claimed a one-half share in the Crown lands.

In the first place, it must be said that Ke'elikōlani's *legal* claim was debatable. Both the Supreme Court and the legislature had "set forth the view that the crown lands were meant to descend only to successors to the throne."[95] It was a group of attorneys including both supporters and opponents of Kalākaua who advised Spreckels that her claim was viable and that his purchase was legitimate. Former Attorney General Edward Preston issued his opinion on 17 May 1882 that not only were the princess' claims valid but that the "decision of the Supreme Court and the law declaring these lands inalienable are inoperative and void . . . and I do not hesitate to say that under his conveyance he [Spreckels] is entitled to one half of the so called 'Crown Lands.'"[96]

Preston, whom Kalākaua had made attorney general when the water licenses were granted, was reappointed three days after issuing his opinion. But it was the assembly, against the opposition of Nāwahī mā, that decided to grant title to the Wailuku ahupua'a to Spreckels in exchange for extinguishing his claims to perhaps 500,000 acres of Crown lands. Doubtless, most of the Native legislators believed that a sorely needed compromise was reached that narrowly avoided the loss of a half million acres with no compensation to king or government. As far as the haole were concerned, however, there was now a breach in the law protecting the Crown lands from future sale. This was also how the Native opposition perceived the situation. Pilipō's address to the assembly on 18 July 1882 sought to forestall the bill to convey the 24,000 acres that was introduced by Minister Preston: "I cannot understand the Ministry at all. . . . I consider a bill of this kind like an attempt to undermine the King on his throne. . . . I said this Ministry is weak. I still say so; I still think it. They are the protectors of the King, and should defend him to the last. Now the order is reversed. . . . If they fear the consequences, they should stand behind us."[97]

It was an interesting charge by Pilipō that the king's own advisors did not have the stomach to fight the loss of the king's lands. But the elder Kona representative made it clear that the king, too, showed real weakness: "It may be that the Ministry are doing what they are told to do by a higher power. Is it the King? What is the matter with our King? Is he in the power of the same man?"[98]

In all likelihood, the king was indeed involved in this transaction, but perhaps he was not merely being manipulated by Spreckels. Kalākaua was able to circumvent the law limiting his control over the Crown lands, enabling him to grant a special favor to a wealthy and powerful haole who had already made promises to loan millions of dollars to the government. Furthermore, having sold her interest, Ke'elikōlani's claim to a share of those lands was neatly disposed of, leaving control of them to the king's discretion.

What sort of ruling chief could Kalākaua have been without lands to wield,[99] especially since he did not appear to possess the authenticity of a Lota Kapuāiwa, or even a Lunalilo, to so many Hawaiians?

In truth, it is impossible to understand Kalākaua's behavior, especially his "corruption," without factoring in the very real obstacles to his recognition as king by his own kānaka and by the importance of prosperity to that recognition.

Kame'eleihiwa described the importance of "conspicuous consumption" in her analysis of the traditional Ali'i Nui and their tendency to spend lavish sums of money and goods while incurring huge personal debts at the end of the eighteenth century. She wrote:

> The word 'ai means "to eat" and also "to rule." Therefore, by consuming, the Ali'i would rule and direct the mana of the Akua . . . in their search for control over the foreign element in their world, the Ali'i Nui were determined to 'ai (consume and rule) the physical manifestations of the foreigner—his goods, his food, and his "sparkling water" (liquor). Such a display fed the mana of the Ali'i Nui and made it grow in the eyes of the people. . . . After all, Western royalty consumed riches in great quantities, and how could Hawaiian Ali'i Nui prove their divinity to foreigners if they did not behave in the same manner?"[100]

It is not only possible but compelling to view Kalākaua's behavior as a modern reification of traditional behavior. That is, that what motivated Kalākaua was not the pursuit of personal wealth, but the pursuit of legitimacy. It is a compelling argument because it is the same one made for every other competing political element in this society. Wealth, for a king lacking the unanimous aloha of his people, was a means to his asserting leadership over them. In much the same way, foreigners, especially the Hawaiianized haole, used wealth as a means of asserting their superiority, their moral right to be in Hawai'i, and their appropriation of the resources of the Islands.

It should also be said that denying that wealth and prosperity to the Mō'ī was a very traditional way for the Native opposition to diminish his authority. As early as 1876, Nāwahī mā were busy introducing resolutions questioning the spending of the king's ministers,[101] and there were even petitions from the countryside favoring reducing the king's salary. Their favoring of government retrenchment and careful monitoring of the Crown's expenses was no less sincere just because it also humiliated the king to have his expenses scrutinized. Indeed, their resistance to the king was so much more effective because they were sincere in their belief that the king spent money foolishly and that his opulence weakened the nation. Nāwahī said as much in a speech at Hilo: "Is this enlightened politics if one dollar is my income for a day and my spending for the day is two dollars? No. That is ignorant politics; and it is understood that one would die early in his life if his deeds were such. It is the same with a nation. . . . What is the good and the value of cannons purchased at $20,000, the ranks of island soldiers costing $60,000, and the unnecessary expansion of other appropriations? What is the value of these insignificant things to show off?"[102]

Many Native voters invested their trust in men such as Nāwahī despite the fact that their very presence in the legislature not only weakened the king, but strengthened the haole Independent Party and the political fortunes of men whom the Hawaiians did not trust. Thus, the key political quarrels were between those kānaka who saw in the king the only real hope for the nation's continued independence and those kānaka who believed that he was the nation's biggest threat.

The haole were not the center of this controversy. Having no particular loyalty to this or any Native monarch, their only concern was their apparent exclusion from the inner circles of power, even as their personal prosperity expanded. That did not prevent them from delivering their own demeaning attacks on the king, and along with them a further belittling of the nation that he led: "Kalakaua is chief of a tribe of not quite 50,000 people, and his grandfather, if not his father, was a naked cannibal savage; but after being feted on terms of equality in London, Rome and Vienna, it is no wonder that he should go back to Honolulu resolved to live on his paltry revenue in as fine a style as his brother sovereigns in civilized countries. What we wish our Kalakauas and Cetewayos to see is just what they are least able to comprehend; what they observe and remember most is just what it is least expedient that they should aspire to copy."[103]

The indignation of the haole at being shunted aside in favor of newly arrived competitors was not about mere economics. Their resentment sprang from the noticeable change in the demeanor of this king, his willingness to dispense with their guidance, and the fear that he reflected what every other kānaka really believed: that the Hawaiians deserved a greater share of the attention if not the riches of their own nation.

As for the Native opposition, their resistance to Kalākaua forced the king to lean ever more heavily on his own Native supporters and a small coterie of haole advisors and financiers led by a political newcomer, Walter Murray Gibson. It was Gibson and Spreckels, primarily, in whom the king placed his trust and reliance, and their influence most offended both the established haole and Nāwahī mā. It was that new partnership that would encourage them to unite in a single party in 1884.

The Nation's Values

The racial antagonism that characterized the electoral campaigns during the 1880s was not the result of some newly emergent mistrust of the haole fanned by the king and his supporters. Rather, that animosity was a continuation of a steadily growing divergence between the economic and social fortunes of haole and kānaka, as well as a nearly total separation between them in terms of their national identification and loyalty. The animosity was also due to racist portrayals of kānaka in the haole press and the Natives' disgust with the foreigners' arrogance.

It is not surprising that haole believed the political controversy involved them so intimately, when it was really not just about them. Despite the fact that they did not believe that they belonged to the nation in the same way that the kānaka did, they continued to see themselves, or at least their leadership, as indispensable to it. Although it was certainly true that some Native political leaders, *never the king*, would campaign with the admonition that Hawaiians should not cast their votes for any non-Native, the truly virulent accusations were leveled between kānaka.

After the session in August of 1882, Nāwahī and Pilipō appeared at a gathering at Hilo Boarding School where Nāwahī leveled this scathing indictment of his fellow representatives and nobles: "Yes, the Land, that cherished thing, the place where the feet of the famous Conqueror stood and where his weariness was rested; that very valuable land, 24,000 acres on the plain of Kama'oma'o, has been lost. . . . Would you think that if these representatives were true patriots they would grant the land? No. This is simply from their traitorous concerns. It is because easy money was brandished before the eyes of these traitors, with positions and other oily reasons, and they were overcome and granted the land, a thing not easily obtained." [104]

The real controversies in the turbulent years of Kalākaua's reign were principally over how the nation, its members, and its values were to survive. The haole were only tangentially involved in these most difficult and perilous disputes. They were not dying by the hundreds of smallpox, or being isolated by the thousands at Kalawao. They were not being driven from their lands by either disease or economic necessity. They were prospering and would apparently continue to prosper, they believed, no matter what became of the kānaka or, for that matter, the kingdom.

Furthermore, the Hawaiians had grave problems on their hands, crises that could not be resolved by haole leadership and solutions. Every crisis pointed directly to the steady and seemingly unavoidable perishing of the race. What, indeed, could be done to put an end to leprosy? How could the government improve medical service without serious investment in hospitals or without educating kānaka in medicine and related fields, investments that would surely require either a change in the priorities of government spending or larger taxation of the kingdom's wealth? Finally, who would be the nation if the kānaka continued to die?

The king and the Native opposition each believed that they knew best how to deal with these crises. The king would spend the nation's resources on finding the ideal "kindred race," sparking the sugar industry to pay for their introduction, and using the government's revenues to pay for things that would project a favorable image of Hawai'i internationally.

The Native opposition would try to limit the sugar industry, slow immigration, and maintain frugality in the government's spending, believing that the revenue of the kingdom should be spent on the Native people themselves, on education, medical care, and assistance in setting up farms and businesses. They did not favor debt or spending money to improve the nation's image and believed that Kalākaua's unconcern with laws embarrassed the kingdom and could not be redressed by building palaces and armies.

Both the Native opposition and Kalākaua supporters used the motto "Hawai'i for Hawaiians" in different elections. They meant to define the meaning of being Hawaiian at this most critical juncture of the kingdom's history. They meant to distinguish the people who belonged to the nation from those who simply owned a piece of it. "Hawai'i for Hawaiians" was a favorite saying of Emma and of Walter Murray Gibson and did not exactly disparage the haole as much as it dismissed them, but it did assert that the whites were not a part of the nation. They were not Hawaiians. That was a simple truth.

7
Bayonet

A Sovereign who frankly accepted his position under the
constitution, and then used it judiciously, could have had his
own way a great deal of the time and have avoided serious
difficulties for the rest of it. But this is the kind of sovereign
that neither King Kalakaua nor Queen Liliuokalani was willing to be. Each was determined to encroach upon the powers
of other departments at every turn, and to destroy the whole
system of responsible government at the first opportunity. If
the Kings reigning in Hawaii since 1887 had been ready to
follow the road laid out for them by the constitution, it is
likely enough that one of them would be on the throne today.
The relation of the kingdom of Hawaii to the United States
would necessarily be one of dependence or alliance or affiliation of some sort; we have examples in the republics of Cuba
and Panama.

Thomas Marshall Spaulding,
Cabinet Government in Hawaii: 1887–1893

It was not until Wednesday afternoon, 6 July 1887, that a small committee of haole individuals brought a hastily scripted constitution to
the king and forced his signature that destroyed his authority as Mōʻī
and significantly altered the meaning of citizenship and nationhood
in the kingdom. But well before that day the political and cultural discourses that had constantly marginalized the Natives, as human
beings, laborers, rulers, and, eventually, as citizens, paid large divi-
dends to a haole elite who were determined to control the Natives,
even if that meant the annexation of Hawaiʻi to the United States. In

this chapter we will examine the political climate of the mid-1880s, describing Native participation in the elections of 1884 and 1886 and their response to the new haole order in 1887.

The Bayonet Constitution has been portrayed in many different ways. It is not surprising that Lorrin Thurston, who helped draft it, defended it as "a revolutionary document" not unlike the American Declaration of Independence.[1] At least one prominent twentieth-century historian, Ralph Kuykendall, insisted that although the constitution's revisions were drastic, the political and social conditions in the kingdom explained, if not warranted, the change.

But his judgment is not exactly sympathetic to the Native Hawaiian citizenry. In the same chapter he noted that the new voting privileges "extended to resident aliens gave to the haole as a group a greatly increased power in the government and reduced the Hawaiians to a position of apparent and, for a while, actual inferiority in the political life of the country." In his next breath, the author defended the promulgation of the constitution, comparing its coercive character with the Magna Carta.[2]

Thomas Spaulding in his article "Cabinet Government in Hawaii" was more representative of the prevailing American opinion in the 1920s, an opinion preoccupied with power and thus untroubled by the loss of Native civil rights: "There is something to be said for a genuine monarchy; there is something to be said for a republic; there really seems to be very little to be said for a government which preserves the expensive and meretricious features of a monarchy while sacrificing its possibilities of usefulness. Yet this is exactly what was set up in Hawaii in 1887, and quite rightly so, for conditions and not theories were what confronted its founders. Genuine monarchy was tried; it had worked well at first, and at last badly. Nominal monarchy was now to have its turn."[3]

The utilitarianism that characterizes this assessment of the kingdom both before and after the Bayonet Constitution is typical of that period in American and European intellectual tradition, which reduced most political considerations to the simple issue of whether or not such policy, law, or treaty strengthened or weakened the nation. Realpolitik, a philosophy of government exemplified by individuals such as Prussia's Otto von Bismarck in the nineteenth century, defines good government as successful government and is most comfortable at a distance from discussions of morality, human rights, and national ideals.

With that orientation, it is not altogether surprising that Spaulding did not discuss the constitutional changes affecting the electorate, but focused entirely in his thesis on the confrontation between the king and the haole members of the Hawaiian League who forced Kalākaua to discharge his cabinet and submit to the new constitution drafted by Lorrin Thurston.

The eclipsing of the Native voters from this discussion does provide an intriguing argument based on realpolitik principles. Spaulding insisted that genuine monarchy had been tried, as though the nation had been nothing more than the product of some rational consciousness that tinkered with the apparatus of the state until it settled on the oligarchy of a cabinet-controlled government. This may have been how the haole reformists understood their position and place in Hawai'i at the close of the Kalākaua dynasty. Perhaps they believed that the government had always been theirs to experiment with, and the Native "tribe" and their "savage" rulers were nothing more than compounds and elements to be combined and manipulated under their guidance and control. Certainly, the haole and the scholar who memorialized them saw no need to consider the wishes and resentments of the Native subjects whose relationship to the king was complicated, as we have seen, by a very real historical devotion to the Mō'ī.

Other authors and scholars have been less charitable to haole in their descriptions of this constitution. One writer, Sean Kelleher, simply denounced the letter and the spirit of the Bayonet Constitution, claiming that: "the popular branch [of the legislature] could be outvoted by the propertied branch. The goal of universal suffrage, brought to the Islands by Americans and championed by them in 1852 and 1864, had been abandoned."[4]

Looking back from the beginning of the twenty-first century, one can see a steady progression of viewpoints and analyses of Hawai'i's modern history that gradually placed the seizure of Hawai'i in its more proper colonial context. But it is important to note that until the last decade of the twentieth century, with the publication of works by Native historians and academics such as Davianna MacGregor, Haunani-Kay Trask, and Lilikalā Kame'eleihiwa, there was little attention paid to how Native Hawaiians viewed their own colonization. More than a simple theft of government, the Bayonet Constitution was a demonstration of haole control. The indignant voices of Natives were heard but only for a time. With the loss of political sovereignty, those voices were gradually muted until they seemed to disappear altogether.

Why did they disappear? Certainly the fact that haole control over the printed media, the curriculum of elementary and secondary schools, the very history of our people culminating in the annexation of Hawai'i by the United States had something to do with the quieting of Native voices. But the nature of this colonization, too, resulting in the accommodation of those who conspired against our queen, also had an effect on how the kānaka resisted her overthrow and the loss of the kingdom. Our people were silenced by uncertainty. Not uncertainty about their cause, because in every situation in which their opinions were solicited or even allowed they demonstrated an overwhelming loyalty to the nation and a clarity about their choices. Their uncertainty was over who could be trusted to deal fairly and honestly with them.

The extent to which the national interests had become essentially the interests of the white-dominated commercial enterprises had not, even during the highly contested elections of the 1880s, caused Hawaiians to actually reject their own government. On the contrary, Native opposition to the government was linked to haole factions that were representative of the "missionary-planter-business" interests.

Meanwhile, Native resistance to haole control was, by 1884, vested in the party that supported Kalākaua's government: the Nationals as they called themselves, ho'apili mea 'ai (clinging to the food) as they were known to their detractors. In other words, resistance to the rich and powerful elite was greatly obscured by the fact that Native nationalists such as Nāwahī and Pilipō were enlisted as members of the Independent Party in the early 1880s. While taking on the principal burden of criticizing the king and his cabinet and encouraging the election of haole, some members were increasingly in favor of eliminating monarchy and even ending independence altogether.

Thus by 1886, the Native voters faced the necessity of making one of two absurd choices: support an embattled king who was almost certainly conducting some of his business transactions outside the law, or support a haole-led party that promised no real leadership for Natives and included members that wanted outright annexation, but presented itself as uncorrupted. That Hawaiians chose their king is not surprising, but their choice, which included sending the two greatest defenders of Hawaiian independence into political obscurity, hastened the haole determination to do away with the Native-run nation once and for all.

As for the haole subjects the choices were not nearly so difficult. Those who loudly insisted that Hawaiian independence should be maintained were nevertheless opposed to the continuance of the king's leadership under the cabinets formed by Walter Murray Gibson. Even the foreign residents could have applied for citizenship and brought their numbers to bear in the legislature. Their unwillingness to do so, stemming in part from their inability to assume an identification with the nation, in no way diluted their belief that they had a right to control the political direction of the kingdom because of their control of its resources. As one Maui resident wrote:

> While the holders of the bulk of all property in the Islands are foreigners, only a few of them are legally citizens, and as such are able to share directly as well as indirectly in the business of government. They pay an immense share proportionally of the taxes, but cannot control expenditure. They can neither elect members of the Legislature nor occupy seats therein. It is natural that the American and Englishmen do not willingly surrender their nationality for that of this very small kingdom. . . . On the other hand, for the permanent residents . . . there can be no better way to secure the best future for their children, the best security for their property than by identifying themselves with the country of their adoption, and placing themselves in the position where they can bring their most active powers to bear upon its welfare.[5]

The Bayonet Constitution allowed the whites political control without requiring that they swear allegiance to the king. Indeed, the constitution removed every paradox that had previously confounded haole citizens and other white residents by making the nation belong to them without requiring that they belong to the nation.

In 1886, the most powerful and influential haole in the kingdom formed the Hawaiian League, an organization devoted to "good government." Their opposition to the Gibson cabinets was intensified by their concern for the renewal of reciprocity in 1887 and resulted in a compromise between the rabid annexationists and those who wanted more political control within the government. The Bayonet Constitution was the institution of that compromise.

But in 1883, there were still a large number of highly influential people who were willing to confront the kingdom's administration with a political party that would challenge the king's support, nearly all of them Natives, in the House of Representatives. They created the party known initially as the Independents, financed by contributions from wealthy plantation owners, shippers, and other businessmen. They intended to "send a good representation to the legislature" and held their first meeting within two months of the official coronation of David Kalākaua at 'Iolani Palace. Their agenda included recruiting members of the Native opposition like Nāwahī and Pilipō and running them alongside haole candidates committed to eroding the power of the Kalākaua/Gibson administration by controlling the assembly.

Ultimately, the Independents' failure to significantly detach the Native subjects from the king, despite their arguments of his unworthiness, prompted the haole in that party to take drastic measures to "reform" the government. At the same time, the king's attempts to resurrect the Native culture and incorporate traditional arts and sciences in his administration enraged and worried even the most conservative of the haole elite and embarrassed the kanaka members into virtual immobility. Unwilling to support the king and his "excesses," the Hawaiian members of the Independent Party, nevertheless, had no real power in the fashioning of the opposition against their king.

The Crowning Insult

The organization of the opposition party was a response to what some perceived to be a loss of haole representation in the assembly. Several newspaper articles, cited in the last chapter, offered the perception that haole were underrepresented in the legislature, not because of their actual numbers, but rather by a conception that the white community's fiscal contribution to the kingdom's tax base entitled them to greater influence in the government.

Close analysis of the ethnic composition of legislatures just before and during the Kalākaua years yields some interesting comparisons.[6] In 1872, seven of the twenty-six representatives (27 percent) elected were haole. However, six of the fourteen nobles (43 percent) were haole, many of them leftover appointments going back to Kamehameha IV. Overall, 32 percent of the assembly was white. In 1872, Caucasians (not including Portuguese)[7] numbered 2,520 compared with Hawaiians and part-Hawaiians, who numbered 51,531. Haole, in plain numbers, made up about 4.6 percent of the voting population, though actually less, if one factors in the hundreds of Asian (mostly Chinese) citizens.[8]

Moreover, despite perceptions to the contrary, haole representation *grew*, and significantly, during the Kalākaua years to 40 percent, with the election in 1882.[9] In fact, it can be argued that, strictly on the basis of ethnicity, the Caucasians enjoyed greater representation during the Kalākaua administration than at any time since the two legislatures had been combined in Lota Kapuāiwa's constitution.

Ethnicity was not the only consideration. Walter Murray Gibson was the prime example of a haole whose views and politics, and certainly his Mormon affiliations, were antithetical to the Hawaiianized white families in the Islands. Representing a new group of haole insiders with strong connections to the ruling monarch, much about Gibson was reminiscent of the early missionary community.

This visionary, who had arrived in Honolulu in the summer of 1861, possessed a commission as an elder in the Mormon Church after being baptized only the year previously. Gibson proceeded over the next few years to establish himself on Lāna'i Island, designated by previous elders as the "gathering place"[10] for the Mormon community in Hawai'i. By 1872, perhaps restless from living in a small community of less than three hundred, he moved to Honolulu, where he published the newspaper *Nuhou,* using it as a platform to discuss and shape his own political ideas.

Gibson's sense of personal identification with Hawaiians and belief in their national destiny made him, in his own mind, different from other haole. Even the whites who worked for him on Lāna'i did not understand his attachment to the Natives: "My love for a race is a myth to them. Now I am South Carolinian and believe somewhat in the subordination of races, and yet feel strong attachments to brown and black people. To these young men educated under Puritan congregational philanthropy the kanaka is a digger [*sic*], a darkey, while I view him as an interesting yet feeble younger brother, a subject of an oceanic empire."[11] His comments have interesting implications for Native Hawaiians, because he was the closest advisor to the Native king for five years. His views also made him the very symbol of everything dangerous to the Hawaiianized haole in the Islands, whose fiscal conservatism was so clearly mirrored by an equal aversion to the still persisting Native traditions.

Their mutual animosity was exemplified by the coronation of Kalākaua on 12 February 1883 at the newly completed 'Iolani Palace. In the first place, the coronation was clearly orchestrated by Gibson in his new capacity as premier and minister of foreign affairs. According to one biography, Gibson had seated himself in the most prominent position possible while relegating the other haole notables, "who had been the most vehement in protesting the cost and childishness of this celebration," to less-favored seats.[12] It is also clear that at least some of the missionary families who attended the coronation found more to be outraged about than their seating placement. One was the money that the kingdom spent on the ceremony—an egregious expense, they felt, considering the costs of constructing the palace.[13] The other was the ceremonial prominence of the hula.

The importance of the coronation as a symbol of Kalākaua's prestige is unmistakable. Despite criticism from both haole and Native sources that it was foolish to crown a monarch in the ninth year of his reign, it must not be forgotten that there were those who continued to believe that he was not the rightful Mō'ī. His sister, Lili'uokalani, wrote in her memoirs that the expense was more than justified because the ceremony gave to the country people and neighbor islanders "a renewed sense of the dignity and honor involved in their nationality, and an added interest in the administration of their government."[14] Furthermore, she argued, "Honolulu had been benefitted in the mean

Figure 16. The coronation of Kalākaua and Kapi'olani after the completion of 'Iolani Palace, 12 February 1883. Courtesy of the Bishop Museum, Honolulu. CP 121,821.

time financially, the merchants and traders of every degree reaping a bountiful harvest by the free expenditure of money by every class."[15]

But her comments about the individuals who criticized the expense of the coronation are also noteworthy, reflecting her clear identification of the class distinctions that separated the Native Ali'i Nui from even the wealthiest of their detractors:

> The men who "carry the bag" are not always the best judges of royal obligations. It was necessary to confirm the new family, "stirps"— to use the words of our constitution—by a celebration of unusual impressiveness. There was a serious purpose of national importance; the direct line of the "Kamehamehas" having become extinct, it was succeeded by the "Keaweaheulu" line, its founder having been first cousin to the father of Kamehameha I. It was wise and patriotic to spend money to awaken in the people a national pride. Naturally, those among us who did not desire to have Hawaii remain a nation would look on an expenditure of this kind as worse than wasted.[16]

The opposition agreed with her on that last point. The Hawaiian-language newspaper *Ka Nupepa Kuokoa*, whose publisher since 1879 had been Kawaiaha'o Church's Reverend Henry Parker, scolded both the king and those who would have anything to do with the event even before it actually took place: "Oh, ye people! By mixing yourselves up with this frivolity you are making light of your own burdens and dancing at your own funeral."[17]

The grim image conjured by Reverend Parker may seem merely puritanical, but his remarks cast the king and Gibson as indulgent fools carousing through the nightmare of a recent smallpox epidemic and the continuing misery of leprosy. The fact that these and related disasters to the health and strength of the Natives were never severe enough to interfere with commerce was plain enough to anyone who attended the sessions of the assembly. But a number of people expressed concern that the extravagance of the celebration, Lili'u's claim notwithstanding, was threatening to the Islands' financial reputation and could even affect renewal of reciprocity. The *Saturday Press*, whose publisher and editor Thomas Thrum contributed to both the Reform Party and the more pro-annexation Hawaiian League, wrote:

> We are just beginning to feel the near approach of the troubles that might have been expected to come from such silly, wasteful and pro-

voking tom-foolery as the Coronation has been shown to be. We hear from the other side of the water the talk it has occasioned against the continuation of the reciprocity treaty. "If the Hawaiian government can afford to squander money in that style, the treaty will do harm rather than good: and the Hawaiians will be no better off for the three millions of dollars that the United States has let them have in the Customs revenue that the treaty has remitted." If the American residents cannot prevent such silliness and wastefulness, the three million dollars the United States government has *let them have* [italics mine], has been money thrown away. [18]

It was a fascinating argument that reciprocity, which allowed haole sugar planters to realize incredible personal and corporate profits through a virtually unlimited market into the United States, actually rewarded the Hawaiians, rather than the planters themselves, through the U.S. government's relinquishing of three million dollars in tariff revenues. Furthermore, the idea that it was the American residents' responsibility to prevent such "silliness" made veiled distinctions between Native and Hawaiianized subjects who chose to attend. Most of the ceremony's detractors actually came to the coronation and the celebrations that followed. Presumably their attendance was not silly because they were only observers.

The choice of whether or not to attend was the critical question for prominent Hawaiians. *Ka Nupepa Kuokoa* noted for the record that neither Queen Dowager Emma nor Princess Pauahi and her husband Charles Bishop would attend the festivities. Whether, in fact, they were offended by the large expense of the treasury for the affair, or perhaps were simply unwilling to legitimize Kalākaua's confirmation is difficult to say. In any case, they spared themselves the political embarrassment of being linked to a spectacular exhibition of the once-forbidden hula.

The coronation itself was a blending of Hawaiian and European symbols. Each ritual was punctuated by the choral singing of Christian anthems and led to the king actually crowning himself with a gold diadem before turning and crowning his queen. On the other hand, the king was also invested with a lei niho palaoa, kāhili, and an 'ahu 'ula (feather cloak) that had once belonged to the family of the Conqueror. The celebrations that followed were highlighted by some of the most lavish demonstrations of the ancient art of hula that had been seen, at least in public, since the 1820s. Those hula so disturbed William

Castle that he brought charges against publishers Robert Grieve and William Auld, who had printed the program (in Hawaiian), for publishing obscenities. The *Saturday Press* gave this opinion:

> Who shall draw the line between the *hula* dancing of Saturday afternoon and the horrible bestialities that were exhibited before a crowd of eager, impatient spectators as night came on? . . . We do but half disclose the awful blasphemy and the horrible filthiness of the actions and the language when we say that *meles* were sung deifying with rite of phallic worshiping in whose honor (?) these *meles* were composed, and glorifying him most of all by representations of vilest licentiousness. . . . We ask this community, if every one here has not lost all sense of propriety and dignity, how far is this thing to be allowed to go on?[19]

Nothing better describes the vast cultural abyss separating the kānaka and the haole than these remarks. It was not just that the mission children conceived the hula to be evil, but that its enjoyment was the clearest sign of weakness and degradation of the Natives. Once, when it was heard that Emma was entertaining guests in her home with the hula, a concerned haole sent this stern admonition: "It remains after all, a miserable relic of barbarism, the presence of which and its encouragement by the chiefs is unfavorable to the growth of pure morals among the people. Now I would ask, is it consistent with membership in any Christian Church to encourage the Hawaiian hula by being present at its performance, much more by setting it in operation at ones own premises? I was both surprised and grieved to find the Queen Dowager lending herself to such things. Where are her spiritual advisors?"[20]

Perhaps some of the foreigners in attendance also understood the political implications of the hula's presence at the coronation of the king. Hula was never just entertainment. It represented the very finest art of an ancient civilization and was itself political because many of the mele were praises of the Aliʻi genealogies and their relationships to the akua. This, along with its overt sexuality, made the hula a vehicle for blasphemy, and thus it had been suppressed by missionary doctrine and by law since 1827. Although it had persisted through the reigns of the Kamehamehas, danced in secret and performed discreetly for Alexander Liholiho and Lota Kapuāiwa, this was one of the first affairs of state in which it had been so privileged in over half a century.

Its performance put the missionary families in their place, as spectators, far more effectively than Gibson's seating arrangements. As resistance it might not have had quite the thrill of a military engagement, but it would be difficult to find a more significant contribution by this king than the rehabilitation of the dance. Whatever Emma's opinion of Kalākaua may have been, there is no question that by defying missionary conventions and glorifying the hula, the king was also ennobling her.

There were, however, some Native individuals who were as appalled by the hula as any missionary. One was Representative George Pilipō, who appeared at the trial of William Auld and testified for the prosecution that several of the Hawaiian words to the "Hula Kui" and the "Mele inoa," published in the program, were obscene. The fact that he had to be recruited for this testimony because William Castle did not understand the Hawaiian words sufficiently and assumed their obscene content by the performance of the dance itself is quite meaningful. The *Pacific Commercial Advertiser* reported: "Mr.

Figure 17. Reverend George Washington Pilipō, representative from Kona, Hawaiʻi, between 1860 and 1884. He led the attack with Nāwahī on reciprocity and the policies of Kalākaua until his death early in 1887. Photograph by Montano, courtesy of the Bishop Museum, Honolulu. CP 126,135.

G.W. Pilipo gave evidence as to what he believed to be the meaning of the words marked in the manuscript. (By order of the Court, this part of the testimony cannot be published.) Witness said that he had known people to be mistaken as to the precise meaning of words in their mother tongue. The words in question are in common use. He had seen them in hulas or meles before. Hulas of a certain nature always shocked his moral feelings. The advanced school children would be able to put a construction on those words." [21]

Native "informants" were necessary tools in the prosecution of their own culture. Moreover, Pilipō's testimony implied that the Hawaiian language contained such veiled meanings that ordinary translation into English would not reveal the obscenities that advanced (Native) schoolchildren would understand. This placed any haole ignorant of the language at a real disadvantage when it came to rooting out the masked corruptions in Hawaiian culture. This may well have been one of the issues prompting haole to assert that the language of the nation, sooner or later, would have to be English.

The symbols of this coronation, the hula, the feasting and revelry that continued for days, and the fact that it was open to even the poorest of the Natives, all of these were reproductions of an earlier time before there were haole. In every sense, therefore, this coronation was an affirmation of the *Hawaiianness* of this king. That these symbols also included a very real deference to Christian forms in the hymns and prayers in no way mitigated against the indignation of the missionary families, many of whom came away from this celebration with a renewed sense of opposition to Kalākaua and all of the Native traditions that he represented.

A Crowning Commerce

Why did the king consent to this remarkable spectacle, which at least some observers believe was calculated to offend some of the most powerful interests in the kingdom? The press and a good number of observers and historians came to believe that the king was simply being led around by his nose, and that the real instigator of every indignity to the haole was Walter Murray Gibson. [22] That belief, well represented in the haole press, led to the steady growth of opposition specifically to Gibson, while at the same time the fiction was maintained that the king himself was incapable of such designs.

But it is possible that Kalākaua did not spend over $50,000 of the kingdom's money to scandalize the missionary descendants. It is possible that Lili'u's explanation for the coronation is closer to the truth: that the king was reaching out to his Native subjects, providing an arena in which they could all come together and share an appreciation for the things that made them Hawaiian. It is not at all coincidental that the very aspects of the coronation that the haole objected to, the hula, the week-long feasting, the *expense*, were precisely those things that made it possible for over 5,000 people, most of them kānaka, to enjoy the hospitality of a ruling Mō'ī for the first time in anyone's memory.

Then again, no Mō'ī had ever had to strain so much to assure himself of the adoration or even the loyalty of the people. Here we are reminded anew that in a colonial milieu few cultural expressions are without political consequences. Perhaps the king was able to convince at least some of his kānaka that he was, indeed, one of them. Despite very well financed political opposition, the king's party would continue to lead, if not dominate, the legislative assembly in the next two elections.

Still, the king's choices could certainly be questioned from the standpoint of realpolitik values. By choosing to "ingratiate" himself with the relatively powerless Hawaiians, even going out of his way to insult the wealthy foreigners and haole citizens, Kalākaua appeared to be following a sure script for political suicide. Furthermore, it is possible that he was a foolish and inept leader, although very few of his contemporaries viewed him that way. They denounced him as a corrupt, untrustworthy monarch with strong pagan tendencies, but even Lorrin Thurston believed that he was also a very astute politician. [23]

However, Kalākaua was more than a politician; he was also a Native Ali'i Nui, born and reared to lead if not to rule. The circumstances of his period may not have been the most favorable for an Ali'i Nui; his people were almost a minority in fact and the prospects of ruling the arrogant haole may have been hopeless. But he would be the king of his people, if they would let him.

At the same time, the coronation and the responses to it were not just political postures. Some of the haole were deeply offended to see the work of their parents and grandparents disparaged. Their press referred to the coronation celebration as a "retrograde step of heathenism and a disgrace to the age" on top of being an unnecessary expense. The *Saturday Press* for one was not content to criticize the affair without calling for action: "Some of our people have been all too content to let this Coronation business go on and on. . . . When business is demoralized, when the good repute of this little kingdom for morality, thrift, carefulness is destroyed, when financial disasters threaten with their accumulating burdens of distress and sorrows, then such people will be the first to say, 'Why was not something done to prevent all the trouble?'"[24]

What exactly was the trouble? Surely one root of the foreigners' concerns was the prospect of "financial disasters." These concerns tended to be fixed on the continuation of reciprocity with the United States, which, as stated in the last chapter, had brought tremendous increases in land under cultivation, immigration of labor, and profits, especially to certain favorably placed planters and agents. By 1884, some seventy plantations valued at over 16 million dollars were producing over 60,000 tons of sugar annually.[25]

Not everyone was profiting, however. In fact, an 1884 recession in the United States brought a plummeting of sugar prices in the Islands and the financial ruin of several planters, including nobles George MacFarlane and Archibald Cleghorn. The former was in debt to Claus Spreckels for nearly one million dollars and was "stripped by Spreckels of his sugar agencies and just about all but his liquor business."[26] Spreckels was not the only shark feeding on the smaller fish, but he was the largest. Moreover, his near monopoly of the refining end gave him a powerful edge in determining the raw sugar prices in the kingdom. In 1884, in fact, only two sugar factors, Theo Davies and C. Brewer, were able to withstand Spreckel's pressure to bring the prices down. Nevertheless, the smaller American market that year reduced Davies' profits dramatically.[27]

Spreckels' economic power, coupled with his political influence with Kalākaua, did not only make him a powerful competitor for the other established haole planters and factors. The planters also viewed him as an outsider, a malihini interloper whose success threatened the close-knit collaboration of the other sugar firms.

Spreckels' domination of the sugar industry in Hawai'i was an uncomfortable and ongoing reminder of the downside of reciprocity with the United States. For clearly it was the successful ratification of the treaty that had brought the millionaire to Hawai'i in the first place, and the higher profit ceiling that kept him here. Furthermore, his economic power was growing. Largely through his personal influence with the king and Gibson, Spreckels had, by 1884, managed to practically monopolize the shipping of freight and passengers for his shipping company, Oceanic Line, with generous government subsidies for carrying the mail.[28] But more worrisome to the older "established" planters, merchants, and the Native opposition were Spreckels' intrusions on the very real banking monopoly of the Bishop Bank.

In one of their few legislative victories in 1884, the Independents were able to defeat the national bank bill that would have given wide-ranging financial opportunities and significant influence on the Hawaiian government's fiscal policy to a new bank owned by Spreckels in partnership with William Irwin and F. F. Low, former governor of California. In the face of widespread condemnation by the business community, the assembly voted 35 to 2 to table the bill indefinitely.[29] On the other hand, some of the legislators recognized that the kingdom's businessmen could use another source of capital. When Spreckels and Irwin eventually opened their bank, they forced Bishop to "resume payment of interest on savings accounts" and eventually "brought about lower interest rates on loans."[30] Historian Jacob Adler summed it up nicely: "There can be little doubt that by pursuing bold policies the Spreckels bank forced the conservative, well-managed Bishop bank to adopt bold policies to meet the competition. This created a banking atmosphere suitable to Hawaii's expanding economy in the postreciprocity boom."[31]

Perhaps this boldness inspired some of the antipathy that the Hawaiianized haole felt for Spreckels, Gibson, and the king himself. Everything had once been so nicely managed, with sound, conservative businessmen like Bishop maintaining a slow, steady, predictable growth and with the government spending money on practical things that would serve the continued expansion of industry. It had once been their kind of Utopia, really. The Natives, including the rulers, knew their place and were willing to be instructed on the mysteries of law and constitutional government. Even Kapuāiwa, with all of his monarchical will, had never interfered with the prerogatives of business.

In 1884, all of that seemed to be changing. The king was unpredictable and with Gibson's perverted guidance was willing to spend the tax dollars of the foreigners on frivolous attempts to woo the affections of his people. The older haole families were now the political outsiders with no way back in unless it was through control of the legislature. But even as the planters and merchants girded themselves for electoral battle, it must have rankled the Hawaiianized haole to have slipped so far from the influence that they and their fathers had once enjoyed and were now forced to scuffle with Native representatives for election. Worse, they would usually be outvoted in the assembly by the combined power of the king's representatives and the king's nobles.

Finally, reciprocity, which had brought prosperity to some, had also caused the kingdom and the planters themselves to become dependent on American economic and foreign policy, just as Nāwahī and Pilipō had predicted. In 1882 the prospects of extending or renewing the treaty were dealt a severe blow, it was felt, when Congress passed the Chinese Exclusion Act. Many local businessmen began to fear that Congress might withhold any extensions of reciprocity while Hawai'i was still importing Chinese labor. In fact they doubted that the kingdom could secure renewal without some kind of concession, perhaps even the cession of Pearl Harbor.

But that meant that the merchants were also dependent on the decisions of the king, who had steadfastly refused to consider the cession of Hawaiian lands. Kalākaua was not oblivious to the needs of the sugar industry; he himself had traveled to Japan in 1882 and had secured agreements with that government to increase Japanese labor in the Islands. One question was how long would the king continue to support the objectives of haole businessmen and planters? The fact that the government continued to be generally favorable to the sugar agenda was reassuring to some of the foreigners and white subjects who were reluctant to pursue any drastic changes in the government. But the failure of the Independent Party to significantly ameliorate the haole conception of helplessness would eventually reduce the influence of the conservative members like Bishop and encourage the younger, more aggressive factions in the white community. Indeed, the words of the very cautious and conservative Charles Bishop, written more than a decade before in a letter to former Minister Elisha Allen, are quite revealing of the white subjects' mounting frustration with Hawaiian monarchs, their new advisors, and even with the legislative system in place:

> You will, I know, be surprised, disappointed and almost offended, when you hear the proposal to cede Pearl River as a part of the basis for negotiation for Reciprocity, has been withdrawn. . . . The impression was general that His Majesty was at heart opposed . . . and unscrupulous efforts of Ward, Rhodes, Gibson and others was creating a strong prejudice in the minds of the natives, not only against

the Ministry, but against foreigners and especially Americans which would have secured certain defeat in the Legislature. . . . Of course, Gibson, Ward and Co. are in high glee, and I hear that Ward tells of the number of "old and influential" natives that he sent to talk privately with H.M. against cession. Is it not humiliating, discouraging and disgusting to be in such a position? Do you wonder that I wish to be free and away? But what good to Hawaiians, or anybody else, would come of my "throwing up the sponge?"[32]

In the end, it was not merely the fate of reciprocity that drove the haole to ever-escalating challenges to the king and the ministry. It was their sense that the king, the ministry, the legislature, the entire government was a foolish and comic apparatus without their leadership and control. Participation they had, but participation without control was "humiliating, discouraging and disgusting." It was this discourse, that the Hawaiian government was a mockery of "real" government, that convinced Native leaders such as Nāwahī to join the disaffected whites. As we shall see, the Native association with this party was vital to the party, not just for the Native voters they attracted, but for the legitimacy they offered to the white members.

Reform or Independence?

The first meeting of what would be known initially as the Independent Party took place on 16 April 1883 in the offices of the Hawaiian Planters' Labor and Supply Co. on Merchant Street in Honolulu. It was an organizational meeting attended by thirteen haole businessmen and lawyers who were intent on sending more business-oriented representatives to the assembly in the following election. Most of the members were Hawai'i-born sons and grandsons of ABCFM missionaries and included former legislators such as William Castle, George Wilcox, A. S. Hartwell, S. L. Austin, and William O. Smith.[33]

From the discussions that took place in their initial meetings, it is clear that these members considered themselves spokesmen for the planters and the businessmen. Stafford L. Austin, who had been a representative during the special session of 1855, indicated that "the time had arrived for the planters to take concerted action."[34] But although they had no problem presenting themselves as the party of business and sugar, they were quite unwilling to be labeled a "missionary" party. "Mr. Spaulding urged that in approaching persons to make it appear that the committee is a committee of prominent Honolulu businessmen—and not a 'missionary' movement, nor that of any clique." Though nine of the thirteen founding members listed above were sons or grandsons of ABCFM missionaries, the executive committee fully endorsed the motion.[35]

This executive committee consisted of S. B. Dole, Castle, and Smith, who generally met thereafter without the other members present. The executive committee was charged with recruiting support, including contributions from business leaders and planters. They were also to gather a list of names of suitable candidates for the legislature from the other islands. The members were to submit lists after approaching their friends and associates to join and pledge funds.

At the same time, the Independent Party made determined efforts to include Native candidates on their ticket and continually tried to exploit the political ambivalence of the Native voters toward the king and his administration. However the party did not ask any Natives to sit on the executive committee or to serve as officers.

By 10 May, the executive committee had met three times and had managed to construct a plan for financing the upcoming election. Estimating that the total cost for running candidates from every district would be as high as $40,000, the executive committee directed $14,000 to Oʻahu and $11,000 to Hawaiʻi Island. Their apportionment reflected their understanding of the political strength of their candidates in each respective district. Hāmākua, Kaʻū, and Kohala, each represented by only one legislator, were budgeted $3,000 apiece. Hilo, with two legislators, was allocated only $2,000, an obvious recognition of the political strength of its candidates.[36] One of them was to be Nāwahī. Two weeks earlier, Castle had been authorized to go to Hilo and "consult with Nawahi as to the wisdom of him, Pilipo, and Kalua making tours about the Islands and addressing the people and as to his view of the best methods and times—and to state that expenses would be paid. But not to communicate details as to amount of proposed fund etc."[37]

It was an interesting constraint for Castle who had, in the very first meeting, expressed his belief "that the organization should be open to all, its meetings and minutes not be secret and that even Spreckels would join."[38] That proved to be a vain hope, because of Spreckels' connections to the king and Gibson. But the executive committee's decision does seem to reflect a closing of the ranks, as the party organizers appear to have shared a more trusting relationship with wealthy sugar planters and a different relationship with Native candidates, even those with such anti-Kalākaua credentials as Nāwahī.

What little that haole and kanaka candidates had in common was further compromised by the Natives' inherent inferiority in this relationship. If there was an ideological common ground, it was the issue of the government's monetary policies. Both the Native and haole opposition believed Gibson to be the real culprit leading the king down the path of fiscal irresponsibility that could, for the foreigners, bring financial instability and even ruin. But for the Native opposition, it was the independence of the entire nation that was at stake.

The very term independence had different meanings that were not altogether compatible. Nāwahī had used the word kū'oko'a (to stand apart) in several of his speeches and clearly understood it to mean not only opposition to the administration, but also national sovereignty. *Ko Hawaii Pae Aina* editor Joseph Kawainui reinforced the idea that national independence was threatened by the government's spending and subtly alerted his Native subscribers to a discomfiting truth: "We are not comfortably situated due to the fact that our spending exceeds our revenues. One thing is understood, the aina [the land] has entered a mire of debt of $84,700 inside of the past three months. Some individual haole are better off than the nation" [translation mine].[39]

The kingdom's debt, such as it was, placed the Natives in a disturbing position vis-à-vis the haole. The debt was evidence to men like Nāwahī that the kingdom was incompetently managing its own affairs. The symbolic and real declarations of autonomy from haole influence and leadership coming from the king and the premier only worsened matters because it made the administration solely at fault for the debt. Over time, the administration's spending initiatives on matters relating to expanding the kingdom's role in foreign affairs and rejuvenating Native traditions would all be criticized as a waste of the nation's revenues.

Moreover, at least one candidate, George Pilipō, engaged in highly personal attacks of Kalākaua's National candidates on the island of Hawai'i, calling D. H. Nahinu of South Kona "a liar for the Ministers' party," and Hāmākua's Z. Kalai a man with "a full mouth and a fat belly."[40] These condemnations implied that those representatives' legislative votes were essentially bought by the administration, which rewarded them with civil service jobs in addition to their elected positions. Pilipō thus portrayed the administration as nothing more than a patronage system for supporters of the king.

There was some truth to his accusations. Nevertheless, from the standpoint of Kalākaua's loyalists, the kingdom had actually been and continued to be a vast patronage system for the sugar growers and merchants in the Islands. In fact, both Gibson and the *Pacific Commercial Advertiser* strenuously argued that the kingdom's debt sprang mainly from the government's underwriting of sugar:

> From 1878 to 1886 there had been 12,233 immigrants introduced by the Hawaiian Government. The cost to the public treasury for immigration from 1864 to 1885 inclusive was $951,679.79 and to planters $567,449.70, making an expenditure all told of $1,519,129.49. . . . These figures furnish a key to the increase of the public debt, about which Opposition writers puzzle their brains to such little purpose. The present Administration borrowed, under the Loan Acts of 1876 and 1884, in round numbers, $980,000, and has expended in immigration during the last two biennial periods, $672,191.41, the balance of loan being applied to other public purposes provided for by law. . . . This is a very admirable showing, and should satisfy the class which is now displaying the greatest hostility against the Government, that whatever faults may be charged against the Administration, neglect of the planters' interests is not one of them. [41]

Although the newspapers often disparaged kānaka as uneducated or too inexperienced with the intricacies of modern government to properly conduct their offices, Pilipō's attack demonstrates that even Natives were willing to indirectly support that allegation to strengthen their own opposition to the king. By assuming that appointments of Natives were evidence of government corruption, Pilipō reinforced the notion that the government was run by unqualified or incompetent kānaka.

From March 1883, the Hawaiian newspaper *Ko Hawaii Pae Aina* continuously monitored the public debt, publishing the kingdom's spending record right up to the election in February. In December, this Native newspaper edited by J. Kawainui issued one of its regular criticisms of the administration's legislative supporters: "The representatives who attach themselves to the Ministry and the Nobles, who cling to government positions, who take bribes, who fail to execute justly the will of the makaainana, who enact harmful laws that increase the Hawaiian government's debt, who only spend the government's money on works that do not stand for the wishes of the nation, are enemies of the nation" [translation mine]. [42]

In previous issues, Kawainui had gone on record supporting the Independent slate of candidates, specifically targeting members of the legislature, all political allies of Gibson, to be voted out of office. His newspaper was particularly fond of referring to those representatives as the Hoopili Meaai party, a derogatory term that literally meant "to attach oneself to the food." However, there is evidence that Kawainui's political support of the Independents was also bought. In the 29 May meeting of the executive committee, this was entered in the minutes: "Castle reports arrangements made with Kawainui to subscribe for such number of the Ko Hawaii Pae Aina as Castle shall name[,] to be for quarterly in advance, provided the paper conforms with the views of Castle, and advocating such candidates as Castle should name. Kawainui agreed to the proposition."[43]

This does not necessarily mean that the *Pae Aina* editor was insincere in his support for the Independents. But Castle's insistence on making this editorial support a business proposition and emphasizing that the subscriptions were conditioned on that support certainly indicates that the haole party members were leaving nothing to chance whenever they dealt with Native partisans.

It was a strangely conducted campaign. The harshest criticism of the administration came from the Native opposition and from extremely sarcastic and malevolent editorials, some of them by Lorrin Thurston, in the *Hawaiian Gazette*. Meanwhile the rest of the haole candidates were free to conduct much more moderate campaigns, which, in all likelihood, strengthened their appeal among Native voters.

Independent candidates were largely successful, outside of Honolulu, in the February elections. As most of the newspapers and journals noted with pleased surprise, "Every foreigner who ran, outside of Honolulu, was elected, and in most instances by considerable majorities. . . . In every district in which a foreigner was elected, the native voters are in an overwhelming majority."[44] Native electoral support was unquestionably the determining factor in the election of haole in this and other years.

Although the heaviest concentration of foreigners lived in Honolulu, it is also true that those eligible to vote were still a pronounced minority, perhaps as few as 300 of 2,700 qualified voters. As the *Advertiser* reported, "The total number might probably have reached 3000 if all of them had paid their taxes and claimed their privileges."[45] Here again was the accusation that the haole were, even in this elec-

Table 9. Kingdom-wide Election Results,[a] February 1884

DISTRICT	ELECTED	OTHER CANDIDATES
Hilo	J. Nāwahī (I) 500 D. H. Hitchcock (N) 485	D. B. Wahine (N) 196 J. K. Akina (N) 157 E. P. Hōʻai (I) 20
Puna	Honorable J. M. Kauwila (I) 117	E. Kekoa (N) 99 J. W. Kumahoa (N) Reverend J. N. Kamoku (I)
Kohala	Godfrey Brown (I) 335	G. P. Kamauoha (N) 225 J. W. Moanauli (N) 90 D. S. Kahoʻokano (N) 5 William White (N) Z. Kalai (N) Z. Kanealai (I) 2
Hāmākua	J. K. Kaunamanō (N) 135	C. Williams (N) 104 J. Welewele (N) W. A. Mio (I) P. Kaʻaekuahiwi (I)
Makawao	J. Kamakele (N) 225	J. Kalama (I) 118 Kapule (N) 13
Wailuku	L. H. P. Kaʻulealio (?) 358 W. O. Smith (I) 355	George E. Richardson (N) 255 W. B. Keanu (N) 143 M. Kealoha (N) 69 J. Haole (I) 48 S. Maule (N) 34 T. B. Cummings (I) 22 Makekoa (I) L. W. P. Kānealiʻi (I)
Lāhaina	J. W. Kalua (I) 190 Luther Aholo (N) 181	Kia Nāhaolelua (N) 140 D. Kamaiopili (N) 99
Kaʻanapali	J. Richardson (N) 75	J. Kaukau (N) 38 J. K. Nahaku (N) 12 Kaluahino 1

(continued on next page)

Table 9 *(continued)*. Kingdom-wide Election Results,[a] February 1884

DISTRICT	ELECTED	OTHER CANDIDATES
Hāna	J. Gardner (I) 154	W. H. Halstead (I) S. W. Kaʻai (N) C. K. Kakani (N) J. K. Hanuna (N)
South Kona	D. H. Wahinu (N) 154	C. W. P. Kāʻeo (N) S. Kāʻeo (I)
North Kona	G. W. Pilipō (I) 136	J. G. Hoapili (N) 79 J. K. Nāhale (?) 36 J. W. Keliikoa (N) J. Palapala (N)
Kaʻū	J. Kaʻuhane (I) 198	J. N. Kapahu (N) 136
Molokaʻi and Lānaʻi	S. K. Kupihea (N) 208 J. Nakaleka (N) 208	E. Jones (N) D. Lokana (N) A. P. Pākī (N) S. K. Keaweolu (N) W. A. Kukamana (N) J. W. M. Poʻohea (I) S. Paulo (I) D. Kalauaokalani (I) M. Kāne (I)
Līhuʻe and Kōloa	S. B. Dole (I)	T. Kalaeone (N)
Waimea and Niʻihau	W. E. Rowell (I)	J. Kauaʻi (N)
Hanalei	Honorable G. B. Palohau (N)	D. W. H. Kaʻupena (I) J. H. Kahilina (I) J. H. Kawelo (I)
ʻEwa and Waiʻanae	Honorable Frank Brown (I) 234	J. P. Kama (N) 93 J. Kaʻanaʻana[b] (N) A. Kaʻoliko (I)

(continued on next page)

Table 9 *(continued)*. Kingdom-wide Election Results,[a] February 1884

DISTRICT	ELECTED	OTHER CANDIDATES
Koʻolaupoko	Asa Kaulia (N) 207	J. K. Kaoliko (I) 88 G. Barenaba (N) 11 S. M. Kaʻaukai (N) 6 Kalaʻaukane (N)
Koʻolauloa	Cecil Brown (I) 100	J. M. Kauaikaua (N) 64 J. Kanui (N) 55 Honorable J. Kaluhi (N) 24 J. L. Naʻili (I)
Waialua	J. Amara (N) 97	S. P. Kaʻakua (N) 58 J. N. Kaiaikawaha (I) 41 S. K. Mahoe 8
Honolulu	J. L. Kaulukou (N) 1,129 James Keau (N) 1,123 J. T. Baker (N) 1,118 E. K. Lilikalani (N) 1,112	J. O. Carter (I) 829 A. K. Kūnuiakea (I) 804 J. U. Kawainui (I) 800 A. P. Kalaukoa (I) 793 Frank Pahia (N) 1

Source: From *Daily Bulletin,* 5 February 1884, p. 2, col. 4.

Note: Party designations: (I), Independent; (N), National.

[a] Missing results were not reported in this issue of the *Bulletin.*

[b] J. Kaʻanaʻana, an experienced legislator from these districts (1878, 1880), died a few days before the election. *Pacific Commercial Advertiser,* 9 January 1884.

tion, largely indifferent, unwilling still to participate as voters, much less run for office.

One statistic the newspapers did not print was the number of white candidates, recruited by the party's executive committee, who ended up withdrawing their names from consideration before the tickets were printed. Had Lorrin Thurston run from Waialua, for example,[46] it is possible that he would have defeated the National candidate Jesse Amara. Fellow annexationist Sereno Bishop might have done the same in Kāʻanapali. Altogether, some fairly well placed individuals and original members of the party such as Henry Baldwin (Makawao) and William O. Smith (Lāhaina) declined to run on their party's ticket, leaving in each case a clear field for a National candidate.

These results suggest that despite the claim that a color line existed in Hawaiian electoral politics intended to keep haole out of the legislature, in reality race consciousness worked, if anything, in their favor. This the *Hawaiian Monthly* quickly recognized, but then proceeded to denounce the Nationals for not putting up a single haole for election: ". . . we say that very heavy responsibility rests upon the managers of the Government side, for the attempt to introduce a distinct and positive 'color line' into the recent contest. It can hardly be by accident that every candidate on the government ticket in every district, was a Hawaiian."[47]

Perhaps there was a deliberate attempt to keep whites from enlisting in the National "Party," but because there appeared to be no formal organization, certainly nothing like that of the Independents, it is probable that the "color line" was assumed. Moreover, with the steady representation of the Nationals as the party of extravagance, corruption, and bribery in the English and Native newspapers, it may have been difficult for the Nationals to recruit haole candidates in the first place. Certainly, the Nationals' motto "Hawai'i for Hawaiians" left little doubt that their agenda was to place Natives in key government positions, but haole candidates, even those who professed not to belong to either party, chose to run on the Independent ticket. The *Pacific Commercial Advertiser*, which, despite its protestations of objectivity, usually favored Gibson's policies in its editorials,[48] actually endorsed J. O. Carter in Honolulu, bemoaning the fact that he ran as an Independent: "For Honolulu there is but one white candidate in the field. If he should lose his election it will be because he has permitted his name to be put upon a ticket which is recognized as that of a faction of disappointed men. . . . This gentleman, J. O. Carter is eminently fitted to this city, and he has authorized us to say that he has no sympathy with the party—a noisy but not a large one—whose sole bond of union is the desire to overturn the present administration."[49]

Finally, there was some ambiguity about the political leanings of several candidates. D. H. Hitchcock, who was listed as a National candidate for Hilo, actually voted with the Independents in the assembly and was one of at least three candidates, including Sanford Dole and William Rowell, who benefited from the help of both the Independent Party and government officials. Indeed, the affiliations were so confusing that the historian Kuykendall was misled by some very sloppy newspaper reporting. He listed David H. Hitchcock, son of missionary Henry and Rebecca Hitchcock, as a National candidate and later reported that there were no haole candidates in the National Party. The latter, it turned out, was true because Hitchcock was an Independent.

The scholarly treatment of the 1884 and 1886 elections as narrow victories for the National Party is overly simplistic. The choices presented to the kanaka voters were never only about the race or political alliance of the candidates. Rather, those choices had much more to do with accepting or rejecting the construction of the king's administration as incompetent and corrupt and damning, by extension, all those who voted for their supporters. Very little had changed with regard to the characterization of Native voters as imprudent, except for the presence of a formal opposition that invited the kānaka to prove their worthiness by enlisting with their party.

But the fact that Natives were not at all involved in the platforms, policies, or any of the internal discussions of the Independents substantiated the racial differences between the opposition and the government. When even editorial support in the "Native" newspapers had to be guaranteed by subsidy, it is clear that the party leaders were not especially interested in Native input as much as Native compliance with their views. In the end, the Independents' claim that their party was not the haole party was not credible to anyone: not to the press, the voters, and the candidates, and certainly not to the government, all of whom appeared to understand that it was.

Race was an issue that the haole Independents employed guardedly and obliquely. As the *Saturday Press* proclaimed in 1880, "It is not a question of race, but of fitness. Let the Native prove himself qualified for higher office. . . ."[50] Such proof could only come from the willingness of the kānaka to declare their "independence" from the king and join as junior associates in a partnership with whites.

But race was, perhaps, the only issue that could still unite the kanaka voters. By 1886, the Nationals would be much more vociferous in their assertions that any Native who voted for a white man was disloyal to his own race. Jesse Amara, who won election from Waialua in 1884 and 1886, gave a strongly worded speech during the latter campaign in which he "effectively defeated his white opponents by first itemizing their Assembly records . . . their anti-native legislative stands, and finally concluding . . . 'Is this their love for you, Hawaiians?'"[51]

Another National representative, John Kaulukou, "racked native candidates who sympathized with Caucasians . . . after carefully piling up factual evidence against his opposition concluded . . . that his native opponents 'kissed the hoofs' and 'did the bidding' of white enemies of the Hawaiian race, and that they 'wanted to run the country in their own interests.'"[52]

As in the "riot" of 1874, the attacks were conducted by Natives against Natives over issues of loyalty and kanaka identity. The Nationals certainly campaigned against haole candidates, but not with the same viciousness that they reserved for men like J. W. Kalua and Pilipō. Again, the whites were exempt from this discussion because they were not Native and therefore could not be expected to be faithful to Hawaiians.

Yet there were a few haole who conceived that some form of faithfulness to kānaka was not only possible, but a moral necessity. In 1884 a series of articles from the *Hawaiian Monthly*, a journal that ran for exactly one year, described with apparent sympathy the Natives'

Figure 18. John Lota Kaulukou, representative from 1880 to 1886. He was a strong supporter of Kalākaua and an outspoken opponent of the Bayonet Constitution. Photograph by I. W. Taber, courtesy of the Bishop Museum, Honolulu. CP 73,190.

political difficulties. In these articles, appearing just as the assembly was conducting its business, the *Monthly* tried to conciliate between the political divisions that marked Native and white relations, pointing out to newly arrived foreigners that the Natives' political weakness was not something to be exploited, but understood and assisted:

> [T]he native though numerically strong, is actually weak. Notwithstanding all that has been done for him by well-meaning, but not always judicious friends, he is still placed in circumstances which are in many respects very unfavorable to his success and permanence. . . . Those of us who choose to come here from abroad to reside, should accept the situation in good faith and recognize the fact that we—the white men—are the foreigners. . . . What is wanted is that the people—the bulk of the population both white and brown— including the natives of the soil and those who come here in good faith to make their homes among them, should realize that their interests in this as in so many other matters, are one and the same and should learn to act together for the common advantage.[53]

This characterization of the Native writ large as understudy to the whites when it came to politics was the most reasonable position conceived possible by haole in the kingdom. The *Monthly*'s claim suggested that there were two kinds of foreigners, those who came in good faith and, presumably, those who did not, and called on the "good faith" haole to accept some responsibility for uplifting the Natives and for working toward a common future. Such were the admonitions of the *Advertiser* in 1884:

> They claim for the white foreigner (in which term we include the white descendants of foreigners born in this country) a paramount position in the Government. This is the bond of unity which keeps these heterogeneous elements together. The other party is more compact. It would include the whole native race if personal enmity to, or at least objection to, the King did not cause a certain number of Hawaiians to stand aloof from it. Its binding principle is Hawaii for the Hawaiians. . . . This country is neither for the Hawaiian nor for the foreigner, but for both. We want to see a third party . . . a party of conciliation.[54]

The argument that a conciliation party could remove the racial tensions of the age begged the actual conditions of Hawai'i's political society and drove an ideological wedge between Native electors and candidates. Voting for haole was proof enough of the Natives' desire to be conciliatory. Offering up Native candidates on the Independents' ticket was certainly considered proof enough for that party. However, neither demonstration went to the root of racial politics, which, by discourse, positioned the Natives as inferior to the whites.

At the end of the 1884 session, a reception and banquet was held in Honolulu for the Independent members of the assembly and was well attended by the business community and their wives. Nāwahī, Charles Bishop, and former minister William Green were among the few that did not attend. Both Pilipō and J. W. Kalua were honored that evening along with the other eleven representatives and nine nobles that constituted the opposition party. Kalua's speech especially was deeply revealing of the racial tensions that saturated the kingdom's politics, despite the party's claims to the contrary: "I have been taunted with having no independence; with being a mere satellite of Mr. Jones, of Mr. Castle, of Mr. Hartwell and of being the tail of the missionaries; But I can truthfully say that while believing in the integrity of these gentlemen, I have voted at all times for what I myself thought was the best." [55]

It is interesting that Kalua felt it necessary to proclaim his personal independence from the "missionaries," but that may, in fact, have been the key reason that the Nationals continued to flourish right up until franchise itself was disfigured in 1887. Nāwahī's personal popularity and integrity notwithstanding, there is no question that the Native opposition's alliance with the haole in 1884 brought little to their own individual political strength, and both Nāwahī and Pilipō were defeated in 1886 after extensive campaigning against them by the king.

The banquet itself was an interesting counterpoint to the king's coronation the year before. As a celebration of the modest accomplishments of the Independent legislators, the tone of the affair was generally subdued except when speakers addressed the subject of the king or the subject of race. The welcoming address was given by Noble Godfrey Rhodes, a Kalākaua appointee who had allied himself with the Independents on the first day of the session and was elected president of the assembly. He belittled the character of his former benefactor with his patronizing disappointment:

We all of us bear loyalty to the sovereign [sic]. . . . Yet we consider
it a lamentable thing that the sovereign [sic] of these islands should

not have the best of men in the people by which he is surrounded—
that he is led away by evil counsels, that he has been led away. I
speak it kindly, that it appears by the counsels he follows that he has
the gratifications of his own desires at heart. (Applause) I say this,
sir, not of any unkindness of feeling for him, but in sorrow that he
should be led away by men who have such a lust for place and power
that they will sacrifice every principle of truth and justice to hold
their positions. (Loud applause.)[56]

But it was Noble T. S. Walker's speech that received the most
applause as he took on the whole question of whether haole had any
political legitimacy in Hawai'i. Walker placed the argument in the
most idealistic of contexts:

> There may be attempts made to lessen the importance of this testi-
> monial meeting . . . by the assertion that, being composed to so con-
> siderable extent of people of foreign extraction, this is a demonstra-
> tion in the interests of foreigners. Such a charge against us *is not true*
> and will be the resource only of weak-minded or else absolutely
> unprincipled men. . . . Many of us are born here and educated here,
> and most of us have the whole of our worldly interests existent in this
> country and dependent upon its institutions; institutions which, by
> the law of the land, are to extend their benefits to all, irrespective of
> race.[57]

Walker's assertion that Hawai'i-born haole had a particular interest vested in the Islands was greeted with thunderous applause. Perhaps the notion that their material success in Hawai'i should be
accompanied by a sense of shame, or at least responsibility, chafed
against their own Calvinist upbringing. The ovation that greeted
Walker's claim may well have been an acknowledgment that they were
not, in fact, responsible for shepherding Hawaiians to greater compe-
tence in their political participation. After all, were not so many of
them Native born? What about their rights? Although no one that evening rose to point out that none of their rights was being threatened or
that, in the area of economic benefits, they had enjoyed these in conspicuous contrast with the Natives, it may have dawned on the party
faithful that with men like Dole, Castle, and Thurston, the white community had all the natives that it needed.

Ultimately, it was the king as symbol of the nation's independence
that compromised kānaka unity. The more Kalākaua was constructed

as an unreliable and incompetent ruler, the more daring the haole became in their assertions that monarchy, national independence, or both, were fated to extinction. Such assertions left the Nationals defiantly defending the king and Gibson, but left Nāwahī mā with very little political room to maneuver. The fact that members of their own party were suggesting that the demise of independence was imminent made any accommodation of their rivals in the legislature or any display of support for the king impossible.

Moreover, the linking of the king and the incompetent Native voters together was a remarkable accomplishment for the Independent Party in 1884. It was not particularly successful with the kānaka voters, who, perversely, displayed their resistance to this discourse by electing fewer Independents to the legislature in 1886. But this linkage played a significant role in the construction of the king not just as an embarrassment to the haole who participated in government, but a menace to their freedom and economic future. Thus, when both Pilipō and Nāwahī were defeated by National candidates in the 1886 election, Thurston and other annexationists were able to charge that the Native electorate had finally been corrupted beyond all redemption. Not only had they rejected haole, they had turned away from the only worthy kānaka among them.

A Foundering Independence

At the midpoint of Kalākaua's reign, despite having a firm support in the electorate and a comfortable margin in the legislature, the actual future of his government was already in serious jeopardy. It was jeopardized not so much by the administration's policies but by the haole-formulated discourse that the king, his institutions, and in fact his own people were anachronous relics waiting to be replaced. Whether the Hawaiians were doomed because of their paganism, their devotion to their chiefs, their want of private property, their laziness, their lack of sanitation, or, finally, their opposition to haole, in the end they were just *naturally* doomed.

It was a political debate in which the haole enjoyed, as usual, the advantage of distance and detachment. In one editorial, Lorrin Thurston commented that despite the fact that there was general support for an independent government "in the interests of the native race. . . . When these islands cease to be self-governing the United States will take possession. . . ." For this, Thurston claimed, "The men who are doing the most to produce results which will overthrow this government are those who have the ear of the King; and he, led on by infatuation, is pursuing a course which is fraught with danger."[58]

Others such as Sereno Bishop went further than this, asserting that the end of monarchy and its replacement by an American republic was merely a natural process that Hawaiians should accept "as the true and best form for all enlightened people."[59] Although Sereno Bishop argued that for practical purposes Hawai'i should continue to maintain independence, his comments indicated that such independence could exist only so long as it suited haole: "As in due time the native sovereignty comes to its natural end, whether by the decay of the people, the lack of chiefs, or a general end of its usefulness, there will cease to be any other possible rallying point for a throne, even if there were any further call for such an institution. Republican government will be the natural, fitting and obvious arrangement. . . . It will doubtless be necessary to restrict the suffrage with care in the case of persons with foreign blood to those at home in the English tongue."[60]

These claims, widely read and reiterated, did not only undermine Kalākaua's rule, they savaged the one remaining symbol of any potency connecting kānaka to their traditional past and to any hope for the future. After all, if the Mō'ī were to be discarded, the Natives a poor and fading minority, and English the natural language of the new republic, then what was the point of independence from America, Great Britain, or Canada for that matter? Moreover, if Bishop were right, there was nothing whatsoever to be done. The Native Hawaiians, their language, arts, their very difference would all soon evaporate, willy-nilly, along with their political sovereignty.

It was not at all "frippery and nonsense," as some critics charged, that Kalākaua energetically promoted such activities and organizations as the hula, the creation and funding of a Board of Genealogy by the legislature, the revival of the Hale Naua,[61] and the publication of Hawaiian mo'olelo as well as the epic mo'o kū'auhau (chiefly genealogy) known as the Kumulipo. On the contrary, these were highly assertive of the glory and vitality of Hawaiian traditions and affirmed the cultural distinctions between Natives and foreigners. Furthermore, had they not been published in his reign, while there were still Hawaiians alive who maintained an oral mastery of these texts, it is probable that they would have been lost forever.

Indeed, it is not difficult to imagine how crippled any revival of Hawaiian sovereignty and cultural expression would have been for future generations without the contributions of this Mōʻī. However, his vigorous support of such cultural initiatives further alienated him from what was left of his haole support and has earned him the scorn of their historians. By the end of the 1884 session, Thurston was preparing the editorial slaughter of the king himself, arguing that even if the corruption in government was being engineered by the ministers, the king was ultimately to blame: "What they have done is known to the King. How they have done it is known to the King. How they have choked off investigation by means of their own votes and those of bought and paid for office holders and Government contract jobbers, is known to the King; and yet he maintains them in office and entrusts to them the guiding of the destinies of the nation. Is such a man to be religiously free from criticism, and held to be above discussion by the very men who took him up out of poverty and obscurity and placed him in the position of trust which he now abuses?"[62]

Wherever the king demonstrated his "unworthiness," the Independents were there to assault him, his cabinet, or his representatives. By 1886 a growing list of their complaints would include everything from accusations of corruption to defaming him for his substantial support of Native arts. Ironically, the monarch was no less important a symbol at that point than those who had preceded him. But in 1886, the king symbolized everything that was wrong with Hawaiʻi and its people. The fact that the people (that is, the Native people) refused to join the haole in rejecting their king painted them with the same contemptible stripe.

The election of 1886 was, therefore, a revealing disclosure of the Independents' failure to further separate the kanaka voters from the king. Not only were three fewer Independents elected than in 1884, but haole Independent candidates were defeated by Native Nationals in eight of the twenty districts including Honolulu.[63] More disturbing for the party was the defeat of their prize Native candidates Nāwahī and Pilipō, which they attributed to extensive campaigning against them by the king. Kuykendall explained: "In support of the Government party candidates, the King made two electioneering trips to Maui and Hawaii. He was especially anxious to defeat the three leading native candidates on the Independent ticket, Joseph Nawahi, G.W. Pilipo, and J.W. Kalua. . . . It was reliably reported that 'all Government officials were warned that they must support the Government ticket.'"[64]

If the king did, indeed, bring some intimidation to bear on government officials, it was likely in response to the news reports that several Independent candidates had been supported by government officials in the 1884 elections. Undoubtedly, the king had "his personal influence" and the "weight of his high position"[65] to influence the vote, but it is interesting that the king confined his activity to campaigning against Native candidates instead of also going after haole critics such as Lorrin Thurston, Sanford Dole, and William Kinney. This suggests that the numbers of National candidates elected may not have been as important as divesting the Independent party of Native legislators.

Toward that end, the king was not completely successful, because Reverend Ka'uhane was reelected in Ka'ū. Nevertheless, several influential Hawaiians were turned down at the polls, and when the voting was completed only four of the ten victorious Independent candidates were Natives. At least for 1886, the image of the Independent party as a Native and haole party was seriously compromised by the voters' choices.

Kalākaua may well have benefited from the passing of the three remaining chiefly descendants of the Conqueror: Luka Ke'elikōlani in 1883, Bernice Pauahi in the fall of 1884, and, of special significance, Queen Emma on 25 April 1885. Later in January, the *Pacific Commercial Advertiser* reported that the election campaign "was not a struggle between two great chiefs as in former elections. The Aliis are now all on one side."[66] The queen, an important and unifying symbol for the Native opposition, was gone, and it would have been interesting to see how Nāwahī and Pilipō would have conducted themselves in the legislature had they been elected.

The assertion that the Native nation was destined to either lose its independence or else be increasingly led by whites may have also affected the kanaka voters. It is possible that voters came to believe the arguments of the pro-Administration *Advertiser:* "If a single native votes for a candidate on the Opposition ticket he is attacking the independence of the country and signing away to strangers the graves and bones of his fathers. There is no middle ground to take."[67]

The Independents responded with accusations concerning the conduct of the election, including claims that Kalākaua had abused his franking privileges to supply free gin to government supporters before the election. There is evidence that this was so.[68] There is, however, no evidence to prove that liquor played a larger role in determining how Natives voted than their affection for the king, their favor of indi-

Table 10. Legislative Assembly, 1886. Luther Aholo resigned as vice-president on 13 October and accepted appointment as minister of the interior. J. L. Kaulukou resigned on the same date to accept appointment as attorney general.

NOBLES	REPRESENTATIVES
Luther Aholo*	Luther Aholo (Vice-President)
Charles Reed Bishop	Jesse Amara
John E. Bush	J. T. Baker
Archibald S. Cleghorn	Cecil Brown
Robert J. Creighton*	William R. Castle
John T. Dare*	Charles H. Dickey*
John O. Dominis	Sanford B. Dole
James I. Dowsett	F. H. Hayselden*
Walter Murray Gibson	Simon W. Ka'ai
Charles T. Gulick	J. W. Kalua
Paul Isenberg	J. Kaua'i
Charles H. Judd	John Ka'uhane
J. Ka'ae	A. Kauhi*
Paul Kanoa	J. A. Kaukau
John M. Kapena	Asa Kaulia
J. L. Kaulukou*	John L. Kaulukou
H. Kūihelani	J. K. Kaunamanō
G. W. MacFarlane	J. Keau
J. H. S. Martin	E. Kekoa
John Mott-Smith	Edward K. Lilikalani
Paul Neumann	J. K. Nāhale*
John P. Parker	David H. Nāhinu
Samuel Parker*	A. P. Paehaole*
Godfrey Rhodes	F. Pahia
J. S. Walker (President)	G. B. Palohau
Hermann A. Widemann	G. E. Richardson
Samuel G. Wilder	Lorrin A. Thurston*
	J. Wight *

Source: Lydecker, 1918, *Roster Legislatures of Hawaii,* 156.
* First year.

vidual representatives, or their mistrust of the Independent Party. Nevertheless, some of the newspapers were quick to assume that drink was the only thing that could have impelled Natives to reject the haole party. The *Daily Honolulu Press* editorialized: ". . . it was a sad sight to see the native voters bartering their birth-right of Hawaiian Independence for a glass of gin. It is not a part of prophecy to declare by the testimony furnished by the pages of Hawaiian history, that, if such debauchery is kept up, the Hawaiian Monarchy will be, in a few short years, a thing of the past."[69]

Perhaps it should not have been surprising to anyone that there were still more things that Natives were guilty of that would doom their independence. Although there was no suggestion that alcohol consumption by haole in any way affected their ability to govern or vote, the ascribing of widespread alcoholism to the kānaka also came with its own "proof." It was "known" that Natives were inveterate alcoholics; therefore, the availability of alcohol meant that most, if not all, of those who voted the National ticket were drunk. In one efficient discourse the legitimacy of the king, the Natives in his party, and the vote itself was summarily dismissed.

In the end the positioning of a venal and ineffectual king alongside his drunken or otherwise ineffectual Native subjects finally rid the sons of missionaries of whatever lingering responsibilities they may have entertained for maintaining a Hawaiian nation. For those who supported the king, there were few political strategies available that would dignify them and their monarch that did not involve indignant and racial challenges to that haole discourse. But it was an abrupt lesson in realpolitik administered to the king and to the kingdom in 1886 that demonstrated how vulnerable the nation was to the Western powers' colonial aims in the Pacific. This lesson diminished the kingdom's prestige and, thus, the willingness of the haole to be associated with it.

The Polynesian Federation

In 1885 Kalākaua and Gibson had initiated correspondence with various Western nations, including the United States, Britain, and Germany, over the issue of Pacific Islanders and their continued independence from colonial rule. The origins of Kalākaua's foreign policy are interesting enough and could easily fill a chapter of their own.

Kuykendall and other writers gave credit for the king's "Primacy in the Pacific" to Gibson's long-standing vision of an oceanic empire that would rejoin the Hawaiians and other Polynesians to their ancestral homelands in Malaysia. But a highly assertive foreign policy, doing business, as it were, with the power brokers, was also an important counter to the claim that the Hawaiian nation was in serious decline.

Moreover, there were important ideological reasons for the administration's policies that spoke directly to the issues and principles of national legitimacy. Hawai'i by 1885 had a number of economic and diplomatic treaties with foreign governments from Japan to Denmark. As such, the kingdom was much better situated, the king believed, than other Pacific Islands such as Samoa or the Gilberts that had no diplomatically recognized national entity and therefore were ripe for colonization. As early as 1881, the *Pacific Commercial Advertiser,* then edited by Gibson, had argued that a more forward foreign policy was the prerogative of "real" states:

> If it is to be accepted as a fact incontrovertible that the Hawaiian State is but a group of plantations and a syndicate of traders it may perhaps be nonsense to speak of Hawaiian Primacy in the Pacific. But if it be a recognized Nation with a Governmental and Diplomatic System, a Legislature and an elaborately organized Judiciary, and all the elements of a true Independent State with an established good character, of which there is not the like elsewhere in Polynesia . . . This Hawaiian State is in all respects fit to take upon itself the responsibilities of an advisor, a referee, or a mediator in the affairs of the weaker but still independent divisions of the Polynesian race.[70]

This assertion was important in several respects. In the first place, the kingdom's own historical vulnerability to annexation made the fate of other islands of some political consequence. An 1883 editorial in the *Advertiser* phrased, somewhat delicately, the importance of independence to all islanders: "There is however no good reason why the islands of the South Pacific should become appendages of distant powers. . . . Why would not their independence be as carefully guaranteed as that of Hawaii, . . . The subject is well worthy of consideration by the people of this country. If anyone is to interfere to prevent the further aggrandization of foreign and distant powers in the Pacific, Hawaii ought to do it."[71]

But if Hawai'i had an interest in promoting independence in Polynesia, a claim that was not supported by members of the Independent

Party in 1886, there was still the issue of whether or not the kingdom had the power to prevent the gradual partitioning of the Pacific Islands into colonial quarters. Gibson's claim, that the status of nationhood alone conferred on Hawai'i the right to pursue relationships and alliances with other countries, sidestepped the fact that successful negotiation in the diplomatic sphere rested in part on military power, which the kingdom did not possess.

Nevertheless the administration took a very active role, one might say as active a role as it could under the circumstances, in registering diplomatic inquiries through H. A. P. Carter, the Hawaiian minister to the United States who was appointed envoy extraordinary and minister plenipotentiary to Germany, Great Britain, France, Spain, and the Netherlands.[72] His mission was to "make a political reconnaissance to ascertain whether Hawaii may be recognized as eligible" to play a leading role in a political reorganization of the still sovereign islands of eastern Polynesia.[73] Later, Gibson sent a delegation, led by special envoy part-Hawaiian John Bush, to Malietoa Tanumafili in Samoa to discuss a Polynesian federation between Samoa and Hawai'i in December 1886. Malietoa signed his name to the federation shortly after his first meeting with Bush.

Kuykendall wrote that Gibson's ultimate goal was to establish a Hawaiian-led Polynesian federation of nations. Perhaps it was more ambitious than that. Although the language of Gibson's directive to Carter acknowledged the kingdom's subordinate position to the Western powers, it also appealed to the international community that the powerful nations of the West deal justly with smaller and weaker countries in the Pacific. Gibson offered to "take the leading part in aiding these people in forming themselves into such political communities, and organizing such forms of government under the benevolent favor of the greater Powers; and that Hawaii may receive assurances that such efforts as she shall make in this direction, and such political communities, when organized, shall be recognized and respected by the officials of other Powers."[74]

One can hardly miss the wistful entreaty here that sought to protect the Hawaiian kingdom and its progress toward "civilization" as surely as it sought to be the protector of the other islanders. In retrospect, the administration's initiatives hardly seem either unreasonable or unnecessary in light of the West's rather rapid annexations of New Guinea, Bougainville, New Britain, the Solomons, the Marshalls, the Carolines, the Gilbert Islands, and, finally, Samoa in a partitioning of the Pacific strongly reminiscent of a similar partitioning taking place in Africa.

Samoa in the mid-1880s was embroiled in a chiefly rivalry that was complicated by the presence of several rival foreign groups, especially the British and the Germans. One chief, Tupa Tamasese Titimaea, was encouraged and supported by the German faction in his "revolt" against Malietoa, who was, more or less, endorsed by the British. The United States, with a coaling station at Pago Pago, was an interested party but maintained a measured distance from the conflict.

The presence and aspirations of these Western powers muddled what would otherwise have been a fairly routine competition between rival chiefs into an extraordinary confrontation between imperial Germany, Great Britain, and the United States. Both Germany and Great Britain were outraged that the Hawaiian kingdom had sought to intervene in their colonial dispute. German agents in Samoa followed the Hawaiian delegation wherever they went, and there are indications that the German government believed the Hawaiian mission to be a "stalking horse" for an American plot to annex Samoa themselves.[75] That might have resulted in a naval battle in 1889 had nature not intervened, sending a hurricane that wrecked two warships, bringing their respective nations to their senses and causing them to divide the Islands among themselves.

The diplomatic "tangle" over Samoa was further confused by Bush's mission. But the fact that Hawai'i was not permitted to participate as a representative of Samoan interests in a tri-power conference in Washington on Samoa[76] demonstrated that "Samoan" interests could not be represented by islanders—not by the Samoans themselves, nor by a friendly nation of Polynesians. Hawai'i's treaty with Malietoa did little except to place Hawai'i in direct opposition to the Germans, without any indication from either Britain or the United States that they would support the Hawaiian position.

In fact, the British responded by holding the Hawaiian government responsible for having created "anarchy and disorder, while the three Powers are using their best efforts to restore the blessings of peace and of a stable Government to those islands."[77] The German response was a bit stronger. In diplomatic exchanges to the United States and Great Britain, the German government indicated: "In case Hawaii, whose King acts according to financial principles which it is not desirable to extend to Samoa, should try to interfere in favor of

Malietoa, the King of the Sandwich Islands would thereby enter into [a] state of war with us."[78]

By the time this communication was issued in August 1887, the "King of the Sandwich Islands" had essentially been removed from any semblance of executive power by the Bayonet Constitution; the principal architect of his foreign policy, Walter Murray Gibson, had already left the Islands; and a new haole cabinet and legislature was busy dismantling any remnants of the king's foreign and domestic programs.

The fact that Hawaiian initiatives were not taken seriously and that Hawai'i had no military force to speak of may not have been mere coincidence. To address that deficiency, the Nationals in the legislative assembly had proposed several appropriations for maintaining foreign missions abroad during the 1886 session. One such appropriation was for the purchase of a steamer, the British-built *Explorer*, for the Hawaiian government as a naval training vessel.[79] It was Gibson who decided to renovate the small steamer as a gunboat and send it after Bush to ferry him from island to island and display Hawaiian naval power at the same time.

This symbol of the kingdom's military power was an unqualified disaster. The government purchased the steamer for $20,000 and spent additional money on refitting, repairs, and training. The Independents in the assembly heavily contested these appropriations and, in fact, the entire foreign mission proposal, with Noble Charles Reed Bishop and Representative Sanford Dole leading the opposition. Neither man believed that there was anything to be gained for the kingdom by having a presence in foreign countries. Bishop's typically cautious opinion was that going into debt was no way to project Hawai'i's honor abroad and that "they would gain much more credit by attending to their affairs at home and not being too ambitious to go abroad when they were not asked."[80]

The legislative vote divided precisely by party affiliation, and the Nationals won a decisive victory, 25 to 12, reflecting the Independents' weaker representation in 1886.[81] The *Explorer*, renamed the *Kaimiloa* (The Far Seeker), finally arrived at Apia on 15 June 1887, its voyage punctuated by the embarrassing dismissal of three of her officers for brawling "while drunk," only to have very little of a mission left given the positions of the various antagonists. It steamed about for several weeks with shipboard discipline virtually disintegrating when the commander, a former British junior officer with an alcohol problem of his own, took ill.

One judgment of the *Kaimiloa* came from Henry Poor, the chargé d'affaires of the Hawaiian legation in Samoa, after observing "the continuous insubordination on the ship and utter disregard for all order and discipline" and noting that "with few exceptions, the marines and white sailors behaved badly. . . ." He said, "I must say a few words in praise of the Reform School boys. It was a matter of surprise to me to observe how well they behaved on shore and aboard, and how well they performed their duties: a fact which was commented on favorably in Apia. Had the 'Kaimiloa' been organized differently she might have been creditable as a training ship and been a success instead of [the] wretched and disgraceful failure she has proved. . . ."[82]

Poor's surprise at the discipline shown by Native boys was seen as nothing more than an anomaly, though his estimation that had she been organized differently (without whites?) the training might have

Figure 19. Kalākaua, Antone Rosa, and Paul Kanoa inspecting *Kaimiloa* before it sailed to Samoa in 1886. Courtesy of the Bishop Museum, Honolulu. CB 31,099.

been a success bears some striking correlation to the political discourse of the time. Regardless of the fact that the breakdown in the comportment of the officers and men aboard this ship began with the derelictions of her haole commander, it was the haole press and legislative opposition that became infuriated over one more example of the Native government's deficiencies.

The *Kaimiloa* was recalled, indeed, just as the Native ship of state was already being "recalled" by the sons of missionaries who had helped design her. As a symbol of the Hawaiian kingdom's national stature, the warship-cum-naval training vessel was remarkably appropriate. She was a small ship with a tiny armament that was not intended to be used in earnest. She was rebuilt over a European frame, captained by an English commander, and staffed with a crew of uncontrollable whites and Native boys who tried to make a decent showing for themselves. Her mission was peaceful, yet ambitious. That mission, coupled with her small size and armament, must surely have been a source of ridicule for the seasoned colonial forces that she encountered. To those who understood real force, she was an embarrassment, best scuttled and forgotten.

The "Hawaiian" League

The minutes of the Independent Party in 1885 reveal an interesting change in the party's conduct. Henry Baldwin, a rather reluctant party member, disclosed that too many of their activities were being publicized in the newspapers and "that more and better work could be done by working privately than by publishing what was to be done."[83] William Castle, who at the first party meeting in 1883 had envisioned a party "open to all," said in 1885, "that there were two views on the subject. 1st to work privately 2nd to work publicly and with a platform—that he favored the former under the circumstances here."[84] The circumstances, whatever they were in 1885, appeared to warrant greater secrecy and control by the executive committee.

By January of 1887, the disasters of the previous election and legislative session behind them, a number of party members concluded that the party was not secretive and exclusive enough. They formed the Hawaiian League, a collection of haole businessmen, attorneys, laborers, and artisans whose apparent goal was "Constitutional, representative Government, in fact as well as in form, in the Hawaiian Islands, by all necessary means."[85]

What little is known about this organization comes from the recollections of two of its members, Lorrin Thurston and Sanford Dole. Only two copies of its constitution remain in existence, and Kuykendall could not verify that either copy was true or complete. Lacking actual minutes of their meetings, Kuykendall tried to recreate from a number of written sources the political conflicts that attended this organization. Essentially, the historian believed that there was a radical and conservative faction of the League that differed mainly over what needed to be done to secure "good government" in the Islands. The members were entirely in agreement that the Gibson/Kalākaua administration was not capable of providing that leadership. The more cautious, such as Dole and Castle, simply wanted Gibson out, a cabinet that reflected the business community's interests, and "a drastic revision of the constitution of the kingdom"[86] that would retain at least a form of monarchy. A smaller faction, which included such legislators as Thurston and William Kinney, wanted monarchy ended and replaced by either a republic or outright annexation to the United States.[87]

The question of whether this organization was working toward an "independent" republic or annexation was important to Kuykendall and other mid-twentieth-century writers because America's colonial role in the Pacific was being addressed at the time those histories were written. The American diplomatic histories of the late 1960s on generally portray a highly expansionist policy, driven by such theorists as Frederick Jackson Turner, and policy makers such as William Henry Seward, Alfred Thayer Mahan, James G. Blaine, William McKinley, and others who managed to assert their acquisitive policies over other American policy makers who did not favor overseas possessions.[88]

The intent of the League is important to the discourse on colonialism in the late 1960s. For if annexation was their intent, it lends credence to the theory that the annexation of the Hawaiian Islands was accomplished as a result of a conspiracy between Americans in the U.S. State Department and American businessmen in Hawai'i. Kuykendall appears to have believed otherwise. In a footnote to his discussion of the Hawaiian League, he cited one member, Volney Ashford, who claimed that the movement of 1887 "embraced the establishment of an independent republic, with a view to ultimate annexation to the United States."[89] But Kuykendall, in the same place, called him a not very reliable witness. On the other hand, he cited two others, Sanford Dole and William R. Castle, who in separate memoirs asserted that the annexationist wing of the organization was defeated. The following quotation was attributed to Castle: "this annexation element, after a long and very bitter discussion, was defeated, and the Hawaiians, meaning thereby those of birth, parentage and affiliation, procured a promise on the part of the league that its attempts would be confined to a reformed Hawaiian government, under sufficient guaranties to insure responsible and safe government." [90]

Castle's use of the word Hawaiians to refer to those of Hawai'i birth obscures things rather thoroughly. By lumping together those of Hawaiian "birth, parentage and affiliation," Castle appeared to be saying that some form of common identity bound together the few part-Hawaiians with those missionary children who had been born in the Islands. As for those who were Hawaiian by affiliation, that could have meant anything and nothing at all. More important, for haole to claim that they were also Hawaiian was another very significant appropriation of what had once been an exclusively Native possession.

In any case, to suggest that all those who were native born did not prefer annexation was simply untrue. Both Thurston and William Kinney were "Hawaiian by birth," but quite clearly they both were annexationists. Still, the intent of the League, whether it was to alter the constitution or turn the country over to the United States, while important to the haole who participated in the League, meant relatively little to the Natives. For although the kānaka would continue to oppose annexation, the haole appropriation of their government was at least as unpopular and threatening to their interests.

In the first place, kānaka did not join the League. Of the 405 members of the League, Kuykendall acknowledged, there were "a few members of part Hawaiian ancestry," with no identifiable Hawaiian names on the role. [91] So none of the four Independent Party legislators belonged, and neither did Nāwahī. Should we presume that they were not asked to join?

The question is important because of the attempted secrecy of the League's proceedings and, indeed, its very existence. Members were required to take the following oath: "In the presence of almighty God and of these witnesses, I do solemnly swear upon my honor as a man, that I will never divulge the existence of this league except with the express authority of the Executive Committee; that I will maintain inviolate its secrets; that I will do all in my power to advance its objects, and that I will aid and defend its members who may be jeopardized in its service." [92]

Members of the League were careful about whom they trusted. The fact that they did not include such stalwart Independents as Kaʻuhane and Kalua is curious, but we cannot be sure whether they were considered for membership or not. What we know is that only a few of the Native Independents who had been elected in 1886 as Independents survived the special election of 1887 as representatives of the newly created Reform Party. Native candidates were encouraged to join the "new" party, but none of them was granted leadership in it. Neither were any Natives offered cabinet positions in the new government, although all of the ministers were members of the Hawaiian League.

The fact that neither Nāwahī nor Kalua were part of the League is tremendously suggestive of where the kānaka stood in relation to the haole in the nineteenth century and where they would continue to stand for much of the next century, either outside the powerful and influential or deeply subordinate to them. If they were asked to join the League, they refused, possibly agreeing not to divulge the existence of the League to anyone. However, it is more likely that they simply were not invited.

Lacking conclusive evidence of any kind, the second possibility seems the most likely. Nāwahī was too much of a nationalist to belong to the conspiracy against his own king and people. Kalua, regarded by Thurston as a brilliant speaker, was also a dangerous element capable of working a crowd into a high level of excitement.[93] But the main reason that no Native politician was recruited for the Hawaiian League is simply that Natives were no longer necessary. The Native vote was only necessary if there was to be a vote. If one was to engineer a coup, then all that was needed were rifles and a will.

As for the legitimation of the coup, Natives again were not necessary. The Hawaiian League had all the natives they required: Thurston, Kinney, Halstead, Dole, and Sereno Bishop.[94] These "Hawaiians" would exercise immediate leadership in 1887 and would, with very few changes, engineer the overthrow of the kingdom in 1893, finally achieving annexation in 1898. Nāwahī died in 1897, fighting to restore the monarchy under Liliʻuokalani, the sister of the king he so strenuously opposed.

Bayonet

On the afternoon of 30 June 1887, members of the Hawaiian League and several hundred other mostly white residents held a mass meeting at "the armory of the [Honolulu] Rifles at Punchbowl and Beretania Streets."[95] The Honolulu Rifles, a shooting club that had eventually become an official unit of the kingdom's armed forces, was assembled in full force outside the meeting. Its presence exemplified the treacherous political climate. Commander Volney Ashford, whom Thurston characterized as "thoroughly vicious," informed the League that he had assembled the troop, some four hundred men, because he feared the king might attack the mass meeting. He had, however, informed the king that "he was calling out the Rifles to hold the meeting in check."[96]

With such delicate intrigues on patrol outside, the League conducted its meeting inside with a bit more candor. Generally they agreed that the ministry had to be replaced by one more sympathetic to "the people," that the king's recent scandals over the licensing of opium had to be redressed, and that the king had to promise never again to interfere with elections.[97] Several individuals, notably William Kinney, called for a new constitution that would address all of their concerns, once and for all.

The demand was not unanimous, but nearly so. Paul Isenberg announced his support for the resolutions but opposition to the unlawful promulgation of a constitution. A screaming William Kinney was joined by others who shouted him down. Thirteen men were dispatched to the king bearing the resolutions of the "citizens," to which the king responded the very next day. Acknowledging that Gibson had already been dismissed, Kalākaua claimed that he had already invited "the Hon W. L. Green to form a new Cabinet on the day succeeding the resignation of the cabinet."[98]

Before the mass meeting the politically sensitive monarch had read the signs of unrest in the haole community and had taken steps to relieve the tension. By essentially caving in to all of the League's demands, however, the king helped encourage the determination to force his future compliance with a new constitution. On the other hand, it is difficult to imagine what else he might have done. In a situation where the loyalty of the white citizens was in doubt and where the best trained and equipped armed force was composed of those very whites, the king really had very little choice between combat and surrender.

Sanford Dole's account indicates how confusing the situation was for the king, who, Dole believed, was fairly well apprised that a conspiracy was taking place:

At this juncture it became desirable, if arrangements could be made, that the volunteer companies be under arms and in control of the town. Of course such action without authority, would be a revolutionary step. Fortunately, while it was under consideration, the authorities, recognizing the day to be one of possible unrest, ordered the companies out, which relieved the situation for the time being; while the troops were patrolling the streets under the nominal orders of the government, they were actually under orders of the league, until the crisis was over.[99]

See how Dole so fastidiously maneuvered around the legalistic bases of the coup. Because "the authorities" had themselves called out the Honolulu Rifles, technically, perhaps, no law was broken. On the other hand, there could be no better symbol of betrayal than this group of armed men, ostensibly the protectors of the nation, actually working to destroy the government. As for whether the presence and opposition of the Rifles coerced the king into signing the constitution, we have Clarence Ashford's recall of the occasion: "Revolutions do not go backwards, and there was sufficient determination and force behind the revolution of 1887 (bloodless as it was), to persuade the dusky monarch into subjection. . . . More might be written of the arguments made and the physical attitudes assumed toward the King by members of the Cabinet on that memorable occasion, but let it suffice to say that little was left to the imagination of the hesitant and unwilling Sovereign as to what he might expect in the event of his refusal to comply with the demands then made upon him."[100]

The king's signature ended the twenty-three-year-old constitution established by Lota Kapuāiwa and inaugurated one that would divide the nation because of its content and its origins. For the king, this constitution meant the abrupt and nearly total termination of any executive power or royal authority. For haole, it meant not only an enhanced representation in the legislature and control of the executive, it also retrieved their ability to define the nation and membership in it. For kānaka, the Bayonet Constitution was much more than a change in voting rights or the king's powers and prerogatives. It was the final demonstration of their helplessness with regard to the haole, and that their own government and their sense of national identity counted for little.

Three articles destroyed the king's authority to act as the chief executive. Article 31 in Kapuāiwa's constitution defined the king as the sole executive power, and the king's person as inviolate. Bayonet's Article 31 read, "To the King and the Cabinet belongs the Executive power."[101] Article 41 of the new constitution terminated the king's power to remove a cabinet member once appointed without a legislative vote of "Want of Confidence" and required all of his acts to be countersigned by a cabinet member. Finally, Article 78 provided that: "Wherever by this Constitution any Act is to be done or performed by the King or the Sovereign, it shall, unless otherwise expressed, mean that such Act shall be done and performed by the Sovereign by and with the advice and consent of the Cabinet."[102]

Because Kalākaua had already appointed a cabinet consisting of members of the Hawaiian League, the constitution's authors quite naturally expected that the king's authority was permanently in their hands. In this, they were quite mistaken. Several cabinet members resigned their seats over the next three years, in part out of their mutual mistrust of each other.[103] When Godfrey Brown left the ministry after only six months, Kalākaua used his resignation to assert that the entire ministry was thereby required to tender their resignations as well.

Though he lost that battle, the king was able, after months of public, legislative, and judicial debate, to secure for himself the right to veto legislation with or without the consent of the ministry. The fact that the members of the judiciary were lined up evenly on both sides of the question and that the Supreme Court voted 4 to 1, with Sanford Dole dissenting, to uphold the king's power is evidence that some of the justices at least regarded the law as something more than a blueprint for political opportunism. But it is also true that although those same justices recognized the illegal basis of the Bayonet Constitution, they were still willing to lend their expertise toward its eventual design. Albert Judd said: "The justices of the Supreme Court were kept in ignorance of the league which resulted in obtaining from Kalakaua the constitution of 1887. Just before its promulgation Justice Preston and myself were invited to assist in its revision, which we agreed to do under a written protest that we did not approve of the method of its promulgation as being unconstitutional."[104]

With the highest legal authorities in the nation doubtful of the legality of the constitution, one might expect that the Natives would be less than awed by its majesty. But when a delegation of kānaka did go to Kalākaua to petition him to abrogate it, the king referred the delegation to his cabinet ministers, saying only that the new constitution was better than the old and enlarged the civil rights of the people.[105] The *Hawaiian Gazette* quoted him: "Under the old Constitution, the people went barefoot or wrapped their feet in ti leaves; under the new Constitution, they wore shoes; under the old Constitution they wore the malo, now they wear clothes like other civilized people; under the old Constitution they sheltered their heads under palm leaves, now they wear hats and moreover, this was His Constitution."[106]

David William Earle, in his 1993 master's thesis, Coalition Politics in Hawai'i—1887–90: Hui Kālai'āina and the Mechanics and Workingmen's Political Protective Union, theorized that the king's language may have been a disguised message sent to his Native subjects, warning them that the new government was as foreign as shoes and hats to them, while alerting them to his unwillingness to challenge it.[107] Perhaps Earle is correct, although the king knew perfectly well that shoes, hats, and new constitutions wore very well on some of his Native subjects. Or perhaps Kalākaua never quite made up his mind about what could or should be done, once the new constitution was promulgated. The king was the nation. A weakened king symbolized, therefore, a weakened nation. His humiliation was the Natives' humiliation. Perhaps he reasoned that there was little such a humbled and weakened people could do against haole.

Kalākaua's reluctance to directly oppose the cabinet no doubt encouraged Thurston to proclaim the king a coward in his memoirs.[108] Perhaps if Kalākaua had vigorously opposed the constitution, his people might have rallied around him and restored his power. Many of his own people believed that. In fact, Robert Wilcox, a hapa haole with Ali'i rank, organized and led an attempted coup in 1889 to restore the old constitution on the strength of the belief that the kānaka would support their king, with warfare if necessary. Apparently, the king did not believe in them. Having perhaps encouraged Wilcox to take over the palace and "force" him to abrogate the constitution, the king did not wait for the Native force to arrive, but took refuge in his boathouse, while the surprised ministry reacted with armed men of their own, killing and wounding several of Wilcox's men.

It is difficult to read the king's actions as anything but a betrayal of his own people. But Kalākaua's own words to the Native petitioners in 1887 suggest how helpless he believed the kānaka to be. Although he might have demonstrated more spine, he might also have precipitated open warfare between his Native subjects and the haole.

Perhaps he, like his sister in 1893, had no stomach for war. Instead, he urged the kānaka to take the oath to support the new constitution and qualify themselves to vote. [109]

But the new voting laws and composition of the assembly made it much more difficult for the kānaka to mount a political opposition to the new constitution. In fact, it was these laws that really offended the Native and Asian citizenry, who met in a series of public meetings beginning in July to voice their opposition. The nobles who had formerly been appointed by the king and who were supposed to represent the "dignified classes" of Hawaiian society were now to be elected for terms of six years. Their numbers were fixed by law at twenty-four, the same as the representatives under the new constitution. However, there were extremely high property qualifications placed on both candidates and their electors that for all intents and purposes eliminated Natives from either running or voting for these seats.

Thus the constitution created what Kuykendall himself called "a special electorate,"[110] whose rights and obligations were not determined by anything except property and wealth. Article 59 specified that these electors must be (males) of Hawaiian, American, or European descent who had resided in the Islands for three years and could read and comprehend a newspaper written in "Hawaiian, English or some European language." But the article also specified that: "he shall own and be possessed, in his own right, of taxable property in this country of the value of not less than three thousand dollars over and above all encumbrances, or shall have received an income of not less than six hundred dollars during the year next preceding his registration for such election."[111]

This was a special group indeed, made even more selective with the final section of this article, which stated that neither the residency nor literacy requirements would bar the franchise from "any persons residing in the Kingdom at the time of the promulgation of this Constitution, if they shall register and vote at the first election which shall be held under this Constitution."[112]

This section was surely designed to entice support from those who had only recently arrived from abroad and who might not otherwise be willing to participate, but the property and money qualifications were absolutely inviolable and sacred. So, too, was the exclusion of Asians, who had formerly been citizens under the monarchy. The enlargement of the House of Nobles along with the constitutional right of the ministers to vote in the legislature guaranteed that this special electorate would have a controlling vote in the legislature no matter how the Native voters responded in the election of their representatives.

But even that electorate was altered in Article 62 to include "Every male resident of the Kingdom, of Hawaiian, American, or European descent, who shall have taken an oath to support the Constitution . . . and shall have been domiciled in the Kingdom for one year immediately preceding the election; and shall know how to read and write either the Hawaiian, English or some European language. . . ."[113] It was the very first time that democratic rights were determined by race in any Hawaiian constitution. This article also came with the provision that neither the residency nor the literacy requirements would be imposed on those currently residing in the kingdom who took the oath and voted in the first election.

Thus, the participation of the Natives in their own government was severely compromised by equating them with virtually any Caucasian, including Portuguese immigrants literally "fresh off the boats." Birth and devotion to the Native Hawaiian nation would count for absolutely nothing because no elector would be required, as formerly, to renounce their own previous nationality and swear allegiance to the king.

Taken together, the enlargement of the franchise cheapened beyond recognition the value of citizenship and national identity that Lota Kapuāiwa's constitution had so clearly demonstrated. It also removed the last pretense that the government existed for any other purpose than to protect the wealthy. Requiring that voters swear to support the constitution placed the Natives in a nearly impossible position. To participate at all, to have any hope of amending the constitution, meant that they had to give their word to support it, a conundrum that severely divided them during the 1887 election.[114]

In a large Native rally held less than two months before the election, several candidates for representative for Honolulu exhorted the crowd to take the oath of allegiance and vote despite their opposition to the constitution. A. P. Kalaukoa, a former Independent Party candidate who had failed to secure election since 1876, spoke on its merits, saying, "Now tell me, have any of you been endangered by this new constitution?" The angry crowd responded with cries of "Nui ka Pilikia. (We are greatly oppressed.)"[115] But even Attorney Samuel Kāne, who appeared on the Opposition (to the constitution) ticket, argued: "We have not yet signed it. . . . If we do not take the oath, of course, we cannot vote. But in this perilous time we are under obligation to take oath under it. No matter if we agree with it or not, we shall have a majority on our side, and then we will be able to change it." [116]

Kāne's speech pointed out the weakness of the Native position in what had, only days before, been their nation and their laws. It was a perilous time indeed, made more so by the fact that it was impossible to know what one's obligations were as a citizen. With the franchise so disfigured by the inclusion of any and every Caucasian merely present in the Islands, what could it mean for kānaka to join the haole in a new nation that humiliated and disempowered Natives and their king? Would they not be betraying their own understanding and definition of themselves by taking that oath?

Joseph M. Poepoe, an experienced Honolulu attorney and candidate for Honolulu, took the stage later that day and called Kalaukoa "The Angel of Death." But his remarks about the nation and its regard for their king spoke directly to the importance of the king to the Native identity and the distinction that so clearly existed between kānaka and haole: "The Americans have no respect for royalty, for they have no king. Therefore, they want to exercise the same power here as they do in their own country. They are doing it little by little, and it will not be long before Hawaii becomes an entire republic. We who cherish our King ought not to allow this to be done." [117]

This was the true danger for the Natives, who had lived through disease, death, the loss of land, and the steady assaults on their dignity. The constitution, an instrument that they had been taught to respect and rely on to symbolize their nationhood, had now been used to remove the last traces of their honor as a people. Their Mōʻī was now a figurehead; what then were they? The Natives' conception that they represented the nation as true, albeit impoverished, citizens was exposed as nothing more than a fabrication. They could still vote, so long as they acquiesced, and they were not yet a minority. But so long as a special, privileged, and alien class could legally control the legislature—as they controlled the executive—the Natives were both symbolically and virtually rendered powerless.

The actual disempowerment of the Natives was quickly manifested in the September elections for a "special" legislature. Native and haole candidates opposed to the Bayonet Constitution called themselves the Independent Reform Party, a meaningful appropriation of past and current names of the party that had betrayed them. Perhaps they called themselves by that name to remind the Reformers that the kānaka were still very much a part of the nation and were still willing to negotiate a shared future with the haole. If so, there is no indication that the haole cared one way or another. No longer needing, or able, to emphasize their independence from the administration and, perhaps, not wishing to maintain the fiction that they supported a completely independent nation, they ceased pretending that their political aims were anything else but change, and change with a decided evangelical bent.

The change was immediate, and although the new election requirements benefited haole candidates, some of the kānaka who had been Independents in 1886 joined the newer version known as the Reform Party and were able to get reelected. They were J. Kaʻuhane of Kaʻū and A. Kauhi of ʻEwa and Waiʻanae. Kalua did not run, and former Independent Party members Nāwahī, Paehaole, and L. W. P. Kānealiʻi joined the opposition against the Reform Party and ran against their former mates in 1887. Only Paehaole was elected, one of two Independent Reform legislators against twenty-one representatives and twenty-four nobles all allied with the Reform Party.

The turnabout between the dominance of the king's party and the dominance of the haole party was abrupt and demonstrated the swift transformation of electoral power generated by the new constitution. It is certain that Native Independents were left completely out of the planning and execution of the coup d'état, which was engineered almost entirely by a "committee of thirteen" individuals led by Lorrin Thurston, who drafted the Bayonet Constitution.

Natives were invited to participate in the spoils, however. A. P. Kalaukoa, who had not won an election since 1876, won in Honolulu along with newcomer D. L. Nāone. In other districts, Nakaleka (Molokaʻi/Lānaʻi) was elected despite having lost in 1886. Even publisher Joseph Kawainui entered the legislative arena and was rewarded with a victory in Hāna over a virtual political unknown.[118] Altogether, Natives made up three of the twenty-four nobles in the 1887 session and eleven of twenty-four representatives.[119] The most meaningful statistic was that the legislative opposition to the Bayonet Constitution was virtually crippled until 1890.

"Good government" (that is, government guided by a firm white hand) had finally been achieved. The instruments that had made it possible were the drastic changes to the power of the king, the transformation of the legislative assembly into a body that represented the business community, and equally far-reaching change in the definition

Table 11. Legislative Assembly, Special Session of 1887 (Ministers: G. Brown, Foreign Affairs; Thurston, Interior; Green, Finance; Ashford, Attorney General)

DISTRICT	NOBLES	REPRESENTATIVES
Hawaiʻi	D. H. Hitchcock	Henry Deacon
	S. C. Luhiau	D. Kamai
	Charles Notley	G. P. Kamauoha
	H. S. Townsend	John Kaʻuhane
	Charles P. Wall	(Vice-President)
	James Wight	William A. Kinney
		J. Maguire
		J. D. Paris
Maui, Molokaʻi, Lānaʻi	E. H. Bailey	James Campbell
	Henry P. Baldwin	W. H. Daniels
	James Campbell	E. Helekunihi
	P. N. Makee	C. F. Horner
	John Richardson	J. U. Kawainui
	Hermann Widemann	J. Nakaleka
		O. Nāwahine
		A. P. Paehaole
Oʻahu	William R. Castle	Cecil Brown
	James I. Dowsett	Frank Brown
	W. E. Foster	James I. Dowsett Jr.
	A. Jaeger	Frank Hustace
	M. P. Robinson	A. P. Kalaukoa
	William O. Smith	A. Kauhi
	Henry Waterhouse	D. L. Nāone
	Samuel G. Wilder	
	(President)	
	Alexander Young	
Kauaʻi and Niʻihau	C. Bertlemann	Francis Gay
	G. H. Dole	William Hyde Rice
	George N. Wilcox	A. S. Wilcox

Source: Lydecker, 1918, *Roster Legislatures of Hawaii,* 172.

of the electorate. However, it also came as the result of tremendous loss of Native confidence in themselves and a very real confusion of what it meant to be Native.

Kuykendall wrote that a variety of acts and policies of the new government "caused antagonism to the Reform Administration." Among these he listed the cession of Pearl Harbor in exchange for a renewal of the Reciprocity Treaty, the ratification of which "was represented as a threat to Hawaii's independence."[120] More than any other action taken by the new government this one demonstrated with the greatest clarity that Native requirements were to be sacrificed for the needs of the sugar planters and the commercial sector that supported them.

But there was little confusion about that. The kānaka understood quite well that a large motivation for the coup was economic and that for the Reformers, good government meant government that supported the industry. Ironically, the renewal of reciprocity did not pay off for the sugar industry in Hawai'i. In 1890, future president William McKinley secured the passage of the McKinley Tariff Act in the U.S.

Figure 20. Lydia Kamaka-'eha Dominis Lili'uokalani, Kalākaua's sister and last ruling monarch of the Hawaiian kingdom. Photograph by J. J. Williams, courtesy of the Bishop Museum, Honolulu. CPBM 54,034.

Senate. The Act provided for a two-cent-per-pound bounty to be paid to all American sugar producers, effectively undercutting the benefits of reciprocity for the kingdom's sugar planters. That legislation sent the Islands' sugar economy into an immediate recession and caused the few kānaka members of the kingdom's legislature to introduce a bill calling for the immediate expulsion of the U.S. Navy from Pearl Harbor, arguing that America was violating the treaty with Hawaiʻi.

Dominated by haole Reform Party members, the legislature steadily divested itself from anything appearing to support the Native culture. Within the first two weeks of the session the legislature abolished the Board of Genealogy and the Hawaiian Board of Health.[121] Before the end of that legislature, there would be virtually no government agencies left to even pretend to minister to the particular needs of Natives. On the other hand, the sugar industry, with reciprocity assured,[122] a firm control of immigration, and the final arbiters of the kingdom's spending and taxation, would be better positioned than at any other time.

It cannot be said that Natives had no place at all in the government. On the very first day of the 1887 session, after Hawaiian League member Samuel Wilder was elected president of the assembly, "The Chair appointed Representative Kawainui a committee of one to conduct the newly elected President to the Chair, which he did in a very gracious manner."[123] There was, after all, an important role for the kānaka to play in the nation. Those who would graciously accept their subordinate status would always be welcomed, even encouraged, to participate. Such Natives would signify the success of the religious and secular missions that had converted them. Those who resisted that status would be either politically marginalized or, like Robert Wilcox and Liliʻuokalani in 1895, prosecuted as criminals.

As for the king, it is likely that the Bayonet Constitution shortened his rule as it personally humiliated him. It cannot be said that he gave up trying to reassert his power, both to veto and to appoint new ministers, but he clearly did not lead the Native patriots in their attempts to abrogate or amend the Constitution of 1887. In many ways he disappeared from active leadership, his initiatives feeble and his intentions unclear. His died in San Francisco on 20 January 1891, where he was hoping to make one more journey east to negotiate a new reciprocity agreement. His people grieved and turned their hopes to Liliʻuokalani.

8

Ho'oulu Lāhui

The ideological aggression which tends to dehumanize and
then deceive the colonized finally corresponds to concrete
situations which lead to the same result. To be deceived to
some extent already, to endorse the myth and then adapt to it,
is to be acted upon by it. That myth is furthermore supported
by a very solid organization; a government and a judicial
system fed and renewed by the colonizer's historic, economic
and cultural needs. Even if he were insensitive to calumny
and scorn, even if he shrugged his shoulders at insults and
jostling, how could the colonized escape the low wages, the
agony of his culture, the law which rules him from birth until
death?

Albert Memmi, *The Colonizer and the Colonized*

I have spent a good deal of my middle-aged existence connected to
this mo'olelo and to the scholarly and unscholarly work that went into
its creation. It is time to let go of it, pray for its publication, deal with
the inevitable criticism of its shortcomings. The first of its shortcomings, at least for the academic scholar, is that this is a mo'olelo. In English, mo'olelo translates as history, story, tale, folktale, account. Literally, it means a fragment of a story, as though the teller recognizes that
he is not saying everything there is to say about the subject. I cannot
pretend to say everything there is to say about lawmaking and constitutions and their contextualization in culture. I do not even try to say
everything that I know about this subject, but all that I do know is only
a small part of the truth. Here is an example: How many Native voters refused to vote in 1887 as a serious and intentional boycott of the

new constitution, and how many others because they were rendered hopeless and apathetic by its provisions and its genesis?

I have no idea, even though I do understand how important the question might be to a cultural historian, or to a political scientist, or to a Hawaiian nationalist in the twenty-first century, searching for historical evidence of our people's resistance to colonialism. However, I can think of a much better question. Why did A. P. Kalaukoa stand before a crowd of kānaka who were clearly hostile to the Bayonet Constitution and try to defend it? Did he intend to deceive his people, securing haole support for his election by sowing doubt and disunity among the kānaka? Was he courageously risking his reputation by appealing to the Natives to make the best of the situation and maintain at least a semblance of representation in the assembly? Perhaps he was just a fool.

I think this is a better question, though no more answerable than the first one, because it reveals more of what is important to us as Hawaiians. In the wake of such astonishing changes in our society, have we simply given up trying to be true kānaka and given ourselves over to the pursuit of power, comfort, or haole approval? Are we merely doing the best we can to live as Natives in a foreign culture that seems to regard us as insignificant? Or are we just confused about who we are? Do we even know what it means to be Hawaiian anymore?

These questions demonstrate what over a century and a half of assimilation will do to separate a people from their very selves. We can look back at the confusion of our ancestors over Bayonet and remind ourselves that they, at least, still spoke their language, still worked the land in kalo (taro), and still sustained a majority in the population over the Europeans and Americans in the kingdom. It is a fact that they opposed the Constitution of 1887, overwhelmingly, though not unanimously. But there was even more consensus that the constitution had power over them all unless and until the legislature amended it or the king chose to abrogate it.

All of the most significant transformations in nineteenth-century Hawaiʻi came about as legal changes: in rulership, in land tenure, in immigration, and especially in the meaning of identity and belonging. The Hawaiian saying "I ka ʻōlelo ke ola, i ka ʻōlelo ka make" reminds us that language is a creator and a destroyer, and law is nothing if not language. Our submission to the language of law and especially to its ubiquity and its fickleness is what, I believe, has so altered our sense of ourselves and our inherent sovereignty. It was law that positioned

Natives and haole as subjects and citizens in the kingdom through the promulgation and termination of constitutions, through the election of Native and haole officials, all of which, in the long run, deprived Natives of any meaningful participation in their own governance. In the process the kānaka were continually subjected to the pronouncements of their difference and inferiority, which both enabled and validated their dispossession.

In Hawai'i modern institutions of law and economics did not evolve either naturally or spontaneously. These were already existent structures carried here by white settlers, erected as a framework for conversion, embellished by the accumulated wealth of agribusiness, and fortified by a nascent racism. But neither were Hawaiians merely exploited by an unfamiliar system; they were manipulated into a position of actual inferiority by haole settlers whose names are known and were listed in the membership roles of the Hawaiian League. Even before the existence of that League and its contemptible constitution, the Natives were exploited by the haole discourse that portrayed them as incompetent.

I am a Native Hawaiian, He Kanaka Maoli, 'ōiwi maoli au. This is a simple enough assertion, the meaning of which is as clear as water when it springs from the rock. I belong here, not just to the land but to the other Kānaka Maoli of this 'āina, and they belong to me. This claim is not so clear to everyone, especially those who are not Native, but who, nevertheless, have roots here that are several generations long. Many think that asserting our Nativeness is merely about claiming entitlements. Having identified themselves with America, most residents of Hawai'i do not understand that our self-definition as *Hawaiians* has little to do with trying to gain political and economic advantage over them. It has everything to do with kinship.

In the same way, our goals have much less to do with resources than with inheritance, even less to do with money than with dignity. If my study here has shown little else, I hope that it has demonstrated a consistent and determined struggle by Native Hawaiians to maintain, for better or worse, their kinship with each other. Ravaged by disease, debt, doubt, and the duplicity of law and white men, the lāhui was incorporated into the American republic, against the people's will, one hundred years ago.

But the Hawaiian nation of the nineteenth century was compromised by an ongoing discourse that held the Natives and their nation as inferior to whites and their nations. So the question begs to be asked, which nation was the "real" nation? What nation did we mourn when the American flag was raised over 'Iolani Palace in 1898? Was it the aupuni united by Kamehameha and transformed under his son Kauikeaouli that, early missionaries assured, would create a haven for the kānaka? Was it the assertive kingship of Kapuāiwa? Was it the lāhui of Kalākaua that tried to maintain its distinctive Native identity while pursuing recognition and success in the Western world? Was it the Mō'ī as its chief symbol, or the kānaka as its constituency? Or was the nation the system created by haole to facilitate their hold on the wealth of the Islands and to communicate their superiority to the Native and Asian citizens?

The Nation as Power

These questions are meaningful because although only one form of the nation, the system of distributing wealth and power, survived the nineteenth century, a powerful Native identification with the sovereign kingdom continues to exist and grow a century after annexation. The contemporary sovereignty movement does not distance itself from the monarchy, though few of the movement's supporters advocate a return to monarchy itself. We commemorated the passing of the kingdom as a day of mourning and commitment to the restoration of our nation. 'Onipa'a (immovable), the centennial observations of the overthrow in January 1993, were attended by thousands of Hawaiians at numerous gatherings throughout the archipelago. In commemorations that were political and spiritual, conducted in English and Hawaiian, combining the apologies of Christian churches and the militant assertions of Hawaiian patriots, Christian prayers and ancient oli (chants) to the chiefs and the akua, 'Onipa'a demonstrated that Hawaiian nationalism continues to develop from a cultural coalescence of Native and Western forms.

It is that coalescence that continues to complicate the Native identity in much the same way that accommodation of the haole plagued the Native voters and legislators in the nineteenth century. In the first place, it is difficult for Hawaiians to imagine a nation that includes non-Hawaiians. Even if there were no resentment of the haole for their appropriation of the lands and government, we still feel bound together as Native people in ways that cannot be defined by the structures of our government or by words such as nationalism. The nearest word that we have for the nation is lāhui, a word that means "gathering," "people," "tribe," and even "species." We are, in the end, a distinct people whose commonalities extend far outside the ability of laws and constitutions to define us.

Yet the law does define us. On 23 February 2000, the U.S. Supreme Court decided that the State of Hawai'i could not hold elections for Office of Hawaiian Affairs trustees, while limiting the vote to those of Native ancestry, without violating the Fifteenth Amendment. One result of this decision is that it could initiate a trend to divest the Kānaka Maoli of entitlements that, at this point, represent one of the few hedges against massive poverty and homelessness.

Knowing this, understanding what is at stake, many Hawaiians, myself included, still find it difficult to wholeheartedly support the Office of Hawaiian Affairs, an agency that has not always behaved honorably and whose factions and intrigues have provided ammunition for those who oppose Native self-government. It would be a considerable distortion to compare the Office of Hawaiian Affairs with Kalākaua's administration in 1886, but the lessons are similar. Despite an ongoing and historical experience with a Western legal system that continually denied the Kānaka Maoli the simple right to be kānaka, we Hawaiians continue to be manipulated by American laws and decisions whose ethics and values do not correspond with our own.

The Supreme Court decision demonstrates the inadequacies of American law to treat Kānaka Maoli fairly. No one would deny the necessity of federal intervention in matters of suffrage given the historic problems of race in America. The irony is that until whites took over the government in Hawai'i in 1887, suffrage had never before been connected to race. It is this American obsession that now threatens the meager exercise of self-rule that still exists for Native Hawaiians.

If the story of the Bayonet Constitution has taught us nothing else, it tells us that the law was bigger than we understood. It was bigger than the king and bigger than all of his supporters and opponents. Nothing that any of them brought to bear to the struggle—their lineages, their enormous talents, their courage, not even their numbers and their loyalty to each other—was a match for the law. Indeed the law enabled their talents, courage, and loyalties to work against them as a people, helping to frame them as political parties while eroding their historic kinship with one another. They were marginalized, thrust to the edges of political discourse, while the constitution, this foreign idea, took hold of the center of the controversies that it had created.

A proper moʻolelo delivers lessons from the past that ought to guide our present behavior. We, the Kānaka Maoli of the twenty-first century, are still divided, and we continue to assert political positions that deal merely with the edges of the problems of our survival. Late in 1999, federal representatives from the Department of the Interior came to Hawaiʻi to gather testimony and proposals from kānaka on how reconciliation between the United States and the Hawaiian people might be effected. Kānaka Maoli turned out by the hundreds at every one of their appearances and treated the delegation to generations of frustration, calling for every conceivable kind of redress: monetary reparations, more aid for education and health, return of lands and federal recognition, independence, and restoration of the kingdom.

It became obvious that we were not so much speaking to the American delegation as we were speaking to ourselves, contending over the central problem that had underwritten our loss of sovereignty in the first place. How do we protect our lāhui, our kinship with one another? Do we conform our responses within the framework of the American political system, hoping that we might bring new benefits to our children thereby, or do we insist on clinging to every tradition that we can recover, insisting on our separateness, our distinctness, from a society that seemingly regards such distinction as anachronistic and dangerous?

Some of us fear that the latter option marginalizes us, and that fear itself is hugely ironic. It is as though we have come to believe that we are the ones living on the edges of American life, the center of which contains the true and legitimate criteria for our existence. Though we send our children to immersion schools, we worry when they score poorly in standardized English examinations. Though we demand self-government, the proponents of complete independence are often scorned by those of us who believe that to be an unrealistic dream.

There are ironies in this that would be humorous if they were not so painful. The constitution of the largest of the sovereign Hawaiian governments, Ka Lāhui Hawaiʻi,[1] limits full membership to Hawaiʻi residents of Native ancestry. Founded almost exactly one hundred years after Bayonet, Ka Lāhui has no land, no money, no paid positions to offer its citizenry and leadership. In other words, as a fount of political or economic empowerment, Ka Lāhui has little to offer its citizens. Although its membership is restricted genealogically and thus offers distinction, identity, and purpose to its members, there is no mechanism for confirming a member's Native ancestry.

The State of Hawaiʻi, on the other hand, is wealthy and powerful, wielding an annual budget in the billions, and is, by far, the Islands' largest employer. The state also provides limited assistance to Hawaiians of 50 percent blood quantum or more through both the Department of Hawaiian Home Lands (DHHL), an agency set up by federal legislation in 1920, and the Office of Hawaiian Affairs (OHA), established by the state constitutional convention of 1978. Both agencies have significant assets. In 1993, OHA commanded total assets of 160 million dollars,[2] and DHHL managed 187,413 acres of land.[3] These assets make both agencies fairly potent political actors in the state. In addition the law defines the beneficiaries of these agencies more stringently and requires scrupulous documentation of one's ancestry to qualify as a beneficiary. Thus, one would assume, the beneficiaries would possess an even stronger sense of identity as Hawaiians, but neither agency has ever been a catalyst for Native sovereignty.[4]

In fact both have been censured by the public and by other agencies for failing to meet their responsibilities to their Native Hawaiian beneficiaries. Criticism of OHA has come from sources as varied as Dr. Haunani-Kay Trask and the state auditor.[5] Trask, an outspoken and fiery member of the faculty at the Center for Hawaiian Studies, called OHA an embarrassment to Hawaiians for, among other things, its internal squabbling and failure to protect important sacred and historic sites from urban development.[6] Most interesting is Trask's comment that "the worst aspect of OHA is its continued collaboration with the State Democratic Party."[7] Trask and other Hawaiians in the sovereignty movement hold a special contempt for Natives whose political advancement, they believe, has not advanced the conditions of the Natives. We are much harsher in our criticism of other Hawaiians than we are of non-Natives, including haole.

The point is that agencies do exist that can conceivably enrich and empower Native Hawaiians who wish to participate in "mainstream" haole society. Why is this not enough? Why, in fact, has this option never been enough? For if this work has shown nothing else, it demonstrates that the political, social, and economic structures of the kingdom, largely constructed by haole to incorporate the Natives into an association with European and American values and ambitions, consistently failed to erase a distinct kanaka identity. Whether we focus on the Maka'āinana petitions of the 1840s, the racial politics of the 1870s and 1880s, or the organization of Native resistance to the Bayonet Constitution, we find a significant number of kānaka unwilling to surrender their identification and community with each other.

Such unwillingness has extracted extraordinary sacrifice. I believe that Kalākaua himself sacrificed what might have been a long and comfortable reign if he had identified more closely with the wealthy missionary families instead of his own impoverished and discredited people. Likewise, his sister Lili'uokalani risked not only her reign, but her life by responding to the petitions by her people to restore the 1864 Constitution in 1893. For this, not only did her haole ministry betray her, so did the United States government, landing troops to threaten the palace and guard the conspirators against the queen.

The kingdom's government became a retainer of power. But the government never empowered the Natives to materially improve their lives, to protect or extend their cultural values, nor even, in the end, to protect that government from being discarded. As far as the kānaka were concerned, the deficiency of the kingdom was never that it was too small, too poor, or too vulnerable to conquest, but rather that it failed to be responsible for its people. This was not the fault of the legislatures, the Ali'i, nor the Mō'ī, including Kalākaua. The government was neither responsible for nor responsive to the Natives because it could never be as responsive to human beings as other human beings can be. The kingdom was designed to compartmentalize power and authority as a way of increasing productivity and economic power. Its design was strongly influenced by a haole value system that ultimately considered the Natives expendable. Yet despite this, the kānaka never lost their sense of loyalty to the nation. To understand that aspect of nationalism, we must look beyond the nation's ability to empower the individual.

Nation and Identity

The kingdom, despite its inability or unwillingness to promote the economic status of Natives, nevertheless was deeply meaningful as a symbol of their survival as a distinct and unique people. Hawaiians consistently demonstrated a willingness to share their nation with foreigners. Even in 1845 when Maka'āinana petitioned to deny haole general access to land and citizenship, they did so only to protect their own identity as the true people of the land and their Ali'i as their true leaders. "Good haole," they argued, did not need an oath of allegiance, and bad haole would never be bound by it.

As the Hawaiians' worst fears materialized, and they continued to die or live in poverty while the haole flourished, the Natives continued to support the government. Even during the 1880s when "Hawai'i for Hawaiians" became the rallying cry for both supporters and enemies of the king, the kānaka were never so unhappy with their government that they were willing either to revolt against it or even to cease their electoral support for white candidates. By then, of course, the kingdom was all that they had left to demonstrate their survival as a people.

The accommodations that Native political parties made with the Reform government after 1887 did not return significant political power to the kānaka or protect their sovereignty as a people for very long. Here we are left with important questions, not so much about their strategies, but about the assumptions that kānaka leaders and voters made about how the political structure could or would protect their independence. They decided to participate; that much is clear. But did they imagine that they would retrieve political power as a voting bloc, or did they participate because they saw no other way to protect the fragile sovereignty of their nation and their own frail identities in the process?

This is no small question. On one hand, we must wonder how important political influence and the exercise of power can possibly be if one is forced to sacrifice belief, values, and the dignity of one's heritage in the process. On the other hand, without political power, how can one effectively assert, protect, and extend one's cultural ideals? Although I submit that moralists and realists have absolutely no problem answering these questions for themselves, most people struggle with the definitions of power and principle, muddling along, compromising where they can afford to, and maintaining their integrity as far as they possibly can.

One thing is clear to me. The individual's integrity is quite intimately bound to a sense of cultural distinction and difference. Hawaiians did not resist their homeland becoming an extension of America because they felt that they could never become adequate American citizens. They resisted because they were Hawaiian. They resisted incorporation even though many were impoverished, the vast majority landless, and they themselves had been reduced to an almost impotent electorate by the Constitution of 1887. What is nationalism but that? If their actions and defiance appear inexplicable, they are no more inexplicable than any other culturally assertive gesture, from the insistence on speaking a language that has no universal prestige, to the worship of gods whose sacred places have been inhabited by buildings and golf courses and desecrated by bombs and tourists. 'Ae (yes), we are Hawaiians still, and like our great- and great-great-grandparents are still finding it nearly impossible to accommodate our cultural distinction with our political powerlessness.

Yet it may be that the kind of empowerment implicit in a people's assertion of their identity is more dynamic than a well-financed administration or even a well-equipped military. When Native peoples insist on displaying fealty to tribe, clan, or unrecognized nation in the face of numerous social pressures and enticements to discard those loyalties, we must wonder about the vitality of our culture to have withstood the most efficient colonizer in human history. The culture may not have survived intact, but it has unquestionably survived.

Beginnings

The kingdom, however, did not survive. Perhaps, however, the aupuni was the mōhai (sacrifice) required for Hawaiians to recognize the inability of government, any government, to truly represent the nation, the lāhui. The kingdom was never more than a shell containing the living flesh of the nation, which was its people, its chiefs, its Mō'ī, and, of course, the 'āina. For the most part, we are all still here, though somewhat the worse for wear.

We are, unfortunately, still a beleaguered race, and our problems come not only from our poverty and homelessness, but from a lingering sense that our "failure" is the result of our own inadequacy as a people. That sense is the result not only of our political oppression, but an insidious discourse that portrays the Western conceptions of government, economics, education, and ideals as the only proper and "realistic" models for contemporary societies. This discourse, this language was woven into the cloak of the colonizers in Hawai'i. To reject that colonization necessarily entails rejecting the discourse as well.

It is tragically possible that many Hawaiians may not do either one. Not every Native is an activist for sovereignty, and quite a large majority of those who identify themselves as Native are uncertain about their political options and hesitant to make any drastic changes. A poll conducted by the *Honolulu Advertiser* found that although a majority of Hawaiians favored some form of sovereignty, 81 percent of the respondents felt that more time was needed to decide issues related to sovereignty.[8] On the other hand, 83 percent agreed that "Hawaiians deserve reparations in land or money to make up for the overthrow of the Monarchy."[9]

The promise of reparations is the worst threat to the recovery of the Natives. In the first place, a monetary amount cannot be fixed on the loss of a people's identity. Nor can reparations, no matter how high the amount, do more than expiate the guilt and dissolve the responsibility of the United States. It cannot relieve the colonized from the status of victim. In fact, reparations perpetuate the victim's status as a helpless recipient of America's largesse, the colonizer's sense of justice. We will have advanced no further than our nineteenth-century ancestors if we settle for reparations.

But more important, I think, we will surrender what our ancestors refused to surrender—our identity, our difference as a race, our pride in our nationality—if we persist in the belief that some other agency can restore our dignity for us. If it does nothing else, history should instruct the living, not merely memorialize the dead. We have placed far too much reliance on the rituals and promises of others. Let us 'imi haku again. We must search for our chiefs, insist on their accountability, sacrifice when necessary, and live as a people again. Let us turn away from the fiction that power is threatening and that ethnic distinction is bigotry. If we wish to live as Hawaiians alongside other Hawaiians, with rules and customs of our own making, why should we be discouraged? We have long since forsaken the authority of the missionaries over us. Why should we continue to submit to their laws?

In the end, nationhood is identity. A nation's constitutions, laws, and elections are never more than symbols of the will of the people to think, worship, and behave as a people. We have lived long enough with the laws and rituals of others and, despite that, have survived. What might we do in a society where custom, law, and leadership reflect our own desires and aspirations? What old and new forms might we rediscover, what meaningful relationships might we recreate between humans and the earth, between the world of nature and the world of gods, without the stern remonstrations of the missionaries and the deceptive binds of their laws? How tragic it would be for us not to make the effort.

Notes

Chapter 1: Aupuni

1. One famous cartoon featured in *Harper's Weekly* portrayed the American avuncular symbol dragging a dark woman named "Hawaii" to the altar.

2. Kuykendall, 1940, Constitutions of the Hawaiian Kingdom, 48: Article 59, paragraphs 1, 3, Constitution of the Hawaiian Islands, 1887.

3. Kamakau, 1991, *Ruling Chiefs of Hawai'i*, 396. This work was compiled from a series of newspaper articles written between October 1866 and February 1871 by the author, a historian and member of the House of Representatives. They were published first in 1961 and then reprinted with indexes in 1991. This passage originally appeared in the newspaper *Ke Au Okoa* on 20 May 1869.

4. Ibid., 412. Originally in *Ke Au Okoa*, 26 August 1869.

5. Ibid., 230. There is some ambiguity about what it is, exactly, that Kamakau meant by "the old days" (ka wa kahiko). In Hawaiian usage, it could mean anything over fifty years in the past. Many of his examples of the troubles of chiefly society, however, come from the era of the Conqueror, Kamehameha, a posthaole period.

6. The nearest word that we have for the nation is lāhui, a word that means "gathering," "people," "tribe," and even "species."

7. Kamakau descended from an 'Ewa, O'ahu, lineage.

8. Aupuni is a term that is used in Hawaiian-language newspapers and other sources as interchangeable with the kingdom. In this first chapter I use the word as distinct from kingdom, a state form created by the Constitution of 1840. In my interpretation, there was no kingdom before 1840.

9. See Kame'eleihiwa, 1992, *Native Land and Foreign Desires*, 58–64. Actually the conquest by Kamehameha ended a warring period, several centuries old, between the great Maui and Hawai'i lineages. This warfare had also resulted in the destruction of the great O'ahu chiefs following the defeat of Kahahana by Kahekili in 1783.

10. Kamakau, 1991, *Ruling Chiefs of Hawai'i*, 138.

11. Malo was reared in the family of this learned chief and from him developed his remarkable skills of memory as well as his knowledge of the old religion. Whether or not he was hānai in the complete Hawaiian sense of the word (that is, adopted) I am not certain.

12. Stannard, 1989, *Before the Horror.*

13. Young, 1995, Moʻolelo Kaukau Aliʻi, 264.

14. Bushnell, 1993, The "Horror" Reconsidered, 115. Bushnell believed that contemporary estimates of the pre-Contact Native population were too low, but objected to Stannard's revision to 800,000, preferring a more moderate estimate of 400,000–500,000. However, Kameʻeleihiwa believes that Stannard's estimates are too conservative and that the population of prehaole Hawaiʻi was at least one million. See Kameʻeleihiwa, 1992, *Native Land and Foreign Desires,* 81. For "official" estimates of pre-Contact population and census documentation of the Native decline in the nineteenth century, see Schmitt, 1977, *Demographic Statistics of Hawaii,* 7, 25.

15. Kameʻeleihiwa, 1992, *Native Land and Foreign Desires,* 81.

16. For a discussion of the Hawaiian concept of pono (correct behavior, a state of balance and correctness in the universe), see Kameʻeleihiwa, 1992, *Native Land and Foreign Desires.* The author's focus was on the Aliʻi Nui in this work, but I doubt that she would contest the notion that Makaʻāinana were equally influenced by these values.

17. Schmitt, 1977, *Demographic Statistics of Hawaii,* 7.

18. In the eleventh hour of her illness she was finally baptized by English pastor William Ellis, of the London Missionary Society.

19. Richards was part of the third mission delegation that arrived in 1823, three years after the ABCFM established themselves under the Reverend Hiram Bingham.

20. Kaukaualiʻi were chiefs of descending lineages whose principal value was that they could enter into the company of sacred chiefs without being harmed by the incredible mana of that chief. They could, in turn, convey the wishes and orders of that chief to the Makaʻāinana.

21. Kameʻeleihiwa, 1992, *Native Land and Foreign Desires,* 283: Table 21. Davida Malo was given his Mahele award on Molokaʻi.

22. Ibid., 282: Table 20.

23. "Papa Inoa o ke Kula Nui o Lāhaināluna," in *Ka Hae Hawaii,* 19 May 1858, pp. 26–28.

24. Kameʻeleihiwa, 1992, *Native Land and Foreign Desires,* 281: Table 19.

25. It would be scandalously rude to their descendants for me to conclude that they were Makaʻāinana. Evidence from family histories may someday shed light on their identities.

26. Malo, 1951, *Hawaiian Antiquities (Moolelo Hawaii)* (original publication, 1898), viii.

27. Ibid., ix.

28. Andrews, 1835, letter of 24 November to Secretaries of the ABCFM, Missionary Letters, vol. 6, 50–51.

29. *Polynesian,* 16 October 1841. Notwithstanding the *Polynesian's* high praise for the Native scholars, it is likely that the document was principally drafted by William Richards. The Native scholars Malo and Boas Mahune acted as translators and mediators with the Mōʻī.

30. Kamakau, 1991, *Ruling Chiefs of Hawaiʻi,* 370. Kamakau said that it

was Richards who drafted the constitution. He went on to say that "the king selected Boas Mahune to represent him and Jonah Kapena to represent Kinau in drawing it up."

31. Ibid., 282. Also see my description of this event in chapter 3.

32. Ibid., 283.

33. Schmitt, 1977, *Demographic Statistics of Hawaii*, 35.

34. Wagner-Wright, 1992, When Unity Is Torn Asunder, 39–60.

35. See Schmitt, 1977, *Demographic Statistics of Hawaii*, 25. There are no estimates of population by ethnicity before 1853, when Caucasians numbered 1,687 of a total population of 73,137.

36. The Mōʻī was the supreme ruling chief of large districts of lands. By the fifteenth century, powerful historical forces were pointing toward the eventual centralization of the entire archipelago by a single Mōʻī. That, of course, was accomplished by Kamehameha the Great at the end of the eighteenth century. His successors ruled as a dynasty until 1874, with the election of Kalākaua.

37. L. F. Judd, 1880, *Honolulu: Sketches of the Life*, 81–82.

38. Bingham, 1981, *A Residence of Twenty-one Years*, 60–61.

39. Bishop, 1838, An Inquiry into the Causes, 57.

40. Dibble, 1838, *Ka Moolelo Hawaii*. Dibble in his preface acknowledged that most of the writing was done by students with some additions by their teachers who edited the 1838 manuscript. Although some of those teachers may have been Natives like Malo or Kamakau, I feel certain that the last two sentences of this passage were added by a haole. In Hawaiian the text reads, "Ma hea e huli nei ko kakou alo, ma mua anei I ke ao [literally, to the past light]? Ma hope paha I ka po [to the future darkness]?"

41. Calvin, 1951, The Institutes of the Christian Religion, 383–384.

42. From Edwards, 1996, Select Sermons.

43. Bishop, 1838, An Inquiry into the Causes, 62.

44. Kamakau, 1991, *Ruling Chiefs of Hawaiʻi*, 275–276.

45. Ibid., 334–342. Here Kamakau described the pivotal year 1834 when Kauikeaouli's resistance to Christian authority threatened to bring the mission's influence to an early end.

46. Daws, 1968, *Shoal of Time*, 97. Daws reported that by the beginning of 1838 nearly ninety missionaries were in the field, thirty-seven of them ordained ministers.

Chapter 2: Law and Lāhui

1. Kamakau, 1991, *Ruling Chiefs of Hawaiʻi*, 343. See also Kuykendall, 1938, *The Hawaiian Kingdom*, Vol. 1, *1778–1854*, 157. Kuykendall named some of the members of this "school": Daniel and John ʻĪʻī, Timothy Haʻalilio, Mahune, and Malo. Boas Mahune never served in the legislature; he died intestate in 1847. But eight of his classmates (out of a class of forty-four) served as representatives between 1841 and 1870. They were Oliwa ʻĀlapa, Asa Hopu, Kaʻanaʻana, Kaʻaukai, Kahoʻokuʻi, John Kapena, A. Moku, and Davida Malo.

2. Kamakau, 1991, *Ruling Chiefs of Hawai'i*, 344.

3. Ibid., 345.

4. Kingdom of Hawai'i, 1840, Foreign Office and Executive, *He Kumu Kanawai a me ke Kanawai Hooponopono Waiwai.*

5. Ibid.

6. Kamakau, 1991, *Ruling Chiefs of Hawai'i*, 371.

7. Chambers, 1896, Constitutional History of Hawaii, 13.

8. Cited in Kuykendall, 1938, *The Hawaiian Kingdom*, Vol. 1, *1778–1854*, 158. From *The Letters of Dr. Gerrit P. Judd, 1827–1872*, Preserved in the Archives of the A.B.C.F.M., Boston, 110–112.

9. Kamakau, 1991, *Ruling Chiefs of Hawai'i*, 397. The other representatives were Jacob Malo and Kapae for Hawai'i, Paul Kanoa and L. K. Hala'i for O'ahu, and David Pāpōhaku for Kaua'i.

10. Ibid., 397.

11. Malo, 1951, *Hawaiian Antiquities (Moolelo Hawaii)*, 198.

12. Ibid., 187.

13. Ibid., 198.

14. Kingdom of Hawai'i, 1845, *Journal of the Legislative Council.*

15. Kingdom of Hawai'i, 1845, Foreign Office and Executive, *Privy Council Minutes*, Appendix O. Gerrit Judd was secretary.

16. A Kona Petition: "Would Not Sell Public Lands to Foreigners." Cited in Kame'eleihiwa, 1992, *Native Land and Foreign Desires*, Appendix.

17. Kame'eleihiwa, 1992, *Native Land and Foreign Desires*, 202.

18. Kingdom of Hawai'i, 1846, Department of Foreign Affairs, Answers to Questions. Prepared by R. C. Wyllie, minister for foreign affairs.

19. *Friend*, August 1845, p. 2.

20. Kingdom of Hawai'i, 1845, Department of the Interior, Miscellaneous Files, November.

21. Kingdom of Hawai'i, 1840, Foreign Office and Executive, *Privy Council Minutes.*

22. Kingdom of Hawai'i, 1847, Department of the Interior, Miscellaneous Files, book 2. 8 October.

23. Other kingdom representatives who served as assistant instructors at Lāhaināluna were L. S. Ua, D. H. Nāhinu, Luther Aholo, and J. Kakina.

24. Kingdom of Hawai'i, 1848, *Journal of the Legislative Council.* Entry for 7 June. The Mō'ī eventually quieted—he did not settle—the argument.

25. They were the chiefesses Kekāuluohi, Hoapiliwahine, Kekau'ōnohi, Konia, and Keohokalole and the male Ali'i Kuakini, Pākī, Kahekili, Leleiōhoku, Kekūanaō'a, Keli'iahonui, Kana'ina, John 'Ī'ī, Keoniana, and Ha'alilio.

26. Its official name was the Board of Commissioners to Quiet Land Titles.

27. Kingdom of Hawai'i, 1848, *Journal of the Legislative Council*, 334–337.

28. Ibid.

29. Kingdom of Hawai'i, 1845, *Journal of the Legislative Council*, 23.

30. This was a significant event in 1843 and was covered by Kame'elei-

hiwa, 1992, *Native Land and Foreign Desires*, 183–185. Acting on advice from Gerrit Judd, Kauikeaouli ceded the kingdom to Great Britain under protest when threatened by British Commander Georges Paulet. The kingdom was under Paulet's "government" from February to July of 1843. The kingdom was restored to Kauikeaouli by British Admiral Richard Thomas. This restoration appeared to have justified Judd's advice and made him the most influential man in the kingdom for several years.

31. Kingdom of Hawai'i, 1845, Foreign Office and Executive, book 4, 15.

32. Malo, 1839, On the Decrease of Population.

33. Kingdom of Hawai'i, 1845, *Journal of the Legislative Council*, 21.

34. *Friend*, August 1845, p. 119.

35. Chun, 1987, Biographical Sketch of Davida Malo, xiv.

36. Kingdom of Hawai'i, 1845, *Journal of the Legislative Council*, General Records, Series 222.

37. *Friend*, August 1845, p. 118.

38. Kingdom of Hawai'i, 1845, *Journal of the Legislative Council*, General Records, Series 222.

39. Kingdom of Hawai'i, 1837, Foreign Office and Executive, Malo to Kīna'u, 18 August.

40. Castle, 1915, Sketch of Constitutional History in Hawaii, 24.

Chapter 3: 'Āina and Lāhui

1. Kingdom of Hawai'i, 1848, Supreme Court Letter Book of Chief Justice Lee, 4 January. It was standard practice for deeds issued to contain the disclaimer "subject to the rights of the Native tenants." William Little Lee, member of the Land Commission and chief justice of the Supreme Court, in 1848 wrote responding to a concerned ABCFM pastor, "the tenants however, will not lose their rights should they fail to send in their claims, for I will see that no Konohiki has a title to lands except on the condition of respecting the rights of tenants."

2. Kuykendall, 1938, *The Hawaiian Kingdom*, Vol. 1, *1778–1854*, 291.

3. Wyllie to Judd (no.10), 19 November 1849, in *Report of Secretary at War*, 1855, Appendix, 7–8. Cited in Kuykendall, 1938, *The Hawaiian Kingdom*, Vol. 1, *1778–1854*, 291.

4. Kame'eleihiwa, 1992, *Native Land and Foreign Desires*, 30–31.

5. Kuykendall, 1938, *The Hawaiian Kingdom*, Vol. 1, *1778–1854*, 293.

6. Judd, 1880, *Sketches of the Life*, 116–117.

7. Kame'eleihiwa, 1992, *Native Land and Foreign Desires*, 295.

8. Kingdom of Hawai'i, 1850, *Journal of the Legislative Council*, 9 July.

9. Ibid.

10. Ibid.

11. Kingdom of Hawai'i, 1850, House of Nobles and Representatives, *Hawaii Penal Code and Session Laws*, 146–147.

12. Schmitt, 1977, *Demographic Statistics of Hawaii*, 25. It is unfortunate that we have no corresponding numbers for identical years. The Interior Department of the kingdom had lists and numbers for 1851, and statistician

Robert Schmitt had population estimates for 1853, 1860, 1866, 1872, and 1878. Note that the Caucasian (haole) numbers do not include Portuguese, who were counted as a separate ethnicity.

13. Cannelora, 1974, *The Origin of Hawaiian Land Titles*, 38.

14. Ibid.

15. Clech-Lam, 1989, The Kuleana Act Revisited, 272.

16. Kameʻeleihiwa, 1992, *Native Land and Foreign Desires*, 44–47. Kameʻeleihiwa described ʻimi haku (searching for a lord) as an issue for Kaukaualiʻi. A similar custom involved Makaʻāinana who took the step of leaving the place of their birth.

17. See Cannelora, 1974, *The Origin of Hawaiian Land Titles*, 39–44.

18. Cited in Linnekin, 1983, The Hui Lands of Keʻanae, 176.

19. Cannelora, 1974, *The Origin of Hawaiian Land Titles*, 41.

20. Jones, 1934, Naturalization in Hawaii, 17.

21. Ibid. Lawmakers did not make any legal provisions for alien women who might wish to marry Native men.

22. Kingdom of Hawaiʻi, 1848, *Journal of the Legislative Council*, 3 June, 118–120. Kekūanāoʻa may well have been thinking about the recent marriage of High Chiefess Bernice Pauahi to the haole businessman Charles Reed Bishop.

23. Kamakau, 1991, *Ruling Chiefs of Hawaiʻi*, 281.

24. *Friend*, August 1845, p. 119.

25. Jones, 1934, Naturalization in Hawaii, 17.

26. *Sandwich Island News*, letter from Scrutateur, 23 June 1847, p. 2. I am not at all certain, but this letter and the one signed "Brevitas" may have been written by the same individual, Abraham Fornander, future minister of education and future justice of the Supreme Court. Other letters that he admitted writing were signed with Latin pseudonyms. See note 35.

27. Kingdom of Hawaiʻi, 1850, *Foreign Office Letter Book No. 11*, Wyllie to U.S. Commissioner Anthony Ten Eyck, 403.

28. *Friend*, 9 October 1844, p. 91.

29. Gerrit P. Judd, minister of foreign affairs, Letter to the Secretaries of the ABCFM, 5 September 1844. Cited in Jones, 1934, Naturalization in Hawaii, 77–79.

30. *Friend*, August 1845, p. 119.

31. Cited in Kuykendall, 1938, *The Hawaiian Kingdom*, Vol. 1, *1778–1854*, 265–266.

32. Kingdom of Hawaiʻi, 1850, *Statute Laws*, I, 79–80.

33. Porter, 1918, *A History of Suffrage in the United States*, 113.

34. Ibid., 114.

35. *Polynesian*, 22 September 1849, p. 3. Letter by Brevitas.

36. Independent Hawaiian-language newspapers willing to publish Native political views did not come into existence until 1861.

37. *Polynesian*, 11 August 1849, p. 3. Editorial by E. O. Hall.

38. Kuykendall, 1938, *The Hawaiian Kingdom*, Vol. 1, *1778–1854*, 266.

39. Kingdom of Hawaiʻi, 1851, *Journal of the House of Representatives*, 16 April, 9. Most of the irregularities had to do with failures to strictly follow the

letter of the law. There are no examples from this period to suggest that prospective legislators tried to cheat their way into office. Rather, the opposite occurred in 1851 when Lokomaika'i of Moloka'i and Wahinemaika'i of Hāmākua were not seated with the other representatives on the opening day of the legislature. Their election was irregular because they were not elected on the first Monday of January as was required by law. Two other men who were elected on the proper day had declined to serve, forcing those districts to hold a new election a few days later.

40. Kingdom of Hawai'i, 1847, *Journal of the Legislative Council*, 11 May, 136.

41. Schmitt, 1971, Voter Participation in Hawaii, 53.

42. *Polynesian*, 11 January 1851, p. 138, col. 2.

43. *Polynesian*, 16 October 1850, p. 3.

44. Daws, 1968, *Shoal of Time*, 130. Some of Robertson's charges included interfering with the administration of other kingdom offices, appropriating public money, misdirecting funds, using his personal influence for personal profit, and incompetence.

45. These Lāhaināluna lawyer/representatives were, in order of their legislative service, Z. Ka'auwai, Z. Kauma'ea, Oliwa 'Ālapa, Kolia, W. P. Kahale, H. J. Wana, J. W. E. Maika'i, John Kalili, and S. M. Kamakau.

Chapter 4: A House Divided

1. *Polynesian*, 29 November 1851, p. 114, col. 1.

2. Kingdom of Hawai'i, 1851, *Journal of the House of Representatives*. It is worth noting that the kānaka continued to petition the House of Representatives throughout the decade. Very few petitions are in evidence that were authored or signed by haole.

3. See Dibble, 1858, Student Roster of the Lāhaināluna Seminary, 26–28.

4. Kingdom of Hawai'i, 1851, *Journal of the House of Representatives*, 27–36. These pages contain the entries for 13 May through 19 May 1851.

5. Ibid.

6. Ibid., 37.

7. Ibid.

8. Kingdom of Hawai'i, 1852, *General Records of the Legislature*, Petitions, 77. The italicized words were underscored by the translator.

9. Ibid., Reports. Undated.

10. Kingdom of Hawai'i, 1851, *Journal of the House of Nobles*. See entries from 30 April to 6 May.

11. Turrill, n.d., The Joel Turrill Correspondence, 35.

12. *Ka Nupepa Kuokoa*, 5 December 1863, p. 2. Articles and editorials lamenting the death of Alexander Liholiho describe the procession of thousands of Hawaiians, who filed past the body of their Mō'ī for more than a week.

13. Varigny, 1981, *Fourteen Years in the Sandwich Islands*, 55.

14. Kamakau, 1991, *Ruling Chiefs of Hawai'i*, 411–412.

15. Turrill, n.d., The Joel Turrill Correspondence, 37.

16. Ibid.

17. Chambers, 1896, Constitutional History of Hawaii, 19.

18. Kuykendall, 1953, *The Hawaiian Kingdom*, Vol. 2, *1854–1874*, 116.

19. Kuykendall, 1938, *The Hawaiian Kingdom*, Vol. 1, *1778–1854*, 267.

20. Turrill, n.d., The Joel Turrill Correspondence, 52.

21. *Weekly Argus*, Mat. K. Smith, ed., 4 February 1852, vol. 1, no. 4. This letter was signed with the pseudonym "Alpha," who was identified several weeks later as Abraham Fornander, a Scandinavian who eventually headed the kingdom's educational system, became a legislator and Supreme Court justice, and authored several highly regarded works on Hawaiian history and lore.

22. Lydecker, 1918, *Roster Legislatures of Hawaii*, 12. Lydecker included copies of the various constitutions in his work. This is cited from the section entitled, "The House of Nobles."

23. The following members of the 1841 House of Nobles were dead by 1852: eight Ali‘i Nui: Hoapili, Kahekili, Keāhonui, Kekāuluohi (female), Kekau‘ōnohi (female), Keohokālole (female), Konia (female), and Leleiōhoku. The remaining six were Kaukauali‘i according to Kame‘eleihiwa (1992, *Native Land and Foreign Desires*, 308): Kuakini, Timothy Ha‘alilio, Keli‘iahonui, Julie Kauwā Alapa‘i (female), Kānehoa (James Young), and Nāmau‘u.

24. *Polynesian*, 2 May 1852. Not all of the supporters of monarchial power were British. Both Sheldon and Metcalf were Americans.

25. Ibid., 1 May 1852.

26. Ibid., 24 April 1852.

27. Kingdom of Hawai‘i, 1852, *General Records of the Legislature*, Committee Reports. Signed by Marshall with Metcalf, Ka‘auwai, Barenaba, and Kamakau in attendance. Dated 16 April.

28. *Polynesian*, 20 December 1851, p. 126, col. 2.

29. Ibid., 1 May 1852.

30. Ibid., 3 January 1852, p. 134, col. 2.

31. Simpson, 1847, *Narrative of a Journey Round the World*, 253.

32. Buck, 1986, The Politics of Culture, 182.

33. Friends of the Hawaiian Judiciary History Center, 1984, Searching for the Hundreds.

34. *Weekly Argus*, 14 January 1852.

35. George Robertson did not run from Honolulu in 1852 due to a change in the laws requiring three months' residence in a district before election. He ran instead from Hāmākua, where he survived a much closer race than he might have in Honolulu.

36. *Polynesian*, 10 January 1852, p. 138, col. 3.

37. Kingdom of Hawai‘i, 1852, *General Records of the Legislature*, Petitions.

38. Daws, 1968, *Shoal of Time*, 146, 441n. In the fall of 1851 Judd fired William Jarrett from his position as auditor in the Treasury, essentially making the young man a scapegoat for Judd's own problems. Daws said that Judd "pursued him through the courts and eventually ruined him."

39. *Weekly Argus*, 14 January 1852. It would be ironic in the extreme if

the representative that this anecdote referred to was Honokaupu, a likely pick because Kekaulahao had served in 1851. For when the House voted on whether to strike Article 23 from the constitution, Honokaupu and a minority of representatives voted to keep it in. If he was, indeed, the beneficiary of missionary persuasion in Honolulu, he apparently did not feel obligated to return the favor.

40. *Polynesian*, 20 December 1851, p. 126, col. 2. Editorial. There is no byline on this editorial. The newpaper's editor was E. O. Hall, a former ABCFM missionary.

41. Ibid., 5 June 1852.

42. Kingdom of Hawai'i, 1852, *Journal of the House of Nobles*. See entry for 3 May.

43. *Polynesian*, 8 May 1852.

44. Hobbs, 1935, *Hawaii: A Pageant of the Soil*, 88.

45. Ibid., 87. For a comprehensive description of missionary land transactions, see Hobbs' Appendix "B," 157–178.

46. Ibid., 157–158.

47. Ibid., 88.

48. Ibid., 43.

49. *Weekly Argus*, 14 January 1852.

50. *Polynesian*, 3 January 1852, p. 134, col. 2.

51. Kingdom of Hawai'i, *Journal of the House of Representatives*, 20 April 1852, 144. The motion to strike Article 23 from the draft constitution passed. In favor: Marshall, Kaho'okui, Richardson, Metcalf, Z. Ka'auwai, Barenaba, Kama'ipepekane, Naiapaakai, Funk, Kamakau, Pali, and Kapehe. Against: Robertson, Wakeman, Sheldon, Laanui, Kalili, Kalauhala, Honokaupu, and G. Rhodes.

52. *Polynesian*, 1 May 1852. Alexander Liholiho favored the article initially and was supported by Wyllie, Kanoa, Pākī, Kā'eo, Lota Kapuāiwa, and Kana'ina. Armstrong moved to strike the article and was supported by Judd, Kapeau, Kapena, 'Ī'ī, Pi'ikoi, and Nāmakehā. Alexander Liholiho broke the tie by casting the vote to erase the article. The nobles took the entire day to decide this question.

53. *Weekly Argus*, 1 May 1852.

54. *Polynesian*, 28 February 1852, p. 166, col. 1.

55. Hawaiians outside the legislature tended to steer clear of the debate over Article 23. But one petition from a congregation in Wailuku, introduced by John Richardson, called for striking the article. It had over two hundred signatures. See *Polynesian*, 24 April 1852, p. 199, col. 2.

56. Kamakau, 1991, *Ruling Chiefs of Hawai'i*, 425–426.

57. Ibid., 402–407.

58. Ibid., 399–402. Samuel Kamakau was one of those who drafted petitions from Lāhainā asking the Mō'ī to replace the foreign cabinet ministers with Ali'i.

59. Ibid., 402. Kauikeaouli's response to Kamakau is especially interesting because the king singled out G. L. Kapeau as an especially promising

Native official. Although Kamakau acknowledged that Kapeau had been appointed, he never once concurred with the king's high opinion of that future noble.

60. William Little Lee's address before the Royal Hawaiian Agricultural Society. See L. F. Judd, 1880, *Honolulu: Sketches of the Life,* 167–168.

61. Lee concluded his speech to the Royal Hawaiian Agricultural Society with these words, "Then if our last hope fail, if all our efforts to send a quickening life-pulse through the heart of the wasting nation avail not, we can but commend it to Him, in whose hands are the issues of life and death—to Him who numbreth the nations as the small dust of the balance, and taketh up the isles as a very little thing."

62. Kingdom of Hawai'i, 1852, *General Records of the Legislature,* Petitions.

Chapter 5: Conventional Beliefs

1. Lydecker, 1918, *Roster Legislatures of Hawaii,* 48. "Mode of Amending the Constitution."

2. Kuykendall, 1953, *The Hawaiian Kingdom,* Vol. 2, *1854–1874,* 119–122. In 1858, the representatives, at the suggestion of the king, introduced five amendments that would have reduced their numbers from twenty-four to twenty-one (the king wanted twenty), paid them a flat rate for each session rather than a per diem (the sessions usually went long), made the king's ministers eligible for election to the House of Representatives, required a property/income qualification for representatives, and a reading test for voters. All but the first amendment passed both Houses, but none of them was introduced to the 1860 legislature because the government failed to publish the amendments three months before the elections. When the king tried to have those amendments and seven others introduced in the 1860 legislature, the House of Representatives passed the new amendments but rejected the five that the previous legislature had passed. The nobles, unwilling to take action on the seven "unsatisfactory" amendments, postponed their vote until the 1862 session. Eventually, the representatives resisted those amendments that affected them.

3. Ibid., 119.

4. Kuykendall, 1938, *The Hawaiian Kingdom,* Vol. 1, *1778–1854,* 412 and Daws, 1968, *Shoal of Time,* 137–142. These two historians disagreed about the reliability of this number. The official published death count was 2,485 deaths resulting from 6,405 cases, but the government archives contain a file that cites over 11,000 cases on O'ahu alone and nearly 6,000 fatalities.

5. Lydecker, 1918, *Roster Legislatures of Hawaii,* 62. "His Majesty's Speech Dissolving the Legislature." Liholiho said, "the House of Representatives framed an Appropriation Bill exceeding our Revenues, as estimated by our Minister of Finance, to the extent of about $200,000, which Bill We could not sanction."

6. For a general description of this group and their activities, see Daws, 1968, *Shoal of Time,* 147–153. But more detailed and reliable remarks can be

found in the memoirs of David Gregg, the American commissioner to the Islands in the 1850s. See Gregg, 1982, *The Diaries of David Lawrence Gregg*.

7. Daws, 1968, *Shoal of Time*, 148.

8. Kingdom of Hawai'i, 1853, *Journal of the House of Representatives*, 16 June. The House records reveal only the most austere details concerning the representatives' votes over the issue of Lathrop's payment. Daws (1968, *Shoal of Time*, 142) focused considerable attention on this doctor/dentist's career.

9. Kingdom of Hawai'i, 1852, *Journal of the House of Representatives*, 16 June.

10. *Polynesian*, 23 June 1855.

11. Lydecker, 1918, *Roster Legislatures of Hawaii*, 72. "Special Message of His Majesty Sent to the Legislature, March 31, 1859."

12. Chambers, 1896, Constitutional History in Hawaii, 20.

13. Kamakau, 1991, *Ruling Chiefs of Hawai'i*, 280. Kīna'u gave birth to a son, David Kamehameha, in the mid-1820s following her marriage to Kekū-'anaō'a. That son was hānai to Ka'ahumanu and Kekāuluohi.

14. Young, 1995, Mo'olelo Kaukau Ali'i, 109–111. Young discussed the paradox for Ali'i Nui whose traditions encouraged noho (mating for the purpose of producing children) with siblings and the Calvinist morality that prohibited it.

15. Kamakau, 1991, *Ruling Chiefs of Hawai'i*, 290.

16. Young, 1995, Mo'olelo Kaukau Ali'i, 266. Young stated, "The monarchy was sustained beyond 1854 because a change in genealogical standards for possible heirs was accepted by the chiefly hierarchy who survived unscathed by the ravaging effects of foreign diseases. When the decision was made in 1839 to give the *Ali'i Nui* children a *haole*-based education, the selection of qualified students centered on offspring from the couples with one partner who was in the 'Best of the Rest' category." Kame'eleihiwa argued, however, that the priority of matrilineal descent in Hawaiian chiefly society made Kīna'u's children true *Ali'i Nui*. Kekū'anaō'a was a high chief, in any case, whose O'ahu family had merely been overcome by the conquest in 1794.

17. Kauikeaouli's selection of Alexander Liholiho is also a prime example of the twin causes of the crisis in chiefly genealogies (death and Christianity) discussed by Young in his work. Kauikeaouli, whose progeny of his nī'aupi'o union with Nāahi'ena'ena did not survive, had no other children with any of the high chiefesses. His hānai son was a reasonable choice because of their relationship. Otherwise, Kapuāiwa, the elder, might have been the more obvious choice.

18. Lydecker, 1918, *Roster Legislatures of Hawaii*, 38. See Article 25.

19. Ibid., 10.

20. Kuykendall, 1953, *The Hawaiian Kingdom*, Vol. 2, *1854–1874*, 124. Kuykendall said, "Immediately after the sudden death of Kamehameha IV, steps were taken to ascertain whether there might be a posthumous heir born to him."

21. This evidently led to a small and very temporary crisis that was described by British High Commissioner Synge: "There seems to have been

some doubt whether the present King's title to the throne was sufficiently clear, or whether, according to the Constitution, the Regency of the Kingdom should not be placed in the hands of the Princess Victoria Kamamalu as Kuhina Nui, . . . until the legislature should elect a King. Such objections, which emanated from a small but not uninfluential section of the American Missionaries who are supposed to hold the Princess under their controul were however overruled by the prompt action of the Privy Council." Cited in Kuykendall, 1953, *The Hawaiian Kingdom*, Vol. 2, *1854–1874*, 125.

22. Lydecker, 1918, *Roster Legislatures of Hawaii*, 11.

23. Ibid., 40. Article 45 states, "The King and *Kuhina Nui* shall have a negative on each other's public acts."

24. Kuykendall, 1953, *The Hawaiian Kingdom*, Vol. 2, *1854–1874*, 115–134.

25. Lydecker, 1918, *Roster Legislatures of Hawaii*, 99.

26. Ibid., 72. "Special Message of His Majesty Sent to the Legislature, March 31, 1859."

27. *Pacific Commercial Advertiser*, 14 May 1864. It should be noted that in the king's original statement the Hawaiian text read, "a no ka noonoo ana I ka hemahema o na Lala o ke Aupuni I mea I hiki ai na hana o ke Aupuni." Literally: for the considering of the incompetent of the branches of the Government to enable the work of the government. This clause in Hawaiian was abridged in the proclamation's second publishing on 14 May and the clause in English read only "to provide ways and means to carry on Our Government."

28. Ibid.

29. Kuykendall, 1953, *The Hawaiian Kingdom*, Vol. 2, *1854–1874*, 140–143.

30. *Pacific Commercial Advertiser*, 2 April 1864, p. 3, cols. 1–2.

31. Whitney maintained such a consistent hostility to government-controlled immigration of labor that he eventually fell from favor with the ever more powerful plantation owners and lost his newspaper in 1870. See Beechert, 1985, *Working in Hawaii: A Labor History*, 74–77.

32. *Pacific Commercial Advertiser*, 2 April 1864, p. 3, cols. 1–2.

33. Ibid.

34. Ibid.

35. Ibid., 23 April 1864, p. 2, col. 4. Ma'aku'ia was a former teacher from Lāna'i, an 1834 graduate of Lāhaināluna whose name does not appear anywhere in the Indices of Land Commission Awards. He was probably landless. He was certainly not illiterate.

36. Cited in Kuykendall, 1953, *The Hawaiian Kingdom*, Vol. 2, *1854–1874*, 116. Memo to Alexander Liholiho, September 1861.

37. Kingdom of Hawai'i, 1864, Foreign Office and Executive, *Cabinet Council Minutes*, 3 March. Quoted in Daws, 1968, *Shoal of Time*, 184.

38. *Pacific Commercial Advertiser*, 31 December 1863, p. 2, col. 2.

39. Ibid.

40. *Pacific Commercial Advertiser*, 1 October 1864, p. 3, col. 2. Samuel Castle, son of missionary/entrepreneur William Castle received the scorn of

the *Pacific Commercial Advertiser* when he ran for the legislative assembly after serving on Kapuāiwa's privy council. The newspaper charged, "The public will be surprised at Mr. Castle's lending himself to be a tool of a ministry which has proved a disgrace to the country . . . the barren honor of a Privy Councillor has completely changed his views of men and things, and the present degradation to a seat in this Assembly, should he retain it, will destroy public confidence in him."

41. It should be noted that Robert Wyllie's plantation at Princeville was a spectacular failure. See Daws, *Shoal of Time*, 1968, 175.

42. *Pacific Commercial Advertiser*, 24 December 1863, p. 3, col. 2. De Varigny was later "rehabilitated" in Whitney's eyes after he published his financial report to the legislature, which the *Advertiser* complimented. Also, de Varigny favored awarding a government contract to the *Advertiser* to publish the complete minutes of the legislative assembly in 1864. He fought Wyllie and Charles Coffin Harris (Alexander Liholiho's attorney general) over it and lost. *Pacific Commercial Advertiser*, 22 October 1864, p. 2, col. 2.

43. Turrill, n.d., The Joel Turrill Correspondence, 90. 20 January 1854.

44. James I. Dowsett was the son of Samuel James Dowsett, a trader seaman. He was specifically mentioned in a *Pacific Commercial Advertiser* reprint of a letter sent to the *San Francisco Bulletin* and published on 13 July 1864: "Mr. Dowsett, having lived here from infancy, (born at sea) is more identified with the natives—having made a fortune here—and understands better their characteristics and their wants than any one in the islands I can name. He is decidedly liberal in his politics, but unfettered by any governmental ties."

45. *Pacific Commercial Advertiser*, 7 January 1864.

46. Five kānaka delegates, Kahananui, Kuaʻea, ʻŪkēkē, Heleluhe, and Kipi, signed a petition forwarded at the convention by Gulick and Green. The other signers of that petition read like a roster of the ABCFM and their children: Gerrit and Charles Judd, D. H. and E. G. Hitchcock, and Reverend Henry Parker.

47. The 1864 elections, held in January, elected twenty-four representatives. But the election was nullified with the promulgation of the new constitution in August. A new election was held in early September.

48. *Kuokoa*, which was founded by the very same Whitney that edited the *Pacific Commercial Advertiser*, was, in the early 1860s, very much a Hawaiian version of the English newspaper. Its opinions usually reflected those of the *Advertiser*. For example, the 14 May 1864 editorial in *Kuokoa* expressed nearly word for word the concern in the 14 May *Advertiser* that the constituting power not be taken away from the legislature.

49. *Pacific Commercial Advertiser*, 7 August 1864, p. 1, col. 1.

50. Kingdom of Hawaiʻi, 1864, Foreign Office and Executive, Cabinet Council File no. 2, March to July. Signed by Wyllie and Harris, 26 March.

51. Locke, 1951, *The Second Treatise of Civil Government*, 421: "Men being . . . by nature all free, equal, and independent, no one can be put out of this estate and subjected to the political power of another without his own consent."

52. *Pacific Commercial Advertiser*, 25 June 1864, p. 2, col. 3.

53. Ibid., 4 June 1864, p. 2, col. 3.

54. Ibid., col. 2 (in the story "Official Delinquents"). See also 21 May 1864, p. 3, col. 3 (letter from Makaainana): "Still, after carefully reading the Attorney General's explanation, one is unable to find in it any definite answer to the most important question that now agitates the public mind, viz: *Is it the intentions of His Majesty's Ministers that the proposed convention shall alter or annul our present Constitution?*"

55. *Kuokoa*, 16 July 1864 (Kauwahi's speech on Article 62).

56. *Pacific Commercial Advertiser*, 21 May 1864, p. 3, col. 4 (letter from Another of the People).

57. Kingdom of Hawai'i, 1864, *Minutes of the Constitutional Convention*.

58. *Pacific Commercial Advertiser*, 9 July 1864, p. 2, col. 3 (letter from "Viddette").

59. Kuykendall, 1953, *The Hawaiian Kingdom*, Vol. 2, *1854–1874*, 39.

60. Turrill, n.d., the Joel Turrill Correspondence, 62, 14 January 1853.

61. This chapter cannot bear another digression. But it should be noted that Wyllie was blamed for having promoted the introduction of the Anglican Church into the kingdom during the reign of Kamehameha IV. When Alexander Liholiho, the royal family, and Wyllie left Kawaiaha'o Church to become members of St. Andrews, the ABCFM lost a good deal of prestige.

62. I have not found any of the king's speeches in which he defends his ministry. Kapuāiwa was a taciturn individual by reputation and rarely spoke at public gatherings outside of the opening and closing of the legislature. I also think that Kapuāiwa may not have been particularly adverse to his ministry acting as a lightning rod for haole criticism.

63. *Pacific Commercial Advertiser*, 30 July 1864, p. 2, col. 2.

64. Ibid.

65. Ibid.

66. The two dissenting nobles were Charles Reed Bishop and the future Mō'ī, William Charles Lunalilo.

67. *Pacific Commercial Advertiser*, 30 July 1864.

68. See Lydecker, 1918, *Roster Legislatures of Hawaii*, 88–93. Articles 31, 43, and 4, respectively.

69. *Pacific Commercial Advertiser*, 16 July 1864, p. 2, col. 4.

70. Ibid., 30 July 1864, p. 2, col. 2.

71. Turrill, n.d., The Joel Turrill Correspondence, 62, 14 January 1853.

72. Ibid., 34–35.

73. In fact, the king also supported closer *economic* ties with America, expecting that such ties would increase the wealth of the government and, thus, the nation. In 1867 he convened a special session of the legislature just to ratify a treaty of reciprocity with the United States. His speech convening that assembly said, "I am satisfied that the anticipated benefits of the Treaty of Reciprocity will not be confined to any special branch of our industry, but will extend over all." See Lydecker, 1918, *Roster Legislatures of Hawaii*, 110.

74. Friends of the Hawaiian Judiciary History Center, 1984, Searching for the Hundreds.

75. See Kuykendall, 1940, Constitutions of the Hawaiian Kingdom, 39:

"In Article 61 (corresponding to Article 77 of the old Constitution) Denizens were no longer eligible to this office. The minimum age was raised to 25 years. The one year residence requirement was changed to three years domicile, the last year of which had to be immediately preceding his election. Most important was the addition of a property qualification, which could be satisfied by ownership of real estate of an unencumbered value of at least $500 or by an annual income of at least $250."

76. *Hawaiian Gazette,* 28 April 1866. On the opening day of the legislature, the representative from Waialua, attorney Keawehunahala, called for this "equal treatment" of all the members.

77. Ibid.

78. Ibid.

79. Ibid.

80. Ibid.

81. Ibid.

82. Bishop was married to the princess Bernice Pauahi, and Dominis was married to Liliʻuokalani, sister of David Kalākaua and future queen.

83. *Hawaiian Gazette,* 5 May 1866.

84. Ibid.

85. Ibid.

86. Ibid.

87. Ibid.

88. Ibid.

89. *Pacific Commercial Advertiser,* 6 January 1866, p. 1. Over thirty-five hundred of these were taxpayers, prompting the *Advertiser* to comment, "A more unequal and unjust law was never devised than the present constitutional law regarding the franchise—unjust because it is really enjoyed only by a few government officials and rich persons—unjust because it degrades the poor man to the level of a slave; aye, below that of a slave, for it taxes him and then deprives him of the right to vote. . . . It degrades the poor man, white or black, for it makes him feel it a *curse to be poor,* and that he is practically outlawed."

90. Ibid.

91. Ibid., 9 June 1866.

92. Beechert, 1985, *Working in Hawaii: A Labor History,* 60. But Lota Kapuāiwa's other economic initiative, pursuit of a treaty of reciprocity with the United States, would, when finally secured by Kalākaua in 1874, so greatly expand sugar cultivation that immigrants from China and Japan would virtually replace Hawaiian workers by 1882.

93. See *Pacific Commercial Advertiser,* 13 August 1864, p. 2, col. 2. "The property qualifications will appear to foreigners to be so small as to be insignificant; but their application will be solely to the native, and will act to exclude from the polls a large portion, perhaps one-half, or even two-thirds of the present voters, because not one in a hundred of the native kuleanas or lands are valued at $150, and a large portion are held in the names of the wives or mothers, and not by males."

Chapter 6: Hawai'i for Hawaiians

1. Schmitt, 1977, *Demographic Statistics of Hawaii*, 9, 25. Estimated population in 1842 was 100,800. Almost all of them were Natives. In 1887 it was 84,500, but only half, approximately, were Natives or hapa (of mixed blood).

2. Ibid., 611. See also Thrum, 1888, *Hawaiian Almanac and Annual*, 34 (Comparative Table of Receipts and Expenditures). In the biennium 1884–1886, the government expenditures show that the Department of the Interior, which was responsible for capital improvements, was by far the largest consumer of public money, spending $1,162,126 of the nearly $3,000,000 budget. By contrast, neither the Bureau of Public Education nor the Board of Health were allotted more than $241,000, and the legislature spent just over $31,000 for its session, which included salaries.

3. Schmitt, 1977, *Demographic Statistics of Hawaii*, 229. Overall literacy was estimated at 75 percent in 1853 when the population was overwhelmingly Native, with Caucasians, mostly Americans, making up the bulk of the remainder. This is important because the census takers determined literacy only in English or Hawaiian. In 1884 with Chinese and Portuguese making up nearly three-eighths of the population, literacy in English and Hawaiian stood at 44.6 percent.

4. In 1884, at least three principal Hawaiian-language newspapers were in operation, all of them weekly: *Ka Nupepa Kuokoa, Ka Elele Poakolu,* and *Ko Hawaii Pae Aina.* The significant English papers were the *Pacific Commercial Advertiser* and the *Evening Bulletin,* published daily, and the *Hawaiian Gazette* and the *Saturday Press,* both weekly. All of these papers were published in Honolulu.

5. See Kamakau, 1991, *Ruling Chiefs of Hawai'i*, 109, 208, in which Kekāuluohi is identified as the daughter of one of the Conqueror's wāhine, Kaheiheimālie, and Kaleimamahū, a half brother of Kamehameha.

6. Kuykendall, 1953, *The Hawaiian Kingdom*, Vol. 2, *1854–1874*, 244. See also Schmitt, 1977, *Demographic Statistics of Hawaii*, 602. Of 12,581 votes cast in the Islands, 12,530 were for Lunalilo.

7. Although the election of the king struck some of the haole observers as a "contradiction in terms," the traditional succession of Mō'ī was only partly based on heredity. According to Kamakau, the great O'ahu Mō'ī Mā'ilikūkahi was elected by a council of Ali'i Nui in the fifteenth century.

8. Kuykendall, 1953, *The Hawaiian Kingdom*, Vol. 2, *1854–1874*, 240–245. See also the *Pacific Commercial Advertiser,* 30 July 1864, p. 3, col. 2: an editorial about the conduct of the 1864 constitutional convention. Article 3, which dealt with the freedom of the press, contained a clause that could limit that freedom in defense of the royal family. Lunalilo and C. R. Bishop were praised by the newspaper's editor for being the only two nobles to vote against restraining the press for any reason.

9. Kuykendall, 1953, *The Hawaiian Kingdom*, Vol. 2, *1854–1874*, 243.

10. Ibid., 244.

11. These attacks came from a distant relative of Kalākaua, Koi'i Unauna, who claimed as early as 1856 (when Emma and Alexander Liholiho were wed)

that Emma was not descended from Keliʻimaikaʻi but from Kalaipaʻihala, a half brother of Kalaniʻōpuʻu.

12. Korn, 1976, *News from Molokaʻi*, 58. See letter from Emma to Peter Kāʻeo dated 14 August 1873.

13. Joesting, 1972, *Hawaii: An Uncommon History*, 209.

14. Thrum, 1874, The Second Interregnum. This is a scrapbook of newspaper articles written about the election and its aftermath and can be found in the Hawaiʻi Collection of Hamilton Library, University of Hawaiʻi at Mānoa.

15. Cited in Thrum, 1874, The Second Interregnum.

16. Daws, 1968, *Shoal of Time*, 197. An oft-cited story was told by legislator C. J. Lyons (1868, 1870), who reported having come upon a poster advertising support of the queen and how it had been defaced by an unknown Kalākaua supporter with the words, "Aole makou makemake e ike i ka palekoki e hookomo ana i ka lolewawae" (We do not wish to see the petticoats putting on the breeches). However, it is quite possible that any number of haole fluent in Hawaiian could have written this.

17. Thrum, 1874, The Second Interregnum.

18. Ibid.

19. A. F. Judd to Theo Davies. Cited in Kuykendall, 1967, *The Hawaiian Kingdom*, Vol. 3, *1874–1893*, 6.

20. Kuykendall, 1967, *The Hawaiian Kingdom*, Vol. 3, *1874–1893*, 5.

21. Ibid., 15.

22. Thrum, 1874, The Second Interregnum.

23. Kuykendall, 1967, *The Hawaiian Kingdom*, Vol. 3, *1874–1893*, 10.

24. Thrum, 1874, The Second Interregnum.

25. Thurston, 1936, *Memoirs of the Hawaiian Revolution*, 10.

26. William F. Allen to Elisha Allen. Cited in Kuykendall, 1967, *The Hawaiian Kingdom*, Vol. 3, *1874–1893*, 10.

27. Thrum, 1874, The Second Interregnum.

28. Ibid.

29. Sheldon, 1988, *Ka Buke Moʻolelo ʻO Hon. Joseph K. Nāwahī*, 273.

30. Ibid., 2.

31. Ibid., 25–35.

32. Ibid., 345–348. His widow ʻAima received no less than eighty memorials from individuals and political associations scattered throughout the Islands.

33. Ibid., 280.

34. Ibid.

35. See Thrum, 1874, The Second Interregnum, 9. Pilipō led the rally held at the queen's residence before the election.

36. Kuykendall, 1967, *The Hawaiian Kingdom*, Vol. 3, *1874–1893*, 14.

37. See Korn, 1976, *News from Molokaʻi*, 229 n. 6. The Hawaiian historian Kepelino was sentenced to death on 12 October 1874 by Supreme Court Justice C. C. Harris, despite his counsel's argument that the petition was not a secret and that it had never reached the French official to whom it was addressed. The king eventually pardoned Kepelino.

38. Ibid., 295. When Naʻili was elected from Koʻolauloa in 1876, the queen wrote, for example, "Naili, they say, is on our side."

39. Kuykendall, 1967, *The Hawaiian Kingdom*, Vol. 3, *1874–1893*, 195. Kuykendall wrote: "Perhaps in anticipation of this situation, the King had, a few weeks before the election, appointed six new nobles, three Native Hawaiians and three of foreign birth, bringing that branch of the legislature up to its authorized strength." (They were Leleiōhōkū, Kapena, Simon Kaʻai, John Mott-Smith, Godfrey Rhodes, and Samuel N. Castle.)

40. *Pacific Commercial Advertiser*, 5 May 1876, p. 1.

41. Ibid., 20 May 1876, p. 3, col. 6.

42. Ibid., 10 June 1876, p. 2.

43. Reported in the *Pacific Commercial Advertiser*, 25 July 1874. See also Kingdom of Hawaiʻi, 1874, *Session Laws of the Hawaiian Kingdom's Legislative Assembly*, 37–38.

44. Korn, 1976, *News from Molokaʻi*, 57.

45. *Hawaiian Gazette*, 17 December 1873, p. 3, col. 5.

46. Sheldon, 1988, *Ka Buke Moʻolelo ʻO Hon. Joseph K. Nāwahī*, 78.

47. *Pacific Commercial Advertiser*, 13 May 1876, p. 2.

48. Ibid., 3 June 1876, p. 2.

49. Ibid., p. 3.

50. Ibid.

51. Ibid., 29 July 1876.

52. See Kingdom of Hawaiʻi, 1874, *Session Laws of the Hawaiian Kingdom's Legislative Assembly*, 110–120. By 1876 all adult male inhabitants were responsible for three annual taxes: the poll tax of $1, the school tax of $2, and a road tax of $2. So each family paid a minimum of $5 per year, and much more if they owned dogs and horses.

53. *Pacific Commercial Advertiser*, 3 June 1876, p. 4. See entry under the Legislative Assembly, 25 May.

54. Ibid., 29 July 1876.

55. Kuykendall, 1967, *The Hawaiian Kingdom*, Vol. 3, *1874–1893*, 47.

56. Ibid., 56. In fact, the chairman of the finance committee, Walter Murray Gibson, called the transaction illegal.

57. Ibid., 55.

58. Ibid., 54.

59. *Pacific Commercial Advertiser*, 29 July 1876. See also Tate, 1968, *Hawaii: Reciprocity or Annexation*, 120. Tate wrote about the benefits of reciprocity to Hawaiians. Under the impulse of the treaty, Hawaiʻi increased her population from 58,000 in 1876 to about 75,000 in 1882 and anticipated a figure of 100,000 if the treaty remained in effect. Proponents of the treaty, however, neglected to say that much of this population increase was due to the importation of Oriental and other contract laborers. Of the entire 35,908 laborers of all kinds employed on the fifty-nine large sugar estates in 1899, 31,623 were Japanese and Chinese, 2,700 were Portuguese and other foreigners, and only 1,326 were Hawaiians.

60. U.S. Congress, 1898, *Senate Journal*, 55th Cong., 3rd sess., no. 16,

The Report of the Hawaiian Commission, 139. Cited in Kuykendall, 1967, *The Hawaiian Kingdom*, Vol. 3, *1874–1893*, 52–53.

61. *Pacific Commercial Advertiser*, 5 February 1876, p. 2, col. 2.

62. *Hawaiian Gazette*, 16 February 1876, p. 2.

63. *Pacific Commercial Advertiser*, 4 March 1876.

64. Ibid.

65. Hillebrand, 1867, *Report on the Supply of Labor*, 26. Hillebrand was the kingdom's first commissioner of the Board of Immigration.

66. *Pacific Commercial Advertiser*, 24 April 1869.

67. See Kuykendall, 1953, *The Hawaiian Kingdom*, Vol. 2, *1854–1874*, 73. He stated, "It is not known how or when leprosy was brought to Hawaii. The Hawaiians applied several names to it; the most common one, *Mai Pake* (Chinese disease), had reference to the fact that the disease was common in China; it is believed that it was brought from that country to the islands, but there is no definite proof that such was the case."

68. Hillebrand was medical director of the queen's hospital and commissioner of the Board of Health. In 1864 he was appointed commissioner of the Board of Immigration.

69. Daws, 1973, *Holy Man: Father Damien of Molokai*, 135–137. The book is about Damien and his self-sacrifice, working among a people afflicted with a disease that was regarded with particular loathing by haole. Except for a few pages devoted to Native helpers (kōkua), rather little is said about the kānaka.

70. Kuykendall, 1953, *The Hawaiian Kingdom*, Vol. 2, *1854–1874*, 257–259.

71. *Pacific Commercial Advertiser*, 10 June 1876, p. 3. The same article contained the text of a bill that S. K. Mahoe introduced on 7 June that would return all the exiles to their homes.

72. *Saturday Press*, 20 January 1883, p. 2, col. 2. The Vital Question. Foreigners who were infected were also sent to Kalawao, although they represented a very small minority. In 1873, 560 persons were sent to Kalawao. Only a half dozen were foreigners. See Kuykendall, 1953, *The Hawaiian Kingdom*, Vol. 2, *1854–1874*, 258.

73. *Pacific Commercial Advertiser*, 3 June 1876, p. 3.

74. Ibid., 18 March 1876, p. 5.

75. Kuykendall, 1967, *The Hawaiian Kingdom*, Vol. 3, *1874–1893*, 159. The king pursued immigration from Japan, sending John Kapena as his special emissary to Tokyo in 1882. Kapena's message to the imperial Japanese government was that the Japanese and Hawaiians were a cognate race, and that the Japanese were welcome to come to the Islands and repopulate them.

76. *Pacific Commercial Advertiser*, 9 February 1884, p. 3, col. 4. The article noted that there were 2,700 qualified voters in Honolulu, compared with 1,900 in 1882. Only 300 of them were haole. "The total number might probably have reached 3000 if all of them had paid their taxes and claimed their privileges."

77. *Pacific Commercial Advertiser*, 7 February 1874. Cited in Kuykendall, 1967, *The Hawaiian Kingdom*, Vol. 3, *1874–1893*, 191.

78. *Pacific Commercial Advertiser*, 31 March 1877.

79. Ibid., 4 March 1876, p. 3.

80. *Hawaiian Gazette*, 8 August 1877, p. 2.

81. *Pacific Commercial Advertiser*, 5 February 1876, p. 2.

82. Ibid., 1 February 1884, p. 2, col. 2.

83. Kuykendall, 1953, *The Hawaiian Kingdom*, Vol. 2, *1854–1874*, 186.

84. *Pacific Commercial Advertiser*, 3 June 1876, p. 3.

85. Adler, 1966, *Claus Spreckels: The Sugar King*, 297 n. 25.

86. *Pacific Commercial Advertiser*, 10 June 1876, p. 3, col. 6.

87. Ibid., 1 April 1876, p. 3.

88. Adler, 1966, *Claus Spreckels: The Sugar King*, 60.

89. Ibid., 14–15. Spreckels spearheaded a determined effort by California refiners to avoid competition from the kingdom's higher grades of sugar. At the same time, the California refineries were dependent on the Islands' production of lower grades. Late in 1875, a sugar agent in the Islands threatened to withhold the entire crop of Hawaiian sugar from the California market unless the refiners dropped their opposition to reciprocity.

90. Ironically, I think, Gavan Daws, a historian with little respect for Kalākaua, collaborated with George Cooper in a remarkable work that documented the profiteering of Democratic Party insiders in the expansive real estate market of the 1960s and 1970s in Hawai'i. Few of those individuals have been prosecuted or even sued. Fewer still have received the kind of scathing criticism that the king endured. See Cooper and Daws, 1990, *Land and Power in Hawaii*.

91. Adler, 1966, *Claus Spreckels: The Sugar King*, 39–41. It is believed that Spreckels paid the king $10,000 and loaned him an additional $40,000 at 7 percent interest with which the king could pay off several loans outstanding at 12 percent interest.

92. *Ka Nupepa Kuokoa*, 13 July 1878.

93. Adler, 1966, *Claus Spreckels: The Sugar King*, 39.

94. Ibid., 37.

95. Ibid., 53.

96. Ibid., 56. Two attorneys general under Kalākaua, Preston and Hartwell, supported Spreckels' claim, as did William Castle, an outspoken critic of Kalākaua and Spreckels in the 1880s.

97. *Hawaiian Gazette*, 26 July 1882.

98. Ibid.

99. Kame'eleihiwa, 1992, *Native Land and Foreign Desires*, 309. Kalākaua had virtually no land of his own. Kame'eleihiwa has told us that his mother Keohōkalole mortgaged so much of her lands that "most of them were gone by the time of her death." What little remained for her children, including Kalākaua, "seemed to accrue to Charles Bishop."

100. Ibid., 146.

101. *Pacific Commercial Advertiser*, 27 May 1876, p. 3. On 22 May, a petition was signed by Nāwahī, Pilipō, Kaua'i, Mahoe, Kahuila, Kāneali'i, Waterhouse, and Kalaukoa to impeach the minister of interior for spending $2,700 on a ball at Ali'iōlani Hale without permission.

102. Sheldon, 1988, *Ka Buke Moʻolelo ʻO Hon. Joseph K. Nāwahī*, 83.

103. *Saturday Press*, 24 February 1883.

104. Sheldon, 1988, *Ka Buke Moʻolelo ʻO Hon. Joseph K. Nāwahī*, 84, 85.

Chapter 7: Bayonet

1. Thurston, 1936, *Memoirs of the Hawaiian Revolution*, 153.

2. Kuykendall, 1967, *The Hawaiian Kingdom*, Vol. 3, *1874–1893*, 370–372. Ralph Simpson Kuykendall died before completing Vol. 3. It is possible that he was not responsible for the final drafts of the chapters on the overthrow. It is almost certain that these chapters were written by Grove Day.

3. Spaulding, 1924, Cabinet Government in Hawaii, 7.

4. Kelleher, 1973, The Politics of Constitutional Revision in Hawaii, 71.

5. *Hawaiian Gazette*, 14 September 1884.

6. These comparisons are based on the actual count of legislators who were elected and served between 1874 and 1882. All of these names were gathered and published in Lydecker's (1918) *Roster Legislatures of Hawaii*.

7. This distinction is not my own arbitrary one. Schmitt, 1977, *Demographic Statistics of Hawaii*, listed in Table 1.12 (p. 25) two distinct categories of Caucasians: "Portuguese" and "Other Caucasians." In 1872 there were only 424 Portuguese. The other 2,520 were of American, English, French, and German stock.

8. According to Jones, 1934, Naturalization in Hawaii, more than four hundred Chinese had been naturalized between 1850 and 1887. But there is no way of knowing how many Chinese were actually citizens in one year without actually going through thousands of names and listing them by year. I chose not to do this because they did not represent a sizable political bloc and thus were not part of the political competition that existed between haole and Hawaiians.

9. Although it is true that the percentage of elected haole fell to 17 percent in 1882 from what it had been a decade earlier, their number in the House of Nobles, most of them Kalākaua appointees, was a staggering 68 percent. Their actual numbers in the assembly went from 13 of 40 (1872) to 22 of 54. They had closed the gap with the Native population, which declined to 44,232 (1884), while "Other Caucasians" had increased to 6,612, making them 13 percent of the combined haole and Native population. However, as more than one newspaper lamented, most of the new arrivals were not, and did not intend to become, citizens. Even more significant than their population increase, however, was the increase of the Portuguese, who numbered almost 10,000 in 1884. See Schmitt, 1977, *Demographic Statistics of Hawaii*, 25.

10. Adler and Barrett, eds., 1973, *The Diaries of Walter Murray Gibson*, xiii.

11. Mcghie, 1958, Diary of Walter Murray Gibson. Entry for 31 July 1862.

12. Adler and Kamins, 1986, *The Fantastic Life of Walter Murray Gibson*, 137–138. This biography, which reads in many places more like a novel, does not document any specific reference to haole dissatisfaction with their seating. But Theo Davies' biographer (Hoyt, 1983, *Davies: The Inside Story*, 111)

referred to Davies' complaint to British Commissioner Wodehouse that he had been given a place in the procession behind several officers of the British navy.

13. Kuykendall, 1967, *The Hawaiian Kingdom*, Vol. 3, *1874–1893*, 246. Kuykendall reported that over $250,000 was spent on the construction of 'Iolani Palace during the 1880–1882 biennium, about four times what had been authorized by the 1880 legislature. This expenditure, along with the emergency allocation of $100,000 to cope with another smallpox epidemic in 1881, was covered by the legal transfer of funds from other items in the legislature's 1880 appropriation bill.

14. Lili'uokalani, 1990, *Hawaii's Story by Hawaii's Queen*, 104–105.

15. Ibid.

16. Ibid.

17. *Ka Nupepa Kuokoa*, 27 January 1883.

18. *Saturday Press*, 27 January 1883.

19. Ibid., 3 March 1883.

20. *Pacific Commercial Advertiser*, 9 May 1874.

21. Ibid., 9 March 1883, p. 2.

22. Adler and Kamins, 1986, *The Fantastic Life of Walter Murray Gibson*, 139.

23. Thurston, 1936, *Memoirs of the Hawaiian Revolution*, 51. "Whatever of slow thinking and mental incapacity may have been exhibited by the King in other respects, there was none when he was organizing and conducting an election campaign and securing affirmation by the Legislature."

24. *Saturday Press*, 3 March 1883.

25. Hoyt, 1983, *Davies: The Inside Story*, 131.

26. Ibid., 118.

27. Ibid., 119.

28. Adler, 1966, *Claus Spreckels: The Sugar King*, 120–122. Of particular interest is the fact that Oceanic was able to destroy its competitors by having the newest and fastest steamships available and cutting its fares long enough to put others out of business.

29. Kingdom of Hawai'i, 1884, *Journal of the Legislative Assembly*, 134.

30. Adler, 1966, *Claus Spreckels: The Sugar King*, 176.

31. Ibid., 177.

32. Kent, 1965, *Charles Reed Bishop: Man of Hawaii*, 77. Letter to Elisha Allen dated 27 November 1873.

33. Information from a file in the Lorrin Andrews Thurston Collection in the Hawai'i State Archives entitled Reform Party Minutes. (Technically, this is an inaccurate title. The Reform Party, as such, did not exist until 1887. Before that, it was known as the Independent Party.) First meeting, 16 April 1883. The following were present: E. P. Adams, J. B. Atherton, S. L. Austin, W. H. Baily, H. P. Baldwin, W. R. Castle, S. B. Dole, W. W. Hall, A. S. Hartwell, W. O. Smith, Z. S. Spaulding, L. A. Thurston, G. N. Wilcox.

34. Ibid.

35. Ibid., 30 April 1883.

36. Ibid. By 8 December 1883 the party had received pledges from twenty-six individuals and four sugar companies for a total of $13,000. However, as

the minutes of their 25 May 1885 meeting revealed, only $9,000 was actually spent on the 1884 elections. Without any detailed budget, it is not known how much money was allocated to individual candidates, but minutes of an 1886 meeting confirm that nothing was allocated to Nāwahī during the 1884 campaign.

37. Ibid., 30 April 1883.

38. Ibid., 16 April 1883.

39. *Ko Hawaii Pae Aina*, 18 July 1885. From the Hawaiian: "aole kakou ka ke kulana paapaana a ma kahi hoi o na hoolilo, aole i malama ia maloko mai o na loaa. O ka mea maopopo, ke hookomoia nei ka aina i loko o ka nenelu o ka aie ma ke $84,700 iloko o ekolu malama. . . . Ua oi ae ke kuonoono o kekahi haole hookahi mamua o ke aupuni."

40. Ibid., 31 October 1885.

41. *Pacific Commercial Advertiser*, 9 January 1886.

42. *Ko Hawaii Pae Aina*, 8 December 1883. The Hawaiian text is "He enemi no ka lahui na lunamakaainana hoopili kuhina, hoopili Alii, hoopili oihana aupuni, lawe i ka waiwai kipe, hooko pono ole i ke kauoha o na makaainana, kau I na kanawai ino hoomahuahua aie o ke aupuni Hawaii, hoolilo dala wale o ke aupuni i na hana kuole i ka makemake o ka lahui."

43. Reform Party Minutes, 29 May 1883.

44. It may suggest that rural voters may have been more heavily influenced by sugar planters and their interests, but this would be difficult to prove with the evidence at hand. Although it is certainly true that Independent candidates were successful in most districts where there were plantations employing Hawaiians, that would hardly explain why George Pilipō was elected in North Kona, where sugar was almost unknown.

45. *Pacific Commercial Advertiser*, 9 February 1884, p. 3, col. 4.

46. In the following election (1886) Thurston ran from Moloka‘i and won a seat against strong opposition.

47. *Hawaiian Monthly*, 1 (3), March 1884.

48. The publisher and editor in 1884 was Fred Hayselden, Gibson's son-in-law.

49. *Pacific Commercial Advertiser*, 1 February 1884, p. 2.

50. *Saturday Press*, 9 October 1880, p. 2.

51. *Pacific Commercial Advertiser*, 18 January 1886. Cited in Ching, 1963, *A History and Criticism*, 8.

52. *Pacific Commercial Advertiser*, 11 January 1886. Cited in Ching, 1963, *A History and Criticism*, 3.

53. *Hawaiian Monthly*, May 1884, pp. 100–101.

54. *Pacific Commercial Advertiser*, 2 February 1884, p. 8, col. 1.

55. *Evening Bulletin*, 25 August 1884.

56. Ibid., 27 August 1884.

57. Ibid., 25 August 1884.

58. Ibid., 27 August 1884.

59. *Hawaiian Monthly*, October 1884. This is a remarkable and oft-quoted article by this son of a missionary and was regarded, even by the administration-friendly *Pacific Commercial Advertiser* as a fair and reasoned argument.

60. Ibid.

61. See Allen, 1991, *Kalākaua: Renaissance King,* 195. Every haole historian has described Kalākaua's affiliation with this "secret society," most with disapproval or even ridicule. Traditionally, the Hale Nauā was an institution of Ali'i Nui society, whose most prominent feature was the recitations of genealogies by each of the chiefs as a means of demonstrating shared lineages and ancestors. Helena Allen, one of the few sympathetic biographers, said, "Its early purpose was to prevent bloodshed by uniting the chiefs under the bonds of kinship, friendship and rank."

62. *Evening Bulletin,* 28 August 1884.

63. *Ko Hawaii Pae Aina,* 6 February 1886. The defeated candidates included incumbents such as Francis Brown in Ko'olaupoko, John Richardson in Kā'anapali, Halstead in Hāna, and Hitchcock in Hilo.

64. Kuykendall, 1967, *The Hawaiian Kingdom,* Vol. 3, *1874–1893,* 282.

65. Ibid.

66. *Pacific Commercial Advertiser,* 22 January 1886. Cited in Kuykendall, 1967, *The Hawaiian Kingdom,* Vol. 3, *1874–1893,* 280.

67. *Pacific Commercial Advertiser,* 22 January 1886.

68. Lorrin Thurston is one of the sources for this evidence. See Thurston, 1936, *Memoirs of the Hawaiian Revolution,* 56.

69. *Daily Honolulu Press,* 4 February 1886, p. 2.

70. *Pacific Commercial Advertiser,* 3 December 1881. Kuykendall quoted only part of this text, making it appear that the editorial was stating for a fact that Hawai'i was fit to be an international player. See Kuykendall, 1967, *The Hawaiian Kingdom,* Vol. 3, *1874–1893,* 313.

71. *Pacific Commercial Advertiser,* 4 August 1883.

72. Kuykendall, 1967, *The Hawaiian Kingdom,* Vol. 3, *1874–1893,* 317.

73. Ibid.

74. Ibid., 318. Citation of letter from Carter to Count Herbert Bismarck, 7 November 1885.

75. See Daws, 1968, *Shoal of Time,* 237.

76. Kuykendall, 1967, *The Hawaiian Kingdom,* Vol. 3, *1874–1893,* 328–329 n. "On April 25, the acting British consul in Samoa wrote that he had been informed by Selu, the chief secretary of the Samoan government, that Carter [H. A. P. Carter] had been appointed 'to represent King Malietoa and Samoan interests at the Conference of the Representatives of the Three Treaty Powers about to be held at Washington.' In London, this report received brief comment in the foreign office, ending with the following minute by Lord Salisbury: 'but of course Mr. Carter cannot be admitted to the Conference.'"

77. From Salisbury to Sir L. S. Sackville West. Cited in Kuykendall, 1967, *The Hawaiian Kingdom,* Vol. 3, *1874–1893,* 332.

78. Ibid., 337–338.

79. This ship, renamed the *Kaimiloa,* was originally proposed to be a man-of-war. Her diminutive armament as well as a political decision to make the ship an "emissary of peace" resulted in the change in designation.

80. Kingdom of Hawai'i, 1886, Legislative Assembly, *Hawai'i Hansard: Proceedings,* 400 (entry for 21 July 1886).

81. Ibid., 414.

82. Kuykendall, 1967, *The Hawaiian Kingdom*, Vol. 3, *1874–1893*, 336.

83. Reform Party Minutes, 30 June 1885.

84. Ibid.

85. Section 2 of the League's constitution. Cited in Kuykendall, 1967, *The Hawaiian Kingdom*, Vol. 3, *1874–1893*, 348.

86. Kuykendall, 1967, *The Hawaiian Kingdom*, Vol. 3, *1874–1893*, 349.

87. Ibid.

88. There are numerous authors of this kind of work, but the scholar who most defines the approach is Walter LaFeber, author of *The New Empire: An Interpretation of American Expansion, 1860–1898*. Part of his preface reads, "The overseas empire that Americans controlled in 1900 was not a break in their history, but a natural culmination. Second, Americans neither acquired this empire during a temporary absence of mind nor had the empire forced upon them. I have discovered very little passivity in the systematic, expansive ideas of Seward, Evarts, Frelinghuysen, Harrison, Blaine, Cleveland, Gresham, Olney, and McKinley and the views of the American business community in the 1890s" (vii–viii).

89. Kuykendall, 1967, *The Hawaiian Kingdom*, Vol. 3, *1874–1893*, 348 n.

90. Ibid. This was quoted in Baldwin, 1925, *A Memoir of Henry Perrine Baldwin*, 55–56. Cited in Kuykendall, 1967, *The Hawaiian Kingdom*, Vol. 3, *1874–1893*, 348–349.

91. Kuykendall, 1967, *The Hawaiian Kingdom*, Vol. 3, *1874–1893*, 348. Kuykendall did not identify who those part-Hawaiian individuals were. It is possible that he simply took Thurston's word for it.

92. Thurston, 1936, *Memoirs of the Hawaiian Revolution*, 133.

93. Ibid., 105.

94. Dole, one of the earliest members, left the League after becoming uncomfortable with its radical elements. Sereno Bishop was one of the last to join.

95. Thurston, 1936, *Memoirs of the Hawaiian Revolution*, 142.

96. Ibid., 138.

97. Dole, 1936, *Memoirs of the Hawaiian Revolution*, 52. Actually the resolution named a committee of four individuals to "assist the King in naming a new cabinet. Kalakaua accepted a new cabinet the next day consisting of William Green, Lorrin Thurston, Godfrey Brown, and Clarence Ashford." All of them were members of the Hawaiian League.

98. Kuykendall, 1967, *The Hawaiian Kingdom*, Vol. 3, *1874–1893*, 364.

99. Dole, 1936, *Memoirs of the Hawaiian Revolution*, 49.

100. Ashford, 1919, Last Days of the Hawaiian Monarchy, 28.

101. This constitution is published in several places, among them Lydecker, 1918, *Roster Legislatures of Hawaii*; the *Pacific Commercial Advertiser*, 3 July 1887; and in the Appendixes to Thurston, 1936, *Memoirs of the Hawaiian Revolution*, 590–604.

102. Thurston, 1936, *Memoirs of the Hawaiian Revolution*, 603.

103. Kuykendall, 1967, *The Hawaiian Kingdom*, Vol. 3, *1874–1893*, 411. Godfrey Brown resigned his ministerial seat after six months, the result of

extreme displeasure with the failure of the legislature to disband the Honolulu Rifles, whose commander he distrusted. William Green also resigned for reasons of health the next year, and Clarence Ashford, Volney's brother, resigned in 1890.

104. Albert Francis Judd, in a statement prepared for the U.S. Senate Committee on Foreign Relations, 4 December 1893. (U.S. Congress, 1893, *Senate Journal*, 439; cited in Kuykendall, 1967, *The Hawaiian Kingdom*, Vol. 3, *1874–1893*, 371.)

105. Kuykendall, 1967, *The Hawaiian Kingdom*, Vol. 3, *1874–1893*, 407.

106. *Hawaiian Gazette*, 9 August 1887.

107. Earle, 1993, Coalition Politics in Hawai'i, 46.

108. Thurston, 1936, *Memoirs of the Hawaiian Revolution*, 21. "Kalakaua displayed diverse qualities: a personal charm and kingly demeanor; an unbalanced mentality and a total inability to grasp important subjects intelligently; a fundamental financial dishonesty; a personal extravagance, which merged into the control of community finances to such an extent that community financial collapse loomed; an immoral disposition, or it might be termed 'unmoral'; a bent to indulge in political intrigue, a reckless disregard for political honor, which made impossible the continuance of honest government; personal cowardice."

109. Ibid. The king spoke at Sunday services at a church in Lāhainā.

110. Kuykendall, 1940, Constitutions of the Hawaiian Kingdom, 48.

111. Ibid.

112. Ibid.

113. Ibid., 49.

114. Earle, 1993, *Coalition Politics in Hawai'i*, 50–51. Earle's meticulous study shows that the Native electorate was divided over a number of issues. One had to do with the attempt to create a coalition with Asian, particularly Chinese, men who had been disenfranchised by the new constitution. Ultimately, the most prominent Native association, Hui Aloha Aina, chose to ally itself with haole mechanics and artisans, whose chief political agenda was to stifle Asian immigration in favor of Portuguese immigration, as the latter were not seen as threats to haole employment. Earle wrote, "Since the Chinese could not help provide votes for the Hawaiians, the Hawaiians were faced with a choice of supporting Chinese and remaining politically marginal, or abandoning the Chinese and taking advantage of the Haole vote. In the end it was the latter choice that was made."

115. *Pacific Commercial Advertiser*, 26 July 1887, "Mass Meeting."

116. Ibid.

117. Ibid.

118. *Pacific Commercial Advertiser*, 19 September 1887. Nāwahī's defeat was very narrow. He earned good returns in Hilo and outpolled his Reform rivals 162 to 12 in Puna. But the results from the sugar plantation communities of Honomū, Onomea, and Laupāhoehoe destroyed him.

119. Ibid. The nobles were Reverend S. C. Luhiau, Charles Notley, and John Richardson. The representatives were A. P. Kalaukoa, D. L. Nāone, A. Kauhi, D. Kamai, Reverend J. Ka'uhane, O. Nāwahine, E. Helekunihi,

J. Nakaleka, and Joseph Kawainui, Reform Party; and Paehaole and Kamau-oha with the Opposition.

120. Kuykendall, 1967, *The Hawaiian Kingdom*, Vol. 3, *1874–1893*, 424. Kuykendall also cited the strict enforcement of the leprosy segregation law and the failure to "take vigorous action on the Chinese question" as significant unifiers of public opposition.

121. Kingdom of Hawai'i, 1887, *Journal of the Legislative Assembly*, 10 November entry. The Hawaiian Board of Health licensed Native health practitioners including kāhuna lā'au lapa'au (skilled in the prescription and preparation of herbal medicine).

122. At least until the passage of the McKinley Tariff Act in 1892, which effectively destroyed Hawai'i's favored status.

123. *Pacific Commercial Advertiser*, 3 November 1887. Wilder was elected 26 to 23 over William Castle.

Chapter 8: Ho'oulu Lāhui

1. Ka Lāhui claims a citizenry of nearly 20,000. The next largest government is probably the Nation of Hawai'i led by Bumpy Kanahele. I would be surprised if it could claim more than 4,000 citizens.

2. State of Hawai'i, 1993b, Management and Financial Audits of the Office of Hawaiian Affairs (no page number).

3. State of Hawai'i, 1993a, Management and Financial Audit of the Department of Hawaiian Homelands, 1.

4. The Office of Hawaiian Affairs did try to assert leadership in the sovereignty movement in 1988, submitting its so-called "Blueprint" to the Native public. It was not taken seriously, and OHA withdrew it.

5. In the two reports from the state auditor (Marion Higa) in 1993 (State of Hawai'i, Management and Financial Audits), the findings were much more critical of DHHL than OHA. However, in her summary (in Overview of report on Office of Hawaiian Affairs), Ms. Higa reported, "The board [of trustees] has fundamental fiduciary duties to the beneficiaries of the trust but does not have a full understanding of those responsibilities. Basic fiduciary duties include loyalty, prudence and the marshaling of trust assets. OHA has vigorously pursued the marshaling of its resources. However, we have found instances in which the loyalty or duty of the trustees to act solely in the interest of OHA beneficiaries could be questioned."

6. Trask, 1993, *From a Native Daughter*, 94–95.

7. Ibid., 95.

8. *Honolulu Advertiser*, 19 November 1995, p. A-1. SMS Research and Marketing Services, Inc. surveyed four hundred "Hawaiian households" from 12 to 31 October 1995. The margin of error was put at 5 percent.

9. Ibid.

Glossary

'Aha Ali'i: conventions by which Ali'i Nui were recognized by other Ali'i; these included the recitations of genealogies, the right to wear the feathered cloaks, and other signatures of Ali'i rank. For a brief time in the early nineteenth century, the small retinue of Ali'i Nui who advised Kamehameha I, Ka'ahumanu, and Kauikeaouli before constitutional government were also known as the 'Aha Ali'i.

Ahupua'a: a political and economic division of land running from the mountain to the sea; the basic administrative unit of territory before the kingdom.

'Aikapu (sacred eating): the traditional practice in which men and women ate separately and that further regulated worship, work, and child rearing before 1819.

'Āina: the land, the island itself and everything living upon it, the child of Papahānaumoku.

'Ai noa: free or profane eating. Men and women eating together or ignoring the periods of separation, prohibited in traditional society, but made acceptable by Ka'ahumanu and Liholiho in 1819 ('Ainoa).

Akua: god or goddess.

Ali'i: the class of Natives who ruled over the land and people and maintained their genealogies through careful mating and by recording their mo'okū'auhau.

Ali'i Nui: chiefs of high rank and status whose very presence was so powerful that they were dangerous to ordinary people.

'Āpana: a piece of land within an ahupua'a.

Aupuni: the unified government established by Kamehameha the Great and ruled by his successors.

'Auwai: the irrigation system developed by Hawaiians to link the streams to wet-land taro patches (lo'i).

Hānai (literally, to feed): it traditionally meant to adopt the child of another into one's own immediate family. That child became indistinguishable from the other children in treatment.

Haole: stranger, foreigner; after 1778, this term came to apply specifically to Caucasians.

Hoa'āina (literally, friend of the land, tenant): used as the legal definition of anyone granted a kuleana patent in the Mahele.

'Imi haku (literally, to search for the lord or chief): the obligation of all lesser chiefs to find someone or some principle to serve that was worthy of one's talents and ambitions.

Kahu: guardian, usually assigned to Ali'i Nui children.

Kāhuna (sing., kahuna): genealogists, healers, priests, and other individuals who were guardians and practitioners of traditional arts and sciences.

Kālaimoku: chancellor; a high official whose power was exceeded only by the Mō'ī. Kalanimōkū was the Ali'i Nui who exemplified this position under the unification of Kamehameha I, as both supreme general and guardian of the treasury.

Kanaka (pl., kānaka): a person, human being.

Kanaka Maoli: Native person, a Hawaiian by ancestry.

Kaukauali'i: lesser chiefs in service to higher-ranking Ali'i Nui.

Kauoha: the verbal will or command of the ruling chief.

Ka wā mahope: the time after; the future.

Ka wā mamua: the time before; the past.

Konohiki: Ali'i who were subordinate to ruling Ali'i and Mō'ī. Considered stewards of the land and people.

Kuhina Nui: a kind of extension of the Mō'ī himself, this position, given first to Ke'eaumoku and then to Ka'ahumanu, allowed them to exercise power in Kamehameha's name. The Kuhina Nui was a kind of second executive and was institutionalized in the Constitution of 1852, which required the Kuhina Nui's co-signature on all executive actions. Kamehameha V did away with this position in 1864.

Kuleana: a relationship of obligation and prerogative. To have a kuleana meant that one had both a responsibility and a right in a particular area.

Kumukānāwa: foundational law; constitution.

Lāhui: gathering, tribe, nation, community, race.

Mā: the people associated with (e.g., Kaʻahumanu mā: Kaʻahumanu and her family who constituted the Council of Chiefs in the 1820s).

Mahele: to divide and to share; also a division or section of land. The Mahele, sometimes referred to as the Great Mahele, created private and public property from the traditional land-use arrangement between Aliʻi and Makaʻāinana.

Makaʻāinana: planter, or people of the land; usually anyone who was not Aliʻi.

Mālama: to care for, nurture, and nourish.

Malihini: newcomer; stranger, foreigner, guest; an unfamiliar person.

Mana: personal spiritual power, possessed by all living things and believed to be concentrated in Aliʻi Nui.

Mele: a traditional song or chant that could be accompanied with hula.

Mōhai: sacrifice, offering.

Mōʻī: paramount chief, usually of Aliʻi Nui rank. Before Kamehameha I, each major island was ruled by a Mōʻī.

Moʻo kūʻauhau: a chiefly genealogy.

Moʻolelo: story, history, tale, legend; moʻolelo were understood to be stories of people, chiefs, and gods, usually with the intent of instruction.

ʻŌiwi (literally, of the bones): a Native person, a Hawaiian by ancestry.

Oli: a traditional song or chant that was not accompanied by hula.

Pono (often mistranslated as righteous—it means balance): an individual, an act, or a behavior that reflects a balance between male and female dualities; therefore wise, judicious, proper, good.

Wahine (pl., wāhine): woman.

Bibliography

Published Works and Manuscripts

Adler, Jacob. 1966. *Claus Spreckels: The Sugar King of Hawaii*. Honolulu: University of Hawai'i Press.

Adler, Jacob, and Gwynn Barrett, eds. 1973. *The Diaries of Walter Murray Gibson: 1886–1887*. Honolulu: University of Hawai'i Press.

Adler, Jacob, and Robert M. Kamins. 1986. *The Fantastic Life of Walter Murray Gibson: Hawaii's Minister of Everything*. Honolulu: University of Hawai'i Press.

Allen, Helena. 1991. *Kalākaua: Renaissance King*. Honolulu: Mutual Publishing.

Ashford, Clarence. 1919. Last Days of the Hawaiian Monarchy. *Twenty-seventh Annual Report of the Hawaiian Historical Society*. Honolulu: Paradise of the Pacific Press.

Baldwin, A. D. 1925. *A Memoir of Henry Perrine Baldwin, 1832–1911*. Cleveland: Privately printed.

Beechert, Edward D. 1985. *Working in Hawaii: A Labor History*. Honolulu: University of Hawai'i Press.

Bingham, Hiram. 1981. *A Residence of Twenty-one Years in the Sandwich Islands*. Tokyo: Charles E. Tuttle Co. (Original publication, 1849, by the Huntington Press, Hartford, Connecticut.)

Bishop, Artemis. 1838. An Inquiry into the Causes of Decrease in the Population of the Sandwich Islands. *The Hawaiian Spectator* 1 (1): 52–66.

Buck, Elizabeth B. 1986. The Politics of Culture: A History of the Social and Cultural Transformation of Hawai'i. Ph.D. diss., University of Hawai'i at Mānoa, Honolulu.

Bushnell, Andrew. 1993. The "Horror" Reconsidered: An Evaluation of the Historical Evidence for Population Decline in Hawai'i, 1778–1803. *Pacific Studies* 16 (3): 115–161.

Calvin, John. 1951. The Institutes of the Christian Religion. Printed with omissions in George H. Knowles and Rixford K. Snyder, eds. *Readings in Western Civilization*. Chicago: J. P. Lippincott.

Cannelora, Louis. 1974. *The Origin of Hawaiian Land Titles and of the Rights of Native Tenants*. Honolulu: Security Title Corporation.

Castle, William R. 1915. Sketch of Constitutional History in Hawaii. Pages 13–27 in *Twenty-third Annual Report of the Hawaiian Historical Society, for the Year 1914*. Honolulu: Paradise of the Pacific Press.

Chambers, Henry Edward. 1896. Constitutional History of Hawaii. *Baltimore, Slavery, and Constitutional History*, no. 1. Baltimore: Johns Hopkins Press (pamphlet).

Chinen, J. J. 1958. *The Great Mahele: Hawaii's Land Division of 1848*. Honolulu: University of Hawai'i Press.

Ching, James. 1963. A History and Criticism of Political Speaking in the Hawaiian Kingdom. M.A. thesis, University of Missouri, Columbia.

Chun, Malcolm Naea. 1987. Biographical Sketch of Davida Malo. Page xiv in David Malo, *Ka Mo'olelo Hawai'i* (1987). Honolulu: The Folk Press.

Clech-Lam, Maivan. 1989. The Kuleana Act Revisited. *Washington Law Review* 64:233–288.

Cooper, George, and Gavan Daws. 1990. *Land and Power in Hawai'i: The Democratic Years*. Honolulu: University of Hawai'i Press.

Daws, Gavan. 1968. *Shoal of Time: A History of the Hawaiian Islands*. Honolulu: University of Hawai'i Press.

———. 1973. *Holy Man: Father Damien of Molokai*. Honolulu: University of Hawai'i Press.

Dibble, Sheldon. 1838. *Ka Moolelo Hawaii*. Translated 1984 by Dorothy M. Kahananui. Honolulu: Committee for the Preservation of Hawaiian Language, Art and Culture, University of Hawai'i.

Dole, Sanford. 1936. *Memoirs of the Hawaiian Revolution*. Honolulu: Pacific Commercial Advertiser, Inc.

Earle, David William. 1993. Coalition Politics in Hawai'i—1887–90: Hui Kālai'āina and the Mechanics and Workingmen's Political Protective Union. M.A. thesis, University of Hawai'i at Mānoa, Honolulu.

Edwards, Jonathan. 1996. Select Sermons (www.ccel.org/e/edwards/sermons/-).

Friends of the Hawaiian Judiciary History Center. 1984. Searching for the Hundreds of 19th Century Hawaiian Lawyers. *The Native Hawaiian* (June). Honolulu: Alu Like, Inc.

Gregg, David L. 1982. *The Diaries of David Lawrence Gregg: An American Diplomat in Hawaii, 1853–1858*. Edited by Pauline King. Honolulu: Hawaiian Historical Society.

Hobbs, Jean. 1935. *Hawaii: A Pageant of the Soil*. Stanford, California: Stanford University Press.

Hoyt, Edwin P. 1983. *Davies: The Inside Story of a British American Family in the Pacific and Its Business Enterprises*. Honolulu: Topgallant Press.

Joesting, Edward. 1972. *Hawaii: An Uncommon History*. New York: W. W. Norton.

Jones, Maude. 1934. Naturalization in Hawaii. Manuscript, Honolulu Board of Commissioners, Private Archives. Hawai'i State Archives, Honolulu.

Judd, Laura F. 1880. *Honolulu: Sketches of the Life, Social, Political, and Religious, in the Hawaiian Islands from 1828 to 1861*. New York: A. D. F. Randolph and Co.

Kamakau, Samuel M. 1991. *Ruling Chiefs of Hawaii.* Honolulu: The Kamehameha Schools Press.

Kame'eleihiwa, Lilikalā. 1992. *Native Land and Foreign Desires: Pehea Lā E Pono Ai?* Honolulu: Bishop Museum Press.

Kelleher, Sean A. 1973. The Politics of Constitutional Revision in Hawaii. Ph.D. diss., Brown University, Providence, Rhode Island.

Kent, Harold W. 1965. *Charles Reed Bishop: Man of Hawaii.* Palo Alto: Pacific Books.

Korn, Alfons L. 1976. *News from Moloka'i: Letters between Peter Ka'eo and Queen Emma, 1873–1876.* Honolulu: University of Hawai'i Press.

Kuykendall, Ralph Simpson. 1938. *The Hawaiian Kingdom.* Vol. 1, *1778–1854: Foundation and Transformation.* Honolulu: University of Hawai'i Press.

———. 1940. Constitutions of the Hawaiian Kingdom: A Brief History and Analysis. *Papers of the Hawaiian Historical Society* 21.

———. 1953. *The Hawaiian Kingdom.* Vol. 2, *1854–1874: Twenty Critical Years.* Honolulu: University of Hawai'i Press.

———. 1967. *The Hawaiian Kingdom.* Vol. 3, *1874–1893: The Kalakaua Dynasty.* Honolulu: University of Hawai'i Press.

LaFeber, Walter. 1963. *The New Empire: An Interpretation of American Expansion, 1860–1898.* Ithaca: Cornell University Press.

Lili'uokalani. 1990. *Hawaii's Story by Hawaii's Queen.* Honolulu: Mutual Publishing Co. (Original publication, 1898, by Tuttle and Sons, Honolulu.)

Linnekin, Jocelyn. 1983. The Hui Lands of Ke'anae: Hawaiian Land Tenure and the Great Māhele. *Journal of the Polynesian Society* 92 (2): 169–188.

Locke, John. 1951. The Second Treatise of Civil Government, from *Two Treatises of Civil Government* (1884). In George H. Knowles and Rixford K. Snyder, eds. *Readings in Western Civilization.* Chicago: J. P. Lippincott.

Lydecker, Robert C. 1918. *Roster Legislatures of Hawaii: 1841–1918.* Honolulu: The Hawaiian Gazette Co., Ltd.

Malo, David. 1839. On the Decrease of Population in the Hawaiian Islands. *The Hawaiian Spectator* 2 (2): 121–130.

———. 1951. *Hawaiian Antiquities (Moolelo Hawaii).* 2nd ed. Bernice P. Bishop Museum Special Publication 2. (Original publication, 1898.)

Mcghie, Frank. 1958. Diary of Walter Murray Gibson. M.A. thesis, Brigham Young University, Provo, Utah.

Memmi, Albert. 1957. *The Colonizer and the Colonized.* Boston: Beacon Press.

Porter, Kirk H. 1918. *A History of Suffrage in the United States.* Chicago: University of Chicago Press.

Schmitt, Robert C. 1971. Voter Participation in Hawaii: 1851–1897. *Hawaiian Journal of History* 5: 50–58.

———. 1977. *Demographic Statistics of Hawaii, 1778–1965.* Honolulu: University of Hawai'i Press.

Sheldon J. G. M. 1988. *Ka Buke Mo'olelo 'O Hon. Joseph K. Nāwahī.* Translated

from the Hawaiian by Puakea Nogelmeier and the Pacific Transla-
tions Committee, Hawaiian Historical Society, Honolulu.

Simpson, George. 1847. *Narrative of a Journey Round the World, 1841–1842.*
2 vols. London: H. Colburn.

Spaulding, Thomas. 1924. Cabinet Government in Hawaii: 1887–1893. *University of Hawai'i Occasional Papers,* No. 2.

Stannard, David. 1989. *Before the Horror: The Population of Hawai'i on the
Eve of Western Contact.* Honolulu: Social Science Research Institute.

Tate, Merze. 1968. *Hawaii: Reciprocity or Annexation.* East Lansing: Michigan
State University Press.

Thurston, Lorrin A. 1936. *Memoirs of the Hawaiian Revolution.* Honolulu:
Pacific Commercial Advertiser, Inc.

Trask, Haunani-Kay. 1993. *From a Native Daughter.* Monroe, Maine: Common
Courage Press.

Turrill, Joel. n.d. The Joel Turrill Correspondence Concerning the Sandwich
Islands, 1850–1860. Manuscript, Hawaiian Pacific Collection, Hamilton Library, University of Hawai'i at Mānoa, Honolulu.

Varigny, Charles de. 1981. *Fourteen Years in the Sandwich Islands: 1855–1868.*
Honolulu: University of Hawai'i Press.

Wagner-Wright, Sandra. 1992. When Unity Is Torn Asunder: The Distressing
Case of Thomas and Lucia Holman. *Pacific Studies* 15 (2): 39–60.

Young, G. Terry Kanalu. 1995. Mo'olelo Kaukau Ali'i: The Dynamics of
Chiefly Service and Identity in 'Ōiwi Society. Ph.D. diss., University
of Hawai'i at Mānoa, Honolulu.

Official Documents and Records

*All references for Kingdom of Hawai'i are located in the Hawai'i State
Archives, Honolulu.*

Andrews, Lorrin. 1835. Missionary Letters. Vol. 6. Hawaiian Mission Children's Society, Honolulu.

Dibble, S. 1858. Student Roster of the Lāhaināluna Seminary. *Ka Hae Hawaii,*
19 May.

Hillebrand, William. 1867. *Report on the Supply of Labor, Etc. by the Hon.
Wm. Hillebrand, M.D., Royal Commissioner to China and India, to
the Honorable Board of Immigration of the Hawaiian Islands.* Honolulu, Hawai'i State Archives.

Kingdom of Hawai'i
 1837–1845. Foreign Office and Executive. Records.
 1840. Foreign Office and Executive. *He Kumu Kanawai a me ke
  Kanawai Hooponopono Waiwai.*
 1840–1845. Foreign Office and Executive. *Privy Council Minutes.*
 1841–1850. *Journal of the Legislative Council. Buke Oihana o ka Ahaolelo,* Helu 1 (1841–1845) (in Hawaiian); *He Buke no ka
  Ahaolelo oke Aupuni,* Helu 2, Buke 2 (1845–1847); *Ahaolelo
  o ke Aupuni o Hawaii,* Helu 3, Buke 3 (1847–1850).
 1845. *Journal of the Legislative Council.* General Records.

1845–1847. Department of the Interior. Miscellaneous Files.

1846. Department of Foreign Affairs. Answers to Questions.

1848. *Supreme Court Letter Book of Chief Justice Lee.*

1850. *Foreign Office Letter Book* No. 11.

1850. House of Nobles and Representatives. *Hawaii Penal Code and Session Laws.* Honolulu: Government Press.

1850. *Statute Laws,* I. Honolulu: Government Press.

1851–1863. *Journal of the House of Nobles.*

1851–1863. *Journal of the House of Representatives.*

1852. *General Records of the Legislature.*

1864. Foreign Office and Executive. *Cabinet Council Minutes.*

1864. *Minutes of the Constitutional Convention.* Honolulu: Pacific Commercial Advertiser.

1874. *Session Laws of the Hawaiian Kingdom's Legislative Assembly.*

1884–1887. *Journal of the Legislative Assembly.*

1886. Legislative Assembly. *Hawai'i Hansard: Proceedings.*

Judd, Gerrit P. 1911. *The Letters of Dr. Gerrit P. Judd, 1827–1872, Preserved in the Archives of the A.B.C.F.M., Boston.* Honolulu.

Reform Party Minutes. 1883–1885. Lorrin Andrews Thurston Collection. Hawai'i State Archives, Honolulu.

State of Hawai'i. 1993a. Management and Financial Audit of the Department of Hawaiian Homelands. Office of the Auditor. Report no. 93-22. Honolulu.

———. 1993b. Management and Financial Audits of the Office of Hawaiian Affairs. Office of the Auditor: A Report to the Governor and the Legislature of the State of Hawai'i. Report 93-28. December. Honolulu. Unpaginated.

Thrum, Thomas. 1874. The Second Interregnum. Scrapbook. Hawaiian Pacific Collection, Hamilton Library, University of Hawai'i at Mānoa, Honolulu.

———. 1888. *Hawaiian Almanac and Annual.* Honolulu: Hawaiian Gazette Press.

U.S. Congress. 1893. *Senate Journal.* 53rd Cong., 2nd sess., no. 227, vol. 1. Morgan Report.

———. 1898. *Senate Journal.* 55th Cong., 3rd sess., no.16. The Report of the Hawaiian Commission.

Newspapers and Journals

The Daily Bulletin (Honolulu)

Daily Honolulu Press (Honolulu)

Evening Bulletin (Honolulu)

The Friend (Lāhainā and Honolulu)

The Hawaiian Gazette (Honolulu)

Hawaiian Monthly (Honolulu) (monthly journal)

The Hawaiian Spectator (Honolulu) (monthly journal)

Ka Hae Hawaii (Honolulu)

Ka Nupepa Kuokoa (Honolulu)
Ko Hawaii Pae Aina (Honolulu)
The Pacific Commercial Advertiser (Honolulu)
The Polynesian (Honolulu)
The Sandwich Island News (Honolulu)
Saturday Press (Honolulu)
The Weekly Argus (Honolulu)

Index

Printed in the USA
CPSIA information can be obtained
at www.ICGtesting.com
JSHW011924281223
54443JS00001B/3